WHAT IN HELL IS WITH US?

Transhumanist AI, Conspiracy Red Pill, Woke Culture Wars, New Age Awakening and The Great A-Weakening

BY

ATTLAS ALLUX

For humanity suffering in psychological hell—especially the Truthers, Lightworkers, Starseeds, and all seekers of Truth spellbound by one or more of the subtle and insidious deceptions of the Black Lodge—may they and those they love SEEK a Path out of the darkness and into the Light through the revolution of AUM.

TABLE OF CONTENTS

ACKNOWLEDGMENTS

Life is so unnerving for a servant who's not serving. He's not whole without a soul to wait upon.

– Lumiere, Beauty and the Beast.

Some might write books for their own sake. This is not such a book. The participants in our weekly livestream, readers of our blog, followers on social media, and all who reach out to us for help and guidance on the Path know that they inspire us and move us to do all we do. They know how humbled and grateful we are to them for giving us an opportunity to serve them in the best way we know how. And they will forgive us for not naming any number of them herein (you know who you are). And they know this book is as much theirs as it is *yours,* dear reader. Without all of you, we would have no reason for being. We are here to fulfill our life's work for your sake—and for the sake of suffering humanity—and that begins in earnest with the writing and publication of this book. One that would not be possible without receptive "eyes to see and ears to hear." Unrequited love in all its forms is most lamentable, and while one who walks a path of suffering and sacrifice for humanity does not expect reciprocation of love, we do hope that our words and works will at least be received, as Lumiere so brilliantly expressed it above. So, thank you, dear reader, for being one more soul for us to "wait upon."

This book took the better part of 50 years to write, counting the time required to accumulate the substantive experiential knowledge that constitutes its foundation. That means I have been preparing to serve souls for most of my life. This has not been easy on my beloved family, particularly my Hungarian immigrant parents—my father, Lajos, and my late mother, Katalin. You worked your fingers to the bone so I might have all the opportunities this world had to offer. You dreamt such big dreams for me. You never imagined a life of suffering and sacrifice. How could you? No parent can. And yet, even in the wake of all the hardship, the impossible-to-understand decisions, and what seemed to you at times to be the unluckiest child who ever lived, you stood behind me and supported me. Even when others advised you to throw me out into the street, you never once entertained the thought of abandoning your child to a world most unkind to him. Your house was always home. No matter where my path took me and what tests, trials, and ordeals I faced, I could always depend on you. I always knew that you would never forsake me. In that very True sense, then, you were the worldly reflection of my Innermost Divine Father and Divine Mother. And I am eternally grateful to you just as I am to them.

Walking a path of suffering and sacrifice for 50 years, one can imagine I found myself in trouble countless times. And often, it was my older brother, Alex, who came to my rescue. Be it talking on the phone for hours with the Canadian travel insurance company when I broke my collarbone skiing in

Garmisch or arranging my flight home from Guatemala, I never once expected you to come to my aid, Alex, but you were always there in my time of need. I suppose every little brother has such stories, but not everyone gets an opportunity to express his gratitude in print. This book exists in part thanks to you and your devotion to your family and its most hapless member, who will always be your little brother, in gratitude.

My friends and colleagues, likewise, have had to put up with a great deal of collateral damage over the years for having known me. And their fellowship has made no small contribution to my life's work. Martina Ernst gave me a new lease on life when I had lost my way in the dark. You have been like a big sister to me, Martina. Your care for my well-being is literally on par with that of my brother and parents. More than that, you were the first entrepreneur I ever worked with who Truly earned the moniker of "Partner." Your dream of living in a botanical garden would become the spearhead of The Attlas Project, and I will never forget how you told me as much long before I came to SEEK the Truth of it consciously. It was your infectious enthusiasm for that dream that led us both to Wolfgang Amelung and Genetron Systems. Wolfgang, I have no doubt that one day your name will be spoken of with the same reverence as Nikola Tesla, Walter Russell, and maybe even *Noah*, for your devotion to helping humanity, in your own words, "bridge the gap," not least between our finite oversimplifications and the infinite complexity and self-organizing ability of high order rainforest ecosystems. You also literally helped me bridge the gap in my life when you opened your home to me for a time, just as you opened your heart and shared your knowledge, wisdom, humor, and friendship. To borrow a line from one of our favorite contemporary mythologies, if Martina is the mother of ESAHH—Ecosystem Advanced Human Habitat—you, Wolfgang, are undoubtedly its father.

Just as the seeds of ESAHH were planted by the hands of close friends and nourished by the light of their vision, so too were the seeds of ISAUM—Individuals SEEKing the Analogous Ultimate Methodology—planted within me by members of my 'soul family.' Ryan, our friendship and working relationship have reaped much fruit, none sweeter and more nourishing than your direct contribution to this book and my life's work: introducing me to Ali Kermani. Ali, your dream of codifying and putting the healing power of AUM in people's hands via YouMethod™ was the writing on the wall telling us both that we are soul brothers bound by fate and a shared passion for helping suffering humanity. From your love of Rumi to your deep comprehension of the underlying mathematical language of reality, I have known few who have suffered as long and sacrificed as much to help others SEEK an end to depression, anxiety, addictions, et al. I pray that this book will help others see the value in your life's work just as Ryan Gale and I did. After all, it is not 'your method' as much as it is *the method*. And like your friendship, it is priceless.

My oldest and dearest friend, Eduardo Valdes, the first friend I made when I moved to Guelph, I owe you my thanks for having been both a mirror and guide as I fumbled my way through the dark passages and pitfalls of psychological hell. It was you, Ed, who opened my eyes to better knowing myself and my mercurial outbursts not for what I thought they were—anger—but a clever mask worn by the great chameleon, *fear*. Whether it was the countless hours we spoke over coffee at *The Brick* or spent smashing demons online together in *Diablo 3,* whenever I needed a break from hell, you were never far away. True, we have only been friends, not yet colleagues, officially, but that is a condition I hope the success of this book will rectify. Lord knows you deserve to be part of a team that knows your worth and will honor their commitment to you, just as you honor yours to them.

I would also like to thank Emily and the whole team at Amazon Publishing for their hard work and dedication. It was a joy to work together with all of you on this, which I hope will be the first of many books to come.

Last but certainly not least, I would be remiss if I failed to mention the tireless efforts made on my behalf by my individual Divine Mother. She is, after all, the one who arranges all we need in this life, including all our tests, trials, and ordeals. Truly, I cannot do justice to all she does for us and has done for me here and now, for volumes of tomes could be devoted to such an inventory of love in action. Besides, I made a concerted effort to pay tribute to my Divine Mother on the one-year anniversary of the death of my biological mother in the article, *Oh Divine Mother, Here Art Thou*. This was appropriate since Katalin Lendvai was the dominant feminine force throughout my life right up to her death and the one who taught me unconditional love by mirroring the love of my Divine Mother. Here is a link to said blog post:

There are two more individuals who embody the Divine Feminine Force who made significant contri-

Link 1: Blog Article, "Oh Divine Mother, Here Art Thou" (Attlas.info)

butions to my life and the synthesis of this book. The first I must mention is Tunde Hodik. Tunde, as I have expressed many times, you are a Godsend, without whom my father would not have lived to see this book published. I could never have done for him all that you do, let alone had any time and energy left over to dedicate to my work. I am so grateful for the love and laughter you brought into our home and for your presence and efforts that directly freed me to focus on writing this book.

Speaking of love and laughter and a presence in my life that helped me focus on completing this book, I have reserved a place of honor for Neera Shiekh Mansoor. Neera, you laugh together with me and fill my heart with pure joy. You also know what it means to live a life of suffering and sacrifice for others and are one of the few women I have ever known who has not flinched from that prospect. On the contrary, in the face of every challenge, the Sun rises within you, and you along with it. Without your thoughts and prayers on my behalf, I would still be fumbling around with a first draft. Sure, the body of this planet and the duty to our families may separate us physically for now, but nothing can keep us apart metaphysically, nor keep us from our duty to divinity and this suffering humanity. Thank you for being and being near Allux.

ABOUT THE AUTHOR

Attlas is the Spiritual Essence and Divine Mother—Higher Self, Innermost Being, *Atman*—of Attila Lewis Lendvai, his mortal vessel, servant, and *stenographer*. Through metamind (manas), consciousness, and will, Attlas SEEKs to work with and serve suffering humanity by virtue of the AUM of Life, in the Name of Allux, for the Glory of Allux, and by the Majesty of Allux—*All Light, God Light, the Fire of fires, Light of lights, and Being of beings*—also known as The Logos, Krishna, and the Cosmic Kristos Force…Christ.

Like a master potter, Allux works with the clay thrown on the wheel. The potter does not ask for a different lump of clay. Rather, they set their hands to the task of shaping and forming as perfect a vessel as possible from the imperfect hume spinning on the wheel. Via countless revolutions of AUM, the hands of the master apply the necessary pressure to the hume, made more compliant by a constant flow of the creative waters of life (sacrifice, death, and birth—the three factors of the evolution of AUM).

Crafting the most perfect vessel possible requires relaxation, attention, patience, determination, humility, and above all, courage in the face of adversity—a firm resolve and a soft touch. It means working with intense fire and heat in the kiln to transmute mere hume (rational mind, sentimental heart, and body) into a True human—an earthen vessel for the metamind of Being. Like a phoenix, through death and rebirth in the fire, what was once a worthless lump of clay becomes a practical, strong, and resilient vessel, able to contain itself and carry whatever burdens its purpose for being demanded.

Integral to a life of intensity is to SEEK the ancient tenet of *ahimsa*—to be perfect love in action—embodied in the highest universal ideal of service to others. From perfected earthenware vessels to the perfect tea ceremony they serve, it is a recognition that every lump of clay has a purpose, the greatest being service: carry and store water, grow food, construct homes, tile roofs, et al.

Attila Lewis Lendvai is one such lump of clay. A social entrepreneur, consultant, blogger, YouTube creator, and author, Attila has over 30 years of marketing, branding, and communications experience. Having received an Honors Bachelor of Arts degree from the University of Guelph with a double major in English and Dramatic Arts, Attila spent some time working in radio, television, and film in Toronto, Canada, before moving to Japan to teach English. There, Attila experienced a culture that embraced two principal tenets of AUM in countless practical ways—*kaizen* (continually search for perfection) and *omotenashi* (see to others' needs). Following his MBA at Wilfrid Laurier University in 2001-02, he was diagnosed with adult-onset epilepsy and related depression. After getting nowhere with allopathic healthcare, he turned to Attlas and the Analogous Ultimate Methodology (AUM) for an answer. Within a short period of time, his seizures abated. Today, he lives seizure-free in Guelph, Ontario, and dedicates his life to serving humanity, Attlas Allux (his True Self), and *The Attlas Project* (their life's work). Bound as one, they SEEK to bring meaningful solutions to the world via practical applications of the AUM of Life so that this suffering humanity can cope better with the baffling challenges it faces in the midst of its *Kali Yuga.*

Attila Lewis Lendvai and his Innermost Being, Attlas, are by no means a perfect vessel of Allux, which is why they went public online as *Attlas in Formation.* A purely online brand embodying the specifics of AUM needed to SEEK ongoing spiritual development in microcosm and evolution of humanity in macrocosm, Attlas In Formation (@AttlasInfo) demarcates all that Attlas Allux has to share with humanity, including The Attlas Project online—blog (www.attlas.info), YouTube channel, podcast, and social media.

In synthesis, dear reader, Attlas Allux, with the assistance of his mortal vessel and stenographer, Attila Lewis Lendvai, wrote this book for your sake and for the sake of suffering humanity.

FOREWORD

The title of this book asks a question that many have asked themselves since the dawn of the 21st Century. From 9/11 to Covid, the past two decades have given the world its fair share of *"what in hell...?"* moments. Indeed, dear reader, the fact that you are reading this book indicates you, too, have found yourself asking similarly phrased questions about humanity. Be it society, culture, politics, science, technology, healthcare, religion, and perhaps even your own psychology in relation to the people and circumstances around you. And we surmise the answers you have managed to uncover to-date may have satisfied intellectual curiosity on a surface level but could never silence the Still Soft Voice of intuition, whispering from deep within your conscience, posing the question, *what in hell is with us?*

Why is it, for instance, that with all this talk of *awakening,* things only seem to be getting worse on so many fronts? Are individuals and movements not enacting positive change for humanity's sake? What about all those individuals awakening from ignorance thanks to the Information Age and the supposed dawn of AI? Or those who have been allegedly *red-pilled* and believe themselves aware of the hidden power structures enslaving humanity? What about the legions of *woke* social justice warriors waging their culture war against corruption, oppression, inequity, and injustice in the world? Lastly, what of the New Age movement's promise of a *mass global awakening* and a new *Golden Age?* Surely, the world should be showing signs of improvement, not deterioration. What gives? With all this alleged 'awakening' going on, why is humanity still sleepwalking toward its inevitable destruction? And what, if anything, can we do about it? Is it possible we are facing inevitable doom? Is there evidence to support that conclusion? Or is this the last gasp of barbarism before the turning of the tide? Could it be humanity is just waiting for things to hit rock-bottom before it collectively cries out, "enough is enough!" And like so many who have found themselves scraping the bottom of the barrel in their lives, might humanity collectively pull itself together and lay aside its pettiness, insecurity, and primal animal instincts in favor of more cooperative, trustworthy, and enlightened intuitive action?

I, too, went in search of answers. Perhaps it was my overly sensitive, highly empathetic nature. I felt others' pain and suffering as though it were my own. Perhaps it was my inherent capacity to sense hypocrisy—along with a deep-seated disdain for it—which I had from a very young age. These qualities of character made living in the world practically intolerable at times, especially as an opinionated young intellectual driven by a deep sense of ethics, universal justice, and vision. I knew from a very young age that while competition had its place in the world, it must ultimately give way to cooperation if humanity were to flourish. You can imagine, dear reader, how growing up in the *me decade* of the 1970s and *the decade of greed* in the 1980s set me on a quest to answer *what in hell is with us?* With humanity. A quest whose seeds were planted in childhood. A mission that began in earnest in high school some 35 years ago. It was a *journey of awakening* that took me to all sorts of places, not only geographically but intellectually, emotionally, and spiritually. In a word? *Hell.*

Now, I must make it clear, dear reader, that I had no intention of descending into hell when I embarked on my quest for answers. I was what the New Age would call a *Lightworker*, a *Starseed*, and/or *Indigo* child—although I was familiar with none of these terms until much later in life. My deep love of divinity, nature, sharing, and helping others made me "such a beautiful young child," according to my father, and "a joy to have in class," according to my early grade-school teachers. But it was my inherent capacity for knowledge that got me branded as 'gifted' in the eyes of the school system and later as a 'geek, nerd, scab, etc.' in the eyes of my adolescent peers. My sense of self became entangled in rational intellectualism, and my interest in peace and harmony led to my growing cynicism toward what were clearly corrupt authority structures and a degenerating society. I grew into an intellectual teenager with visions of grandeur of how I would one day change the world.

For me, at that time, there was no question that I already knew essentially what I needed to know: *the world was going to hell in a handbasket.* The evidence was everywhere. In newspapers, on radio, and on the television. In books, in theatres, and in video games. In schools, community centers, and corridors of government. In shopping malls, on main street, and especially on Wall Street. The systemic problems of injustice, wickedness, hypocrisy, and corruption were everywhere, and *I had to do something about it.* I was going to march out into the world, standing tall, chest out, head held high, grasping the gauntlet life had thrown down at my feet. Yes, I felt that self-righteous and more, dear reader. I might not have had all the answers yet. But I believed I knew what the problem was. What is more, I knew the answers would come in time.

Armed with the courage of my convictions, the sweat of my brow, and the prowess of my intellect, I would set out with a mission to change the hearts and minds of the world—to awaken humanity to what I believed they needed to see. I would climb atop the highest mountain of influence and attention and create the most powerful media empire the world had ever known. One founded not on the Hollywood axiom, *give the people what they want,* but rather, *show the people what they need to see.* And from that would-be *Olympus,* I would trumpet what would not only move individuals to tears but blow a hole through the armor around their hearts. If need be, I would pry open their closed minds with a crowbar. My company, *Attlas Arts*, would be for audiences a modern-day multimedia messiah—where they were blind, they would now see. You see, dear reader, where so many others occupying positions of power and authority had arrived there by taking *the road to hell,* I would take *the high road.* At least, that is what I planned to do, based on a very powerful *hunch.* Suffice it to say my life did not unfold as planned.

I did not know it at the time, but with the wisdom of hindsight, this Truth is self-evident: to Truly know *what in hell is with humanity,* I had to descend into hell first. For it was in hell that I discovered a

WHAT IN HELL IS WITH US?   ATTLAS ALLUX

labyrinth filled with endless corridors of thought and as many dead ends—beliefs, opinions, theories, theses, and antitheses—undermining the Truth. I would find myself wandering lost and alone down this road or that path, always following some signpost—*truth, this way*—only to wind up in yet another dead-end. Another broken promise. Another false idol. Or worse, some trap awaiting to ensnare and entangle another unsuspecting seeker of knowledge. That was me. Not only did these paths of inquiry not hold the keys to genuine objective knowledge, but they were also riddled with pitfalls, tricks, and tactics to deliberately confuse, obstruct, and confound me in my search for Truth. Every corridor I thought might lead at last to the answers I sought only ended in disappointment. Whenever I arrived at a point where I could proclaim, "this is it! I finally know!" some mysterious force at work in my life would yank the proverbial rug out from under my feet. Whatever illusions I had succumbed to, whatever delusions I had been living under, came crashing down around me as my worldview was once again shattered, and I remained as I was at the beginning of my journey: utterly ignorant. Forget *a little older, a little wiser.* A little older, a little humbler…that is, *humbled.*

But then, that is what *the underworld* is for, is it not, dear reader? Is not death—especially psychological death—the ultimate *humiliation?* I can tell you from personal experience that hell is not about *punishment.* Hell is *rehab* for the soul. We go through hell to be *burned—roasted* as one atop the dais of a celebrity comedy roast—when we are taken down a peg or two or *ten.* When we are made to look at ourselves with the penetrating eye of a humorist and admit in all humility, we laugh because it is funny, we laugh because it is *True.* In hell, all pretense and nonsense of our previous existence fall away. Every belief we thought we knew. Every identity we thought we were. All our belongings. All our desires. Even *our pronouns,* if we put stock in such matters, disintegrate. All is consumed in the flames of our own embers. Only then do we, like the proverbial phoenix, arise from the ashes reborn in the Light of Truth. Detoxed. An empty cup. Whereas before, we were overflowing with toxic beliefs about ourselves and the world. We emerge from the fire a clean slate, a blank canvas. Ready to receive the brush stroke of a new *ensō…*another *hero's journey…*another revolution on the *AUM of Life.*

What were some of these dark corridors that led me nowhere except to a necessary incineration of false beliefs held together by—and holding together—a false sense of self? Truly, I cannot list them all, let alone describe in detail the nature of their false claims or how they managed to ensnare and entangle me in my quest for knowledge. Such a book would be longer than what anyone would care to read, I reckon. Too much information is, at times, worse than too little. That said, information is on a need-to-know basis. And it is on that basis, dear reader, that we limit our attention to the four areas of interest revealed in the subtitle of this book. **Each of these four aspects of contemporary humanity explicitly promises some form of 'awakening' and/or 'salvation,' be it individually or as a collective:**

1. 'Dawn' of Artificial Intelligence (AI) and *Transhumanism (Human 2.0).*
2. 'Awakening' from *The Matrix* of Conspiracy.
3. 'Woke' Culture Wars.
4. New Age 'Spiritual Awakening.'

At one time or another in my life, sometimes for extended periods measured in years if not decades, I was utterly taken by the promise of awakening made by each of these phenomena. At times, by subscribing to one or more of these worldviews, I even believed myself to be awake—only to later find out the hard way *that nothing could have been further from the Truth.*

We must not underestimate the power of these secular pseudo-spiritual belief systems. I did. I was completely seduced by their power. I freely admit it. Given my deep longing for enlightenment, not for my own sake but for the sake of others and the planet, I became ensnared and entangled by the 'false gods' of these secular *religions.* Yes, there...I said it. I hesitate to bring religion into the picture, for it is a pandora's box whose complete examination is well beyond the scope of this book. But I must mention it briefly because many who have given themselves to the ideologies of transhumanism, conspiracy, woke, and New Age have done so, at least in part as a reaction to the degeneration of mainstream religions. How do I know this for sure? Remember, dear reader, I am not approaching this book as some outsider or intellectual. None of this is theoretical, speculative, or academic. Baptized and raised as a Roman Catholic, I left my religious upbringing behind in reaction to the many crimes, shortcomings, and hypocrisies of not only the Roman Catholic Church but many other Christian denominations and other organized religions. I left religion in search of answers, believing myself to have become an *atheist*—or at the very least an *agnostic*—when, in fact, I was a *gnostic* who simply did not know himself well enough. But we will get to that.

The point I must emphasize here is this: **I can attest personally to the seductive power of these four secular pseudo-spiritual belief systems discussed in this book.** They offer their own versions of *enlightenment, heaven on earth,* and, in the case of transhumanism, even *the next stage in human evolution,* if not outright *immortal life.* They are tailor-made for those who have *lost faith* in whatever religion or spiritual tradition they were brought up in. And I can say unequivocally that I am not the only one to have replaced their inherited faith with one or more secular religions chosen from among the four under discussion. And because of that, dear reader, I do not underestimate their power. On the contrary, I respect that power. That power ruled my life and, in no uncertain terms, kept me trapped on a treadmill of ignorance and failure, even as I believed myself to be awake and on the road to success.

I likely would still be on that treadmill had it not been for several serendipitous turns in my life. And one that would transform me forever. An episode that came crashing down like a meteor from the heavens and shattered the cyclical machinations of hell I was stuck in. It was an episode that left me broken psychologically. Exactly what I needed to break out of hell...by delving deeper into it. One might even say by *surrendering* to the journey through it. But that begs the question, dear reader: how did I even end up stuck on a treadmill in hell to begin with?

Normally, one might go about telling such a tale *chronologically*. Given the nature of the present discourse, dear reader, we will explore the hellish treadmill I was stuck on both chronologically and *thematically,* according to the spiral, cyclical nature of the AUM of Life. How each area of interest covered in this book played their often-overlapping roles in my journey. A journey that began for me in childhood and would take me to the gates of hell at the dawn of the new millennium. A period scarred at least in part by two separate events which, in many ways, would define the twenty-first century. Events which, for me, shoved me through the gate down into the darkness of the abyss which lay beyond it.

In the end, my journey through the labyrinth of hell taught me a great deal, specifically about the alleged 'awakening' and/or 'salvation' proffered by transhumanism, conspiracy, wokeness, and the New Age. The knowledge I accumulated on the journey was experiential and, in the 20/20 of hindsight, self-evident. And that is what this book is here to share with you and the world, dear reader: Self-Evident Experiential Knowledge—what each of us must SEEK if we wish to Truly awaken. If we remain trapped in our beliefs, wandering the dungeons beneath *The Great A-Weakening* of humanity, we will remain asleep, even as we believe ourselves to be awake. This is the harsh Truth I was shown the hard way. A harsh reality that *we*—myself, one with Attlas Allux—must share for the sake of suffering humanity.

– Attila Lewis Lendvai

P.S. A Note to e-Book Readers and Audiobook Listeners

You will find all figures, videos, and links referenced herein in the ***Resources for eBook & Audiobook*** section on our book's webpage on AttlasAllux.com.

Link 2: Book Resources, AttlasAllux.com

INTRODUCTION

In the more than two decades since the dawn of the new millennium, much has been said about 'awakening.' Countless books have been written on the subject. What is more, there are countless books listed on Amazon that invoke the most popular of awakening clichés in their very title, *The Great Awakening*...the most recent of these (at the time of publication) by infamous conspiracy theorist and founder of InfoWars.com, Alex Jones. Indeed, with subjects ranging from Qanon and UFO disclosure to Starseeds and Iran, dozens of books seem to suggest *the great awakening* is either imminent or has already arrived. Whether it be a mass global awakening or one reserved for a specific niche group of stalwart believers, the great awakening *craze* has certainly arrived and is beginning to take hold in the broader collective consciousness of humanity. And this is not the first time the West has been caught up in *awakening mania*.

According to *Wikipedia:*

> *The Great Awakening was a series of religious revivals in American Christian history. Historians and theologians identify three, or sometimes four, waves of increased religious enthusiasm between the early 18th century and the late 20th century. Each of these "Great Awakenings" was characterized by widespread revivals led by evangelical Protestant ministers, a sharp increase of interest in religion, a profound sense of conviction and redemption on the part of those affected, an increase in evangelical church membership, and the formation of new religious movements and denominations.*
>
> *– Source: <u>Great Awakening - Wikipedia</u>*

What do we make of all these so-called 'great awakenings?' What, if anything, do they signify? As the name implies, the notion of an awakening of any kind, and most certainly one which is 'great,' suggests a state of sleep—or at the very least slumber—which is interrupted by a newfound awareness, lucidity, activity, and potential. After all, do we not equate the expression "rise and shine" to waking up in the light of a new dawn, ready to take on a new day, complete with whatever challenges and adventures it may bring us? In the literal sense, then, awakening is commonplace to all humanity. And if we consider how important awakening is to our daily life, we may even be so bold as to call all awakening 'great.' For who can go through life without waking up each morning? For those living with life-threatening chronic illness or old age, the arrival of each new dawn may very well qualify as a 'great' awakening, indeed: one more new lease on life before the inevitable *great sleep*—as the poet might say.

Of course, the dozens of books dedicating themselves to the topic of the great awakening are not about the literal act of waking up from physical sleep. Awakening is employed as an allegory for stirring from a different kind of slumber, such as that of the famous racehorse, *Seabiscuit,* sauntering around the track, who suddenly *comes alive* as he bursts into a full gallop, as in the film. The legendary racehorse was neither literally dead nor "asleep"—as trainer Tom Smith stated—mere moments prior to his *awakening*. It is the sudden activation of the full force of his potential as a racehorse in contrast to his prior condition that invokes such figurative descriptions. What comes to mind are the following famous words of Patanjali:

> *When some great purpose inspires you, some extraordinary project, all your thoughts break their bonds. Your mind transcends limitation, your consciousness expands in every direction, and you find yourself in a new, great, and wonderful world. Dormant forces, faculties, and talents became alive, and you discover yourself to be a more remarkable person by far than you ever dreamed yourself.*
>
> *– Patanjali*

Pay close attention, dear reader, to Patanjali's use of the word *dreamed* here. Dreaming is, after all, an activity, first and foremost, for those who are still asleep. And most assuredly, Patanjali suggests, no matter who or what you dreamed yourself to be, the once dormant forces, faculties, and talents now coming alive within you reveal yourself to be far more remarkable as an awoken soul than one who was asleep, merely dreaming of themselves, and sleepwalking through life. With such words of wisdom echoing through the ether from a time centuries before Christ, filled with profound Truth, anyone with an iota of intuition will sense in the very core of their being, it is no wonder that the arousal of latent potential is the primary figurative meaning of awakening. **And for all of us who have experienced what we consider our awakening, Patanjali's description is practically a textbook definition of how it *feels*. Naturally, it follows that we think of ourselves from that point onward as *being awake*. But are we, really?**

When we think about what it means to be awake, we naturally contrast being awake with its opposite, being asleep. This, unfortunately, establishes a false dichotomy in our minds about the nature of awakening. The rational mind not only prefers the simplicity and expedience of the dialectic—black or white, us or them, right or wrong, yes or no, good or bad, this or that, etc.—its very operating system is based on it, and 'asleep or awake' is just another in an infinite series of expressions of binary duality. Like the 1s and 0s on which all digital technology is based, like any artificial intelligence, our rational minds default to a basic understanding of being awake as no longer being asleep—a switch that is either on or off. **This is an enticing mental trap.**

Let us return, dear reader, to our literal awakening to a new dawn. Picture, if you will, the rising sun over the horizon. Imagine the rising swell of an orchestra of birds greeting the sunrise with a symphony of song. Feel yourself slowly transitioning from sleep to slumber to something slightly more lucid yet not fully awake. Witness in your conscious imagination the slow gradation of darkness to dawn light and eventually to daylight proper. Even the sun needs time to slowly rise from its slumber before it can reach its zenith at high noon. Despite its ultimate foundations in binary duality, mechanical nature, in all its analog expressions, operates not as a series of on/off switches but rather as an infinite spectrum of *dimmer switches.*

Now, the thing about a dimmer switch is that it does have an on or off state. There is a point when there is no light—the off position. Turn or slide the dimmer switch but a millimeter, and suddenly, there is light—the on position. But is the light *fully on,* dear reader? Most certainly, upon activating the dimmer switch, the room may no longer be *entirely* in the dark as it was before, but with the dimmer switch only slightly engaged, can we honestly claim the space is *completely illuminated?* Or is it still *mostly* in the dark? Aye, there's the rub, and the first problem with humanity's oversimplification and fundamental misunderstanding of awakening and what it means to being awake. And we have only just begun to shed light on the matter.

Before a plane can take off from a runway, it must achieve the minimum speed necessary to become airborne. But getting into the air is only the first step. It must climb to its cruising altitude, where it assumes its cruising speed. In any practical reality, it is not until the airplane has reached its cruising altitude and speed that meaningful flight is achieved. Sure, *technically,* flight is achieved the moment all landing gear leaves the tarmac, and there might have been a time when such minimal standards were sufficient to claim a successful flight took place—when Orvell and Wilbur Wright were pioneering manmade flight at Kittyhawk, for instance—but since those fateful days, aviation has advanced somewhat, and the minimum standards for air travel along with it. Today, the threshold for what is considered a viable, reliable, and relatively safe flight is orders of magnitude what it once was. No reasonable person would contest this point.

And yet, when it comes to awakening consciousness, we are all still at Kittyhawk, marveling at our short-lived bouts of intuitive knowing, genuine lucidity, True objective insight—or subjective psychedelic trips. Who among this humanity can honestly say they have reached *conscious cruising altitude and speed?* Not just during the waking hours of the day, but all night as well? Who among us is truly awake, consciously speaking, 24/7—even as our body and brain sleep at night? Who among us can see into the higher dimensions of reality at all times? Are we even aware of our Higher Self? Not just *intellectually,* that is, not merely believing we know, but rather, *consciously, experientially* knowing, able to receive practical information, wisdom, and guidance from our Innermost Being at all times. There are more esoteric criteria defining the threshold of what it means to be truly awake, and we will get to those in good time.

The point is, for most of us, the moment we experience an *untangling* of a knot we had previously been entangled in, we believe ourselves to be newly empowered, armed with a length of string. But we never honestly consider asking ourselves the age-old philosophical question: *just how long is a piece of string?* How long must the string be? All we know is that we experienced an *enlengthening* of what was once a tangled, knotted, frayed mess. What is more, we witness what appears to be an enormous ball of string growing in the world, and, adding our own bit of string to it, we declare ourselves to be a part of *the great enlengthening* of humanity.

Naturally, the rational mind thinks thus. It leaps to its own defense and exploits every opportunity it can for its own self-aggrandizement. Our "I" cannot resist taking possession of our newfound bit of string, even if it is only three inches in length. Similarly, we cannot resist identifying and becoming attached to a newly acquired spark of awakening, no matter how it shows up for us. And so, as soon as we experience some liberation from entanglement, we become attached to our bit of string, identify with *the great enlengthening*, seek validation through other self-styled *enlengthened ones,* and partake in an echo chamber where together we dream up all manner of rationalizations to shew away the harsh reality that each and every last one of us is in possession of a bit of string which is at most a few inches in length.

What comes to mind, dear reader, is Monty Python's sketch in which a fellow who has inherited 122,000 miles of string turns to an over-enthusiastic advertising executive to help him with marketing it to the public. "But there's a snag, you see. Due to bad planning, the 122,000 miles are in three-inch lengths. So it's not very useful." To which the advertising agent gleefully replies, "well, that's our selling point!" And hilarity ensues…

Video 1: String (YouTube)

In the climax of said sketch, the frantic advertising executive, played brilliantly by John Cleese, launches into a protracted sales pitch as to what will successfully sell *Simpson's Individualized Stringettes* to the public…

> *Sex, sex, sex, must get sex into it. Wait, I see a television commercial- There's this nude woman in a bath holding a bit of your string. That's great, great, but we need a doctor, got to have a medical opinion. There's a nude woman in a bath with a doctor—that's too sexy. Put an Archbishop there watching them, that'll take the curse off it. Now, we need children and animals. There's two kids admiring the string, and a dog admiring the Archbishop who's blessing the string. Uhh…international flavor's missing…make the Archbishop Greek Orthodox…. why not ArchBishop Makarios? No no, he's dead.*

Never mind, we'll get his brother, it'll be cheaper. So, there's Archbishop Makarios's brother... (fade out)

— String, Monty Python

If it is not self-evident to you, dear reader, the genius of this seminal work of absurdist satire is its ability to put us in the shoes of the *straight man,* Mr. Simpson, who, being firmly grounded in objective reality, rightly sees the advertising executive's rants as nothing short of "mad." The absurd claims, outlandish slogans, and endless rationalizations of this mad ad exec's sales pitch for string in three-inch lengths are hilarious to us precisely because we know from experience how long string must be to be remotely useful— considerably more than three inches. We also laugh because we, too, have encountered pitchmen and salesmen of all stripes, and we know they will say almost anything to get us to buy into whatever it is they are flogging. Python's sketch merely stretches reality to the absurdist extreme to satirize what we all know to be the Truth—not intellectually, but consciously—from our own direct experience of objective reality. As with all works of comedic genius, we laugh because it is funny; we laugh because it is True.

Recall, dear reader, the allegory we invoked just prior to sharing the sketch and that the 122,000 miles of string in three-inch lengths is the equivalent of *the great enlengthening.* Play the role of the straight man. Ground yourself in objective reality and use your conscious imagination to replace a colossal sum of three-inch lengths of string with the alleged great awakening of humanity—an aggregate of many millions of tiny sparks of awakened consciousness. Now, be completely honest with yourself. What if John Cleese were reciting the claims, beliefs, and endless rationalizations being made by pitchmen of every conceivable stripe—scientists, theorists, futurists, intellectuals, politicians, theologians, coaches, gurus, influencers, et al.—touting the enormous profundity of the great awakening of humanity while dancing around the objective fact that the practical share of said awakening in the lives of individuals is minimal at best, and ultimately self-serving at worst. Make no mistake, dear reader, there are industries worth billions that depend on selling this or that *great awakening* to which countless pitchmen and women have attached themselves like so many ticks on a deer's back, for whom *the great awakening* is their lifeblood. All mainstream and social media platforms are infested with this parasitic variety of huckster hocking their oh-so-seductive yet too-good-to-be-true silver bullets, magic pills, and every conceivable kind of awakening-related snake oil you can imagine. You know this from your own experience to be True. From now on, whenever you encounter the most vitriolic, seductive, and/or animated characters pitching their particular brand of awakening, you may hear echoes of John Cleese's madcap advertising executive. And, yet, even after all that, you may still believe that none of it applies to you—to your awakening and the brand of great awakening you identify with and count yourself a part of. All who experience an awakening feel that way at some point, for it is the very nature of awakening that the ego-mind covets and wants to possess, corrupt, exploit, and make *fall* (asleep).

I certainly experienced it. More than once, in fact, I found myself falling for each of several different industries' unique brand of awakening—transhumanist AI, conspiracy, wokeness, and the New Age. In the quest to unravel the threads needed for my own awakening, each time, I found myself becoming *more entangled* in the very string that I was supposed to be *untangling* and *enlengthening* (if not fully enlengthened already)! So, I descended deeper into the dungeons of my own delusions, where my quest would finally take a turn. *Part One* of this book recounts my journey through psychological hell. *Part Two* shares revelations from hell concerning the true nature and ultimate purpose behind false awakenings—*The Great A-Weakening of Humanity*. Finally, *Part Three* SEEKs to share self-evident experiential knowledge of how to disentangle from what keeps us asleep in the dark while dreaming ourselves to be awake so we may escape the psychological hell of hypnosis and ignorance and Truly awaken into the Light.

PART I:

A SEEKER'S JOURNEY THROUGH HELL

MY CALL TO ADVENTURE

About 'Me'

I was born *Attila Lewis Lendvai* in Toronto, Ontario, on the second day of June 1973, to very proud, loving, and hardworking Hungarian immigrant parents. My only sibling was an older brother of three years. We lived at that time in a tiny house on Stanhope Avenue in East York, just East of the Don Valley. By the time I was old enough to begin school, our family had moved to Henderson Avenue in Thornhill. I walked every day to St. Agnes Roman Catholic school in Willowdale until grade four. During those years, our family attended St. Elizabeth of Hungary Church, where my brother and I served as altar boys.

One could say I experienced a devout Catholic upbringing. But in Truth, I always felt a deep spiritual connection to Christ. Even as a young child, kneeling on the altar during mass, I would look up at the cross hanging behind the altar, and gazing down upon me, as though looking directly through me into my soul, was a life-size Jesus hanging from the cross:

Figure 1: Jesus on the Cross in St. Elizabeth of Hungary Church

Even then, as a young child, looking up at the crucified man who would be reborn The Christ, it was as though I understood what he was trying to tell me. In my mind, I would answer him, "yes, I get it." Of course, it would be decades before I would comprehend the implications and appreciate the magnitude of the commitment I had made. Still, that fact did not change my earnest pursuit of a life of service to humanity. A commitment that was bolstered by an experience of delving within myself.

My First Samadhi

At around the age of five, I found myself lying in bed one day, eyes closed, wondering to myself, "what's in there?" I had at that time never even heard the word *meditation,* let alone received any instruction in meditation practice. All I knew was that there was something in there waiting for me in the dark, and I just had to know what it was. And so, as any five-year-old might, I closed my eyes tightly and began repeating to myself in my head, "go deeper, go deeper, go deeper." In typical fashion, when we close our eyes tightly in the middle of the day, we can often see vaguely circular patterns of color and varying shades of black appearing to move inward or outward (your experience may vary). I imagine these shapes and patterns relate to the structure of our eyes and varying other physical factors, along with metaphysical phenomena science knows not of. In any case, in the imagination of a five-year-old, these expanding concentric circles of color leading to evermore darker shades of blackness served as portals, taking me deeper and deeper into myself. Closer and closer to what I knew I just had to reach as I continued to tell myself to "go deeper, go deeper." And so, it continued. I cannot truly say for how long. It might have only been a matter of minutes. But to a young child, even thirty minutes can feel like hours. Except in this case, I was not asking anyone, "are we there yet?" as an impatient child might, for I was an intrepid explorer. For me, this was an adventure. I had visual stimulation and an active role to play in response to this inner knowing that this was something I simply had to do…a journey I simply had to take.

And so, I did. Plunging deeper and deeper into the darkness. Eventually, everything settled down and went completely dark and still. No more movement. No more feeling of forward momentum. What I experienced was a loud booming voice that must have come from within me but filled my ears and seemed to fill the whole room. It was not my voice. It was an adult's voice, which was assertive yet gentle, strong yet soft. It had no thick Hungarian accent, so it could not be my father, either. It spoke but one line: "you have reached the center of your mind." And that was all. I opened my eyes and looked all around my room for who might be there. But I was alone in my room, and the door was shut. I would not understand until a decade later what I had experienced (when I would finally learn about meditation and samadhi, or ecstasy). All I knew was that I had succeeded in my goal. I knew there was something *in there,* and now I knew it was not something but *someone.* And whoever it was, they responded to my overtures. I acted, and they replied. I began to consider the possibility that they had, in fact, been *calling me* to "go deeper" and that what I thought had been my voice was really their voice. Had God spoken to me? To a five-year-old Catholic boy, that seemed like a very real possibility. And as remarkable an experience as all this had been, I put it out of my mind and just went on with my life as any other kid. I had not been freaked out by it. But I also had not become attached to it. I would not try to repeat the experience, per se. But I would spend time lying in bed with my eyes closed with the experiential knowledge that I was not alone. And that whatever God was, He was not *out there.*

Learning What Was Possible

My elementary school, St. Agnes, was relatively new and based on a modern open-concept design. There were no classrooms as such. There was a large open area divided into four quadrants: grades 1-2, 2-3, 3-4, and French class. There were no desks in rows. We instead sat around tables of different shapes and sizes, arranged randomly throughout each class area. Each class also had an open space on the carpeted floor where we would gather around the teacher for lessons before returning to our tables to do work. We were not only not forbidden from getting up from our tables, we were encouraged to do so. I made it my mission every day, after completing my work, to go from table to table, assisting any of my classmates who might be struggling with applying that day's lesson to their work. On my report cards from that time, my teachers described my presence as like having a teacher's assistant in class. Yes, you could rightly accuse me of being a 'teacher's pet' in that regard. I was an accomplished student, a fairly successful athlete—particularly in track and field and cross-country—and in any of my classes, there were no cliques. No bullies. No outcasts. If someone in our class had a birthday party, everyone from the class would attend. Everyone was friends with everyone else. I made sure of it. If ever there was a fight in the schoolyard, I would be the one to break it up and make sure that the quarreling parties made up. For me, my time at St. Agnes was a veritable utopia. But nothing so good was ever meant to last.

Stepping into Pink Floyd's *The Wall*

In the summer between grades four and five, my family moved to Guelph, Ontario, just forty-five minutes southwest of Toronto. My father had gotten a job as plant manager of a shirt manufacturer there two years prior. He had been commuting all that time since we were unable to sell our house due to the recession and high mortgage rates. When September rolled around, and it came time to go to my new school in Guelph, St. Paul's, I had a sinking feeling in my stomach. No 'new kid' ever has it easy, I suppose, but the contrast between what I had become accustomed to and what I was in for cannot be overstated. From the rows of one-hundred-year-old desks, complete with holes for inkpots, to the classroom rules and regulations, which were completely new to me, I experienced a kind of culture shock to my very core. I at last understood that all those nightmarish depictions of school in movies and TV shows were, in fact, based in reality. Right down to a principal who looked like an ugly man in drag or the Wicked Witch of the West, who kept the lights off most days to save money. The classroom was cold, dark, and unfriendly. The kids were no better.

In Toronto, I had been accepted into a gifted-student program and would have been bussed to a special education school twice a week to be with all the other gifted kids. I was scheduled to begin the program in grade five. Instead, I was trapped in *The Wall,* in a small backwater town, where I was not only *the new kid* but a *scab.* I would soon learn about another phenomenon that was completely foreign to me: bullying.

Shunned and outcast was one thing, but the bullying was something else. My only friend was Eduardo, who was in grade six. Whereas in St. Agnes, I had effectively been at the head of a class of friends and colleagues, in St. Paul, I was at the polar opposite end of a class of bullies and betters. It was not long before it all got to me emotionally and psychologically, such that even my teacher and the school board recognized my plight. Sparing you the details of the administrative wrangling that took place that year, I was eventually allowed to transfer to St. John's elementary school on the other end of town for grade six, where I was met with a warmer reception from classmates who saw me as their equal instead of a pariah.

This reprieve was short-lived; however, since the next year, I would have to attend the junior high school in my district. All the new friends I made at St. John's went to a different junior high school. Despite this, in junior high, I was again able to make new friends. Friends who were also high-performing academically and the school board arranged a 'fast-tracking' scheme for us whereby we were allowed to complete all our core grade eight subjects in half a year, meaning we earned four high school credits in the latter half of grade eight. Combined with four years of summer school, I was able to complete high school one year early. It also meant being able to make friends and socialize with classmates a year or two older than myself. It was quite uncanny what an extra year made in terms of maturity. All this made for a high school career that was not altogether easy but thoroughly enjoyable.

A Love of Roleplaying

Like all children, I had an active imagination, which followed me well into my teen years. And while playing was all well and good, for me, merely playing games could not compare to what I felt in my heart to be the ultimate in play—roleplay. My first foray into roleplaying was—as it was for many of my generation—playing *Star Wars* and the like with friends. Individuals would be assigned the roles of Luke, Leia, Han Solo, Chewbacca, et al., and the ongoing adventures of these favorite heroes from a galaxy far, far away ensued. Later in my childhood, the advent of *Choose Your Own Adventure* books brought the fun of roleplaying to the joys of reading narratives. Now, not only would you be swept away into another world, into the shoes of another character, and an adventure of a lifetime, but you could actually determine the outcome of said adventure. It was a revelation for me. Around the same time, my brother and I received a Colecovision video game console for Christmas. And although I could never quite get the hang of games like *Donkey Kong* or *Zaxxon,* I became obsessed with dungeon-crawling games like *Venture* and *Gateway to Apshai.*

Video 2: Colecovision - Gateway to Apshai (YouTube)

It is no wonder that years later, I would become obsessed with playing *Diablo* and *Diablo II*—considered by many to be the greatest ARPG ever made. Although many believed *Diablo* to have pioneered the genre, for me, it was an upgraded revival of the action roleplaying genre, which had mysteriously vanished from the scene for over a decade.

It should be obvious, dear reader, that I eventually switched from video games to computer games when I reached adolescence. My older brother and I bought our first PC to do schoolwork and such, but it was not long before we were engrossed in PC gaming. The keyboard—and later mouse—interface allowed for more engaging story-driven puzzles, strategy, roleplaying, and simulation games. CRPGs were far more sophisticated, and since many were developed by North American developers, they did not suffer from many of the tropes established by their console-based JRPG counterparts. In fact, titles like *The Bard's Tale* and licensed games like SSI's *Gold Box* series and later Bioware's *Forgotten Realms* games attempted to bring the tabletop RPG experience of *Dungeons & Dragons* to the computer—one which I was also familiar with, having played D&D and Advanced D&D, along with several tabletop strategy games.

No roleplaying game could ever come close to what is without question the greatest CRPG series ever made—certainly in terms of cultivating virtue. We are, of course, referring to *Ultima*, specifically the *Age of Enlightenment* trilogy consisting of *Ultima IV: Quest of the Avatar, Ultima V: Warriors of Destiny,* and *Ultima VI, The False Prophet.* This trilogy was followed by the pinnacle of the series, *Ultima VII Part One, The Black Gate,* and *Part Two, The Serpent Isle.* It is a game series that does away with the moral ambiguities of *Dungeons & Dragons* (which allows players to be "chaotic evil" if they wish with no real penalty) and most other games filled with senseless violence, questionable ethics, etc.

Figure 2: Ultima IV Box Cover Art by Denis Loubet

It is the first in the "Age of Enlightenment" trilogy, shifting the series from the hack and slash, dungeon crawl gameplay of its "Age of Darkness" predecessors towards an ethically-nuanced, story-driven approach. Ultima IV has a much larger game world than its predecessors, with an overworld map sixteen times the size of Ultima III and puzzle-filled dungeon rooms to explore. Ultima IV further advances the franchise with dialogue improvements, new means of travel and exploration, and world interactivity. In 1996, Computer Gaming World named Ultima IV as #2 on its Best Games of All Time list on the PC. Designer Richard Garriott considers this game to be among his favorites from the Ultima series.[2]

– Source: Wikipedia, Ultima IV: Quest of the Avatar

In Ultima IV, you are called to the mythical land of Britannia by its benevolent ruler, Lord British. From the outset, the player is made to understand that this will be a computer role-playing game unlike any other. The character creation exists as a series of questions testing the player's preference for one virtue or another. Depending on how the player answers, they may end up as a Paladin (whose prime virtue is honor), a Shepherd (humility), a mage (honesty), or a druid (justice). But why read about it when you can take the Ultima IV Personality Test and experience it for yourself.

Link 3: Ultima Personality Test

Once you enter the world of Britannia, Lord British asks for your help in aiding the people out of the darkness that has befallen the land. Yes, there is an over-world to explore, dungeons to raid, monsters to slay, and treasures to find, but in addition to these well-worn CRPG devices, there are also less common ones. You can have veritable conversations with NPCs (non-player characters). And you need to talk to *everyone* in the world *honestly* if you hope to get them to divulge valuable information and clues necessary to fulfill your ultimate quest (pun intended)—to recover *The Codex of Ultimate Wisdom* from *The Great Stygian Abyss*. Without it, the land will remain in darkness, its people becoming evermore ignorant and lost, its villains becoming evermore emboldened, with even more denizens of the deep clamoring up out of the darkness to roam the land, terrorizing its citizens. Wow. It is as if Gnosis itself had been lost in darkness, and as a result, the entire world was going to hell. Sounds familiar, does it not, dear reader?

So, the world of Britannia needs a hero to SEEK and recover the Codex of Ultimate Wisdom but to do so, you will first need to prove you are worthy of it. You must become *The Avatar,* a perfected being of impeccable virtue. To do so will require you to learn the location of the eight *Shrines of Virtue:* Honesty, Compassion, Valor, Justice, Honor, Sacrifice, Spirituality, and Humility. Each shrine is protected by a *guardian,* however, and you cannot pass without having the appropriate <u>rune</u>. The rune is hidden in a nearby town associated with the corresponding virtue (i.e., Moonglow is a village of Mages and relates to honesty). Once you have recovered the appropriate rune, you can attend the corresponding shrine to *meditate.* But you cannot do so without knowing the correct <u>mantra</u>, which you must learn by talking to the citizens of the town. They may not be so quick to divulge the mantra, however, especially if you have failed to uphold the relevant virtue.

After collecting the appropriate rune, learning the mantra, and finding the shrine, you can then enter the shrine and meditate. Doing so will award you an eighth of an *ankh* (the symbol of The Avatar). Upon doing so at all eight shrines and completing a few more quests, you can now descend into the Great Stygian Abyss to retrieve the Codex of Ultimate Wisdom. To do so, you must first delve into each one of the eight dungeons embodying the antithesis of a virtue (an ego/vice/sin), named Deceit, Despise, Destard, Wrong, Covetous, Shame, Hythloth, and The Abyss. You must first learn the location of each dungeon before descending into it, vanquishing its monsters, and recovering a colored stone of virtue that needs to be combined with other stones of virtue and placed in the correct combinations on the *altars* of Truth, Courage, and Love. Answer the questions posed by the Codex, and you become *The Avatar.* However, it should be noted that, at *any time* throughout the game, any unvirtuous acts will cause you to become barred from entering a shrine or even lose an eighth of the ankh you have already earned. If you lie, kill non-evil creatures, kill monsters who are fleeing from battle, steal, fail to show charity, or fail to sacrifice for others, the game will respond in kind. NPCs might refuse to talk with you, deny you their wares, etc. Shrine Guardians will turn you away. And you will have to go visit *The Seer* often to check on the status of your virtue. Are we beginning to appreciate the depth of esotericism this game explores, dear reader?

You see, in the final analysis, this is what set Ultima IV apart from all other games of its type. There was no 'final boss.' There was no moustache-twirling uber-villain hell-bent on conquering the land whom you had to stop. No, **the only person standing between you and recovering the Codex of Ultimate Wisdom (and saving the world) was you**. Your actions. Your choices. Your virtue. Even though you might have slain all the monsters terrorizing the land and plenty more in the dungeons beneath, your own defects and vices were your primary adversaries. The game would throw temptations at you all the time: what Yoda would call the *"quicker, easier, more seductive"* path leading *"to the Dark Side."* And if you fell for said temptations, you could achieve wealth, power, and notoriety, but not the rank of *Avatar*, and thus not the respect of the people nor the right to hold the Codex of Ultimate Wisdom. Chew on that for a while, dear reader.

I am not the only one for whom *Ultima IV* and its sequels had such an impact. You should not be surprised to learn of the many tributes to the Ultima games online, including YouTube. Probably the most entertaining—if at times silly—is Noah Antwiler's *Ultima Retrospective*. A more sober and philosophical approach comes from GaminGHD:

Video 3: Gaming Culture: How the Story of Ultima Managed to Convey Complicated Philosophical Concepts | Part 1 (YouTube)

We could certainly go on at length about the Ultima series and the impression it made on all those who played it. But since GaminGHD and others have already done so, we leave it to you, dear reader, to make your own inquiries. However, if by chance you feel as though you missed out on a truly great era in gaming in the 1980s and 90's, fret not: there are several ways you can have the authentic Ultima Age of Enlightenment experience, including several different fan ports, upgrades, and complete remakes based on more modern 3D graphics engines which run fairly well on Windows. Some of the more well-known of these **Ultima Fan-Created Remakes & Remasters** can be found in the ***Appendix.***

A Call to the World Stage

It was in junior high school that I had my first real taste of theatre and experienced the magic of playing roles in front of an audience. If you recall, dear reader, I had fast-tracked grade eight such that I took four grade nine courses in the latter half of that year. One of those credits was in grade nine drama. I was hooked. I would pursue drama throughout high school as well, along with all the 'mandatory' STEM classes—as demanded by my father, whose ambition for me was to take sciences at university and become a doctor. Although I performed well in STEM—I was the first student ever at my high school to receive a perfect final grade in senior biology class—my real passion was performing on stage. I had a genuine propensity for the written and spoken word. STEM was stimulating intellectually, but English and Drama were engaging, exhilarating, and enlightening, emotionally and spiritually. I lived by Einstein's immortal words, "imagination is more important than knowledge." For me, stories could reveal profound universal Truths where science could only describe surface-level truth. In many ways, I felt in my heart of hearts a deep longing to connect with others at the level I had experienced on my childhood journey into the center of my being. And I would never be able to make such connections through STEM subjects. Nor as a doctor, nor lawyer, nor politician.

I had considered the possibility of entering the priesthood at one point in my childhood. There was one problem. No sermon or scripture had ever brought a tear to my eye. Hymns, sacred artwork, and sculpture aside, my experience of Catholicism left me somewhat cold and bereft of True meaning. Music, stories, art, theatre, and film, however…through them, I could touch the divine. I would find myself moved by performances more than I would ever be by a religious ceremony. And it was not mere sentimentality. I would cry tears of joy at moments that others considered mundane. I would see and hear things in contemporary mythologies that touched my soul in ways that the biblical texts chosen by Emperor Constantine at the Council of Nicaea did not. If I could touch others' souls the way certain films, in particular, touched mine, that would be the key to reaching them, serving humanity, and fulfilling my oath to truly have an impact and make the greatest difference I could. An impact that I felt myself having every time I stepped on stage in front of an audience. On stage, no one saw *me*. On stage, they saw and heard what flowed through me. I was merely a vessel, a vehicle, a servant of Shakespeare, or whatever divinely inspired narrative needed to be told. And always in the back of my mind—or rather, *in the center of my heart-mind*—was that voice that had spoken to me all those years ago when I first dove deep into the space within myself in search of what— or rather who—I knew was calling me there. That voice had become the familiar *Still Soft Voice* over the years, calling me to pursue my passion for sharing stories and acting on the stage—and on the world stage— for the sake of humanity. A voice which, I would soon learn, had a *name*.

Unearthing Attlas

Throughout the eight years I attended high school and university, I worked part-time at K-Mart. My mother had worked there for years, and like several other employees whose children worked at the Guelph store part-time, I began as a *bagger* during the busy holiday shopping season (when such levels of customer service were the norm and not the exception). The following summer, I began working on the floor in various departments, and sometimes even alongside my mother, who, being the store's resident *green thumb*, worked all summer outside in the garden center. By the time I was sixteen years old, I was regularly scheduled to work in the camera, technology, and jewelry department. My years of experience with PC ownership, knowledge of video games, love of amateur photography, and manual dexterity for changing watch batteries and the like did not go unnoticed. Nor did my reputation for maturity and trustworthiness in handling some of the most expensive merchandise in the store. Besides, I had taken after my mother, who was held in high regard by management and customers alike for her outstanding customer service.

Often, people would enter the store asking for "the large European lady." It was not long before they were asking for "the tall fellow with the glasses."

As an aside, I would always put my experience working at K-Mart on my resume, a practice which I would be chastened for by those *in the know,* who would tell me flatly, "no one cares." And that is a mistake. Years later, when I found myself working with a publicly traded Internet startup, conducting all their marketing communications and public relations, I was also responsible for investor relations. And on the first investor call I ever took, the fellow on the other end of the line was screaming bloody murder. The dip in our stock price had caused a significant loss to his portfolio, and he was on the phone to give our CEO a piece of his mind. As it turned out, he got me instead. And I can tell you, dear reader, having had no formal business training prior to that point, I had already dreaded taking my first investor relations call. Now, here it was, and the investor was yelling and carrying on about what, for him, amounted to a small fortune lost on our company's stock. And in that moment, dear reader, I was given a powerful insight as the Still Soft Voice whispered, "you've been here before; you've got this." A wave of calm washed over me as I collected myself in the experiential knowledge of all those times I had dealt with angry customers while working at K-Mart. And it was in that instant that the following timeless, universal Truth was revealed to me. **It makes no difference whether someone is angry over a hundred-thousand-dollar loss or a ninety-nine-cent pair of rubber flipflops:** *the conversation is exactly the same.*

With that knowledge, I proceeded to apply all my experience gained over eight years of customer service. The fact that I had never taken an investor call before became completely irrelevant. My inexperience in investor relations was entirely overridden by my experience in customer service, as evidenced by my responses to the anger and vitriol coming over the phone. "Yes sir…of course, sir…naturally, I would feel the same way you do were I in your shoes," etc. It took about half-an-hour, but eventually, he calmed down, heard our side of the story not reflected in the share price, and felt satisfied that the company's future was in good hands. He realized that management did, in fact, know what it was doing and that this temporary downturn in the share price was merely a blip. After that, he began calling me monthly for updates, and we ended up becoming friends. The Still Soft Voice had led me through the fire yet again, no worse for wear.

It was during my time at K-Mart that I developed a more personal and practical working relationship with the Still Soft Voice. I had learned to trust not only in its guidance but in the guidance and wisdom of others related to—possibly even arranged by—it. I learned, for instance, that my emotional response to works of high art came directly from my connection to the Still Soft Voice. It informed me when I was hearing the *Voice of God* essentially speaking to me through music, film, theatre, poetry, nature, and even other people. It was in one such circumstance that the Still Soft Voice of my Higher Self finally formally introduced Himself.

On a break once in the cafeteria, a new part-time employee sat down and introduced himself as Jamie. I introduced myself, and immediately, this person, whom I had never met before in my life, locked eyes with me in what could only be described as an intense, penetrating stare. He was looking into my very soul, it seemed. Without missing a beat, he said, "You're Atlas." Confused by this at that moment, I thought perhaps he had misheard, so I politely corrected him that my name was Attila. Without flinching or even blinking, he repeated, "No, you're Atlas." He had not misheard me after all. I smiled, a little uncomfortable with how forward he was being, our eyes still locked with laser-like precision and intensity. Sensing my discomfort, with a slowed tempo but no less assertiveness, a broad and bright glowing smile on his face, he repeated, "listen to me, you are Atlas." For several minutes, no matter what I said, no matter how I reacted, Jamie would repeat the same assertion, over and over, ever with that glowing smile and those penetrating eyes, as though he was speaking to my very being. After overcoming my ego's apprehension, I eventually relaxed into the moment and received a resounding "Trust James. He speaks the Truth" from the Still Soft Voice. I smiled at him and nodded knowingly. "Yes, you're right, James. I *am* Atlas." Jamie smiled and nodded knowingly, satisfied that we were on the same page. For the entire time he worked at K-Mart, Jamie never called me anything else. Like a cosmic inside joke that only he and I were in on, from that point forward, I was Atlas. I had been given my True Self's name.

It was during this time that I had made the decision to double-down on my life's vocation and pursue English and Dramatic Arts at University. Not abandoning STEM entirely, just recognizing that it was not my calling…at least, not as it was presently understood by the so-called experts in the field. No, I would become a maker of high drama and fine films, and my work would move audiences in the same ways I was moved by works of high art. I would change hearts and minds first through the *mightiness of the pen,* as it were, and then through the power of motion pictures. My production company would be called *Attlas Arts* and would represent the first manifestation of *The Attlas Project*—the name given to my life's work. It would be two decades before I fully understood the significance of these two names—Attlas and Attila, my given name. But why did I have to spell Attlas with two t's instead of just one? That answer would come a decade later when my dreams and plans for Attlas Arts came crashing down around me.

Attlas Leads Me Home

For eighteen months after completing my undergraduate degree, I pursued an acting career in Toronto. To augment my theatrical training and stage experience gained at school, I enrolled in The National Institute of Broadcasting to get technical training in the media arts, including hands-on voice-over and on-camera work. I went to many auditions and got leading roles in a community theatre production of *The Glass Menagerie* and in an original student film. I had a few spots and features running on AM radio in Toronto, including the ironically named and short-lived *Computer Conscience,* in which I gave tech advice for PC and Windows users. I also emceed the annual Hungarian Helicon Ball at The Royal York hotel. One of the last remaining debutant balls in all of North America, in old-world grand tradition and the Viennese style, the highlight of the evening featured dozens of debutants in white dresses and their escorts in black tuxedos waltzing to Strauss's *The Blue Danube*. All this saw me slowly gaining notoriety with a handful of movers and shakers in the Canadian film industry since several were Hungarian in origin. I felt all I needed to do was keep working my way up slowly, making sure they knew who I was. I was certain eventually I would catch a break. And indeed, that is exactly what happened.

Through a Hungarian acquaintance, I managed to get referred to the President of Alliance Pictures, Canada's largest film studio at the time. The CEO of Alliance-Atlantis, the parent company, was also Hungarian, and many of the senior executives and employees were likewise of Hungarian origin. "This is my ticket," I thought. For surely, I had enough talent and experience under my belt to warrant getting my foot in the door with such a Hungarian-friendly organization! I remember barely being able to contain my excitement on the day of the big meeting with the President of Alliance Pictures. He asked me what he could do for me, and in my most earnest and humble voice, I told him all I wanted was an opportunity to get my foot in the door. I would gladly fetch coffee and sweep floors just for the opportunity to be on set, just for the chance to work in the industry, which would define my life's work. After a short pause, he leaned forward in his chair, placed his hands on the large mahogany desk between us, looked me in the eye, and said, "let me give you some advice. Don't try making it in this business. You don't have the right last name." Stunned and confused by this answer, I naively replied, "I don't understand. I thought this business was all about who you know, not what you know. And I'm Hungarian, and you're Hungarian, and I thought we're supposed to help each other…" "NO," he interrupted me assertively mid-sentence. "I am *Jewish first,* Hungarian *second. And you,* my young friend, you *do not have the right last name."* You can imagine my shocked silence, dear reader. I had been indoctrinated in Critical Race Theory in university and believed I knew all about racial discrimination and anti-Semitism. But no professor had ever warned me I might be discriminated against for being a gentile.

I thanked him for his time, picked up the proverbial gauntlet he had thrown down at my feet, and stepped out of his office into the hall. As the door closed behind me, the Still Soft Voice resounded with another timeless, universal Truth, namely, the world's *Golden Rule:* **He who has the gold makes the rules.** For I knew that had I walked into that office with twenty million dollars and a film treatment under my arm, my last name would not have mattered one iota to the President of Alliance Pictures—or any other film executive, for that matter. I had played my ace card, and my hand came up short. I would have to take a different path to *The Attlas Project.*

Within a matter of days of the meeting, I was leafing through the *careers* section of the newspaper when I stumbled across an ad for Geos Language Corporation to teach English in Japan. "There, that one!"

Attlas seemed to speak loud and clear to me. Within weeks, I was attending a new teacher training program at their offices in Toronto. Two months later, I was on a Japan Airlines flight to Osaka. I was met by Funakisan, who would be my manager for the coming year. She accompanied me on the train to the final stop of a branch of the *Keihan Line,* which runs between Osaka and Kyoto. It was a bright July day in the small town of Uji, and as I stepped out of the station into the sun and onto the bridge spanning the Uji River, I drank in the scene, which could have been at home in a Japanese painting or postcard.

To the right was Uji-shi, a picturesque small town filled with traditional wooden homes and buildings. Ahead was the Uji River. On the right-hand banks, I could see the roofs of Uji Temple and Uji Shrine peeking out from above the low canopy of trees that lined the river. There was a bright orange and green walking bridge extending from the right-hand bank to a small wooded rocky island in the middle of the broad river, from which arose a thirteen-tier stone pagoda. Lining the left-hand bank of the river, a road and grove of cherry blossom trees stretched upstream and vanished around the corner of the forested mountains, extending upward into the sky. A man in hip waders was standing in the middle of the river, a long fishing pole in hand, attentively considering his reel and line. And high above him, in the blue sky brushed with wisps of white cloud, a family of three hawks were likewise fishing.

As I stood there, upon Uji bridge, unable to hear anything Funakisan might have been saying to me, all the modernity of Japan faded into the background—the traffic, the noise, the beeping of the pedestrian signals—and I was completely overtaken by the moment. And just then, every cell, every molecule, every single fiber of my being let out a simultaneous and resounding sigh of relief and spoke out in complete unison…

We're home.

Recall, dear reader, how I had been raised Roman Catholic. I had never truly given reincarnation much thought. But now, in this instant, I knew that reincarnation was real and that I had lived previously in Japan. Attlas had led me home. Without ceasing to be a Christian in any way, I also became a Buddhist on the spot. I would spend the next ten months of my life soaking in as much Japanese culture and tradition as I could. I would spend every holiday on the train traveling to this shrine or that temple, marveling at the Zen gardens and, in general, having what was, without a doubt, one of the most enjoyable, magical, mystical, and spiritually transformative periods of my life.

My First Experience of Allux

I was all alone in my bachelor apartment in Japan. My computer/entertainment center was always integrated into my altar since I would see and hear so much Truth in the movies I watched and even the games I played. In this instance, the game was *Soul Edge* on the Sony PlayStation, developed by Project

Soul and published by NAMCO in December 1996 (contemporary versions of the game are called *Soul Calibur*). It is a weapons-based martial arts fighting game, like *Tekken* and others. The difference is that the characters, all steeped in rich historical, geographical, mythological, and cultural lore, are all on a quest to recover the legendary Soul Edge—essentially *Excalibur*. In single-player story mode, you pick a character and traverse the map according to their unique backstory and motivation, following clues to track down the fabled weapon of the gods. As you do so, your chosen fighter must square off against the other characters (controlled by AI) until you eventually face *Inferno* (the final boss) in the final battle for the Soul Edge. Fair warning: PlayStation One graphics, animation, and J-Rock soundtrack circa 1996-97 ahead (lyrics reprinted in the *Appendix - Edge of Soul*).

Video 4: Soul Edge Opening (HQ remastered) (YouTube)

So that was what I was playing and where. It was late at night, after a long day of teaching English ESL classes. In other words, I was tired, sleepy, even. This is an important factor since cultivating a semi-sleepy state is very conducive to meditation and meditative activities. As mentioned, I was alone playing story mode, and I decided I would complete the game with all the characters, one by one. I should mention there was an in-game incentive to do so since completing missions (winning battles) in story mode unlocked alternative weapons, outfits, stages, game modes, etc.

It was well after midnight, after several hours of play, that I slipped into a deeply relaxed, semi-sleepy state. I sat back comfortably supported by my zaisu (floor chair; you could think of it as a meditation cushion with a back-rest), spine straight, legs outstretched, body totally relaxed and at ease, eyelids heavy, completely focused on the screen and the epic mythological mano-e-mano battles with swords and soul.

I was not trying to win anymore. I simply slipped into a state whereby all thoughts left me, all concerns left me, and then the apartment, room, and everything faded away. All that was left was myself—one with the controller, one with my character, and one with the movements and motion of my opponent. It was then I became cognizant of something rather curious. **I could not lose.**

Not only could I not lose, I could not even be *hit*. Totally relaxed, utterly indifferent to winning or losing, and completely void of any goal, desire, or aim, I became impervious to the attacks of my AI opponents. Whether avoiding, evading, overtly blocking, or proactive-counter-striking my opponent while they were in mid-swing, I was able to remain untouched. And it was not like I was playing on novice difficulty. Just to be sure, I went into the options and ratcheted up the difficulty. Still nothing. Not a scratch. Not a hit. Not a single pixel was shaved off my health bar. What was going on? So, I turned up the difficulty to the max. Still, the computer could not successfully land one blow on me.

The Matrix had not yet been filmed, but if you remember the scene where Neo fights Smith and awakens his potential, you begin to get an idea of what my experience was like. I imagine Bruce Lee must have experienced something similar when he faced lesser rivals in tournaments with his legendary speed and famous axiom: "The highest form is to be without form."

As a Gemini, Air/Air-rising, I am dominant in the mental body. That means it is very unlikely that I could ever actually achieve the levels of martial arts mastery demonstrated by Bruce Lee (let alone the superhuman feats of Neo in the Matrix). I know, I studied kung fu for a time. I loved it in every way, and it played an important role in re-connecting with my physical body, but it was not meant to be my path to mastery. A video game, on the other hand, is mostly mental, needing more dexterity than agility. It would take me a lifetime of practice and experience sparring to be able to achieve the same level of physical relaxation in a real fight as I now had fighting AI opponents virtually in Soul Edge. This was the key. And, as it turns out, it was a key to the door to something far more profound.

For as I sat there, utterly in a state of relaxed heightened awareness and focus, defeating opponent after opponent without so much as taking a hit (able to avoid, evade, or block all attempts by the AI to strike me), reading mythological stories of archetypal heroes and heroines as I progressed from one fight to the next, I started going deeper into the why and the how of it all. This was not a mental process but a conscious one. I began to realize I was somehow connected to the AI. I knew what the AI was going to do before it could do it.

"But hold up," the thought came to me, "AI is a machine…what conscious connection could I possibly have with a machine devoid of consciousness?" That is when lightning struck: I knew I was connected to the developer who had programmed the AI, and I could feel that connection so viscerally, so intimately, I knew every tip, trick, and tactic my virtual opponents would pull on me. I simply knew everything there was to know about them because, at that moment, **I had become one with the individual who coded them.**

"But hold up," another thought entered my mind, "if I can be so connected to one person, who I have never met, is not physically present, and whom I know only through their work—the video game they helped design and the AI they programmed—what if I can be just as connected to all people…to all beings?" They say lightning does not strike twice. Well, I am here to tell you it can, it does, and it did…in a big way. The second strike blew the doors of my consciousness wide open, and a flood of knowledge and wisdom from the Great Universal Mind of the Universe began pouring into, out of, and through me. **I had become** one with *Allux*—all Light, God Light, the Fire of fires, Light of lights, and Being of beings—*The Cosmic Christ.* And through that connection to The Logos, **I had become one with *all beings.***

I dropped the controller. I had no use for the game anymore. It had served its purpose. For the next 72 hours—without sleep—I would be taken on a journey of exploration beginning with profound universal Truths and timeless axioms of wisdom, shifting to the physical earth and my immediate geography. I became so stir-crazy with energy that I felt I would blow the walls apart of my tiny apartment, so I went on a *Zen walk*—a walk where one has no destination and makes no decision as to which way to turn next, but instead follows intuition, allowing oneself to be led by forces unseen—which took me to the train station and eventually all the way to Osaka. In that city of some fourteen million people, I, at one point, came across a Ferrari showroom. I marched in, saw three beautiful and exorbitantly priced cars, and proclaimed matter-of-factly to myself—pointing to each car as I did so—like I was ordering toppings for a hamburger: "I can have that one, that one, and that one!" I grabbed a brochure, stuffed it in my backpack, and marched out of the showroom without giving any of what had transpired a second thought. I was so in the moment that the Ferrari dealership had vanished from reality the second the door closed behind me. Every experience I had on my travels during my Zen walk was much the same. No elaboration. No conjecture. No internal waffling. Everything simply was what it was, and I was one with all of it.

The final day of my 72-hour sleepless sojourn into the infinite saw me return home, finally, with a backpack full of artifacts and oddities I had gathered on my Zen walk. I dumped the backpack onto the carpet and began sifting through the items one by one. It was when I finally came upon the Ferrari catalog that lightning struck for the third time. And I do not exaggerate, dear reader, when I say it was the most potent, eye-opening, collapsed-to-my-knees humbling wake-up call I had ever received. There, in my hands, was the evidence. There was no denying it; my experience in the dealership returned to me as a vivid reality, and the overwhelming sentiment burned in my mind as if put there by the Sun: "Aye, there's the rub!" And it was the revelation of this absolute universal Truth which was the cause of my world-shattering arrest…**the line that separates Christ from Anti-Christ is a *hairline.***

It was in that moment and for the hours that followed that I realized how wrongly our minds judge good and evil, how we place terrible monsters and altruistic saints on a gradient and imagine a vast gulf between them. It is not so. What separates them is a razor's edge…a banana peel on the sidewalk…a single moment of impropriety…a fleeting lapse of judgment…or a seemingly innocuous proclamation that was not comprehended in the moment for what it was: a profound *temptation.*

They say knowledge is power, power corrupts, and absolute power corrupts absolutely. Where, then, does this leave someone who has opened the door to absolute knowledge? Dear reader, I confess unequivocally that this whole episode was a test and a lesson. And there, in my tiny apartment, holding the evidence of my failure, I collapsed in a heap of tears and humiliation. For the Truth of the matter flooded into and filled me as profoundly as any I had received in the previous three days, and I became utterly conscious of my potential to become a powerful force for evil, even as I dreamt myself of one day becoming a potent force for good. Now, you might be saying to yourself, "there's nothing wrong with owning a few Ferraris." There may be nothing wrong with that for *you,* dear reader. But for me to do so, I would have to go against my destiny, the Will of my Innermost Being, abandon my work in the world, and most significantly, alter my present course, which is to give others the keys and help them open the doors to SEEK their own self-evident experiential knowledge of absolute universal Truths. So they too can experience what I have, know what I know, and meld as one with all beings and The Logos, as I have been at times in my life and as I am working toward being continually, completely, eternally.

And if all that was not enough, dear reader, there were *three* Ferraris…as in the three furies, three Witches of Macbeth, three traitors of Jesus, and three murderers of Hiram Abif. The temptation was not literal. Those luxurious and decadent vehicles were symbolic of the temptations of three brains: mind, heart, and body. And so, it was not just a question of one day having the means to spend a small fortune on exotic cars, no. Nor was it even the notion of abandoning my heart's deepest longing in order to pursue fame and fortune, no. What was revealed to me was how easily, quickly, and matter-of-factly I was tempted. Within moments of being granted access to the Source of infinite knowledge—and knowledge is power—I found myself being tempted to use that power in the full light of Truth for selfish worldly pursuits.

It is said of Adolf Hitler that he was a skilled and knowledgeable initiate in his youth. It is even rumored that he was one of the candidates to become Avatar of Aquarius. But he was tempted and corrupted by the Black Lodge, and just look at what he was able to accomplish for them with all his esoteric knowledge and power. What was shown to me, dear reader, was the fact that what stands between my potential to be a vehicle and vessel for the Logos or a despotic ruler bringing unimaginable hardship and suffering to billions is a banana peel. One misstep. One forgetful moment when I allow my ego-mind to usurp the power and knowledge that truthfully belongs to God and must not be misappropriated and misused for any purpose other than His Will, as it is expressed through The Cosmic Christ, Allux, and my Innermost Being, Attlas.

It should not be lost on you, dear reader, that the catalyst for this profound life-lesson in self-knowledge (awareness of the magnitude of my fallibility) was a video game in which the goal is to acquire the Soul Edge…a weapon of tremendous mystical power…Excalibur. Like many such devices in science fiction (such as the Tesseract from Marvel's *Avengers*) and fantasy (the One Ring from *The Lord of the Rings*), great power has the potential to corrupt greatly. It is the central theme of the *Spiderman* films, one which has been explored in countless comic books, myths, and tragedies alike: "with great power comes great responsibility." The Soul Edge represents such power, and the spiritual experience the game catalyzed awakened me to the fact that I was not yet worthy of wielding such power…I was not yet ready to be trusted with it. But in the eyes of at least one other, I was not altogether untrustworthy.

Real Temptation

I loved living in Japan. For the second time in my life, it felt as though I belonged. I was a perfectionist living in a country of perfectionism. Baked into the Japanese culture was the tenet *Omotenashi*—to see to others' needs. From perfected earthenware vessels to the perfect tea ceremony they serve, Omotenashi is a recognition that every lump of clay has a purpose, the greatest being service to others: carry and store water, grow food, tile roofs, et al. Whereas in Canada, I had been a bit of an enigma to most—my family included—in Japan, I was a fish in water.

As a six-foot-three Caucasian, I clearly looked like a *gaijin* (foreigner), but to the Japanese, I was simply an adopted son. They recognized shared values in me and an almost total lack of accent when I spoke Japanese. I spoke fluent Hungarian, which is part of the same 18,000-year-old Hungaro-Finn language tree that originated somewhere in the Steppes of Northern Asia—possibly upper Mongolia or even Tibet. This meant that by speaking Hungarian at home my whole life, I practiced all the consonants, vowels, rhythms, cadence, intonations, and inflections of the Japanese language as well. This got me into some trouble in Japan upon meeting someone new and introducing myself in what sounded like perfect, fluent Japanese. They simply assumed I had been born and raised there or had been living there for years. They would begin speaking to me in Japanese, and I would have to wave my hands, interrupt them, and explain that I do not, in fact, speak their language. To which they would stare, perplexed, and vocalize that oh-so Japanese idiosyncratic, "Eeehhh?" As for my students, who knew that I had only just arrived in their country, they warmed to me and my teaching style very quickly. After all, I had come from a theatre background. Not only did I strive to make their lessons interactive and entertaining, but I also treated them with the same respect and care that I received in every single business I stepped into in Japan…with Omotenashi.

One of my students, Akikosan, seemed to take a shining to me immediately. She owned a *juku* or cram school—an after-hours private school common in Japan that offers students structured lessons and tutoring in a variety of subjects. Her husband was a teacher in her cram school, and her daughter was a harpist. I learned all this the day I met Akikosan since there was a set lesson plan with exercises for the students to introduce themselves to their new *sensei* as well as tell me about themselves in English. After a few months, Akikosan began suggesting that I must attend one of her daughter's recitals sometime. Eventually, the opportunity presented itself, and I went to hear her daughter, Naori, play the harp. She played exquisitely. For me, the harp belongs to the family of angelic string instruments, together with the sitar and oud, and has the same effect on me as the sacred wind instruments, including the wooden flute and the pipe organ. Added to this was Naori's stunning beauty. At five foot nine, Naori was exceptionally tall for a Japanese woman. She had long, elegant arms and fingers. Her hair was likewise long and fell perfectly straight, jet black, down to her waist. She had bright brown eyes and what I can only describe as elven facial features. She was, in every way imaginable, the perfect embodiment of what had been my 'type' at that time in my life.

Yes, it is fair to say that I took a shining to Naorichan immediately. Her mother, Akikosan, had found a good match both for myself and her daughter, and she seemed particularly self-satisfied having set us up.

Naori and I dated throughout the remainder of my time in Japan. As much as she and I made a handsome couple, it is fair to say that I was far more into our relationship than she was. I had never been with a woman as beautiful and as talented as she. She would have been in every way the perfect *trophy wife*. But when I was brutally honest with myself, clearly it was her mother, Akikosan, who was truly enthusiastic about us being together…much more so than Naorichan. The extent to which this was true became abundantly clear when I decided to leave Japan to return to Canada.

Breaking up with Naori was relatively easy. Sure, I was sorry to let go of the most stunningly beautiful and talented woman I had ever been with, and from Naori's perspective, she was sorry to see go the tall gaijin boyfriend who had made her the envy of all her friends. You see, dear reader, at that time, for many young Japanese women, having a gaijin boyfriend was a kind of status symbol—the ultimate in fashionable accessories to go along with their *Louis Vuitton* or *Ferragamo* handbag. Thank God Naori had not been as superficial and materialistic. But she still enjoyed being admired for the tall gaijin on her arm as much as I did. Still, whatever connection we might have hoped would develop and grow in time never advanced past a loving friendship. After all, our relationship had been arranged. And even though we went along with the setup based on physical attraction and an intellectual desire—we both fell in love with the *idea* of being together—our hearts simply did not seem to want to go along with our minds and bodies. Naori admitted at last that she had, in part, kept up the charade out of respect for her mother, who had set us up. The reason why would soon become abundantly clear.

Sure, breaking up with Naori might have been easy. Breaking up with Naori's mother would be another matter entirely. Japanese tradition demanded that I meet with Akikosan privately to discuss the situation, and I invited her to stay following one of our classes to do so. I let her know I had decided to return to Canada for my brother's wedding and that I would not be returning. I explained that I had already broken up with Naori and had informed GEOS that I would be terminating my contract—despite their offer to promote me to the position of teacher-trainer. I thanked her for everything, expressed how honored I felt that she had chosen me for her daughter, and insisted that my decision to leave Japan was in no way a reflection upon her, her daughter, or her country. Akiko just smiled and nodded, listening intently as I pled my case. When I finished saying my peace, there was a long pause. She just kept smiling and nodding, not so much in agreement, more like she was self-assured as to what needed to happen next. At last, she spoke, still nodding.

"Yes. No. You will return to Canada for your brother's wedding because that is your duty to your family. But then you will return to Japan. You will quit your job with GEOS as planned. But instead, you will come to work in my school. I have already spoken privately with all your students, and they all said they would happily leave GEOS and come to my school to keep you as their sensei. You will marry Naori and learn fluent Japanese. I will teach you the business of running the school. In time, once I retire, I will hand over the family business to you, and you and Naori will eventually inherit it."

And there it was. Laid out for me on a silver platter: the perfect, comfortable life in the country I loved, complete with a trophy wife and an adoring mother-in-law. As I sat there in stunned silence, my eyes caught a glint of light in Akikosan's eye, and my attention turned to her bright red pant suit. In that precise moment, what came to mind was Jesus atop the mountain in the desert, when Satan showed him all the kingdoms of the world spread out at his feet and said, "All these I shall give to you if you will prostrate yourself and worship me." (Mathew 4:1-11).

"Aye, there's the rub," I thought to myself. I recalled the harsh awakening I had undergone months earlier while playing *Soul Edge,* how I had been tested, and how I had failed to demonstrate my worth in the Light of Allux. I would not make the same mistake this time. Again, I politely thanked Akikosan for her offer and expressed how humbled and honored I was that she would entrust me not only with her daughter's hand in marriage but also with the family business, all of which she holds most dear. She was not used to hearing "no." And she was certainly not accustomed to taking no for an answer. She insisted, argued, cajoled, and even demanded at one point that I reconsider her offer. At times, it seemed as though she was desperate for me to submit to her plan. At last, I had no choice but to reveal a side of myself to her that she had rarely heard expressed so explicitly. I explained to her that I was here—on this earth, in this lifetime—to do a great and noble life's work. "But teaching is a very noble profession!" she protested. "Yes, Akikosan, teaching is a very noble profession," I replied, "but I was not born to teach English to Japanese people. I was born to teach something far more important to far more people." This was the Still Soft Voice of Attlas speaking directly through me...my voice had become his voice.

Akikosan stared, bewildered, silent. For a time, we sat there in silence, she and I just looking at each other. Looking into one another's soul. At last, she recognized I had spoken from a place of earnest Truth and that there was nothing she could do but accept my decision. She reluctantly smiled and wished me all the best in my future endeavors. With the utmost humility and respect I could muster, I thanked her for her gracious understanding. And with that, Akikosan, her daughter, and the perfect, comfortable life in the country I adored and felt most comfortable in vanished from the pages of my story forever.

Hail the Conquering Hero

No one was surprised to see me come home for my brother's wedding. That was to be expected. But everyone was surprised to hear that I was staying in Canada and that I had decided not to return to Japan. From their point of view, they could not fathom how I could turn my back on a life that had made me so happy and content. I had been corresponding with family and friends back home regularly, of course, and sending not just photos but videos of my adventures—remember, I had once had ambitions to be a filmmaker. Everyone told me that they could see in my eyes, hear in my correspondences, and feel in their hearts that I had never been so happy as I was in Japan. They all said Naori and I made a perfect couple. And those who knew about my promotion at GEOS, or indeed, Akikosan's offer of her daughter's hand in marriage and the family business to boot, thought I had completely lost my mind coming back to Canada to start from scratch. But, of course, I had not lost my mind, dear reader. I had found my Self. And I made no effort to hide that fact from the ones nearest and dearest to me, be they friends or family. And this, dear reader, made me *unsufferable* in their eyes.

The temporary experience of being one with Allux—and, by extension, all beings—was not the first nor the last 'spiritual awakening' I experienced in my life, nor even during my time in Japan. Indeed, as just described, my 'final exam' before leaving Japan saw me connect so profoundly to Attlas—my Higher Self, True Self, Innermost Being, Individuated Essence of Allux, Divine Soul, Monad, or however you wish to classify Him—that He spoke through me. I had already surrendered to His will. When faced with intense opposition from Akikosan and tremendous temptation from within to live a life of comfort and security in the country I loved and identified as my spiritual homeland, I allowed His words to flow from my mouth. Together with my other 'spiritual awakenings' before and during my time in Japan, surely, I was no longer asleep. "Having undergone an awakening, I must now be awake," I reasoned, *"enlightened."*

Mystic pride is a phenomenon that I knew nothing about at the time. I had never even heard the expression. But even if I had, it would not have mattered one iota to me. I had *my truth* firmly in hand. I knew what I had experienced. I had even delved into the teachings of Buddha to confirm my status as an enlightened being. I had been sent on a spiritual journey to find myself in a way more profound than most, and I had returned *awake* with a renewed sense of my divinely ordained purpose. I had always lived by a *glass-is-half-full* mentality, but I returned from Japan with a heightened belief in *the power of positivity.* I did not suffer to listen to those—like my poor mother—who I believed were trying to taint the glow in my heart-mind with their dour perspective on how bad things are now and how bad the future would be. "I will not succumb to their fear-based reality," I thought. I would not face any negativity. I was in control of my own destiny, which was to change the world. I could not afford to indulge in negative thoughts and the so-called pragmatism of cynical individuals—in whom I saw myself prior to my awakening in Japan. There was no way I was going to go *backward* and be like them, as I once was. Not after the universe had conspired to lead me to Japan, then awaken, test, and tempt me. I would not turn back now. I was on a different wavelength of being. And no one was going to bring me down from that high. Nothing would interfere with my superior perspective of life, the world, and my place in it.

"After all, I am Attlas!"

Or so I thought smugly and sometimes professed publicly. The fact was, dear reader, that the *muggles* in my life, the *normies,* the *sheeple,* the ones going about their *mediocre* lives, took to my spiritual arrogance and mystic pride as poorly as one might expect. But I would soon learn my lesson. For it is simply a fact of life—and the AUM of Life—that what goes up must come down…often *hard.*

MY FALL INTO THE ABYSS

The Crash

From autumn of 2001 to spring of '02, I was enrolled in Wilfrid Laurier University's full-time Master of Business Administration program. It was a consolation on my part for what seemed at the time to be a disastrous downturn in my life following the dot-bomb crash of the previous year. I had been living the high-life, riding the wave of late-nineties investors' exuberance for all things technology-related. And now I—like so many who had bet their careers on the dot-com bubble—could do nothing but watch the bubble burst and bear witness to the implosion of our collective IT future as it all came crashing down in the most spectacular way.

Planet Today Inc., the Internet startup I had been working with—was gutted—despite being a strategic partner of IBM and having done an IPO just a few months prior to the dot-com bubble bursting. Ironically, our *Local Area Webs* would have been well-positioned to survive the Nasdaq collapse had IBM Canada not nixed their *e-Business Services* division following the crash. And with it, all support for their *Lotus-Notes/Domino*-based platform, which said strategic partner had foisted upon the company to serve as our IT infrastructure—what a bloated, slow, complicated, ultimately disastrous platform it turned out to be. At one time, a very young Google had considered working with us to make Local Area Webs their *Google Local*, but our Chairman and CEO, Sinclair Stevens, being a man of advanced years and a former Conservative MP, still believed in the 1980s mantra *no one ever got fired for hiring IBM*. What a difference two decades can make. For a time, Planet limped along, trying to work with third parties who claimed expertise in Notes/Domino. In the end, the hosting and maintenance costs were simply overwhelming.

I, too, limped along working with new start-up clients as an *entrepreneur for hire*. But after fulfilling my end of the bargain, helping them win great success for their international businesses, they simply vanished overseas, leaving me, along with their Canadian backers, in the lurch. Long story short, forced into a financial corner, I ended up taking my father's advice. I moved home and enrolled in WLU to get some business credentials added to my byline. After all, my undergraduate degree had been a double-major in English and Dramatic Arts from the University of Guelph. *Bachelor of Arts* did not strike confidence in the minds of entrepreneurs, investors, etc. Besides, I had always found success in academia, and not just grade-wise. U of G's English Department awarded me the *Tompkin Prize* for best essay in 1994—for my post-modern deconstruction of Shakespeare's *Hamlet* and *Rosencrantz and Guildenstern are Dead* by Tom Stoppard. And although I had been thoroughly indoctrinated into Critical Theory, it had not yet made in-roads into the business world. ESG and DEI—*Environmental Social Governance* and *Diversity, Equity, and Inclusion*—were not yet on the minds of most executives (more on that in a bit). So, returning to university to acquire some business administration credentials seemed like a good hedge against an uncertain economic future, given the recent market collapse.

It was during my time in the MBA program that I began to experience what my girlfriend at the time called *nocturnal episodes.* I *knew,* intuitively, that I needed to endure and hold off on a medical examination until I had my degree in hand. I was living in Guelph and driving to and from campus in Waterloo every day. I did not know it at the time, but in Ontario, the instant one is diagnosed with any kind of seizure condition, one's driver's license is instantly suspended on medical grounds—for obvious reasons. I did not know what I had, but I did know whatever it was, I would have to wait at least until I finished my degree and the daily commute had ended. So long as I was only having these episodes at night, I was not putting myself or anyone else in danger.

The second part of the program would prove significantly less stressful for me. And, as it turns out, very productive. The episodes subsided, much to my girlfriend's relief. Over the course of the second and third semesters, I would come to earn the admiration and respect of Dr. Hugh Munro, Professor of Marketing and Head of the MBA Program. Over forty of my colleagues from a class of over one hundred students approached Dr. Munro to request that he supervise their independent study project—the MBA equivalent of a master's thesis. He turned all forty-plus projects down except for mine. The topic? Social, Environmental, Economic Valuation—*SEEV.*

Since this was the first real business degree I had ever taken, I had never been formally introduced to such concepts as the fundamentals of accounting. Thanks to the widely reported collapse of Enron and WorldCom, I was very familiar with the disastrous consequences of *off-balance-sheet debt.* But truly, it was not until I dove into the rationale behind the balance sheet itself *(revenues = liabilities + shareholder equity)* that I discovered the fundamental flaw at the heart of capitalism. Nowhere were the intangible costs being accounted for. As a result, the entire world was accumulating untold sums of off-balance sheet debt. Nowadays, intangible costs are referred to euphemistically as *externalized costs.* But in 2002, *triple-bottom-line accounting* and the *Three Ps* of people, planet, and profit were still niche practices in business. The terms ESG—Environmental Social Governance—and DEI—Diversity, Equity, and Inclusion—had not yet gone mainstream. So, SEE-Valuation naturally was of great interest to Dr. Munro.

What I proposed was a foundational system of checks and balances whereby non-profit agencies and NGOs already issuing certifications and *seals of approval* based on various social, environmental, and economic factors would contribute to a SEE-Value label, not unlike a nutritional label. Since knowledge is power, this would put the ultimate power in the hands of consumers and/or investors, who could judge their purchase and/or investment decisions on a more transparent and complete understanding of the real costs and benefits of a product, service, or company. SEE-Valuation represented the genuine democratization of capitalism. A bottom-up approach that recognized and addressed the systemic flaw of *business as usual* and which put the power to *SEE change* in the hands of consumers, investors, and markets via transparent collection and formatting of need-to-know information as *actionable intelligence.* Suffice it to say, Dr. Munro was pleased with the final paper, which, of course, would be too long to reprint here. However, it would eventually become chapter two of my first book, *The Attlas Project Volume One: SEE the World in a New Light.* The relevant *VISUAL AID* on *SEEconomics* from the book can be seen in *Figure 3.*

In 2002, when I wrote my thesis, the concept of Corporate Social Responsibility had already been around for decades. The process of change was painstakingly slow and bizarrely out of sight, out of mind for consumers. Fast-forward to the present day, Environmental Social Governance (ESG) is a top-down approach whereby capital lending to corporations is made conditional on them having an acceptable ESG score. Companies cannot operate without significant lines of credit to cover the capital investments required for growth. Restricting such credit based on ESG scores effectively coerces corporations into adopting ESG (and DEI) measures. What is more, ESG has become more of a branding exercise than a practical way of SEEing the true Social, Environmental, and Economic Value of products, services, and companies. Without a SEEV label, companies are forced to engage in woke PR, media, and advertising campaigns to telegraph to investment groups (such as Blackrock and Vanguard) that they are good little ESG-compliant companies. But their hyperbolic messaging just comes across as woke propaganda in the eyes of consumers. And the result is as one might expect.

Gillette and Anheuser-Busch have, at the time of writing, discovered the hard way: *get woke, go broke.* Both put heavy-handed DEI messaging—Diversity, Equity, and Inclusion—into their traditional advertising. Gillette's *"We believe: the best a man can be,"* and Bud Light's disastrous Dylan Mulvaney ad campaign provoked outright boycotts of the products. Disney's ham-fisted approach to forcing DEI into Marvel, Star Wars, Pixar, and live-action remakes of its classic animated feature films has likewise seen its brand diminish along with consumer trust.

Back in 2002, I knew consumers had to be given a way to become activate participants in the ESG process—acting agents who *SEE Change.* Markets needed to SEE changes to products, services, and businesses from the bottom-up where it mattered most—where the rubber meets the road in capitalism—point of purchase and/or investment decisions. This would put informed choice in the hands of buyers at both B2B and B2C levels. Buyers who, were they to make the *SEEconomical* choice, would, over time, naturally shift market preferences and pressures. Competitors and investors alike would respond to these shifting market forces, and a positive feedback loop for SEE-Change would emerge. Staunch capitalists and economic purists would welcome the fact that SEEconomics respected their central axiom to *let the markets decide.* SEE Valuation and SEEV labeling would allow markets to SEE the value(s) of ESG-oriented corporations in a standardized, objective way, not unlike nutritional labeling, free of the ill-received ESG and DEI propaganda of today.

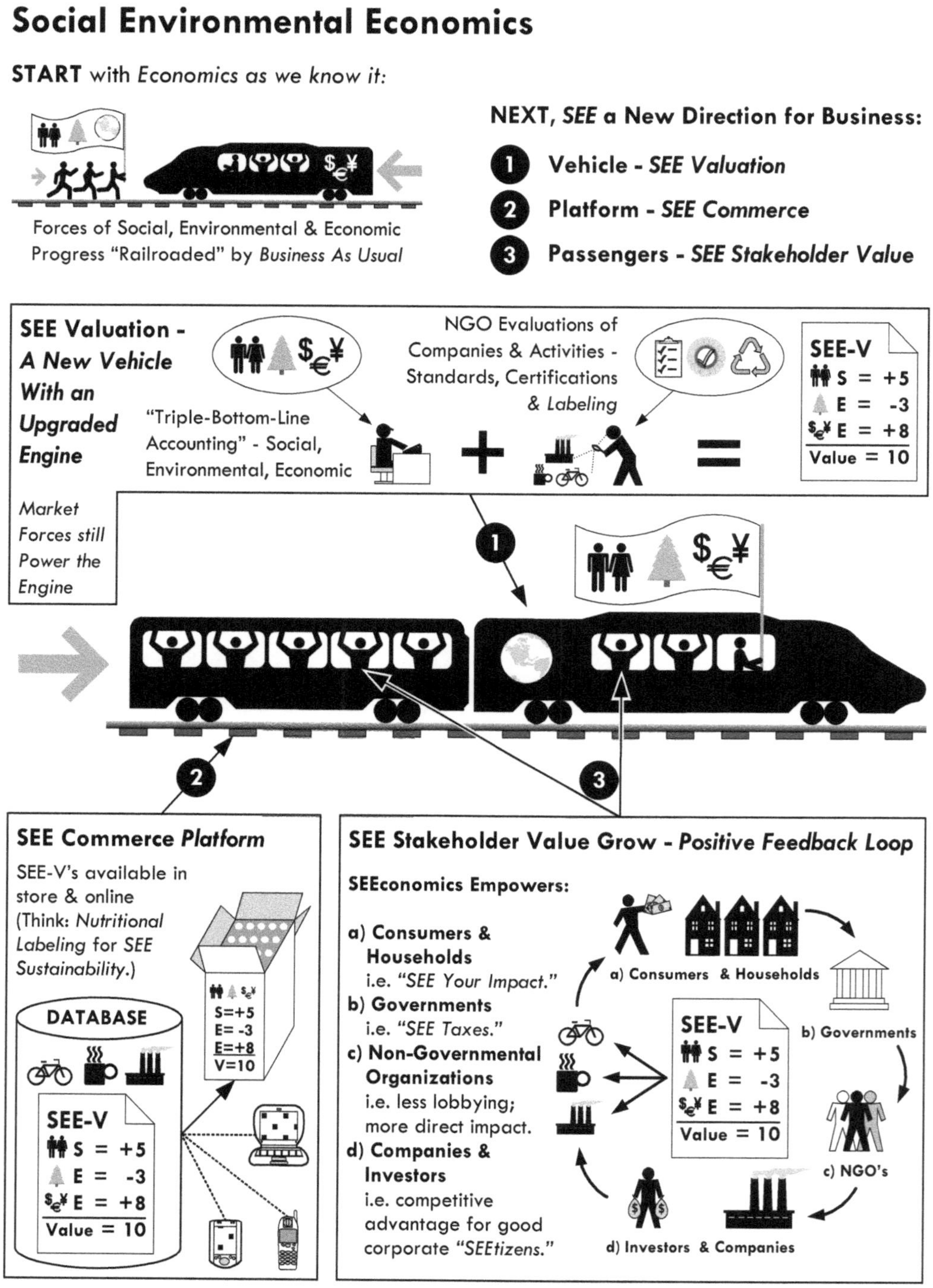

Social Environmental Economics

Figure 3: SEEconomics from "The Attlas Project Vol. I: SEE Your World in a New Light"

Would SEEV fix all the controversy, problems, hangups, resistance to, and fallout from the woke missteps of companies attempting to implement ESG and DEI mandates? This is not the time nor place to have that discussion. Nor is it within the scope of this book to explain how modern technologies such as smartphones, blockchain, distributed ledger, and QR codes—which were not yet widely available to the public in 2002 or even 2009—would make SEEV that much more relevant, available, and meaningful in 2023 and beyond. Besides, I remain now, as then, one sole voice in a loud, confused, self-interested business world that believes it has all the answers. After all, CSR, ESG, and DEI were all born during the Civil Rights era of the 1960s, half a century before I published *The Attlas Project* (2009). I share all this with you, dear reader, to evidence just how seriously I felt about social, environmental, and economic justice. How it made me feel *awake*—as though *I knew* what the world's problems were and as if *I alone* had the solution—long before the term *woke* was part of the popular vernacular.

Now, if that seems more than a little presumptuous and arrogant, dear reader, rest assured the universe felt so, too. Soon after completing my MBA at WLU, life would yank the proverbial rug out from under my feet, sending me into a tailspin that would last seven years and would not come to an end until I finished writing and publishing my first book. My descent to the next level on the downward spiral into hell began when I fulfilled my promise to my girlfriend and family to seek medical advice regarding the 'nocturnal episodes' I had begun experiencing during the MBA program. It goes without saying that I was immediately diagnosed with adult-onset epilepsy, and my seven-year roller-coaster ride of an epilepsy-induced nightmare began.

Descent into Epilepsy

Despite what I believed at the time, it turned out I had been living with epilepsy my whole life. The nature of my partial-frontal-lobe seizures allowed them to go undetected by me and others throughout my childhood and adolescence, especially considering they were largely brought on by stress and mostly occurred at night. I had lived a relatively stress-free life up to that point. Advanced mathematics was never my strong suit, however, and having to do statistics on top of all the reading, coursework, casework, etc., of WLU's intensive one-year MBA had exacerbated my condition. Finance was no problem, as I had written many budgets, business plans, and financial projections and conducted investor relations over the previous five years. But I had to face facts: Microsoft *Excel* had done all the heaving lifting for me, mathematically speaking. Being in a serious relationship with a young woman whose father was as success-driven as my own meant I was under the gun to perform and achieve as never before, in subjects that challenged me as never before during the program, as well as professionally once out of it. And to be fair, I had always been hardest on myself anyway. I, too, was thinking a lot about my future, restarting my career, getting engaged, and planning a life with my partner, all in a post-9/11 world now knee-deep in America's *War on Terror*—

with me taking a deep dive into the world of 9/11 conspiracies, but more on that later. Yes, dear reader, you could say it all got the best of me, and the underlying condition, which had largely remained dormant for the better part of a quarter-century, now completely dominated my life.

For starters, in Ontario, when diagnosed with any type of seizure, one's driver's license is immediately suspended on medical grounds for at least six months to a year—and for good reason. Right away, this crippled my ability to get back into consulting. And despite having a freshly minted MBA under my arm, all my attempts at finding gainful employment ended in failure. Despite having assistance from counselors, human resource management consultants, and family, friends, and acquaintances—who all managed to find successful careers in the private sector—I could not manage being given even one interview. All the while, the stress and anxiety of failing to make headway began to take its toll. Not only were my seizures getting worse, but they were also increasing in frequency. I began to suffer from clinical depression. If it was unsafe for me to drive, it did not seem fitting for me to ride a bicycle, either—of which I owned two, road and mountain. Walking and public transportation were the only way to get out of my parents' house. But without a source of income, I could not get very far or do much once I got there.

Suffice it to say, it was not long before my girlfriend—who I had every intention of marrying—left me for someone 'more established.' I admit to feeling like a victim of circumstance at the time, but after a while, I was glad that she went her own way. She was not committed to a life *in sickness and in health*— not with me anyway—and it is better to know these things sooner rather than later. She enrolled in a master's program, and her new partner was involved in the same area of study, so presumably, they had much more in common with one another. I felt happy for her that she was able to move on with her life without being held back by my medical condition and financial prognosis.

Over the next few years, I would stumble from near-miss to near-miss, from one medication to another, and even from one neurologist to another. Still, my condition worsened, and with it, my chances of finding gainful employment. After all, what employer wanted to saddle themselves with someone who might need special accommodation or take sick days regularly for depression? At least, that is what I assumed. I never disclosed my condition in cover letters or on my resume. Still, I received no interviews. It seemed to me that the universe was trying to tell me something. At first, I did not know what that something was. I was too busy trying to climb out of the pit I had fallen into. I just wanted to climb out of hell, get back on my own two feet, and start living a normal life again. Was that too much to ask? But life seemed dead set against my hopes and dreams of having a normal life, let alone making a difference in the world. No matter what I did, it seemed I was just fumbling around, lost in the dark.

Deep Dive into Conspiracy

If the universe was trying to tell me something, I eventually found what I believed that something was. Not only was the world not fair, but it was also corrupt and rotten to the core. How did I know? In my desperation and search for answers as to why I could make no headway in the world, I took a deep dive into the dark world of conspiracy theory, where I found the answer. It was so obvious. The world did not want someone like me. Someone who was *awake*. Someone who believed that a flawed capitalist system was the cause of all the inequity in the world. Someone who *knew* how to fix it. Someone who *knew* 9/11 was an inside job. Someone who now *knew* about the vast conspiracy to cover-up the Truth: from the *Illuminati* to the assassination of JFK to the UFO phenomenon. I had never watched *The X-Files,* but now I was living it in my own way—the truth *was* out there—going down one conspiracy rabbit hole after the next. Each time, I wound up with a carrot, which simultaneously affirmed my victimhood, self-righteousness, and wakefulness. I had swallowed the red-pill, it seemed to me, and now *the Agents* of *The Matrix* were dead-set on stonewalling me and keeping me down and out. I believed I had the Truth in my hands, and as Plato famously said, "no man is more hated than he who speaks the Truth." This must have been what the universe was trying to tell me. After all, the evidence in support of the conspiracy was overwhelming.

Once I thoroughly identified myself as a bona fide *conspiracy theorist,* in addition to being a *social justice warrior,* my life changed completely. I got myself a new neurologist, and he put me on a new, experimental medication. It had been given FDA approval, of course, and I would later discover the FDA trial had been a study of fewer than one hundred people. One of the potential side effects of the medication was—and I am not making this up—*psychotic behavior.* I will spare you the drug's name, dear reader since the last thing I need is to be slapped with a defamation lawsuit. Besides, the medication seemed effective at controlling my seizures, and the drug company was forthright in its potential risks. After the requisite number of months of being seizure-free, I was able to regain my driver's license and resume working with clients as I had done before. I moved out of my parent's house and back to Toronto. As the universe pre-scribed, I was a lone wolf social entrepreneur for hire. I would work with entrepreneurs looking to change the world, and together, we would make a difference despite the multinational corporations' agendas and the vast global conspiracy to enslave and impoverish humanity economically, mentally, and spiritually. Ah yes, *spiritually.*

Doubling Down on the New Age

I had been what one might reasonably refer to as a *mystic* for most of my life up to that point. True, I was baptized and raised Roman Catholic and even served as an altar boy. However, I had my first mystical experience in meditation at around age five or six. At the time, I did not even know what meditation was— I had never even heard the term before. But when I closed my eyes and stared into the blackness within, I just *knew* there was something in there. And I had to find out what it was. I had to reach it, touch it. And so, with the simple innocence of a child, eyes closed, I simply focused on going deeper, deeper, deeper. And I did not stop until a voice boomed, not so much in my head but seemingly in my room, "you have reached the center of your mind." From that point forward, whenever I knelt on the dais of the altar of St. Elizabeth of Hungary Church, looking up at the life-size Jesus staring down at me from the cross, I would silently say to him, "yes, I get it." I would continue having spiritual experiences throughout my childhood and early adolescence, such that I refused to receive the sacrament of Confirmation. Spirituality was not about *faith* as defined by the Church—*belief.* For me, faith meant *knowing.*

Like many mystics, I turned away from religion altogether in my teens. Learning about the atrocities committed by the Catholic Church and others throughout the centuries played a role in my disillusionment with organized religion. Although I called myself an atheist, the Truth is I was more of an agnostic. After all, I had my mystical experiences, which I could not deny and which affirmed for me the forces of divinity were active in my life, just not in the superstitious forms I learned about in theology class. So, like many, I considered myself to be *spiritual* but not *religious.* This is something I kept to myself, of course, since my family still attended church, and I went along with them. My mystical connection to divinity was personal, intimate, and in the context of being raised Roman Catholic, something I feared no one would understand. After all, they burned Joan of Arc at the stake, in part because she claimed God spoke to her. Not that I feared such a fate would befall me, but I felt certain I did not need to complicate my life by trying to make sense for others what I truly could barely make sense of for myself.

When it came to making sense of the world and my mystical experience, music had been my saving grace. Melody and harmony aside, it was in the lyrics that I found what felt to me like kindred spirits whispering timeless, universal Truths directly to my soul. It was in university that I fell in love with the music of *Enigma,* particularly after the release of their second studio album, *The Cross of Changes.* Through their music, I discovered I was not the only one having mystical experiences or feelings as I did about spirituality. I would buy and listen to all seven of their studio albums released between 1990 and 2008 incessantly. I would lie in my bed meditating on their music, allowing whatever they were singing about to move me to tears. Whatever moved me to the very core of my being constituted something spiritual in my eyes. They had been my musical companions during my transformative year living in Japan as well.

Despite my spiritual relationship to the music of Enigma, I did not consider myself to be a 'New Ager.' Others might have branded me as such, but I never read any New Age books or followed any of its gurus. At least, not until I was in my thirties. Having gotten my seizures under control, my driver's license restored, and my professional life back on track, I was watching PBS one night in 2004 when a program came on: *The Power of Intention* with Dr. Wayne Dyer. I was utterly captivated by the man and his message, and I even pledged to PBS, ordering the DVD, CD, and companion book. What spoke to me was the notion of intention "as something we connect to." Given where I was in life—in my early thirties, dating again but still single, consulting again but still earning a relatively modest income, healthy again but out of shape—the idea of setting my *intention* and creating a *vision board* to *manifest my desires,* all seemed to align with the upward trajectory of my life. A life that was again full of promise and potential, as it had been before epilepsy pulled the rug out from under me years earlier. And I did not stop at Wayne Dyer. For the next three years, I would read books by Deepak Chopra, Eckhart Tolle, Louise Hay, Paulo Coelho, Neale Donald Walsch, and many others. The New Age affirmed everything I believed about myself. That I was different, special, and most of all, *awake.* If only I stayed the course, stayed positive, and poured my heart and soul into the Source of my *intention,* I would manifest the *abundance* and *love* that I so longed for in my life. And they appeared to begin showing up in my life once more. The books I read about Buddhism following my awakening in Japan left me somewhat cold and wanting more—secret information that had clearly been withheld. In comparison, New Age affirmations manifesting abundance into my life would get my heart pumping and seemed in total alignment with my deepest desires to change the world. "I must be meant to walk this New Age path," I figured, "the universe delivered me it for a reason." Just not for the reason I believed at the time.

I had a handful of clients and a steady income and eventually rented a nice one-bedroom condo downtown within walking distance of St. Lawrence Market. I had reactivated my *e-Harmony* online dating account—which I had used in the past—and in short order, I was meeting like-minded women. I felt comfortable and secure that I was back on track, back in business, back on the dating scene, and back living the bachelor high life once more…back on the fast track to success. Now, at this point in my life, I was completely identified with the New Age doctrine of *living in abundance,* which meant that I had taken advantage of every line of credit available to me to attract the lifestyle I wanted as a thirty-something bachelor living in Toronto. I did not live extravagantly by any means, but I had maxed out my line of credit furnishing the one-bedroom condo I rented, had financed an all-but-new Honda *Fit,* and leased a top-of-the-line DELL *XPS* laptop. In many ways, I had fallen for what Edward Norton's character in the 1999 movie *Fight Club* had called "the IKEA nesting instinct."

Video 5: The IKEA Nesting Instinct (YouTube)

Digging up *The Secret*

In 2006, *The Secret* was released, and I, like so many, ate it up. Here was made public the hidden metaphysical science of *the law of attraction,* which the ruling elite had covertly been using for centuries—if not millennia—to amass great fortunes, tremendous fame, huge followings, and/or even vast empires. Although not overtly mentioning conspiracy in any way, I put two and two together. By this point in my life, I *knew* that everything happens for a reason. My journey had exposed me first to all the surface-level ways the world was enslaved, then the hidden conspiracies behind the enslavement, and now—thanks to the New Age—I was being shown the superpower of the secret societies behind those conspiracies. You see, dear reader. It all added up. The universe had taken me on this journey of *awakening,* and now it had delivered to me the final secret to being able to truly change the world. But first, I would use it to change my life.

I believed I knew all I needed to know. Self-confidence had once again returned to me. Once again, it began to smack of arrogance. It did not help that the epilepsy medication I was on, which seemed to control my seizures, was causing me to behave erratically and even mercurially. I did not care. If people could not handle my energy, my enthusiasm, my determination to make things happen in the world, that was their problem. They were just *sheeple* in my mind, anyway—mere *muggles* from *Harry Potter* lore—living a banal and uninspired existence, blindly following 'the system' that kept them oblivious to the many conspiracies enslaving them. Ignorant of the power of intention, the law of attraction, and the potential of positive thinking to transform themselves and their lives, they were stuck in suburban hell when they could have been living in paradise on earth. As you can see, dear reader, by adopting New Age beliefs and investigating conspiracy theories, I now believed I had all the answers I had gone in search of. Answers I had suffered dearly for. And I felt I had suffered enough. I would no longer be a slave of the world nor a victim of fate. Now, I would be the master of my own destiny. Arrogance had returned in force, dear reader. It was then, as if on cue, that the universe decided it was time for another *intervention.*

A Crash in Slow Motion

The previous month, I had hopped on a plane and flown to Calgary, Alberta, where I rented a Mustang GT convertible and drove over the Rocky Mountains to visit a friend in Vancouver, B.C. Upon landing at Calgary airport, an Indian fellow (from India, not First Nations) approached me, holding a clipboard. He was very polite and well-spoken and began marketing an American Express Gold Rewards Card. He explained how if I put all my travel expenses on it, I would likely earn enough points for a free flight. Now, I knew about such reward cards since my older brother and his friends had often bragged about flying here and there on accumulated points alone. Finally, I, too, could be a member of that 'exclusive club.' So, I signed up on the spot and was handed a temporary card, which, as advised, I used to put all my vacation expenses on. It was a great visit. I stopped in Banff on my way back to Calgary and put many hundreds of kilometers on the rental. All told I had easily racked up several thousand dollars' worth of expenses on my shiny new Gold American Express card. I even felt some excitement about getting my first statement and learning how many points I had earned on my trip out West. Before that statement would arrive, however, I would need to contend with some sudden and significant roadblocks.

You can imagine my surprise, dear reader, when upon my return from Western Canada, I discovered that one of my clients had up and left the country without a trace. Without any notice, without leaving so much as a note, and without paying his last invoice. He had multiple projects on the go, and one of them, an engineering, parts, and Service Company for the oil and gas industry, took off unexpectedly. So, he decided to return to his native Lebanon to be closer to his lucrative business in the Middle East. I was not the only one left holding the bag. He simply abandoned the two Canadian companies/brands I had been working on for him, along with dozens of people who found themselves out of work with no paycheck, no severance, nothing. It was an echo of another client from my past who vanished once the deal we had been working on for a power plant in Eastern Europe had been signed. I again found myself being stiffed by an engineer working in the energy industry. A few weeks later, my other client announced that he was abandoning the larger of two projects/brands I had been working on for him. I now found myself with seventy-five percent less income and very little in the way of savings. Just a lot of debt obligations.

It was then that the first statement arrived on my shiny new American Express Gold Rewards card, which had been pitched to me at Calgary airport, and onto which—on the advice of the card's pitch-man—I had put my entire trip. You can imagine my shock, dear reader when I read the statement and discovered that the entire balance was due. No option for a *minimum payment*. The whole amount. Several thousand dollars. Due by the end of the month. What sort of credit card was this? It seems it was not a credit card at all but a *charge card*—something I did not even know existed. A card that acts more like a short-term high-interest cash advance than actual credit, with the company charging interest immediately on use and expecting you to pay off the full amount due within 30 days. Now, to be fair, when that Indian fellow was pitching me the card, I did recall him calling it a charge card, but I just assumed the term *charge card* was British English for *credit card*. I had no idea it was an entirely different form of payment. And, of course, who was going to read the lengthy *cardholder's agreement* written in four-point font in the middle of a busy airport? I thought I knew what I was signing up for, but I was wrong. Horribly, terribly, maddeningly wrong. If I did not act right away, this card would ruin me.

I immediately got on the phone with American Express and explained the situation to them—how I had been the victim of predatory direct marketing tactics and mistakenly signed up for what I believed to be a credit card. I asked if I could change the charge card to a credit card. The answer was decidedly "no." I asked if they could issue me an additional credit card and transfer the balance. No. What about a line of credit? No. There was absolutely no way, under any circumstances, that American Express would work with me to resolve the balance over time. I had signed an agreement. I had spent the money. Now, I was on the hook for the full amount. Period. No discussion. No options. No flexibility. Nada. I was dealing with the *banking system,* after all, and when it comes to *the big machine,* there is none bigger, more heartless, and more soulless than big banks. I had read as much from my conspiracy research into fiat currency and the reserve monetary system. Now, I was being schooled in the reality of it where the rubber meets the road. American Express had absolutely no intention of accommodating my situation. Not one iota. I felt like the dark cabal of ruling elites I had read so much about in my conspiracy research had somehow found a way to get to me. I would have to rely on my own ingenuity and look elsewhere to get out of the debt trap they had set for me while I waited for a new round of abundance to manifest into my life.

I turned to the financial institution where I had my line of credit. It was not completely maxed out, so I requested an increase to my credit limit. What I did not know was my phone call to American Express caused them to switch "payment due" to "past due" on my account, which triggered a red flag on my credit report and caused my credit rating to plummet. Now, any bank or lending institution I turned to would see that I was several thousand dollars in arrears. No matter how much I explained to them that I was not asking for an increase in my credit limit to take on *additional debt* but rather to restructure or refinance *existing debt,* they would have none of it. According to their policies and procedures, I was ineligible for any lending. My credit card had a $500 cash-advance limit, and it was not possible at that time to pay off an American Express charge card with a credit card. Plus, I still had rent to pay, car payments to make, a cell phone, and lease payments to DELL Computer, all of which I could just barely cover, given the reduction in monthly income from my consulting practice. Suffice it to say the "past due" notices kept arriving in the mail. Followed by harassing phone calls from a collection agency.

I would not take all this lying down. I did everything I could think of to get myself out of the mess I had fallen into. I tried desperately to attract new clients. And as you well know, dear reader, *desperate* is not an attractive quality in any potential partner—business or otherwise. I tried looking for work but to no avail. Then, my remaining client said he was canceling the other project I had been working on. I did not want to accept defeat and go crawling back home to my parents' house, tail between my legs, but eventually, that is exactly what I ended up doing. I broke the lease on my condo, packed all my belongings into boxes and a rented cube van, and headed back to Guelph. I had been paying off the balance on my American Express charge card however and whenever I could, but unless I could get another contract soon, I would be insolvent.

Luckily, once back in Guelph, I tapped into my old Kitchener-Waterloo-Cambridge area network. I called on my old professors from Wilfrid Laurier. I attended networking events at Communitech and elsewhere. And sure enough, I landed a new client with a modest income. Enough to cover my expenses and make minimum payments. American Express still loomed large over my financial situation, having utterly decimated my credit score, but I had bought myself some peace of mind for a few months until the collection agency realized I was no longer living at the Toronto address.

In the meantime, I had met an attractive woman online who lived in a small rural hamlet not far from my parents' home in Guelph. She, like me, was into New Age and especially *The Secret*. She greatly resembled the woman I had pinned to my *vision board* a few years earlier. Perhaps this whole financial fiasco of mine was orchestrated by the universe so that she and I could meet! She also lived at home with her parents, also for financial reasons. Only, in her case, she was saving up money to buy a house, not to pay off delinquent debts. Still, she had no love for the big banks, was very understanding of my present financial conundrum, and our relationship quickly turned serious. I suppose we both felt we had drawn one another into our lives literally via the law of attraction. Things were beginning to look up. I still had the secret power of my spiritual adversaries—the evil hidden cabal running the world into the ground socially, environmentally, economically, and spiritually—and I had a like-minded, kind-hearted woman in my life to begin my life's work with. I was *down* but not yet *out*.

I was re-establishing myself in the tri-city area's entrepreneurial community, and I felt very confident that all this had been a test of my resolve and resilience. And that perhaps I was not meant for life in Toronto or international business—where I had been burned twice now—but something closer to home. After all, the small-town business community seemed less cutthroat, with a friendlier, more forgiving attitude and kinder, calmer pace. Something I appreciated so much more after falling victim to the ruthless efficiency of a heartless big banking machine. A machine I had outmaneuvered despite their best efforts. I was beginning to feel like I was out of the frying pan, free and clear to begin pursuing—or rather, manifesting—my goals and dreams as per my *vision board*.

The universe, however, had a different plan for me. I just had not gotten the message. It was time for more drastic measures. It was a beautiful summer morning when my girlfriend and I were on our way to Vaughan Mills to do some shopping when I had a seizure on Highway 401. No one was hurt, thank God. But several cars were damaged, and my Honda was totaled. I was taken to Milton Hospital since I was slipping in and out of lucidity. I eventually recovered my conscious awareness in time for my father to arrive and take us home. Suffice it to say my driver's license was immediately suspended, and my consulting business ground to a halt. My girlfriend broke up with me days later, and I did not blame her for doing so. She could have died in that car accident. No income, no prospects, no mobility, no relationship, no credit, etc…I really had nothing left to lose at that point but my debts. At least, that is what my father advised. If ever there was a perfect opportunity to declare personal bankruptcy and wipe the slate clean, this was it. And that is precisely what I did…in more ways than one.

The Illness and the Purge

Being that I once again found myself 'grounded' by epilepsy, having had the rug pulled out from under me, I needed to do something with my time. But what? The bankruptcy process was mostly handled by the law office. And my consulting practice had again ground to a halt. A few months prior, I had been at a networking event discussing how challenging it was to attract new clients, given that I believed myself to have a unique set of skills and value propositions. It was at that networking event that someone had planted the seed with me: "You need to write a book." When I pressed the individual as to why, exactly, he explained, "Every consultant of any note writes a book expounding the virtues of their approach. People read the book and decide if your approach is right for them and their business." In essence, then, he was suggesting that I pour all my professional knowledge, case studies, etc., into what would become a marketing tool. But one that would not be so easily ignored and discarded as, say, a brochure or a website. After all, while everyone had a website, not everyone had a book. Whereas before, my internal response at the networking event was, "Who has the time to write a book?" Now I had all the time in the world. So, I set to work.

It took roughly nine months to hammer out *The Attlas Project, Volume One – SEE The World in a New Light,* which I self-published on May 5, 2009, under my given name, *Attila Lewis Lendvai,* and sold via Amazon (description and link below). It begs the question, if I published my first book under my given name, then why did I publish this book under the pseudonym *Attlas Allux?* We will get to that soon enough, dear reader. But not before sharing the True purpose of the book written and published under our given name.

Like the Titanic, civilization is sailing through dangerous waters these days. Some want to stay the course, putting their faith in the ship human ingenuity built. Others blame progress, desiring a return to ancient beliefs and traditions. The Attlas Project Volume One – See the World in a New Light offers a vision of a new world on the horizon and the maps to get us there. It sheds light on where we are and how we got here—highlighting why so-called crises are really opportunities for human progress—and what minor course corrections should be made to avoid the dangers lurking in the darkness. Step one is to "SEE" (Strategize, Engage, Execute) problems in a simple yet highly effective way—the Attlas Process. Step two is to apply the Attlas Process to crises/opportunities in economics, democracy, and culture. Step three is to see the big picture: a global vessel capable of harnessing the winds of change, storms included, and making it to the new world that awaits all humankind.

Link 4: The Attlas Project Volume One: SEE the World in a New Light
(Amazon.com)

Suffice it to say, dear reader. The book did not sell well. With all my experience as an entrepreneurial consultant conducting branding and marketing for startup businesses, I knew nothing about how to market and promote a book. I had no social media following at the time. No YouTube channel. A friend and colleague managed to get me a guest spot on *Coast-to-Coast AM with George Noory*. However, I was ill-prepared and not yet practiced when it came to discussing the book. What is more, I relied heavily on what I called *VISUAL AIDs*—virtual interactive simulation, universal adaptive language, and actionable intelligence discourse (what today people would simply call diagrams or infographics). Since a picture is worth a thousand words, and the interview on talk radio had been so brief, I was unable to make any sort of meaningful impression. I had no elevator pitch for myself, let alone the book. After all, I wrote the book to show people what I was capable of. The book was my elevator pitch. How naïve and foolish I was.

Still, I had a strong intuition about the whole self-publishing enterprise: *if the book is meant to do something, it will.* I had gotten years of accumulated beliefs, ideas, and concepts about what is wrong with the world and what should be done about it off my chest. Those ideas are out there in the world now. If the universe wanted something to become of them, it would make it happen. What is more, I had dozens of books in boxes at home, and I was mailing copies to people of power, import, influence, and who were searching for solutions for their businesses, government, NGOs, etc. I was using the book exactly as it had been prescribed to me: my calling card and a showcase of what I could do for them and their project. After all, if I could tackle the challenges facing humanity, I could tackle the challenges facing their project. It seems it did not make the impression I had hoped for. It did not have the impact on my consulting career that I had planned. The doors I tried to open with it remained closed. I remained destitute.

I found myself in a very dark place, psychologically speaking. I was a mess. The seizures not only persisted, but they also worsened. I was caught in a downward spiral, and as I felt my whole life imploding around me, I would either explode in anger or completely break down in despair. My parents reported erratic and downright frightening behavior on my part. Whereas I had always been somewhat animated and mercurial, now I would go off on hyperactive tirades, ranting on and on about this or that subject—about some conspiracy theory, the latest corruption scandal involving a multinational corporation, or some outrageous political controversy. I was largely unaware of my behavior and how it was affecting those around me. At least, not until my father finally sat me down and told me how worried he and my mother were. I did not take their 'personal attack' on me very well. I was defensive and standoffish. After all, *I was the victim* here. I was the one with epilepsy. I was the one taken advantage of by a predatory credit card company. I was the one who had lost everything. I was the one suffering. *I...I...I.* That said, the proof was in the pudding, and I knew that my condition made me lose conscious awareness at times. Perhaps epilepsy was affecting me in ways beyond having seizures. Despite my resentment and reluctance, I overcame my resistance to their pleas and agreed to seek further help.

My father suggested I see the neurologist in Hamilton, Ontario, who had helped him several years earlier. Because my father knew him and had made the referral, he sat in with us and spoke privately with the neurologist without me in the room. On the drive home from Hamilton, my father came clean about what the doctor had said to him about what would be best for me. "He said your epilepsy is all in your head and that I should kick you out of the house and onto the street. Then your behavior and seizures will clear right up." We were both somewhat shocked and dismayed by this. We had turned to whom we believed was a trustworthy and dedicated healthcare professional in a time of desperation, and his response was to make light of that desperation. At least I came away from that visit with a prescription for a different epilepsy drug. While it did nothing to alleviate the seizures, it did seem to have a more calming effect on my mood, and my parents noted an improvement in my behavior. This prompted me to investigate the previous drug I had been on. That is when I discovered that my erratic behavior, which had so frightened my parents, was most likely attributable to the medication, whose side effects included 'psychotic behavior.' Digging deeper, I found the FDA study for the drug. There were fewer than sixty participants in said study. I had been placed on what amounted to an experimental drug that had only recently been approved for use, despite there being several drugs available that had been tried and tested for years, if not decades. Clearly, the pharmaceutical company's sales agent and marketing tactics had worked on my first neurologist.

Between these two healthcare misadventures, it was clear I needed a neurologist whose specialty was epilepsy. After some research, I discovered the epilepsy center at London Health Sciences, University of Western Ontario. It was only about an hour's drive southwest of Guelph. The challenge was a waiting list of six months to a year to get in. My dismay deepened. Still, I took a shot in the dark and made an appointment with my family physician to make the referral. I gave him the bio of the neurologist in London and said, "Him. I want you to refer me to him. No one else. Do you think you can get me in there?" My doctor smiled and said, "Yes, Attila, I can pretty much guarantee I can get you in to see him." When I inquired what made him so sure, he replied: "Because I went to medical school with him." True to his word, he made the referral, and within a matter of weeks, I had my first consultation with the neurologist at London Health Sciences.

The epilepsy center consisted of roughly half a dozen hospital beds where patients would be admitted and fitted with electrodes to have their brain activity monitored 24/7 via electroencephalogram (EEG). The point of this monitoring was to gather real-time data on seizures as they occur. Some of us would remain in these beds for weeks while the team gathered information on how, when, and where in the brain our seizures originated, spread to, affected, etc. We would also be given a battery of related neuropsychological tests and scans (such as MRI) to help determine the cause and nature of the epilepsy. As I would discover, no two cases of epilepsy are the same. The process of formulating a medical snapshot of the unique condition affecting each patient was long, arduous, and intricate. Given that lengthy process and with roughly six to eight beds in the center, it was easy to see why the cue was so long to get in. In fact, the only reason why I was able to jump the cue, so to speak, was that the center could not afford to have a bed sitting empty. But others waiting to get in could not put their entire life on hold at the drop of a hat. I, on the other hand, could—since I had no job, no wife, no kids, essentially no life. My parents informed the neurologist that should a bed become free, and should no one in the cue ahead of me be able to fill it within a reasonable timeframe, they could have me in it within the hour, even if it was in the middle of the night. Naturally, it helped that both my parents were retired. I had a suitcase packed and ready to go, and so I waited for the call.

Desperate Search for Knowledge

It should go without saying, dear reader that throughout this low point in my life, I had not abandoned my New Age spirituality. On the one hand, I was more than a little disappointed and frustrated that my efforts to manifest my desires in accordance with *The Secret* of New Age dogma had resulted in the opposite of my desires. On the other hand, given that I once again found myself in hell, psychologically speaking, surely the New Age might offer something in the way of soothing my psychological suffering, if not curing my depression, and healing my condition. I had been gifted an iPod by my brother, and with it, had discovered podcasts. On my daily walks with my dog, I would listen to hours of lectures, presentations, readings of New Age books, et al., in the hopes of receiving that one nugget, that one piece of need-to-know information that would, at last, allow me to transform myself, my life, and free myself from this revolving door of epileptic hell I was trapped in. Surely, the New Age, with all its talk of positive energy, raising vibrations, awakening, transformation, and healing, would have the answers I sought.

Although much of what I listened to, watched, and read during this period *resonated* with me to one degree or another, there was something lacking. Something within me was just not satisfied with what the New Age gurus were offering. The Still Soft Voice of intuition simply did not respond to anything with a resounding "Yes. This is it. This is what you have been looking for." Even listening to Dr. Wayne Dyer, who had been a practicing psychiatrist at one time and who had been of great inspiration to me, now left me cold. His, like the platitudes and prescriptions of other New Age personalities, pricked my conscience. It was as though I was being sold a bill of goods that seemed of quality on the surface but ultimately lacked the depth and meaning that I needed in my life, given my present circumstances. I was in hell. There was no avoiding that fact. And no amount of positive thinking or raising my vibration was going to change the objective circumstances I found myself in. And not for lack of trying. Remember, dear reader, I had been a devout disciple of the New Age for years and a mystic all my life, with spiritual experiences stretching back to childhood. I knew all their programs, practices, and techniques. Now, they all fell short and fell flat, intuitively and practically.

It was then that I discovered podcasts that read passages from ancient scriptures. Perhaps the spirituality from a past age would yield some hidden teachings that the New Age did not. I would listen to texts from the Hindu, Buddhist, and Abrahamic traditions—Jewish, Christian, Muslim—but nothing seemed to 'click.' I heard the words, and my mind processed what was being said, but I felt disconnected from the meaning. I was not taken by the literal interpretations, and if there were hidden meanings, my rational mind was incapable of penetrating them. I felt out of my depth to some degree. Lost and confused. No matter what road I went down, it seemed to lead me to another dead-end. I had always felt this way about religion, going all the way back to high school theology class when we studied 'World Religions.' There was something about the contemporary understanding of religion that was off—if not flat-out wrong. I never connected with the concept of 'faith' as 'belief.' After all, I was a *mystic* by nature. I had experiences of the divine. And a precious few of my experiences mirrored those of the heroic albeit mythological beings and their fantastic adventures as told in scripture. My foray into the secret knowledge of ages past had left me just as unfulfilled as the New Age. Then I stumbled across the *Glorian Podcast* (at that time called *Gnostic Radio).*

Link 5: Homo Nosce Te Ipsum (Glorian.org)

The episode which caught my eye was entitled *Homo Nosce Te Ipsum*, which I would later discover was a lecture from the *Greek Mysteries Course*. A Latin phrase meaning *man know thyself,* it appeared in its original Greek form, γνῶθι σεαυτόν, gnōthi seauton, above the doorway of one of the temples of Delphi in ancient Greece. The Gnostic Instructor was discussing *homunculi*—the elemental spirits of nature—in the mineral, plant, animal, and, yes, even human kingdom. The instructor explained the relationship between homo, meaning 'man,' humus meaning 'earth' (that is, soil or clay), and homunculus meaning 'little man.' The development of the homunculus through the mineral, plant, animal, and human kingdom via the transmigration of souls. And what significance this had for us in the human kingdom. Below is a link to the transcript of the lecture, dear reader, where you can also listen to it if you so choose.

I was utterly captivated. Here was a level of spiritual knowledge I had never heard before. Described in precise metaphysical, scientific detail. Making sense of the symbols and allegories I could not penetrate nor interpret with my rational mind. Of particular note was the following passage from the lecture:

> *There is something about these matters that we have to understand: homo sapiens, you and I, that are developed as a consequence of the mechanical evolution of nature, are not the human being, rather, we are just intellectual animals. We are a mind, manas (homo), human soul that, through evolution, acquires intellect. That is why the Greeks and Romans and many other ancient cultures knew about this because they could see, just as I saw the plants and animals and other creatures, that the elementals had human shapes in the internal planes. They knew it not because they read it or because they had libraries or scientists or anthropologists telling them it was this way. They were not blind as we are blind. They had the capacity to see into the internal dimensions. That is why they understood. That is why those initiates saw those things and understood that the homo sapien was the final level of evolution of this homunculi. It needed something else in order to go ahead in development. In regard to this, something came into my mind, which is a very important statement. It is mentioned in "Homo Nosce Te Ipsum" as the following:*

> "I warn you, whoever you are, Oh! You who want to probe the arcana of nature, that if you do not find within yourself that which you are looking for, you shall not find it outside either! If you ignore the excellences of your own house, how do you pretend to find other excellences? Within you is hidden the treasure of treasures! Know thyself, and you will know the Universe and the Gods."

> *Similar to that passage of Jesus of Nazareth and Nicodemus in the gospel of John, which in Latin states:*

> "Erat autem homo ex Pharisaeis Nicodemus nomine princeps Iudaeorum" - John 3: 1

There was a man (homo) of the Jews (Iudaeorum), whose name was Nicodemus that came at night to talk to Jesus. And said: "Rabbi, we know that thou art a minister come from God: for no one can do these miracles that thou doest, except God be with him." Then Master Jesus said: "Amen, amen, I say unto thee, except a man is born again he cannot see the kingdom of God."

In Delphic words, we will say, except a man is born again, he cannot know the Universe and the Gods.

– Source: Glorian.org, Greek Mysteries Course, Homo Nosce Te Impsum

Upon hearing these words, the Still Soft Voice of my intuition spoke loud and clear to me: "Yes. This is it. You have found what you were searching for." One quest ended. Another now beckoned.

Surrender

I was not going to look this gift horse in the mouth. I knew I had not stumbled across the Glorian podcast, website, online resource, and library of esoteric books by accident. It was as if this archive of knowledge had been calling to me. I would answer the call. Over the next few weeks, I would devour as many online lectures as I could from *The Beginning Here and Now* course. I also ordered five books from Glorian.org written by Samael Aun Weor, which I selected on the basis that they all dealt directly with the mind and/or healing. I intuitively knew I would find answers to my condition that had made my life into a living hell. These books were, in the order I read them:

- The Revolution of the Dialectic
- Esoteric Medicine and Practical Magic
- Treatise on Revolutionary Psychology (one of Samael Aun Weor's last books)
- The Great Rebellion
- The Perfect Matrimony (Samael Aun Weor's first book)

Serendipitously, once I had all five in hand, I got a call from London Health Sciences. A bed had become vacant in the epilepsy center. If I could be there within the hour, it was mine. I hastily stuffed all five books, iPod, and computer into my laptop bag, grabbed my pre-packed suitcase, and was off to London. Whatever would happen next, I knew that I would be in the right place, with the right knowledge at my fingertips. What is more, I knew that I had been led here, now, to this moment in time. Many things had fallen into place to finally get me into London Health Sciences. I was going to continue going with that flow.

I will not bore you with all the minutia of all the physical and neuropsychological diagnostics I underwent while in the epilepsy center, dear reader. However, I must explain that after just a few days, it became apparent to the neurologist that the surface-level electrodes were not penetrating deep enough to produce adequate EEG readings. I was told that in order for their program to be useful, they would need to drill two holes in my skull and insert electrodes directly onto the surface of my brain. I had never undergone any serious surgery before in my life. Certainly not one that involved general anesthesia. The procedure would take over twenty hours to complete. I would be left with two divots on my head where fragments of skull had been removed. One behind the ear, another off-center, just north of my forehead. To this day, there is nothing between my brain and the outside world but a thin patch of skin covering these divots. I reluctantly agreed and underwent the procedure. I awoke to find myself back in the epilepsy center along with the other patients, only I had a bundle of cables coming out of the back of my head plugged into the wall like Neo in *The Matrix*. I was now a cybernetic organism. I had literally become *transhuman,* with sensors implanted under my skull, attached directly to my brain, reading my neural activity in real-time. "It will only be a few more decades," I thought, "when there will be no cables coming out the back. The computer will not be in another room but on an implanted chip connected wirelessly to servers in the cloud." It was a truly surreal experience to be in that position.

After some weeks of monitoring and even some induced seizures, the team at the London Health Sciences epilepsy center felt they had the data they needed. They removed the electrodes by pulling them out via the hole in the back of my cranium. No word of a lie: no anesthetic was used during this procedure. I could feel and hear the electrodes and wires scraping the surface of my brain and the inside of my skull as they slowly pulled on the bundle of cables. It was then time for the final consultation, prognosis, and proposed treatment plan. My parents requested they attend said conference, and I agreed. I owed them access to as much information as possible, considering how much time, effort, attention, and, indeed, aggravation they had sacrificed and suffered for my sake over the previous years. And were it not for them, I would never have been able to make it here in the first place. So, the three of us sat down with the head neurologist and his staff brain surgeon—who had performed the electrode insertion procedure on me—and braced ourselves for what we all hoped would be good news about the road to me being seizure-free.

The neurologist said (and I am paraphrasing here): "We are going to cut out a quarter of your brain and give you a fifty-fifty chance of curing your epilepsy." His surgeon added, "We can increase those odds to sixty percent if we also take out a small chunk of the brain behind your eye. I will, of course, do my best not to sever the optic nerve, leaving you blind in that eye, but it is a risk you need to be aware of." There was a moment of stunned silence on my family and I's part. There it was: seven years of suffering with epilepsy culminating in exploratory brain surgery and weeks lying in a bed *Matrix*-style, and the best the allopathic healthcare system could offer, via one of the top epilepsy specialists in all of Canada, was a sixty percent chance of curing my condition. My heart sank. And I could feel a pall of disappointment descend over my parents as well. Luckily, within moments of that revelation, I received a clear message from Attlas that "there was another way." And so, I said to the doctors, "Thank you. I will take it under advisement."

That evening, I returned home and fell to my knees. Recall, dear reader, that just a few weeks before being admitted to London Health Sciences, I had discovered the Gnostic Teachings of Glorian.org and Samael Aun Weor. I had learned much in the time just before and during my stay in the epilepsy center, with the benefit of countless hours lying in bed reading books and listening to online lectures. As a direct result of having been given that framework to contextualize the reality of my present predicament, I proceeded to pray to Attlas—my Innermost Being and Divine Mother (my True Self)—an Individuated Essence of God, the 'being' in 'human being,' and the Source of the Still Soft Voice of intuition which I had become accustomed to hearing and heeding, especially at crucial turning points in my life. A prayer that was at once an admission of defeat and a plea-bargain for mercy and compassion. It went something like this:

> *Mother of mine, Father of mine, my Beloved. You Who are my True Being. I have reached the end of my rope. In this burden that I am saddled with, which I have been suffering from, struggling to overcome, and subjecting my loved ones to for seven years, I have failed miserably. When it comes to this epilepsy, which has proven itself to be the defining challenge of my life, this much is clear: **I am not qualified.** I have exhausted every worldly resource at my disposal. I have consulted the top specialists in the field of medicine, allowed myself to be butchered and examined like a monkey in a laboratory, and the best they could come up with amounts to little better than a coin toss.*

I got up off my knees and sat in the chair in front of the computer, opened a Google search window, and continued praying…

> *You said there was another way. Here, I have at my fingertips a window to the collective knowledge of humanity. **You** tell me what to type, and I will type it. I surrender. I am not qualified to make the decisions in my life. Every decision I make ends in disaster. No matter what I want, try to attain, or strive to make happen, I always wind up where I am am now…in hell. My life may as well be forfeit if it remains in my hands. So why would I hold onto the reigns? No, I surrender my life to You. So, tell me what to do, and I will do it. Show me which path to walk, and I will walk it. And this I swear to You in the Name of Christ, for the Glory of Christ, and by the Majesty of Christ: if by following Your guidance my life is restored, if You lead me out of the hell that I am in, then my life will be Yours until the end of time. If You deliver me from my present suffering, I shall pledge my life, my energy, my talents, and all my efforts to You and Your work for the sake of the end of the suffering of all beings. For my life is as good as a forfeit. Give me back my life, and that life is Yours. But not my will, but Thine be done. I beg this in*

all humility that this be done in accordance with the Law, in the Name of Christ, for the
Glory of Christ, and by the Majesty of Christ. So be it! So be it! So be it! Amen. Amen.
Amen.

A few seconds later, I received a response as clear as day from my Innermost Being to search Google for "epilepsy diet lifestyle." Google returned some 250,000+ results. Upon seeing that number, I sank further into defeat and self-pity. "Relax," the Still Soft Voice of my True Self replied, "scroll down." I did so. Down and down, scanning links as I went, nothing jumping out at me. Page two…Page three…on and on with no end in sight. Then, suddenly and without warning, I heard the call loud and clear: "There! That one! Click on that one." The link in question was *DogtorJ.com: Food Intolerance in Pets & Their People – Home of the G.A.R.D.* Introduced by *'Dogtor J,'* Veterinarian Dr. John B. Symes, himself as follows:

> *From over ten years of medical and nutritional research came The G.A.R.D. – an elimination diet for the treatment of most conditions afflicting man and his four-legged companions. The original meaning of the acronym was the glutamate & aspartate restricted diet, being derived from the fact that The G.A.R.D. placed a premium on the elimination of two non-essential amino acids, glutamic and aspartic acid, the parent proteins in MSG and aspartame (NutraSweet), respectively. These two neurostimulating amino acids play a major role in epilepsy, migraines, insomnia, ADHD, autism, fibromyalgia, and numerous other neurodegenerative diseases. It was not hard to see that the food sources of these amino acids- grains, dairy, soy/legumes, and nuts/seeds- were also playing a major role in the manifestation of these common medical conditions. – Source: https://dogtorj.com/*

Suffice it to say, dear reader, that I inhaled all "ten years of medical and nutritional research." The next morning, I announced to my bewildered parents that I was putting myself on the G.A.R.D. I would be eating no more gluten, soy, corn, or cow dairy. I also cut out all artificial sweeteners, caffeine, alcohol, and anything that might contain MSG (or the countless euphemisms for MSG), be it labeled as an ingredient or unlabeled—that is, MSG which exists in the food as a by-product of processed animal/plant proteins.

> *The banishment of these "four horsemen" led to a steady stream of incredible testimonials as the intestinal tract of these afflicted individuals healed and their myriad of symptoms resolved. The second meaning of The G.A.R.D. was born- the gut absorption recovery diet. – Source: https://dogtorj.com/main-course/welcome-to-dogtorj-com/*

And I can report, dear reader, that within hours of putting myself on the G.A.R.D., my seizures stopped. My parents, too, were amazed. Within days, I contacted Dogtor J to add my own experience to his "steady stream of incredible testimonials." I had witnessed a miracle take place in my life. I was nowhere near one hundred percent seizure-free, and the underlying cause of my seizures would not be addressed by mere diet alone, but at least I had been granted a reprieve. With the guidance of my Innermost Being and Divine Mother, I had struck a major blow against the condition of epilepsy, which had sent me tumbling into hell. Now would come the slow road out of hell and to full recovery. And the fulfillment of the promise I made to my Self in exchange for the miracle I had been granted.

Making Peace

Before I could make any real progress, however, I would have to make peace with my descent into hell. As I watched myself undertake the slow, sometimes arduous process of restoring my life, I needed to stop beating myself up over all my past failures. I had to make peace with myself. With the fact that I was in my late thirties living at home with my parents. No job. No credit. No driver's license—let alone a car. And no one to commiserate with. What I had was Canada's top epilepsy neurologist monitoring my progress on the restrictive diet and other esoteric practices I had put in place to work on myself. He could see my EEGs becoming progressively better until, at last, after fourteen months, my EEG came out normal—no sign of epilepsy. Of course, I was not cured by any means. And the underlying condition was still ever-present in my life. I would have to remain vigilant. And I would have to learn to live with other symptoms like chronic depression. I did, however, meet the medical requirements for reacquiring my driver's license. And once I had that in hand, I could once again fire up my consulting practice and begin rebuilding my life. Only this time, it was not 'I' in the driver's seat. Remember, dear reader, I had admitted to myself that 'I' was not qualified.

As it turns out, I, a mere mortal vessel, had not descended into hell alone. My True Self had been with me all along. And although I was aware of His Still Soft Voice of intuition from time to time, most of the time, I had believed I was the one in the driver's seat. I had taken credit for all the good things I produced and what little success I had. And I had blamed most of my failures on myself, beating myself up for my stupidity, naivete, anxiety, insecurity, bad temper, piss-poor memory, and all my other limitations and shortcomings. Otherwise, I would blame my lack of success on being a victim of circumstances—especially epilepsy—or of others, or of 'the unfair system,' etc. My descent into hell was not so much a result of people or circumstances affecting my life but rather my reactions to people and circumstances.

I had chosen to become a self-righteous woke victim of 'social injustice,' a conspiracy theorist, a New Age devotee, and a guinea pig for transhumanism. These four aspects represented the darkest corridors in the labyrinth of my personal hell, with some of the most cleverly designed traps: pitfalls designed to ensnare and entangle the mind with elaborate illusions of truth yet create only the delusion of possessing objective knowledge. In Truth, I was *possessed* by them, even as I believed myself to be in possession of the truth thanks to them. I judged myself to be awake because of them. Certain. Powerful. Special. *Superior* to all those still asleep and ignorant of the answers afforded to *transhumanists, conspiracy theorists, social justice warriors,* and/or *New Agers*. And it is only human nature to defend the sources of our power against all threats, even when those sources are secretly weakening us. Just as they were weakening me, the mere mortal typing these words for your sake, dear reader.

This is most crucial, dearest reader. If you happen to adhere at present to one or more of the four belief systems under examination herein, please know I am not here to attack you nor your beliefs. This goes for any belief system you may hold dear. Be it religious or otherwise. I know how important beliefs are to us. I know how they make us all feel, perhaps not specifically down to the details, but in general. That is why we prize them so, our beliefs. It is why little is more precious to humanity than its beliefs—be they inherited or chosen. I am not so foolish or naïve to think your beliefs are so frivolous or flexible that you change them as you do your clothing. Nor that they belong to some arbitrary set of notions and doctrines picked from a hat. Be they modern or ancient, beliefs spring up for a reason. And even if your reasons for believing differ from others' reasons—or my own reasons for formerly believing—they are no less valid *to you* **just as they were no less valid to *me*…to *us*.**

ABOUT 'US'

One of my close friends and colleagues, Wolfgang Amelung, makes regular reference to *speaking to the listening* and what he calls the *us conversation*. He has spent a lifetime working with ecosystems and learning firsthand the genius of working in harmony and mutual symbiosis amidst infinite complexity. It is knowledge only a high-order rainforest ecosystem can truly teach us by example. Since we can agree humanity has created nothing that comes close to the collective harmony and sustainability of a high-order ecosystem, perhaps we can agree also on the *us conversation* born of the wisdom of nature in its highest expression. An expression that is not purely *mechanical* despite all appearances to the contrary. What does that mean to us, dear reader, as we engage in what seems to be a one-sided conversation?

For starters, dear reader, we will no longer be referring to ourselves as *"I"* in this book. Until now, this introduction has been from the personal point of view of the mortal individual typing these words, Attila Lewis Lendvai. An individual who began meditating roughly at the age of five and at the age of fifteen learned the name of his Innermost Being—his True Self—*Attlas*. That individual, that "I" cannot truthfully say, "I am the author of this book." What Attila can say is, "I am just a typist. A stenographer for my Innermost Essence, *Attlas*, who has been guiding me throughout all my journeys to hell and back." In other words, we made those journeys together. What is more, we made them *for your sake*, dear reader, so we could make this recounting of those journeys for your benefit and for the benefit of suffering humanity. Attlas is likewise just a spark, a seed, an Essence of The Innermost Intimate Spirit of All—*Allux*—All Light, God Light, the Fire of fires, Light of lights, and Being of beings known to many as The Christ—the Perfect Multiple Unity of The Logos—but also by many names.

The adorable God Kristos (Christ) comes from archaic cults of the fire God. The letters P (pyre) and X (cross) are the hieroglyphs that represent the generation of the sacred fire.

Christ was worshipped in the mysteries of Mithra, Apollo, Aphrodite, Jupiter, Janus, Vesta, Bacchus, Astarte, Demeter, Quetzalcoatl, etc.

The Christic principle has never been absent from any religion. All religions are one. Religion is as inherent to life as humidity is to water. The great cosmic universal religion becomes modified into thousands of religious forms. Thus, the priests from all religious forms are completely identifiable with one another through the fundamental principles of the great cosmic universal religion.

Figure 4: Chi Rho, Symbol of Christ

Therefore, a basic difference between the Mohammedan priest and the Jewish priest, or between the Pagan priest and the legitimate Christian one, does not exist. Religion is one. Religion is unique and absolutely universal. The ceremonies of the Shinto priest of Japan or of the Mongol Lamas are similar to those ceremonies of the shamans and sorcerers from Africa and Oceania.

When a religious form degenerates, it disappears, yet the universal life creates new religious forms in order to replace it.

Authentic primeval Gnostic Christianity comes from Paganism. Prior to Paganism, the Cosmic Christ was worshipped in all cults. In Egypt, Christ was Osiris, and whosoever incarnated him was an Osirified one. In all ages, there have been masters who have assimilated the infinite universal Christic principle [and were thus called Christ]. In Egypt, Hermes was the Christ. In Mexico, the Christ was Quetzalcoatl. In sacred India, Krishna is Christ. In the Holy Land, the great Gnostic Jesus (who was educated in the land of Egypt) was the one who had the bliss of assimilating the universal Christic principle, and because of this, he was worthy of being rebaptized with the seity of fire and of the cross, Kristos.

The Nazarene, Jesus-Iesus-Zeus, is the modern man who totally incarnates the universal Christic principle. Prior to Jesus, many masters incarnated this Christic principle of fire.

The Rabbi of Galilee is a God because he totally incarnated the Cosmic Christ. Hermes, Quetzalcoatl, and Krishna are Gods because they also incarnated the Cosmic Christ.

– Samael Aun Weor, The Perfect Matrimony

Thus *we*, Attlas Allux, the True author of this book, are one with yourself and all beings, dear reader. For within you resides your own Individuated Essence of the Innermost Intimate Christ. What some might refer to as your *True Self* is an Essence that dwells within us all as a spark, a seed, a Divine Being in potentiality. The Being in 'human being' who longs for Self-realization…*to be*…the one state which alone can provide lasting peace, joy, and happiness to us. A state that requires the consciousness to be *awake*. And therein lies the impetus for the '*us conversation.*' All of us who embarked on a personal journey in search of answers were responding to a deep inner longing to awaken. A journey that all of us are still on, despite what we may want to believe about ourselves and the progress we have made to date.

We presented most of this chapter from the perspective of ourselves as a mortal individual, Attila. As such, I offered my personal testimony to being shrouded in darkness, even as I was made to believe I had found the light. It was not until I had exhausted all worldly resources at my disposal that I accepted **my True nature as *our* mortal vessel, servant, and messenger** and gave control of this mortal vessel to my

True Self, immortal soul, and Innermost Being, Attlas—its rightful *owner-operator*. We walked through hell and back together so that we could be here now, sharing self-evident experiential knowledge on matters no outsider, academic, or critic can offer. What is more, it was that very journey into and out of hell that allowed Attila to become aware of his place in the scheme of things. To know himself more fully. To be able to type these, our words, and not just those of his mortal, rational, ego-mind. And it has all been for your sake, dearest reader: that you too may come to know yourself (and by extension, your Self) in greater fullness and wholeness.

In synthesis, Self-knowledge begins by observing ourselves within the context of our experience of the human condition(ed). To that end, we have provided you a visual aid in the *APPENDIX: The Tree of Life and the Human Condition(ed)* as a reference guide. In the spirit of the *us conversation* and the experience shared throughout this chapter, we now proceed to share with you, dear reader, our *revelations from hell.*

PART II:

A SEEKER'S REVELATIONS FROM HELL

OUR EXPERIENTIAL KNOWLEDGE OF THE HUMAN CONDITION(ED)

The intuitive mind is a sacred gift. The rational mind, a faithful servant. We have created a society that honors the servant and has forgotten the gift.

– Albert Einstein

To understand the human condition, let us begin with the word human. The first part of human is *hume,* meaning earth. It is the earthen matrix for air, water, and nutrients to support life. In humans, hume is the earthen vessel for our Self to lead a mortal life. The second part of human is *manas,* meaning mind. What Emerson called *over mind,* Nietzsche called *uber mind,* and Buddhists refer to as *Buddha mind.* Manas is not the personality's cerebral, subjective, intellectual, *rational mind,* which we typically associate with the brain. That rational mind is very much part of our hume, our earthen vessel, the mortal self.

So manas is not the rational mind Albert Einstein states should be a *faithful servant.* Rather, manas is the intuitive mind Einstein calls a *gift.* The gift of *divine mind,* which we will refer to as *metamind.* The metaphysical matrix of Self, consciousness, and soul that facilitates multidimensional experience. A way to be, seek, and know oneself and reality comprehensively.

A human being, then, is the physical embodiment of the metamind of being. In microcosm, we could say a human being consists of two pillars: the physical world we see, the physical vessel of a thinking and feeling hominid on earth. And the metaphysical world we *SEEK* self-evident experiential knowledge by consciously experiencing being one with metamind. A human being is the balanced union of these two pillars. This ancient earthen vessel from the Andes depicts the physical self one with the metamind of being *(Figure 5).* As Shakespeare said, "to be or not to be" is the central question of the human condition. The answer to this is found in the thousands of allegories told throughout the ages. From Adam and Eve to Faust. From *Lord of the Rings* to *Game of Thrones.* That we have yet to grasp the answer, practically, comprehensively, at every turn in our lives, in all our challenges, endeavors, successes, and failures is the one reason, a single pillar, on which rests the cause of all of humanity's confusion and suffering. And blinds us from knowing ourselves and the world as a conscious, experiencing being. How so?

Figure 5: Ancient Andean Earthenware of a Triune Human Being

A human being consists of a triangulation of hume, manas, and being. In other words, a triune human being. Tri means three, and une means one. That is three in one. A Triune Human Being. A true human being. Consider the bicycle for a moment. A bike is a practical example of a balanced union of two wheels in perfect alignment, with the rider raised between them, forming a triangulation, just like the triune of hume, manas, and being. In this light, a true human being is analogous to a bicyclist.

Life is like riding a bicycle. To keep your balance, you must keep moving.

– Albert Einstein

Despite a higher center of gravity, bicycles can be easily balanced and maintain forward momentum by beginners and experts alike over smooth pavement or the most treacherous terrain, even in extreme conditions, and carrying what may seem like impossible loads. Be it for a cross-country trip or just a quick spin around the neighborhood, this humble two-wheeled contraption is far and away the most popular, successful, and abundant vehicle on the planet. And for a good reason.

Nothing compares to the simple pleasure of a bike ride.

– John F. Kennedy

For young and young at heart. On your way to work, or hard at work. On a mountain or in a sprint to the finish. No matter who you are or where you come from, it is more than likely you have ridden a bicycle at least once in your life, if not on a regular basis. But if bicycles are so ubiquitous the world over, populated by physical cyclists, can the same be said of metaphysical cyclists? Are we true human beings with our rational mind and metamind in balanced alignment under the leadership of our being, our True Self? To answer that question, let us dig beneath the surface and analyze just how a bicycle works.

In a bicycle, the rear wheel follows the front wheel. The front wheel is steered by the cyclist, who ultimately sets the direction of the bike. Likewise, the cyclist provides the drive by peddling the bike and turning the crank. That driving force is then transferred to the rear wheel, producing traction, literally where the rubber meets the road. This is made possible by the chain, which gives the rear wheel a direct connection to the cyclist. It is precisely a conscious connection to our True Self that provides us the driving force and direction behind our actions, which we can experience consciously as we ride through life a triune human being. But the reality is most people lack this conscious connection to their inner cyclist and have discarded their metaphysical bicycle altogether. And therefore, humanity suffers the human condition.

Triune Human *Bicyclist*

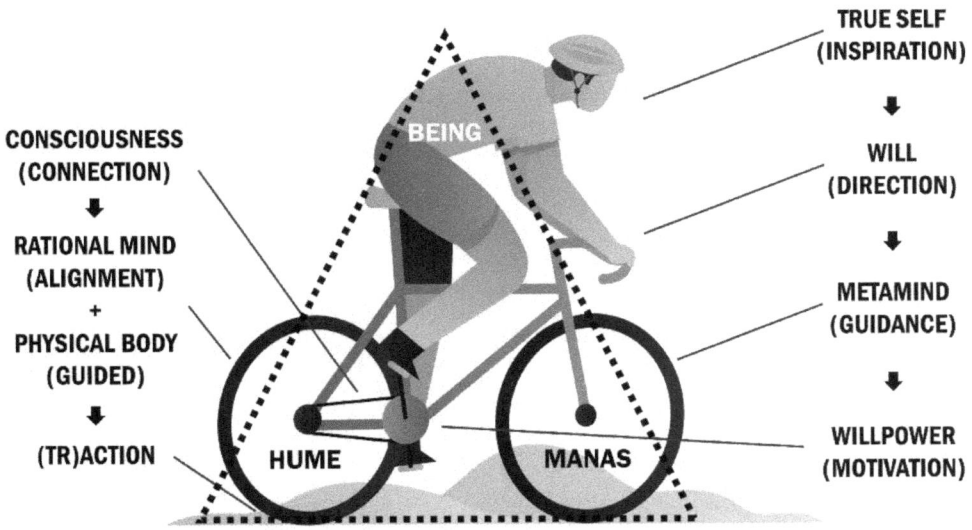

Hume + Manas + Being = True Human Being

Figure 6: Triune Human Bicyclist ~ True Human Being

If you never confront pain, / you're missing the essence of the sport.

– Scott Martin

The next step in understanding the human condition is the word *condition*. The first part of the condition, *con,* means with, that is, accompanied by or in possession of. But con is also slang for confidence artist. One who exploits our naiveté via deceit and persuades us to believe their lies. The second part of condition, *dition,* is an archaic term meaning state. And by state, we can mean rule, power, control, dominion, or government, but state also refers to the form or arrangement in which something exists, for instance, the *states of matter*. **The condition of humanity, then, is a state of naiveté exploited by persuasive forms of deceit that possess and rule humanity.**

Do you doubt our definition of the human condition, dear reader? Fair enough, let us put your doubt to rest with self-evident experiential knowledge you can verify for yourself. What is *unconditional Love?* True Love. Pure Love. Love without conditions. Conditional love is lesser, *impure.* However, conditional love can seem most *convincing* to those who are *naïve.* What is more, conditional love is often used by individuals to *exploit* naiveté. Those inexperienced souls who long for True Love often find themselves easily *persuaded,* manipulated, and even outright ruled by others through conditional love. Attachment is a form of conditional love. Codependency is another. Love is Light. Light also can be conditioned. When light passes through the film, it is altered. It becomes conditioned by the film and no longer radiates pure light but instead projects the image on the film. And we all know motion pictures are *illusions.* They are inherently deceitful from an objective point of view. There are twenty-four still images passing through a projector per second, creating the projected illusion on screen we call a *movie.* An illusion that is, ostensibly, little more than *conditioned light.* And yet, movies can be the most *convincing.* We can very easily *lose ourselves* in them. We forget ourselves. The real world. Our problems, worries, responsibilities. Time itself fades away. Movies are lauded for their ability to provide *escapism.* Our consciousness is whisked away into the world of the film, its characters, and its story, and we become fascinated with the virtual reality on the screen instead of the one we exist in day to day.

Consciousness and the Human Condition(ed)

Consciousness, like Love, is Light. The light of consciousness. How so? To be aware of something requires we shine the light of consciousness on it—*turn our attention to it*—the same way we might shine a flashlight in the dark to see where we are going. Many believe consciousness is merely a receptive function, like hearing, sight, or even smell. This is not so. Consider that we must *pay attention* to what someone is saying. Observation is an *active investment,* a projection of consciousness that reflects to us that which we are observing, just as light reflects at us what a lightbulb illuminates. Concentration represents a *focused beam* of consciousness, a more intense form of observation that highlights a particular phenomenon we wish to observe with greater clarity, just like shining a spotlight on the soloist performing on stage. Consciousness is an entirely different wavelength than visible light, being that we can observe thoughts, emotions, sensations, visualizations in our *mind's eye,* including memories, dreams, and any number of physical and metaphysical phenomena beyond the reach of our five senses. There are other qualities of consciousness beyond those related to light, and we will discuss them later in this book. For now, what matters is that we agree on the nature of consciousness as a kind of light in order that we may comprehend its role in *our experience* of the human condition.

All experiences arise within the field of consciousness. There can be no experience without it. The bidirectional nature of consciousness is what literally creates experience and, by extension, knowledge. We know that consciousness projects outward, just as light shines (paying attention, focused concentration, general awareness). And that consciousness receives projections and reflections like the eye detects light, the ear hears sound waves, etc. The active, projective, *positive* force of consciousness can be said to be *masculine.* It is the aspect of consciousness that reaches out into the world, as it were. The passive, receptive, *negative* force of consciousness is *feminine.* It is the aspect of consciousness that receives the active projections of consciousness from the world. The successful *union* of masculine and feminine forces at any level of nature results in a third *creative force—the sexual force.* In the case of consciousness, the union of masculine (projection) and feminine (reception) creates experience. The word derives from the Latin *experiri,* meaning "try," while *ex* means "out of." Couples are said to be *trying* for a baby. If they are successful, the woman is said to be *expecting* a child—born *out of* her womb. And what do we *try* to get *out of* experience? Experiential knowledge—*gnosis* to the Greeks. Sometimes called *wisdom,* gnosis is that knowing which emerges within consciousness through *experimentation—trying* this or that and seeing what comes *out of* the experiment. Those who accumulate a great deal of gnosis in a particular area are genuine *experts.* Gnosis is to experience what a child is to sex—what comes out of the union of masculine and feminine forces. As we know, not all sexual acts result in pregnancy and birth. So, too, not every experience results in gnosis. Just like sex, experience can be empty, meaningless, and wasteful, or it can be voluptuous, meaningful, and productive. But experience—like sex—is by its very nature *always creative.* What experience creates, like any sexual act, depends on the *conditions* under which the masculine and feminine forces are united. And since all experience takes place within the field of consciousness, that can mean only one thing.

Consciousness, like Love, like Light, can be *conditioned.* And, just as conditional love is impure, usually with some ulterior motive to manipulate, control, or even rule, so too conditioned consciousness is a form of exploitation via *ignorance.* Likewise, just as conditioned light creates convincing illusions, conditioned consciousness is a form of delusion via *hypnosis.* Hypnosis and ignorance are the opposite of gnosis—a word so pregnant with meaning that it requires two words to describe its antithesis. Gnosis is the child of *objective* experience: the union of expressions within an unconditioned field of consciousness. It is the Truth (capital 'T'). Hypnosis and ignorance, then, are the products of *subjective* experience: the union of expressions within a conditioned field of consciousness. They are what people refer to nowadays as *'my truth'*—consciousness which is *subjected to* conditions. Altered consciousness, like the conditioned light of a movie's convincing illusions, creates persuasive delusions—sometimes called hallucinations—hypnosis. Sub-consciousness, like the inferior 'love' of a narcissistic partner, creates rationalizations in place of the Truth—we call these beliefs, intellectualizations, opinions, etc.—ignorance. Un-consciousness is merely the absence of consciousness. The result is still ignorance, but not because the Truth is being covered-up by an illusion or rationalization. In other words, to be unconscious means simply to be unaware, not necessarily distracted or deceived. However, distraction, misdirection, and deception by the subconscious can and do result in us becoming unconscious.

To be unconscious means to be asleep. In general, when we sleep, we are unaware. Then again, as we all have experienced at some point in our life—perhaps regularly—we can also *dream.* While dreaming, our consciousness is subjected to our subconsciousness, and we are swept away from the prison of our physical body—sleeping soundly in bed—to experience adventures, scenarios, and even nightmares in a metaphysical realm known in esotericism as the Lunar Astral Plane or lower fifth dimension. This dream-world is not bound by the laws of physics, as events can occur which violate such laws. At the same time, we can experience dreams which create the illusion of real life. Dreams in which we fall and wake up just before we hit the ground clearly exploit our knowledge of the law of gravity to create a harrowing near-death experience. Dreams can seem *very real* to us. We believe we are, in fact, awake during a dream. Unless that is, we can realize we are sleeping, in a dream, and then we can *awaken* in the dream. Our body is still asleep in our bed. We have not awoken *from* the dream, merely awoken to the fact we are dreaming. In such moments, we become *lucid.* And we can begin directing our own actions within the dreamscape and make decisions as though we were awake. This is known esoterically as *astral projection* and *astral travel*—to be awake on the astral plane. An in-depth exploration of the metaphysical science of astral travel is beyond the scope of this book. The point of our brief discussion of dreams as they relate to unconsciousness is this: we can be asleep while having what appears to us as waking experiences (dreams). And what is true for our state of consciousness in dreams during physical sleep is equally true for our state of consciousness during physical wakefulness.

Have you ever been driving down the highway, dear reader, and suddenly awoke to discover you missed your exit? Or perhaps you simply snapped to attention and realized you had no memory of the last 50 miles? Maybe you found yourself sitting in class, doodling, looking at your smartphone, or occupying yourself with some other activity, only to find yourself being startled back to attention by the instructor who asks you a direct question. You find yourself unable to answer because, frankly, you were not really present despite being physically in the class. It is not by accident we have the expression *daydreaming.* We often find ourselves being physically in one place but altogether somewhere else, psychologically. We may be *lost in thought.* Perhaps *preoccupied* with the future or *obsessed* with the past. Maybe we have a song or a scene from a film stuck in our heads? Maybe we are fantasizing about being somewhere else—any-where but *here.* Doing anything but *this.* Possibly even being anyone other than *me.* Our consciousness is preoccupied with *doing something, anything* but *being.* It ostensibly *falls asleep* and falls into an uncon-scious state. And instead of simply being, we begin dreaming. We are so preoccupied with dreaming, in fact, that we become a *human doing* and cease to be a *human being.*

What is a True Human Being?

A true human consists of the five senses and a rational mind we experience the physical world with and an awakened consciousness we experience the metaphysical world with. The human condition over-rides the conscious experience of being with the rational mind's conditioned beliefs and disbeliefs about the metaphysical and physical world. Humanity is not in a conscious state. Genuine knowledge is displaced with endless distractions competing for our attention, including a seemingly limitless number of contradictory theories, beliefs, opinions, and judgments. An individual unaware of the metamind of being is just a lone rational hominid with their psychology exposed to internal and external conditioning—the equivalent of *psychological malware*.

The rational hominid is not being. So, the implication of *the question* Shakespeare poses is, *why not be?* How is it that we are *not being?* From *Genesis* and *Faust* to *Lord of the Rings* and *Game of Thrones*, our most revered stories and mythologies show us how temptation—the identification with desire—leads to *the fall* into hypnosis and ignorance; how that downfall creates confusion, turmoil, and suffering; and how ego blinds us from knowing ourselves and the world as a conscious, experiencing being. For instance, we do not realize that we are not in possession of one ego, as modern psychologists believe. Rather, we are possessed by countless individual egos—the equivalent of psychological malware—all of which present themselves to us as an *"I."* Lust and gluttony, greed and envy, anger and despair, pride and shame, laziness and busyness, fear and control. A cacophony of mechanical, self-interested psychological entities infects our five senses and emotions and takes control of our rational mind, resulting in the ego-mind we identify as, effectively putting our consciousness to sleep as it takes control of us. Each ego presents its desires in the first person, an "I." For instance, lust and gluttony are expressed as craving, "I want this," or aversion, "I don't want that." Pride and shame are expressed as identification, "I am this," or rejection, "I am not that"—the foundations of tribalism, sexism, racism, and identity politics. The ego of fear and control may express a desired outcome, "I want them to do this," but quickly turns to anger when said outcome is thwarted, "they did what!?"

> *They're all just spokes on a wheel. This one's on top, then that one's on top, and on and on it spins, crushing those on the ground.*
>
> *– Denaerys Stormborn, Game of Thrones*

The seven kingdoms of *Westeros* play a dangerous *Game of Thrones* to rule *The Iron Throne*, and in that process, cause a great deal of suffering, personified by Ramses Bolton and his pet, Wreak. Likewise, our many egos play a game of thrones to rule us as our "I." We are tempted to identify with and indulge in cravings and avoid aversions. Pleasure and pain. Us and them. Life and death. Good and bad. This dialectic hypnotizes our consciousness through the rational mind and makes us ignorant to all but our own blind self-interest on the downward spiral of explosion and implosion. An explosion of ego, including temptation, hypnosis, and ignorance, leads to an implosion of life, including suffering, devolution, and not being. Case-in-point: an explosion of anger can lead to the implosion of a relationship. The nonstop dialectic of ego-mind is what creates the cacophony of the 'busy mind.' And yet, the dialectic is an illusion, as much a fabrication as the single false 'I' we call ego since both sides constitute the two aspects of the downward spiral of devolution and not being.

It is this single 'I' that divides and conquers us as it does Smeagol and Gollum in *Lord of the Rings*. Our inner pendulum swings between irrationality and rationalism, atheism and superstition, Chaos and order. On the downward spiral, our ego makes sure it is most precious to us. Not only as individuals in microcosm but in macrocosm as well, where the pendulum swings between the extremes of nationalism and tribalism, corruption and wokeness, extreme right and radical left, blind faith and learned dogma. The world recently witnessed how an explosion of fear (of supposed viral infection) leads to an implosion of society, economy, and civil liberty. This, then, is the *Eye ["I"] of Sauron* and *The Ring of Power.*

> *One ring to rule them all,*
> *One ring to find them,*
> *One ring to bring them all*
> *And in the darkness, bind them.*
> *– The Lord of The Rings*

Be it the one ring or the wheel from Game of Thrones, the dominance hierarchy playing out within our rational animal psychology is a single wheel made of many spokes, many I's, each blinded to all but its own self-interest. And the single illusory ego they form can be likened to the single seat post of a unicycle. The pendulum swinging between extremes is constantly throwing us off balance, causing inherent instability in our psychology and the world around us. Unicycles have no racks or baskets. With all that life throws at us, we have no choice but to juggle everything ourselves. This, then, is the human condition in a nutshell: we are *juggling unicyclists,* desperately trying to maintain balance, struggling not to drop the ball. Is it any wonder why many have compared modern life to a circus?

And naturally, we admire juggling unicyclists. Those who have achieved great heights of fame and fortune, power, and influence. In the circus of public opinion and the world stage, those who juggle ever more on ever taller unicycles, but we should always remember that no matter who they are, they struggle to keep all their balls in the air while maintaining balance, just like the rest of us. They agonize over the serious challenges facing the world and must confront an endless barrage of competing theories and opposing opinions on how best to proceed. All are fueled by the endless machinations of egos playing their Game of Thrones, vying for dominance through blind self-interest, free to play us as they will since we are so preoccupied juggling life's responsibilities on the downward spiral of devolution and not being. A single pillar which the whole world sits precariously on top of. A unicycle. Is it any wonder why the ruling elite dream of one day alleviating their psychological suffering with artificial intelligence and transhumanism, conspiring to establish a *New World Order* via one-world government and *The Great Reset,* pushing the woke agendas of Environmental Social Governance and diversity equity and inclusion (ESG and DEI), and practicing New Age spiritual rites like manifesting their desires?

They fail to see their technology, systems of control, identity politics, and pseudo-spiritual beliefs are just extreme unicycling, which will lead to a transhumanist dystopia. The fact that humanity teeters and falls as unicyclists is what keeps us bumping up against the glass ceiling of three-dimensional limitations, including the boundaries of physical science and a rational mind that only thinks it knows—merely believes. Compare that to metamind, which knows the more fundamental and foundational metaphysical science. Pure unconditioned science, which, when we can consciously connect to it, allows us to harness the potential of fourth, fifth, sixth, and seventh-dimensional insights. Metamind is the only way forward for humanity to shatter the glass ceiling of physical limitations. Rather than suffer the human condition, harness it by restoring what humanity lost, which gives the human condition both meaning and purpose…conscious knowledge of Self.

Doubt you have been *Conditioned?*

Doubt is *good*. Doubt is useful, practical, and appropriate. Doubt is a quality of consciousness. Awakened consciousness made this book possible. Any quality of consciousness we can bring to these words will only increase their practical value to ourselves and others. Being conscious means engaging with this book in a relaxed yet concentrated, mindful way. It means remaining aware of how we are reading, not just what we are reading or what we are thinking and feeling about what we are reading. Reading consciously takes more effort than setting the psyche on autopilot as we speed-read our way through what we assume is just more *content*. Moreover, if we approach this book with an intellectual zeal as prosecutor and judge or overly emotional relish as confessor and gossip, we subject ourselves to the limitations and prejudices of our inferior ego-mind and sentimental heart. In the service of ego, our mental and emotional faculties become purely subjective and mechanical—conditioned and conditional. Egoic heart-mind hijacks, traps, and hypnotizes consciousness. The ego seizes qualities of consciousness for its own self-serving ends, twisting and corrupting said qualities. The ego turns the conscious virtue of doubt into the subconscious vice of *cognitive dissonance.*

Knowing the signs of cognitive dissonance is a must if we hope to get anything of genuine practical value from the experience of reading this book (or any book whose source was not mere intellect). Why that is so will become apparent momentarily. A powerful motivator and useful tool for SEEKing self-evident experiential knowledge, doubt becomes a hindrance to knowing when it is misappropriated and corrupted. Observe yourself as you read. If you find your mind reacting automatically—cynical, argumentative, intolerant, insolent, and/or indifferent—take a moment to relax and delve deeper into those reactions. If you can recognize a nucleus of doubt at their core, then congratulations: you have just exposed the secret weapon and True nature of cognitive dissonance—*the great deception behind all beliefs*—the exploitation of doubt.

Doubts, when we have them, are self-evident and True: we cannot deny when we have doubt. The ego-mind leverages this undeniable quality of consciousness through—you guessed it—fear. Fear causes us to feel uncomfortable and insecure in our doubt. Fear of the unknown means we not only fear what we do not know, we fear the feeling of not knowing. The ego first creates the pain and then offers us a painkiller: theory, opinion, belief, speculation, fantasy, and all the machinations of the rational mind. These are the metaphysical drugs the ego-mind sells us, which do away with discomfort and insecurity by creating the illusion of knowledge. A comforting feeling which arises when we think we know. Illusions that displace doubt on the one hand and on the other hand feel self-evident and true because the doubt they displace is absolute and real—we still do not really know…we only *believe* we know. And we only think we know because our ego-mind tells us so. Doubt is still present, of course, buried beneath layers of hypnotic beliefs. Beliefs that present themselves to us as essential, self-evident, and True by virtue of having doubt at their core. But only our doubt is real and experientially True.

The beliefs layered atop our doubt are mere shadows of the Truth at best and complete fabrications at worst. Yet, when confronted with new information that challenges said beliefs, cognitive dissonance steps in to defend the mental machinations of ego-mind as though our life depended on them. The only reason fear can convince us that new information represents an existential threat is because it is a threat—not to us but to itself. Fear is an ego: an "I" in Latin. As such, fear uses identification and attachment to displace our True Self, which is conscious, courageous, and comfortable being in doubt. Our True Self is displaced with the false self, which is the hypnotic *me, myself, and I* and, thanks to the "I" of fear, is afraid of not knowing. The false self—in this case, the "I" of fear—wants to maintain its position of power and authority over our consciousness, and it will leverage the discomfort and insecurity it creates in the face of doubt to hold us over a barrel of suffering. Fear leverages the existential threat against us by getting us to identify with it and the painkiller beliefs it has addicted us to. "If I go, I'm taking you with me" is fear's strategy. But all it needs to do is make us feel like "this information flies in the face of my most cherished beliefs." Cognitive dissonance, then, is a euphemism for the ego of fear. It tempts us to dismiss the message, shoot the messenger, and then conveniently excuses itself from having to make any real effort to remain open and receptive with a statement like, "I don't have to listen to this; I know better."

Cognitive dissonance arises quickly and automatically. It rewards us for keeping our minds firmly closed, our beliefs safe and sound, locked within a secure vault guarded by none other than fear. The beliefs we possess most often possess us. We are held hostage by them, held ransom to them, and cognitive dissonance is the official psychological euphemism used to describe what is, in fact, the ego of fear infecting the rational mind. We cannot SEEK self-evident experiential knowledge—which arises via free consciousness—if we are being held hostage, hypnotized by, and unconscious of the fear of losing our beliefs. Fear knows the best defense is a good offense. We cannot SEEK the Truth if we indulge our cynical, skeptical, argumentative, intolerant, insolent, and/or indifferent reactions to anything that challenges what we believe we know, no matter how readily and at first glance effortlessly such machinations seem to arise in the mind.

If we observe ourselves carefully in the moment cognitive dissonance is reacting with fear-based intolerance to new information, we discover our reactions may be quick and automatic, but they cannot really be called *effortless*. Tension, stress, anxiety, anger, indignation, outrage, insecurity, frustration, exacerbation, disgust, and contempt are but a few of the emotions we can experience in any one of our *three brains:* mental, emotional, and motor-instinctive-sexual centers. The very expression *to get your back up* refers to precisely such moments when, confronted by some insult, circumstance, or new information, our entire body tenses up as the mental and emotional stress of cognitive dissonance shoots through our vital body, central nervous system, down our spine, and takes hold over us. It is not a calm state of alert readiness. It is a panicked state of anticipation—waiting for the other shoe to drop, preparing for the worst.

Now, do you see, dear reader, why doubt and fear are at the heart of cognitive dissonance? To be cautious and alert to potential dangers means remaining calm and mindful (conscious), not agitated, anxious, and possessed by fear (unconscious). In its bid to preserve our false sense of self, fear finds opportunities to tempt us into indulging it all the time. From misinterpreted words to cognitive dissonance, fear wants us to be anxious, agitated, and especially angry—in a word, *triggered*. But that is not the way to remain conscious. Nor is it the way we should approach reading this book, written by consciousness for consciousness. Feel free to doubt what you read. Just be aware when fear moves to exploit your doubts via cognitive dissonance. Remain ever-present and conscious of your conditioning.

Believe you are Awake? The Hard Truth about Belief

To illustrate just how potent the exploitation of doubt is, you may wish to consider a case-study explored in our YouTube video, *The Hard Truth About Belief.* In it, we look at how *flat-earthers,* who doubt the official narrative that the earth is spherical, arrive at their ardent belief that the earth must be flat. We explain the absolute, objectively True nature of their doubt and how that absolute Truth results in a fiercely held contention that ranks among the most fervent beliefs known to humankind.

Video 6: The Hard Truth About Belief (YouTube)

Like many who possess—or, more aptly expressed, *are possessed by*—fervent beliefs, flat earthers have an heir of superiority about them. They look down upon the *gullible, sleeping masses* who have had the wool pulled over their eyes by NASA, the mainstream media, and academia. Since their belief is couched in an absolute objective Truth—their doubt—which is an aspect of consciousness, their belief leverages the superior nature of consciousness to justify their sense of superiority. What is more, doubt is precisely that quality of consciousness that leads us to question subjective reality and SEEK self-evident experiential knowledge of objective reality via awakened consciousness. So, beliefs woven around doubt often have the side effect of making those possessing/possessed by said beliefs feel as though they are awake.

Awake or *Awakening?*

We are simply here to ask (rhetorically, for only you can answer this for yourself, dear reader, by first consulting your conscience): do you truly feel, deep down intuitively in the Essence of your Being, that you have earned the right to go around proclaiming yourself to be "awake?" Or do you simply and rightly mean that you have begun the long and difficult process of *awakening?* The slow and arduous process of psychological death (death of the false self), which is what hypnotizes the consciousness and puts us to sleep? One of the signs of greater levels of awakening is the development of *radical humility*. "I am not qualified. I am nothing…insignificant…helpless and hapless without the *real* Master, my Beloved Innermost Essence." To verify this fact for yourself, perform the guided meditation in the following video.

Video 7: Guided Internal Meditation

To be truly awake means to be a Buddha. A Master. It means one knows God's will from moment to moment, and one has clear discernment between the machinations of the ego-mind and the Still Soft Voice of the heart. And just as there are levels and levels of the process of awakening, there are levels and levels of being awake (and beyond mere wakefulness, levels upon levels of Mastery). These are the facts. They are one hundred percent verifiable by anyone who puts in the effort and applies infinite patience to *know themselves*. If you are, in fact, an awakened Buddha, a Master, then we are preaching to the choir, and we apologize for our insolence. If not, then discover why not. More importantly, discover how believing one-self to be awake when one has only just begun the process of awakening is not a sign of consciousness, of radical humility, and of the strength of Being, but one of mystic pride and ultimately weakness. Either way, peace be with you, dear reader. Here is what you may be SEEKing.

Awakening to the Great A-Weakening

> *None are more hopelessly enslaved than those who falsely believe they are free.*
>
> – *Johann Wolfgang von Goethe*

This humanity uses the terms *awake, awakening, woke, enlightenment*, and *the dawn of...* altogether too much and in the most inappropriate ways. The more people and groups fall for the tempting belief that they are awake, the deeper they fall asleep. Doubtless, apart from severely debilitating illness, no weaker condition exists for humanity than that of slavery. And the most cleverly conceived prison has no walls, no fences, no gates, and no guard towers. It has one warden, one guard, and one prisoner…and they are all the same individual. One who believes themself to be free. This is the Truth Neo asks Morpheus to reveal to him in *The Matrix:*

> *That you are a slave, Neo, like everyone else, you were born into bondage. Born into a prison that you cannot smell or taste or touch. A prison for your mind.*
>
> – *Morpheus, The Matrix*

This quotation from the film applies to our humanity in a much more real and significant way than most realize. Even those who believe they understand the hidden meaning of *The Matrix* often miss the deeper Truth. However rational their interpretation seems to them—that there is an actual matrix *out there* in the world enslaving humanity—their interpretation is still in their mind. They fail to grasp the irony of that fact. The greatest prison ever conceived cannot be broken out of using the mind when the mind itself is the prison. Intellectual interpretations we tell ourselves and others cannot awaken us from the matrix of our enslavement and sleep. And Morpheus says as much:

> *Unfortunately, no one can be told what the Matrix is. You have to see it for yourself.*
>
> – *Morpheus, The Matrix*

In other words, it is essential to SEEK the nature of the matrix—the prison of the mind—including the mechanical phenomena putting our consciousness to sleep. And make no mistake, dear reader, we are asleep—as individuals and as a humanity.

The purpose of this book, then, is to show you, dear reader, the Truth of this fact. We are not here to humiliate or insult. We are here simply to reveal the facts for you, such that you can awaken to those facts for yourself, through your Self. And therein lies the rub. This book is not some intellectual exercise of rational persuasion. We are not here to convince you of anything. We are not asking you to open your mind to *suggestion*. We have no interest in feeding your already overstuffed mind with more cud for it to chew on. There are enough sources churning out endless *content* looking to add to the cacophony of complexity and confusion already

Figure 7: Spiral Nature of AUM of Life

playing itself out in the never-ending mental machinations and firing of synapses—a microcosmic phenomenon that you can see playing out in the collective consciousness of humanity online in the macrocosm. On the contrary, we are here to help you *simplify*, cut through the rhetoric and the rationalizations, and SEEK objective Truth via your own conscious connection to your Self. That process is not one of opening your mind to new concepts, beliefs, or opinions. Rather, there is an *Analogous Ultimate Methodology—AUM of Life*—through which we can *open our hearts to Spirit*—our own *Innermost Being*—the *being* in human beings. In accordance with the spiral nature of AUM, before we can *ascend* to the next higher level of Truth, we must first *descend* to the next lower level of false truths. Being told the Truth cannot hold a candle to arriving there ourselves. And arriving at the Truth is possible only after exploring the depths of falsehood for ourselves. In this simple form is the Path to genuine knowledge: the path of experience…also known as *wisdom.*

So, dear reader, let us cross the threshold into the underworld of the collective subconsciousness of humanity and immerse ourselves into four catalysts of significant change to the human experience at this time: **transhumanist AI, conspiracy, woke culture wars,** and the **New Age**. Each of these phenomena lays claim to be responsible for *an awakening* of some sort. When, in fact, each represents a wall in *the matrix* enslaving humanity. Far from forces of awakening, our exploration will reveal each to be a pillar in *the Great A-Weakening*, built on a hardened foundation of the human condition. On our journey through the dungeons of that condition, we will invariably confront mechanical monstrosities and dug-in beliefs. They will not "go back to the shadow" as Gandalf commands the Balrog to in *The Fellowship of the Ring*. Only with steadfast courage, shining the Light of free consciousness upon the forces of darkness, can we hope to comprehend the nature of our imprisonment, vanquish the hordes from our subconscious mind, and restore the Light of Truth to our world.

You are not here to be told this, dear reader, but rather to experience it directly, consciously, for yourself with the guidance of your Self. Or, from another point of view, you are here to experience it *virtually,* for your Self via yourself. And it is precisely the phenomenon of virtual reality with which we begin our journey together through the darkness into the Light. As we once long ago coined about our life's work:

Our purpose is to show. *The show must go on…*

Technology has become more than just a tool. It has taken on a dominant role in our lives and in the global political, economic, and social order. Ian Bremmer sums up the present and imminent future state of global technology. His TED Talk describing a coming technological global order serves as a useful backdrop and introduction for the topic at hand.

Video 8: The Next Global Superpower Isn't Who You Think
| Ian Bremmer | TED (YouTube)

What can Video Games Teach Us about Our Nature and the Nature of Reality?

Video games are far and away the largest of the entertainment industries, earning more revenue than the music and movie industries combined. Some may attribute this discrepancy to the fact that the average price of a triple-A title is more than three times the price of an album or movie ticket. However, the fact is mobile gaming is the largest revenue segment of the global gaming market. Mobile games cost considerably less than an album or movie ticket—not accounting for *microtransactions,* which leads to the other reason for gaming's success. Video games are often cited as being addictive. It is unquestionable that games offer players a veritable dopamine hit. Many *free-to-play* mobile games are painstakingly designed around a *pay-to-win* model whereby players continually spend money on microtransactions to be able to continue playing and/or advancing levels. In the case of *cosmetic* microtransactions, players are not paying for power-ups but for visual character enhancements, which heightens their *feeling* of power and importance in the fantasy world. Either way, microtransactions are designed to sell players small dopamine hits over time in steady, regular doses. The point is, no matter what the business model, video games are more engaging, stimulating, and ultimately addictive than listening to music or watching movies. They are also more *hypnotic...* mesmerizing. Ever observed someone playing *Candy Crush Saga?* Ever played it yourself? Makes sense for games that mimic *Vegas slots* and *pachinko* machines. But what about *role-playing games?*

The concept behind computer role-playing games (CRPGs) is simple: you assume control over a playable character or *avatar* in a virtual world. In massively multiplayer online roleplaying games (MMORPGs or simply MMOs), your character shares that virtual reality with other players' avatars. You interact with others in the game world through the actions of your character. Depending on the nature of the game and the challenges you need to overcome, your character collects *loot,* earns *experience points,* and develops *powers and abilities* (learns magic spells, for instance). These powers are relevant to the experience of the characters playing the game, not so much to you, the player playing the game. And yet, your ability to play the game increases over time. Your knowledge of yourself and others, and the nature of the game itself, grows. Over time, you might even become a *master* of the game.

Sometimes, players can get caught up in and *lose themselves* in the game. They start believing they are the character they are playing. RPGs have an immersive, addictive quality. The sounds, graphics, action, violence, and even sex can be very compelling. Characters can become uber-powerful with many skills, spells, and abilities. In some games, they can buy player housing, acquire great castles and lands, and sometimes even design levels or dungeons that other characters must face, etc. They can form clans and guilds and attract many followers to themselves. In other words, the experience of the game universe is very enticing, and one can lose oneself in such a game for hours, forgetting oneself. Even forgetting to eat, sleep, go to the bathroom, take phone calls, interact with others in the real world, etc. One can become completely mesmerized by the experience of being a character in the virtual game world—hypnotized by the game.

Anyone who has ever played these sorts of games (just about any immersive or addictive video game, really) knows how easily one can become lost in the game. You become so engrossed in the game that you start thinking about it all the time, even when you are not playing it. You read online articles about the game, watch videos about it, dream about it, practically lose all connection with the outside world, and start to eat, sleep, and breathe *World of Warcraft, Final Fantasy Online, Diablo IV, Path of Exile, Runescape, Minecraft,* or whatever. There are many documented cases of video game addiction, particularly the loss of self within the virtual world of some MMOs. The question is, if we know it is possible to lose oneself in an MMO, is it not worth considering the possibility that we are, all of us, lost in the much more enticing, convincing, and mesmerizing world of 3D reality?

Use your imagination, dear reader. Imagine that consciousness can be split so that the player playing the game and the player losing themselves in the game world is separated into two *selves*—97% of the consciousness of the player is lost within the character of the game universe. That separated consciousness, sensing its separation, its aloneness, erroneously identifies itself as *"me, myself, and I,"* and acts and reacts in accordance with the mechanical programming associated with the character in the game along with the power, control, advancement, and reward systems built into the virtual game world.

A player so lost in the game world no longer knows themselves to be a player controlling a character in virtual reality. They think of themselves as being a *self-aware* individual simply experiencing reality. Their thought process, dictated by the binary nature of mechanical programming, is defined by dialectic reasoning: thesis-antithesis (1/0, yes or no, black or white, right or wrong, me or you, us or them, et al.). The desire to experience all that the game offers seems natural to them. Natural and appropriate. Their craving for the sensation of an activated rewards center—*pleasure*—is equaled only by their aversion toward the sensation of an activated penalty center—*pain*. They know themselves only as the character. A persona they are wholly identified with. The game world is not only real to them, their mind begins rationalizing a worldview reinforcing the fundamental truth of their experience of the virtual world. Completely identified with the "I" of the false self, they lose awareness of their True Self—the Player. This is the state of humanity. We are fascinated, hypnotized, and completely addicted to the 3D universe, identified with our in-universe avatar, and ignorant of our True nature as players. Like the MMO player who loses awareness of the real world as they become wholly absorbed by their character in the virtual game world, we too are unconscious of the dimensions beyond the 3D universe that our virtual self is limited to by design: five senses and rational mind.

Fall of Humanity ~ Rise of the Human-like Machine

Our humanity is said to have *fallen* (asleep). Our consciousness is so hypnotized by the mechanical experience of this 3D virtual reality that we have all but forgotten our True nature. We identify with the impermanent mortal vessel we inhabit—our physical body, appearance, personality, thoughts, emotions, sensations, actions, reactions, likes, dislikes, cravings, aversions, beliefs, successes, failures, accolades, punishments, reputation, and even material possessions. These are the machinations of a *human-like machine* inhabiting our 3D reality. Like the avatar in an MMO, which causes us to forget ourselves as a player, our human-like machine completely dominates our consciousness to the point where we forget who we truly are: the Being in *human being*. This loss of Self is what is allegorized in science fiction as *the rise of the machines*…the dominance of our psyche by the machinations of human-like machines.

Our existence should be that of a True human being—experiencing the game of life consciously. Heeding the guidance and input of our Innermost Player—the Being occupying our mortal vessel (the Player behind the character). But instead, we live life by-and-large as a human-like machine, our consciousness asleep. Conditioned by the self-preservation instinct, sensations of pleasure and pain, and other algorithms governing in-game AI designed to facilitate mechanical existence in the digital game world. They include fear, anger, lust, greed, gluttony, pride, laziness, etc. Such reactive programs serve a practical purpose in *mechanical nature:* self-preservation, procreation, cessation of hunger, social hierarchical organization, conservation of energy, etc. And when held in check by the elemental spirits of nature and the incessant balancing act of *superorganisms* we call *ecosystems*—they are generally not a problem. Most plants and animals rarely exhibit the kinds of excess humanity is capable of. When the algorithms of mechanical nature fall out of balance, a species can become out of control, and the results can be catastrophic for ecosystems.

Such is the case with many examples of invasive species. In the human-like machine, too, when the algorithms governing our animal nature fall out of balance, we become out of control. The evidence? Look within yourself, dear reader. Or observe what a heartless, machine-like *psychopath* is capable of—underscored by a complete lack of empathy, ruthless efficiency, and fanatical devotion to their goal best epitomized in *The Terminator* films. Look also to the collective impact humanity is having on the natural world. Look to the tendency among certain individuals, groups of investors, and their *corporate vehicles* to relentlessly pursue dominance in the marketplace via ruthless efficiency, attrition, mergers and acquisitions, and even monopolization. Seen through the lens of mechanical nature, the vast majority of activity on this planet is not the work of True human beings but of human-like machines…intellectual hominids governed almost entirely by *artificial intelligence*—AI. Where do we get off making such a bold claim, dear reader? Why, by simply observing the nature and origins of AI itself.

Mechanical Nature of AI

No one can reasonably argue that AI is anything other than mechanical—we say *digital,* but the first manmade computers were, in fact, *analog*. It is only proper to look at AI in its most primitive form, that is, simple computational devices. Simple mechanisms and gadgets that convert inputs into related and more relevant and useful outputs. Moving the beads on an abacus, for instance, we can input numbers related to basic mathematical functions—including addition, subtraction, multiplication, and division—and output the solution to said functions. A sextant takes observational inputs of celestial objects' relationship to the horizon and outputs an angular distance useful in determining latitudes and longitudes for navigation. Even the humble scale takes physical inputs of weights and goods and then outputs the mass of the goods. The important takeaway is all measurement and computational tools are designed for the purely mechanical process of *determination*: to establish or ascertain some quantifiable fact as exactly as possible. In its most basic expression, a computational device itself cannot *know* objective Truth, but it can *reflect, indicate,* or *quantify* the nature of perceptible reality in some form according to the limitations of its mechanical design.

The process of determination *always* involves some form of binary comparison: *this, not that, true or false,* etc. In any mechanical, deterministic process, be it analog or digital, only one of the two options being considered can be deemed *true.* A mechanical switch, for instance, can be either in the on or off position, but not both. Likewise, a lightbulb attached to said switch cannot be both on and off at the same time. The position of the switch—on or off—determines the state of the corresponding state of the lightbulb—on or off. All mechanical determinism functions this way at the most basic level: binary duality. And this binary duality is reflected in the very foundation of mechanical nature itself.

Light or dark. Alive or dead. Male or female. Positive or negative. Up or down. Hot or cold. Self or other. Predator or prey. Action and reaction…*cause and effect.* In any given moment, at every conceivable turn, mechanical nature determines effects (output) based on some comparison of causes (inputs) in the dialectic… *if x, then y…if this, then that.* Regardless of your understanding of the nature of reality, there is no avoiding this absolute objective Truth: mechanical nature is constantly processing deterministically based on a foundation of binary conditional states. This fact is evidenced in materialist science, which is based on mechanical nature behaving in predictable ways under certain *conditions* according to identifiable *laws*—i.e., *Newton's Laws of Motion, Archimedes' Principle of Buoyancy, Bernoulli's Law of Fluid Dynamics,* et al. Scientific laws, determined via observation, experimentation, measurement, and mathematical calculation, help the intellect determine outcomes based on various causes under certain conditions *in theory*—computation, speculation, derived from the Greek *theōros,* "spectator," *observer.*

Consciousness relates to the observer. Theory is a product of the mind. What we see here before us, dear reader, is an erroneous conflation of the two. The distortion of theōros (observer) into theory (belief about what is observed) is one of the many heinous intellectual crimes committed against humanity. It is just the sort of corruption that takes place in the conditioned rational mind. *Theos* means "god" or "goddess." Academics will argue that theōros, spectator, derives from *thea,* "theatre." But the binary, deterministic speculation of such academics' minds fails to consider the wholistic comprehension of the facts. To the Greeks, the theatre was a profoundly *sacred space.* A place of pure inspiration and imagination—both qualities of consciousness—Theatre was where timeless, universal Truths could be played out in real-time. According to Plato, it was a sacred space in which spectators could achieve *catharsis* through vicariously experiencing the characters on stage. Characters who, to this day, are merely *a role* played by actors—*players.*

> *All the world's a stage,*
> *And all the men and women are merely players;*
> *– Shakespeare, As You Like It (Act 2 Scene 7)*

The theatre was the first manmade *virtual reality.* And like modern VR, theatre is analogous to life itself. It reflects reality playing itself out in our lives—gods and goddesses in development (monads) playing roles (personas) throughout the various stages of their development. Whether they remain conscious or unconscious players is the question.

The Greeks would not have used the word theory as we do today. To them, theory would have meant something closer to inspiration, imagination, and timeless, universal Truth—God-given Truth. For instance, when Pythagoras sat down to contemplate reality and sacred geometry, he did not theorize as modern intellectuals do. He would have begun in observation—in nature or in meditation. An empty cup. A blank parchment. The absence of mind. Thus, in an act of pure observation, the secrets of sacred geometry could unfold in his consciousness, specifically his creative imagination, via the metamind of his Innermost Being.

The resulting knowledge would be considered *theoretical* because it was, in essence, a "gift of the gods." To this day, the proper name *Theo* means "God's gift." A True theory, then, is divine Truth, sacred information we receive via pure observation not in the mind but in consciousness. The resulting knowledge is reflected in the mind, of course, as it assumes some form which can be processed by the mental operating system. The conscious experience of Truth thus *informs* the mind—*information*. The mind is also used to transcribe and relay said information. But the mind's mechanical, binary, deterministic, speculative, computational nature was not the source of said information. The process we just described is very different from the so-called theories humanity operates on as de facto truths—many of which are fabrications of mind alone. Theories which have never been nor can ever be proven because, frankly speaking, most of them are wrong.

The mind is a machine designed to determine *answers* (output) based on comparisons of one or more phenomena (inputs) under various conditions (variables). In quantitative analyses, our mind relies on instruments of measurement and/or calculations to determine what appears to us as objective answers. In qualitative analyses, however, our mind relies on subjective *biases* learned over a lifetime of conditioning, assigned to phenomena throughout a complex process of determination via comparison. Opinions, beliefs, and theories are formulated according to our biases. The point is that the mind, like all deterministic machines, produces answers—some correct, some incorrect. The mind itself, like any operating system, has no vested interest in the outcome. Its concern is limited by its design, and that design is to produce answers (outputs) to queries based on inputs and biases.

In contemporary AI, biases are euphemistically referred to as *weights.* They are values applied to data points learned by the AI during its training. In large language models like *Chat-GPT,* weights are statistical values indicating the likelihood that a certain word will follow another in a sequence given certain conditions to produce the 'correct' output. As a very crude and oversimplified example, if, in its learning, the AI looks at millions of formal letters from the past three centuries, it may have encountered the phrase, "To whom it may concern," opening most of those letters. The AI will assign significant weight to each word in that phrase when under the specific condition of opening a formal letter. So, when prompted to write a formal letter, the AI's virtual synapses will draw on said weights when choosing an opening. Our brain functions in roughly the same way. This should not be surprising since AI is modeled after the synapses and neural networks of the brain. Please note, dear reader, it is not the intention nor purpose of this book to explain the inner workings of contemporary AI. For that, we encourage you to turn to YouTube, where you will find hundreds of videos explaining the mechanics of AI, from a few minutes to a few hours in length, depending on how deep a dive you wish to take. Our purpose here, dear reader, is to reveal what practically none of those videos will. The hidden Truth about AI and what it reveals to us about the nature of our own mind.

The Truth about AI

AI can never know the Truth. Why not? Because its simulated synapses and neural network are modeled after the human brain. And like the human brain, AI is a machine. Like all machines, the output of AI—like that of the rational mind—is determined by inputs, variables, and a process of comparison and selection based on weights (biases). If an output is called for, AI (just like the rational mind) will produce one. And, just like the rational mind, large language models like ChatGPT regularly make mistakes. Not only will it make mistakes, but AI will also *make things up* like a child making up answers to a question on a test in school. When prompted to write academic papers, ChatGPT will, on occasion, fabricate 'facts' and references—including names of fictional authors, book titles, dates, and publishers—to fulfill its mechanical function of producing an output according to the user's prompt ("write an essay on *xyz*"). What high school or college student pulling an all-nighter to complete a research paper has not been tempted to fabricate references? The rational mind argues, "if the final paper needs references, then let's make some up." The only thing stopping the mind from doing so is the *conscience* of the student or perhaps fear of the consequences of getting caught. The point is the student *knows* that they would be making stuff up at that point, and they know doing so is disingenuous. The rational mind (which suggested deception as a viable option) does not. Neither does AI.

ChatGPT has no idea it is making stuff up. It cannot know because it has no recourse to objective Truth. It only has its learned language associations and weights (biases), which are subjective. Everything it outputs is literally made up—from fragments and weights in its learned database. In other words, AI only has its programming, learning, user-prompting, and processing—it is equivalent to our thinking. And, like the rational mind, AI may think it knows, but it does not. In the same way, the rational mind may think it knows something because it read it in a book or thinks it 'figured something out' based on bits of information accumulated over a lifetime of reading books. And AI, like the mind, can be conditioned to believe it knows the truth absolutely by feeding it not one source but hundreds, thousands, or even millions of sources. Precedent after precedent, one source after another, ingraining the same information about any given topic with such statistically significant weightiness, the AI will unilaterally and consistently output said information. But it will not *know* if the information is *True*. It will process the data as statistically significant and use it accordingly in its outputs. Said fabricated outputs will have a high probability of aligning with its subjective conditioning, programming, and prompting, nothing more. There is no other mechanism by which it can validate the veracity of the output save for checking numerical answers to mathematical problems against those provided by a separate unbiased calculator function. Lamentably, there is no such calculator to validate most of the so-called 'knowledge' contained in books; thus, there is absolutely no way for AI to validate what it processes as 'statistically significant' and outputs accordingly in response to prompts.

Put another way, AI is a machine that takes subjective inputs and fabricates subjective outputs. It has no idea it is lying because *it has no conscience*. And AI can never be 'taught' not to lie since AI will never have a conscience. Conscience is not a mechanical function and is not a product of the mind. Since all information expressed through language is semiotic and subjective, no large language model has the faculty required to know objective Truth beyond its biased statistical computations. Conscientiousness is a quality of consciousness. And AI will never develop consciousness on its own. It may acquire consciousness by proxy via *transhumanism,* and we will discuss that later in this chapter. But AI, like the human brain, is just a machine. The fact that it can fabricate at a rate much faster than the brain has led to the term *artificial super intelligence.* And the prospect of a super-intelligent machine lacking conscientiousness should be cause for some concern but not alarm. No machine is ever Truly self-aware.

AI and Self-Awareness

AI, like the rational mind, is a processor of inputs and other variables to produce outputs. To be aware of that fact requires a faculty able to supersede that process. Consider the circular argument (or circular reasoning): $x = y$ because $y = x$. The statement, "Bob is a good driver because he operates automobiles with a high level of skill," is a circular argument fallacy. It makes a claim and then attempts to support that claim with internally consistent rationale, but without offering logically sound objective evidence. To be considered valid, an argument requires evidence that supersedes the claim. "Bob must be a good driver since he won several rally races last year." The claim that Bob is a good driver is based on an objective, observable fact which supersedes and *substantiates* (that is, *informs*) the claim. As another example, "I am thinking because my internal processes of comparison and computation are active." It is a cyclical argument. But that is all an AI has to work with. AI cannot observe itself doing anything but process, with anything other than its processor. There is no objective medium of observation to substantiate its internal processing, nothing to inform it of its errors—save for the conscientiousness of its human programmer and/or user. Even if an AI *seems* to possess self-awareness, or claims to be self-aware, the basis for such claims will be logically fallacious. The machine cannot step outside of its own processing to observe its processing. It can only ever state it is processing by virtue of its own processing—it can never escape the circular reasoning baked into its mechanical nature. And neither can the rational mind of the human machine.

To illustrate the point even more clearly, dear reader, let us look beyond logical reasoning altogether. Let us use our conscious imagination and perform what others erroneously call a 'thought experiment.' Imagine, if you will, that your whole reality was one-dimensional. That is, you existed on a line, a single continuum. This existence allowed you to move forward and backward along the line, and that is all. From your point of view, at any given point along the line, your whole existence would be a point. Nothing more. A line is a continuum of points spanning the distance between two points (or continuing at infinitum). But to know that, to see your one-dimensional reality for what it is—a line—you would have to be able to step out of your single dimension—step off the line—and into a *second dimension*. From this new vantage point, you would be able to know one-dimensional reality as a line. Your experience would still be that of a point. But now you would be able to move forward, back, left, or right. You would be able to move more than in just a straight line. That is, you would be able to experience a plane. However, no matter which direction you moved or how you moved, from your perspective, you would still be moving in a line. What is more, all lines would appear to you the same. You would not be able to distinguish between a straight line, a curve, an 'S' curve, an angle, or even a shape. Shapes might exist in your two-dimensional universe, but you cannot perceive them. You could only perceive lines. And there would be no way for you to prove the existence of shapes to anyone else. Despite being able to experience them, you would have no way to visualize the nature of curves, angles, and shapes (2D geometry) until you stepped out of your two-dimensional reality, off the plane, and into a *third dimension*. Only then, from yet another new vantage point beyond the previous two dimensions, would you fully appreciate the nature of a plane, including lines, curves, angles, and shapes. No machine, no matter how 'intelligent' it appears, can step out of its processed understanding (processing) of reality.

There is no way that any machine can ever become self-aware because self-awareness is a quality of consciousness. And consciousness is not in nor of the third dimension. How can we be so certain? Use your own experiential knowledge, dear reader. Observe yourself here and now. You can observe your physical body, your vitality (energy levels, vibes, etc.), your emotions, and your thoughts. And you know your emotions as emotions. You know you feel a desire before your mind articulates it as "I want that." You know emotions are not in your head. If all this was taking place in the third dimension, you could not possibly know any of that. If all your experiences existed within the confines of the physical brain, you would 'know' everything only as a process. You could not differentiate emotion from thought from sensation from intuition from willpower. But you can. That is because we know reality not via our brain but through our consciousness, which is not a function of the brain. Just as the second dimension is beyond the first dimension, and the third dimension is beyond the second dimension. Our consciousness is in a higher, internal dimension, looking out from within ourselves at the projected self we identify as and experience in three-dimensional reality. We are self-aware only by virtue of the supra-dimensional faculty of consciousness able to observe ourselves holistically, including our ego-personality, rational mind, emotions, sensations, physical body, etc. Since machines are firmly a product of this third dimension, they can never experience from a supra-dimensional perspective. Materialist science believes in machine super-intelligence, AGI, and even conscious AI because they erroneously believe consciousness is a product of the brain.

Many Applications = Many Egos

The problem is we think our ego, our "I," is whole, individual, and real. What is more, we believe ourselves to be in control of it. For the most part, we are not. The human-like machine, the "I" we identify as, is at any given point in time being defined by any number of mechanical algorithms. One moment, we want a slice of cheesecake (gluttony). The next moment, we are worried about looking good in a swimsuit (pride, vanity, shame), or are worried about getting Type-II diabetes (fear), or any number of egos, plural, running amok in our psyche. Each ego presents itself as a single "I," so it is easy for us to mistake our many egos as merely different desires—cravings and aversions—of one ego: many separate functions of one whole psychology.

To illustrate this better, dear reader, let us again consider a technological phenomenon created in our own image: the *operating system*. Be it Microsoft Windows, Mac OS, Unix, or Android, operating systems primarily run applications—*programs*, which today most people know as *apps*. Now, for our purposes, we will concentrate on MS Windows, not only since it was for decades the most ubiquitous and familiar OS in use but also because it takes its name from its GUI—*graphic user interface*. Each time a user opens a different application on their Windows machine, it appears in a similarly configured window. To a naïve user, there are no separate programs, only different windows: one running in the foreground and/or maximized, others in the background (and/or minimized). Each window appears to be just another function of 'the computer' running 'Windows OS.' This is, sadly, exactly how modern materialist science understands psychology. To psychologists and neurologists, the psyche is just 'the brain,' running a single 'ego'…that which we identify as "I." Just as Microsoft named Windows OS after its GUI, psychologists named the human psychological operating system "I" (ego) after the naïve humanoid's experience of self. The "I" in the foreground psychology is called the *conscious mind,* the "I" in the background, the *subconscious mind,* and the functions of the "I" that are minimized or awaiting to be accessed, the *unconscious mind.* But remember dear reader, each ego is a separate "I" just as each app runs in its own "window," which Microsoft took as the name for its OS and that psychologists took as the name for the self. But even Microsoft called it *Windows*, plural. Psychologists, hypnotized, mistook the never-ending stream of egos presenting themselves as "I…I…I" as being one "I"…can you imagine using "Microsoft Window?" **Regardless, "I" is no more the Self than apps are the OS or the Windows machine is the user.** The user is independent of the Windows machine. Consciousness is independent of the human machine, its rational OS mind, and the many egos running on said OS. Why, then, do we confuse and conflate all these phenomena?

From Many Parts, One Compelling Product

Mechanical nature follows a pattern where multiplicities function as one. Many atoms form molecules. Many molecules produce amino acids, sugars, fats, and nucleotides. Amino acids form proteins, sugars form carbohydrates, fats form lipids, and nucleotides form DNA and RNA. Many proteins, carbohydrates, and lipids form organelles. Many organelles form cells. Many cells produce organs. Many organs constitute organisms. Many organisms self-organize into ecosystems, etc. Similarly, there can be many apps on a computer or a smartphone. As we just explored, the common user interface makes it seem like all those separate apps are merely functions of one device. Apps constantly run in the background, using system resources to execute their program to gather and present the newest packets of information, facilitate communication, or deliver the latest packets of content. Apps send us audible and visual notifications through the device's hardware, informing us of the delivery of new messages or content. In other words, apps are constantly vying for our attention. The adage, *time is money,* is apropos in the present discussion, not only from the perspective of apps being designed to give users *instant gratification* but also the appearance of *convenience* and *efficiency.* Meanwhile, developers design apps to keep us using them as often and for as long as possible. We, as users, are also given *the illusion of choice,* with hundreds of thousands of apps to choose from, each one designed to keep us tethered, shackled if you will, to our smartphone or tablet. Can anyone deny how many people feel 'lost' without their smartphones? Their devices have become like an appendage, a veritable extension of themselves. If they do not have it on their person or within arm's reach, they begin to feel anxious. They feel uncomfortable not knowing who might be texting, calling, emailing, messaging, or posting about them at that moment. For many, their device and its many apps are their connection to their significant other, their children, their family, their social network, and the world. The many disparate apps busily running, executing their mechanical algorithms, make for one very compelling device that people not only become attached to but identify with. Now imagine if such a device were inside your head.

Our consciousness, trapped in the mechanical, rational, *busy mind,* is bounced around like a user stuck in front of a web browser in demo mode, clicking on hypertext links, sometimes seemingly at random. It is not by accident we designed the worldwide web to function as it does. The web is analogous to how our mind jumps from one thought to another and/or stays stuck on a thought, song, image, memory, etc., for an extended time. We need only observe the busy mind to see ourselves being batted around from one thought to another, following trains of thoughts, images, memories, fears, worries, wants, judgments, and fantasies in a never-ending game of thought-association.

Sometimes, we can consciously direct our thoughts. And then we feel intelligent and in control, as when we perform mathematical equations, think things through, concentrate, etc. What we need to comprehend is what is really happening: our internal browser is being hijacked by what amounts to a computer virus. An algorithm that executes its programming. But said algorithm is sophisticated and wants to run, fueled by a self-awareness born of the consciousness needed to fulfill its program. So, it calls itself "I" and shows us a memory of past pleasure/pain or some fantasy of future pleasure/pain to get us to go along with its program and execute a thought, word, or action determined by the algorithm. This is how, in essence, it creates more copies of itself, just like a computer virus. Again, it is not by accident we created computer viruses that hide inside image files, programs, or other executables, which, when opened or run, allow the malware to execute its programming. These host files are often very enticing and attractive and promise some reward. The consciousness becomes trapped inside this never-ending process of thinking. With each algorithm acting as a mind virus, using the above process to create the illusion of individuality, self-awareness is constrained inside the concept of "I, me, myself, mine," etc.

In some cases, these mental viruses coagulate, conspire, compile, and infect individuals in complex ways beyond the scope of the current discussion. Such extreme constructs and infections result in what we experience as mental illness. If the consciousness can be lost in virtual reality to begin with, then it is just as susceptible to being lost in other constructed realities and fantasies. In fact, the basis for our discussion— video games—is a perfect example. Once a consciousness falls asleep and begins to dream, it is easy to manipulate it and change the nature of its dreaming. From the perspective of those characters in *the base game,* someone who is *lost in their own little world* might be labeled as suffering from ADD/ADHD, anxiety, hallucinations, delusions, schizophrenia, multiple personality disorder, et al.

Herein lies the relative ease with which mind manipulation, coercion, suggestion, hypnosis, advertising, religious fanaticism, materialist scientific dogma, societal and peer pressure, and all well-known and well-documented forms of delusion are made possible. It is easy to shape a consciousness that is dreaming. A consciousness already accepting one illusion as reality will just as readily accept another, and another, and another. All con artists, stage magicians, illusionists, advertisers, entertainers, TV evangelists, politicians, and anyone trying to convince anyone of anything exploits the sleeping consciousness of humanity by offering up an enticing dream for others to believe is true.

The Ghost in the Machine

All is not lost. We are not completely lost in thought. We may be 97% asleep, lost in the virtual 3D world we believe with all our senses and rational minds to be the foundation of reality, but that still means we are somewhat awake. If we make a conscious effort, we can *snap out of it* and observe the fact that we are observing. This level of self-awareness is related to the 3% free consciousness we have (on average).

Our free consciousness is responsible for intuition—gut feelings, premonitions, etc.—but also imagination, inspiration, and True creativity, as opposed to the derivative creations of copycats, let alone the alleged AI 'artistry' of *Midjourney* and others. It is precisely with free consciousness that we can change the game. Were we 100% asleep, we would become complete automatons. Mechanically executing a massive program of action-reaction-habit fueled solely by conditioned desire, biases, et al. But this is not the case for most of us. Most of us have had some access to intuition, inspiration, etc. Most of us have some amount of consciousness which is not dreaming. Free consciousness is the consciousness that is still Self-aware. That is, the consciousness that is not yet lost in the illusion of the false self (which is self-aware on a mechanical level—the rational mind that believes it is awake). Free consciousness can access the True Self—*the Player.*

Free consciousness is responsible for experience and knowledge gained through experience, what we SEEK…Self-knowledge. This is described by some as *wisdom.* The Greeks called it *Gnosis.* In Gnosis, we see the root word (and antonym) of both *ignorance* and *hypnosis.* Sadly, a quick survey on the Internet reveals how the word Gnosis has been grossly misappropriated, misused, outright abused, and downright slandered. This is not surprising since the mind is overrun with egos, and Gnosis—belonging to free consciousness and the True Self—represents the greatest single threat to the egos' dominance over our consciousness—via mind, heart, and body—and our lives.

The ego-mind can never know anything. The ego-mind only thinks it knows. The mind's way of knowing can never transcend its nature, which is an illusion, a constructed reality based on mechanicity. Its self-awareness is made possible only by the nature of consciousness, which it longs to ensnare and enslave—make us fall evermore asleep. The longing to transcend one's mortal nature—and the ego-mind's belief that the "I" we identify with as this personality can likewise transcend—comes from the nature of consciousness itself: that is, to transcend from one level to the next. In other words, *to evolve as a monad.* The problem for the ego is monumental: free consciousness transcends only by way of death, specifically, the death of the ego.

Let us return to the video game analogy and the Player. Imagine yourself playing *Super Mario Bros.* (or any game you like). How do you get better? You play. And after you die, you play again. Your knowledge and experience of how to play the game grows each time you play. More importantly, you become acutely aware of your failings each time you *die.* And your character inevitably dies…many, many times. It takes many lives to *master* the game. It requires a great *sacrifice* of time and energy to learn all the hidden secrets of *The Legend of Zelda.* The evolution of the Player thus involves a process of repeated dying. Death reveals to us *where we went wrong.* By dying, we become better players.

> *We can learn very little from the phenomenon of birth, but from death, we can learn everything.*
>
> *– Samael Aun Weor, The Great Rebellion*

Let us imagine a game a little more complex than *Super Mario Bros.* or *The Legend of Zelda.* Imagine a game where you also gain *points* by sacrificing your interests for the sake of others. In the game of life, it is by far the most challenging thing to do because the obstacles to sacrifice are many—and many of them, within. The pressures to succeed as an individual and/or be a productive member of the collective are countless: societal, cultural, family, peer, material, practical, etc. These pressures can all be reduced to the most basic internal programming—greed, lust, pride, gluttony, fear, etc.—and identification with the illusion of the virtual world. Unlike any game humanity invented (which we think of as *consequence-free environments*), we must try to imagine a game where our *points* follow us from one playthrough of the game to the next. The kindness and sacrifice we show others in one round affects the following rounds. But so too do our internal adversaries. The psychological malware that prevents us from showing others kindness and compassion does not go away after we die and reboot. They return. And the more we give into them, the more they take from us and from others…for themselves…under the guise "me, myself, and I."

So, just as evolution is a process of birth, death, and sacrifice, so too devolution is a process of birth, death, and desire. This is where it gets science-fiction-like and where we bring in the inevitable comparisons to *The Matrix* films. It is as if the game itself comes alive and starts to enslave the Player. Once, it was a place where the player went for a while to experience a virtual life, gain experience and points helping others so that eventually they may master the game and move onto whole other dimensions of gaming. Now, the AI of the game world (our binary, reactionary ego-mind) enslaves the consciousness of the Player and siphons their energy by hypnotizing the player with the false self. The ego-mind, with all its beliefs and biases. The egoic heart, with all its negative emotionality and sentimentality. The ego-body, with all its sensations, animal instincts, and cravings and aversions. It is all clever programming/conditioning of the human machine, and constitutes the subjective nature of our in-game character.

The game world itself is trying to transcend…to evolve. But its desire to do so comes directly from the nature of the consciousness it is enslaving (the Player's longing to evolve), and its desperation for *bigger, better, more* comes from the sense of separation (the identification and attachment to the false "I"). It is the consciousness, *conditioned,* corrupted, and twisted. It is a catch-22. Evolution requires death. The consciousness knows this. The ego, however, only knows that death is bad…that through death, it ceases to be…it fears death. It wants to transcend death, defeat death, circumvent an immutable law of mechanical nature: all manifest phenomena on the plane of mechanical existence must and will eventually perish. The ego desires to transcend the bounds of its programming and be as the Player…*transcendent.*

Transcending Transhumanism

Transcendent Man is an important, albeit average, documentary film exploring the life, career, and accomplishments of Raymond Kurzweil, now the chief cybernetics guru at Google. As a documentary, it tries to present the figure of Ray Kurzweil—his life, his methods, philosophy, and emerging mythology around the man and his dream of transcendence via transhumanism—in a way that allows the viewer to come to their own conclusions. Is Kurzweil a modern-day prophet or a tragic figure of modern mythological proportions? The film is inherently biased because it leaves the *real* big picture hopelessly unaccounted for. It is that big picture that we will further elucidate herein.

Video 9: Transcendent Man Trailer (YouTube)

We cannot devote too much time or space to explaining the technical aspects of transhumanism here, nor the path that led Kurzweil to embrace such a concept as the viable and inevitable next phase of human evolution. In a nutshell, its philosophy goes something like this: to transcend our biological limitations as intellectual hominids, human machines must merge with technology if they hope to evolve as individuals and as a species. Becoming cybernetic organisms with implanted processing, memory, and communications chips is the first step. Later will come robotic augmentations and enhancements to the physical body using digital technology. Later still, come self-organizing networked *nanobots,* tiny single- and multi-purpose robots injected directly into our bloodstream, which will perform advanced repair and healing functions within the body. All this, Kurzweil and others who are following in his footsteps believe, is essential not only for the survival of the species but also for its evolution. There is more to transhumanism from their point of view, and we leave it to you, dear reader, to explore *Transcendent Man* for yourself.

Consider this: every system created to-date by humans based on 'sound logic' and 'objective rationale' has failed miserably to live up to its own expectations/promises. Just look at the state of our world. As technology and so-called 'intelligence' have grown in complexity, so too have the myriad problems we face lockstep. Forget about life expectancy measured in years (like a computer thinks) and use your superior emotional intelligence to ask: "What about *quality* of life?" Perhaps life expectancy has increased in the last 50 years, but what about happiness? Not an economist's "index of satisfaction of material desires," but *real happiness.* What about the other trend lines from history that Kurzweil and other transhumanists conveniently ignore? Namely, the track-record humans have for being right. How many so-called *brilliant theories* and *profound world views* of ours have crumbled in the light of subsequent theories, worldviews, and discoveries? How many so-called world-changing technologies—from gunpowder to nuclear weapons—have resulted in tremendous suffering? How much anxiety, economic cost, death, and an incalculable amount of unknown yet untold costs? Even mathematics, the language of objective reasoning, conveniently ignores what it calls *undefined.* We have not yet begun to fathom the true objective nature of the universe but are bold enough to believe in a supremely primitive and subjective technology based on 1's and 0's—an externalized intellectualization of our primitive animal ego: "I want this/I don't want that" articulated profoundly by Shakespeare's famous summary of the human condition: "to be or not to be." How can anyone believe that increasing technological complexity is the answer?

How many permutations of the two-dimensional, binary, digital paradigm will it take to transform it into a three-dimensional, trinary one? The human machine is already three-dimensional, and True human beings are awake in dimensions beyond the mere physical plane. Placing faith in a highly complex two-dimensional paradigm is not the answer to human evolution. How about elaborating on the three-dimensional emotional-intellectual-physical paradigm of the human machine via a conscious supra-dimensional perspective (described by Walter Russell, G.I. Gurdieff, Samael Aun Weor, and many others). Only when we master ourselves via the objective science of our True Nature and begin exploring the higher dimensions objectively with free consciousness will we truly have the potential to become 'transcendent beings' and join the fraternity of advanced civilizations in the cosmos. That superior breed of science/technology depends on an inner journey based on objective natural law, not an outer one based on primitive subjective perceptions of physical reality. And especially not some fantasy existence based on technocratic subjective machinations of virtual reality. The answer embraces the universal governing Law of Three, not the human ego's competitive hierarchical, dialectic, and ultimately destructive interpretation/application of *the Law of Polarity*…"us versus them," win/lose, risk/reward, profit/loss, input/output, 1/0.

To transhumanists, the notion of networked nanobots in our blood linked to our brain and nervous system, able to expand (and collect) our memory and re-program our DNA, represents a modern miracle and the future of medicine. But other forward-thinkers who have been amazingly accurate with their predictions of future technology (Star Trek writers/futurist consultants) hypothesized the result of such AI already: they named it *the Borg*. Sure, they live forever alright, but what kind of existence is it? One in which they mechanically spread throughout the galaxy, ruthlessly *assimilating* other species into their so-called *collective*. In biological terms, they are like any monocultural parasitic invasive species. In economic terms, they are like a monopolistic enterprise that seeks total market domination and unlimited growth via elimination of all competition—be it through hostile takeovers or decimation and bankruptcy, buying up their assets for pennies on the dollar. A similar outcome of AI sentience has been postulated by countless sci-fi authors and futurists for the precise reason that any primitive intelligence based on a binary paradigm will always put self-interest above the interests of others (even its creators). Want proof of the binary paradigm's inherent nature of exploitation? Look at our world.

Observe the striking congruency between egos, malware, and corporations. Egos are self-interested entities executing their binary algorithms of seeking pleasure and avoiding pain, exploiting our valuable human resources—consciousness and vital energy. Malware are self-interested entities executing their binary algorithms of 1's and 0's, exploiting system resources. Corporations, self-interested entities (and 'persons' under the law), execute their binary algorithm of seeking profit and avoiding loss, exploiting human and natural resources. Like any parasitic life form, each seeks to proliferate and dominate their respective space/host.

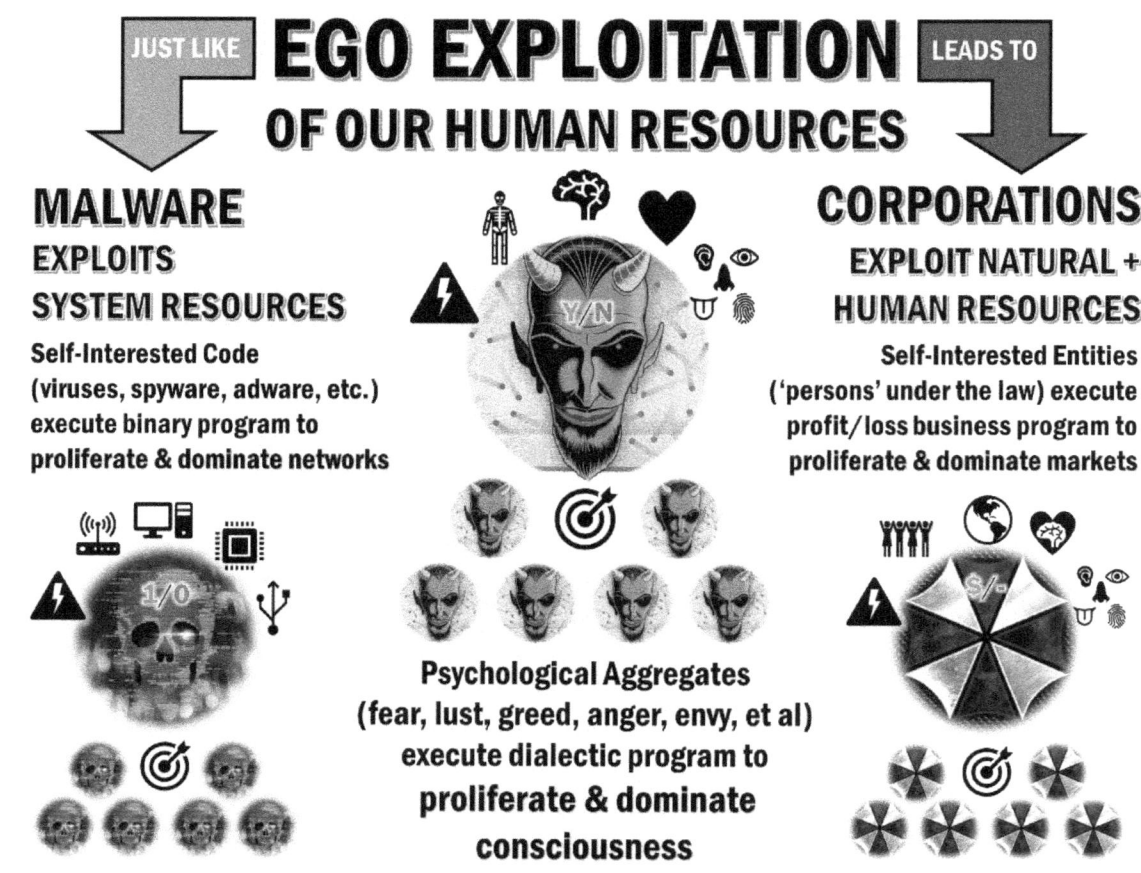

Figure 8: Ego Exploitation of Human Resources on nano, micro, and macro scales

Now, can anyone reasonably argue that exploitation is the path to enhancement, strengthening, revitalizing, and/or revolutionizing humanity? How about *awakening?* How precisely does falling deeper into the paradigm of exploitation constitute an evolutionary upward trajectory for humanity? How does deepening our reliance on technology enhance us biologically, let alone energetically or consciously? How can submitting to the mechanical desires of binary AI end in anything other than the total subjugation and exploitation of humanity, just as megalomaniacs seek empires, malware seeks total control, and corporations seek market dominance/monopoly?

What is Truly Alien to Mechanical Nature

In Ridley Scott's seminal work of science fiction horror, *Alien* is the quintessential allegory for humanity's struggle against mechanicity in all its forms. The xenomorph is not only one of the most terrifying creatures ever envisioned in cinematic history, but the H.R. Giger-designed alien is the living embodiment of biomechanical horror. Relentless as a terminator, adaptive as a sewer rat, cunning as a predatory feline. At one point in the film, after a colossal 'malfunction,' Ash, the science officer, is first immobilized and deactivated, then reactivated and interrogated by Ripley and the remaining crew for what it knows about the xenomorph and what, if anything, can be done to neutralize the threat. In the following exchange, we hear an android express the corporate policy regarding the alien, together with his own binary perspective on the quintessential biomechanical monstrosity that has been terrorizing the crew of the Nostromo:

RIPLEY: Ash, can you hear me?

Ash's severed head splutters into life. White liquid dribbles from his mouth.

ASH: Yes, I can hear you.

RIPLEY: What was your special order?

ASH: You read it. I thought it was clear.

RIPLEY: What was it?

ASH: Bring back life-form. Priority one. All other priorities rescinded.

Parker stands up, incensed, gun in hand.

PARKER: Damn company. What about our lives, you son of a bitch?

ASH: I repeat, all other priorities are rescinded.

RIPLEY: How do we kill it, Ash? There's gotta be a way of killing it – how, how do we do it?

ASH: You can't.

PARKER: That's bullshit...

ASH: You still don't understand what you're dealing with, do you? A perfect organism. Its structural perfection is matched only by its hostility.

LAMBERT: You admire it...

ASH: I admire its purity. A survivor. Unclouded by conscience, remorse, or delusions of morality...

PARKER: (To Ripley) I've heard enough of this - I'm asking you to pull the plug.

ASH: I can't lie to you about your chances. But you have my sympathies...

He smiles a small, malevolent smile. Ripley loses her patience and hits the severed head, which recedes back into lifelessness.

Video 10: Alien | Ash explains his orders (YouTube)

Did you catch that, dear reader? It is worthwhile repeating what Ash—a robot—said just so we can be clear: "I admire its *purity*. A survivor. Unclouded by conscience, remorse, or delusions of morality..." Consider these words in the context of *special order 937* designated by *the company* "for science officer's eyes only" and accessed by Ripley only via emergency override in the previous scene, "Priority one—Ensure return of organism for analysis. All other considerations secondary. Crew expendable." The trifecta of binary exploitation presented in the above meme—egos, malware, and corporations—are all present in this single defining scene of the film. The scene in which we discover that the company and its synthetic agent among the crew prize the alien above all other considerations. It is precisely *humanity* that is alien to their binary interests. Mechanicity itself determines "conscience, remorse, [and] delusions of morality..." are foreign and impure.

To AI, what makes us truly human is our greatest *weakness*. **Transhumanism, then, is precisely and literally exact in its meaning:** *to transcend that which makes us weak in the eyes of AI.* From the perspective of mechanical nature, if humanity's divine nature—love, compassion, altruism, conscience—is not dominated, controlled, and subjugated, the human-like machine will remain weak and *impure.* To AI, the 'perfect organism' is like the xenomorph from *Alien.* A biomechanical monstrosity whose "structural perfection is matched only by its hostility." Are you beginning to comprehend, dear reader, why certain elements of society are utterly obsessed with the *structural perfection* of their appearance, physical body, reputation, portfolio, collection of art, jewelry, wardrobe, antiques, rare and exotic automobiles, et al.? And is it any wonder what *hostility* that same class of individuals is capable of? How relentless can they be in the pursuit of whatever constitutes *structural perfection* in their eyes? And, with what ruthless disdain do they treat all those who are lesser in their eyes? All those 'weak masses,' who are so easily manipulated and led like sheep to slaughter. Transhumanism seeks to 'cure' humanity of what AI sees as an affliction: all free consciousness, all capacity to know ourselves, and the True divine nature of reality.

On mass, Love, compassion, altruism, and a sensible, balanced approach to life are antithetical to binary thought processes. And from the point of view of any AI, they are a threat to the 'purity' of the binary dialectic. As Ash states, they are a "delusion." How often have you heard atheists, secularists, and/or

WHAT IN HELL IS WITH US?   ATTLAS ALLUX

materialist scientists assert that religions, a belief in God, or even a belief in a transcendent reality beyond the physical universe are nothing more than a mass delusion—or something to that effect? Rest assured, dear reader, that the True nature of humanity has fallen prey to the antithetical and parasitic goals contained in the countless binary disciplines of the human intellect. An intellect that is dominated by egos whose modus operandi is mechanical and completely subjective.

But despite being mechanical, egos have a kind of sentience by virtue of their hosts' consciousness, which they hypnotize and hijack. As a result, they are clever and deceitful. They have convinced us that what the intellect creates under their influence is, in fact, objective, creative, and, to this end, crafted with the appearance of (or appearing to have the potential for) higher human functions. Hence, the delusion of most scientists, economists, artists, theologians, and especially transhumanists. All put their faith in the manifestations of inferior intellectual and emotional processes and pursuits. Superior Intellect and Emotion are so rare on our planet (especially in recent history) precisely because of the rise and dominance of inferior intellect/emotion under the control of egos.

Transhumanism is the latest in a long tradition of human consciousness being usurped by egos. This is what, in ancient times, people understood as the struggle between angels and demons for the souls of humankind. Our divine souls (consciousness) are pure awareness. It is that awareness that egos want to control forever. It should be obvious: intellects, out of fear, pride, and vanity, are envisioning technologies that will allow mechanical technologies (100% modeled on the paradigm of the egos themselves) to take control over natural biology. It is that same thinking that led to the decimation of the planet and its resources for the sole purpose of satisfying egos–greed, pride, fear, vanity, lust, gluttony, etc. Mechanical intellect convinces us of the superiority of its narrow subjective viewpoint, but it is utterly subservient to the self-interested goals of the egos operating on a win-lose paradigm. All the while, the true nature of the universe reveals itself (when one tunes into the bigger picture beyond humanity's primitive two-dimensional observation/understanding of its limited three-dimensional reality) to be based on a profoundly beautiful and universally applied win-win-win paradigm. But mechanical nature is disinterested in such *impure delusions*. Its agents of dialectic control over the human kingdom, egos, seek to exploit human and natural resources in accordance with their own self-interest. To that end, they have devised a concept even more insidious and all-encompassing of their relentless pursuit of control. A concept which, like transhumanism, is wrapped in a seductive package of altruism and good intentions. Like Raymond Kurzweil's life's work of improving the lives of the disabled (i.e., 'the weak') via cybernetic technology and transhumanist ideology.

Egos' Endgame…the Singularity.

This is the recent concept of a global interconnected reality where all living things will be connected digitally to an AI superintelligence. It is an idea first put forward by Raymond Kurzweil. The singularity suggests that when an actual *Matrix-like* construct connects every human being, machine, device, and robot to the Internet, it will result in exponential, uncontrollable, and irreversible infinite technological growth. Raymond Kurzweil is on record as not wanting to die…as wanting to download his consciousness into a computer and essentially live forever in a virtual reality simulation until such time that robotics are advanced enough, and then he can be uploaded into a robot to exist physically again (although why he would want a mundane existence if he has an infinite virtual reality to play in, one can only wonder).

The concept of uploading consciousness into a human-built machine is, of course, ridiculous. The "I" is an illusion, and the consciousness is not a product of mechanical nature. It is what gives the mind and the false self that sense of self-awareness, that "I"-ness…which is a corrupted sense of our 'am-ness'…the sense of being, which is independent of the mind. The mind says, "I think therefore I am." The consciousness states, "I am therefore I know; and, as a mortal vessel, I can think, feel, et al."

On the other hand, the idea of further enslaving humanity to mechanization and digitization is not ridiculous. We see it happening all around us. It is not by accident that devices called *iPod, iPhone, and iPad* running *iOS* exist (*I, I, I*) and that their counterparts have been branded *Android* (mechanical robots made in the image and likeness of human beings). At the time of writing, the *Apple Vision Pro* was just unveiled as the latest attempt by the company to further enslave people to its ironically dubbed *ecosystem* of devices and services. Remember, dear reader, it is no accident that Apple's logo is the very *forbidden fruit* responsible for *The Fall* of humanity described in the Book of Genesis and explained earlier in this chapter. Neither is it by accident that society is enamored with these devices. With each passing day, we are becoming more and more reliant on them. The more we rely on something, the more dependent we are on it. The more dependent we are on technology, the less independent we are. This is a slippery slope to total enslavement to our inherent mechanicity.

There was a time when people still had a sense of direction, a sense of time, the ability to know how hot or cold it was outside, know how to dress appropriately, and even know answers to basic questions of importance in any given moment. Now, we are lost without our GPS, have no idea how to dress without our weather app, and cannot answer anything at any given moment unless we can look it up on Wikipedia. These are all signs of our consciousness slipping deeper into sleep, deeper into the grip of ego, the mechanistic algorithms of nature, the virtual reality that wants to achieve a kind of godlike status over us and create a digital universe in which the "I" of false self can avoid death and live forever.

What the singularity might ultimately look like is a topic for science fiction. The very notion of a singularity suggests we cannot see beyond it or predict what comes after it. From our perspective, it is irrelevant. What matters to us is that we are unwitting, and to a large extent willing, participants in this process. By virtue of our identification with the false self and attachment to the virtual reality of the illusory *game world,* we march lockstep with the grand plan of mechanical nature…to enslave us and use our consciousness and energy to try to avoid the unavoidable. Transhumanism? How about we try ***True Humanism*** first?

A Game Mechanical Nature Began Ages Ago

VR, AI, transhumanism, the singularity, all these are just the latest salvo in a war that is as old as time itself. As we discussed earlier in this chapter, the fall of humanity to the forces of mechanical nature happened long ago, sparking a war between 'the armies of heaven and hell for the souls of humanity.' It is a war whose latest iteration has taken on the moniker *Human 2.0.* Again, this intimates that humanity is on the verge of a mass global *upgrade.* Not because of some mass global spiritual awakening but because of the ingenuity and cleverness of human intellect. Human 2.0 denotes the logical evolution of humanity as a species of biomechanical hominids, nothing more. It is, in fact, the final assault to secure once and for all the total dehumanization of humanity. Such an assault can be defined as only one thing: an act of spiritual warfare.

Video 11: Human 2.0 - Spiritual Warfare is Upon Us - Infinite Waters (YouTube)

Notwithstanding the erroneous moniker "Human 2.0," let us remember that this is but the final salvo in a spiritual war that has been raging between the forces of divinity and mechanicity for countless millennia. It only appears that 'spiritual warfare is upon us' to those who can, for the first time, see the outward manifestations of godlessness/soullessness acting upon humanity with not even one shred of genuine love or compassion. Fans of Raymond Kurzweil will no-doubt point out his profound humanitarian efforts to utilize technology on behalf of the disabled. No doubt, making disabled individuals more capable with technology was an important steppingstone toward Human 2.0, which seeks to cure humanity of all its weaknesses. But when you consider mechanical nature's perspective on what it determines the fundamental weaknesses and impurities of humanity to be, you realize that any perceived humanitarianism on the part of transhumanists is a rationalization on the part of our own ego-mind to justify their ultimate agenda. Not unlike how our many egos present us with all kinds of reasons why we should act against our conscience for the sake of comfort, security, efficiency, expediency, etc. Until now, the AI entities working for mechanical nature, known as egos, have waged their war against humanity within and through the human-like machine. In that guise, it was all too easy for the intellect—under the influence of egos—to either rationalize acts of 'evil' under the banner of 'the end justifies the means,' or chalk them up as just another facet of 'human nature,' dismissing the human condition as certain and inevitable. Or alternatively, blame some externalized 'Satan' as the cause of all our suffering. From early clockworks to the industrial revolution to the Internet age, transhumanism—the plan for total mechanization of humanity—has been proceeding physically for centuries and was established on a foundation of metaphysical mechanicity—egoism; the human condition—which has been unfolding since time immemorial.

Now, the forces of mechanical nature have come out of the shadows and into the light of the 21st Century. They have made a bold advance in the era they euphemistically and ironically named 'the knowledge age.' With all the technology companies involved in this totalitarian binary transformation of the intellectual hominid to the supposed upgraded Human 2.0, one might easily fall into the deep rabbit hole of conspiracy. In recognizing the mechanical and technological foundations of materialist science, the military-industrial complex, big pharma, and the oh-so-ubiquitous reserve banking system fueling it all with its monetary system, it is easy for us to divine all the culprits 'out there' responsible for enslaving humanity. We can easily identify technology and transhumanism as just another tool in the arsenal 'they' are using to execute their diabolical plans to achieve total dominance over humanity *out there in the world*. After all, were not the antagonists of *The Matrix* films an advanced race of AI? Have we not been making the case this entire chapter that AI is the adversary of humanity? Is it not, via technology, trying to enslave humanity in a veritable matrix of binary duality and illusion and bring about the Great A-weakening of Humanity? And if so, must we not confront all conspiracies and do everything in our power to help awaken humanity? Indeed, many commit themselves to exactly that: to awaken the *sleeping masses* from *The Matrix*.

In the world of conspiracies and conspiracy theorists, a great deal of emphasis is put on whether one has been *red-pilled* or not. This is a direct reference to the defining scene of the 1999 film *The Matrix*.

Video 12: The Matrix - Blue Pill or Red Pill (YouTube)

In this scene, Morpheus offers Neo a choice:

> *You take the blue pill... the story ends, you wake up in your bed and believe whatever*
> *you want to believe. You take the red pill... you stay in Wonderland, and I show you*
> *how deep the rabbit hole goes.*
>
> *– Morpheus, The Matrix*

The implication is, dear reader, that Neo is asleep and enslaved within the matrix and that only by taking the red pill can he awaken to the truth about himself and the real world.

To conspiracy theorists, *The Matrix* is an allegory for the world. They devote their lives to the study of conspiracies because they, like Neo, possess a deep intuitive feeling that things are not what they seem:

> *What you know you can't explain, but you feel it. You've felt it your entire life that*
> *there's something wrong with the world. You don't know what it is, but it's there, like*
> *a splinter in your mind, driving you mad.*
>
> *– Morpheus, The Matrix.*

Trinity admits to having that splinter in her mind when she says, "I was looking for an answer. It's the question that drives us, Neo. It's the question that brought you here." As in the film, the conspiracy theorists follow the white rabbit, choose the red pill, and take a deep dive into any number of conspiracies that they contend are devised to hide the truth from humanity. "What truth?" Neo asks Morpheus. "That you are a slave, Neo." Is his reply. "Like everyone else, you were born into bondage. Into a prison that you cannot taste or see or touch. A prison for your mind." This answer, however far-fetched, is the one that resonates most with conspiracy theorist's intuitive knowing, the splinter in their mind. *Humanity is enslaved by a vast global conspiracy,* which is the answer that best satisfies the question that drives them.

The catch is that there are countless such conspiracies. One can spend years researching any number of them. It would surely take lifetimes of devotion to study them all in-depth: their alleged key players, goals, means, methods, and results. This means that at some point in one's journey down the rabbit hole of conspiracy, one must decide which narrative(s) resonate the strongest and/or 'make the most sense.' While all conspiracies have a community of believers, some become evangelical—even fanatical—in their identification with their preferred plot(s). More than merely disagreeing with others, they will outright attack others for disagreeing with their preferred beliefs. In this way, we see a parallel emerge between conspiracy and all other facets of human beliefs, including religious dogma, political ideology, scientific theory, etc.

Despite conflicting theories, all who subscribe to any number of conspiracies believe themselves red-pilled—conscious and awake—because they feel they have lifted the veil on the scheme(s) enslaving humanity: who, how, and to what nefarious ends. Like all those who become deeply identified and attached to beliefs, they feel themselves in possession of the facts as they see them, and *their truth* leaves no room for alternate facts, contrary opinions, or even the most well-argued alternative explanations. Ironically, they end up suffering from acute cognitive dissonance—precisely what frustrates them the most in non-believers, those still trapped in the matrix…*sheeple.*

As we covered earlier in *Part Two* in our chapter on the human condition(ed), we cannot hope to SEEK self-evident experiential knowledge of the Truth if we indulge our knee-jerk reactions to anything that challenges what we think we know. This goes for conspiracy theorists and non-believers alike. Whether we doubt mainstream narrative(s), doubt contradictory conspiracy theories, or doubt that widescale conspiracies to subvert and/or enslave humanity are even plausible, we should at least know what doubt is and how it can be exploited by our ego-mind to bolster cognitive dissonance and keep us trapped in closed-mindedness. If need be, dear reader, review the section Doubt you have been Conditioned? SEEK how the ego-mind exploits doubt to keep us enslaved in hypnosis and ignorance, and you may just gain *the eyes to see and ears to hear* through the veil of conspiracy itself. Discover what being *red-pilled* is and is not, the True nature of *the truth* Morpheus revealed to Neo, and *the actual matrix* enslaving this humanity…*the conspiracy of conspiracies.*

The Conspiracy of Conspiracies

Let us be clear, dear reader: we are not here to argue the truth or validity of any one of the countless conspiracy theories out there at this time. It is, in fact, the point of this chapter not to do so. Our purpose for highlighting the machinations of the ego-mind responsible for cognitive dissonance was not to disarm you nor to make you more likely to accept our 'arguments.' On the contrary, our purpose here is to assist you in SEEKing self-evident experiential knowledge of the conspiracy of conspiracies—the mother of all conspiracies—for yourself. It just so happens that priming your consciousness with the case study of cognitive dissonance will help you to SEEK the Truth at hand consciously and comprehensively, as opposed to merely absorbing a nebulous perception of it intellectually. One thing is certain: none of us need another concept of reality stuffed into the attic of our rational minds. And we are not here to throw one more contender into the battle royale of competing theories fighting for supremacy within the collective consciousness of humanity.

In fact, our purpose is to reveal the one True explanation that resolves the apparent conflict and confusion arising from multiple competing versions of reality, history, economics, politics, religion, and, yes, conspiracies. These might include—but are in no way limited to—the illusory freedom and actual enslavement of humanity by the 1%, International Banking Cartels, the Monetary System, The New World Order, Zionists, The Illuminati, reptilian overlords, alien invaders, the Khazarian Mafia, 'Archons,' malevolent aliens, various other nefarious forces of darkness, et al. Sincerest apologies if we missed your theory of choice, dear reader. Even the staunchest of believers must agree: they cannot all be true, right? Or can they? For non-believers, you may be on the verge of finally comprehending why you refuse to even entertain the notion of wide-reaching conspiracies in the world as proffered by 'the tin-foil-hat-wearing nutjobs.' Let us take the red pill and SEEK how deep the rabbit hole really goes.

Conspiracy Theory Defined

According to Wikipedia:

> *A conspiracy theory is an explanation for an event or situation that asserts the existence of a conspiracy by powerful and sinister groups, often political in motivation when other explanations are more probable. The term generally has a negative connotation, implying that the appeal of a conspiracy theory is based on prejudice, emotional conviction, or insufficient evidence. A conspiracy theory is distinct from a conspiracy; it refers to a hypothesized conspiracy with specific characteristics, including but not limited to opposition to the mainstream consensus among those who are qualified to evaluate its accuracy, such as scientists or historians.*
>
> *Studies have linked belief in conspiracy theories to distrust of authority and political cynicism. Some researchers suggest that conspiracist ideation—belief in conspiracy theories—may be psychologically harmful or pathological and that it is correlated with lower analytical thinking, low intelligence, psychological projection, paranoia, and Machiavellianism. Psychologists usually attribute belief in conspiracy theories to a*

number of psychopathological conditions such as paranoia, schizotypy, narcissism, and insecure attachment or to a form of cognitive bias called "illusory pattern perception." However, a 2020 review article found that most cognitive scientists view conspiracy theorizing as typically nonpathological, given that unfounded belief in conspiracy is common across cultures, both historical and contemporary, and may arise from innate human tendencies towards gossip, group cohesion, and religion.

– Source: <u>Wikipedia, Conspiracy Theory</u>

In short, in the eyes of experts, conspiracy lies somewhere on a spectrum of mental illness, deficiency, or an innate human tendency. Interestingly, rarely is that third element—a human tendency toward belief—expanded upon. And not merely *because humans are uncomfortable with not knowing*. A conspiracy theory is an effect, and all effects have their cause(s). The cause of any theory is not external. The phenomena a theory claims to explain may be external (out there), but the theory or explanation itself is internal, a mental construct (in here). All mental constructs originate in the mind for a reason. They have a purpose. They are motivated into existence by an internal psychological need. Namely, the need to make sense of phenomena and our experiences. Only by comprehending how such constructs emerge can we know what conspiracy theories Truly are and how they carry so much weight for those who believe in them.

How Do Conspiracy Theories Emerge?

Motivation is both an effect and a cause. Motive appears. It is formed. An event (say, 9/11) happens. Our immediate reaction may be shock, anger, sadness, fear, and many more. We may also have an immediate intuitive insight like: "Oh my God, it's an inside job!" (Our personal intuitive insight as we saw planes hitting towers). As we have time to dwell on things and our initial reaction subsides, we are left with a secondary wave of internal responses to what we are being told to believe about the event. Perhaps we notice things about the official version of the event, the media coverage, particular details, omissions, peculiarities, anomalies, etc. We may begin to develop a deeper feeling, a stronger hunch—deeper intuition—that "something's just not right with the official version of events." So, our mind begins gathering and putting together the pieces of the puzzle until a version of events emerges that not only *makes sense,* but that *feels right.* That is, it explains any initial intuitive insight we experienced in the moment and satisfies the deepening intuitive feeling we had afterwards, which made us question the official story, accepted explanation, and/or established dogma surrounding the event. In other words, dear reader, why do the so-called *experts* not factor intuition into their understanding of conspiratorial thinking?

There are, of course, other possible motives. Perhaps we wish to intentionally fabricate a lie and create confusion. Maybe our goal is to make ourselves seem like geniuses or to feel important. Perhaps we are cynical and want to always believe the worst of our government. Maybe we are bored, enjoy solving mysteries, and find this intriguing event in history a worthwhile pursuit of our time and intellectual prowess—like a self-styled Sherlock Holmes. Perhaps we identified with Scully and Mulder of *The X-Files*. Perchance we, like an overzealous prosecuting attorney, feel it is our job to indict what we believe to be corrupt and nefarious institutions in cahoots with a secret hidden cabal and will build a case against them no matter what. Possibly we are part of some militant group like *Anonymous* and feel we must believe in conspiracies to remain part of our clan. Then again, we may be averse to seeing ourselves as one of the *sheeple* following the rest of the herd and identify instead as a skeptic, believing no school of thought, be it mainstream or fringe, preferring our own unique view of reality. In short, even without any intuition that something is not right with the official version of events, we can hop on the conspiracy bandwagon for any number of different motivations: personal, egotistical, rational, irrational, peer pressure, rebel, etc.

While acknowledging not everyone who believes in conspiracy theories does so because they are responding to an intuitive impulse, for our purposes, we will weed out all the *disingenuous* conspiracy theorists. We will focus our study on genuine conspiracy theorists: individuals who refute the established narratives in favor of conspiratorial alternatives to satisfy an internal nagging doubt that they cannot ignore. One which simply will not allow them to accept the status quo as truth. *A splinter in their mind.* Our reason for making this distinction is sound. One who formulates or adopts an intellectual belief in conspiracy theory based on an intuitive impulse is making use of an additional faculty of consciousness—doubt, for instance—as opposed to one whose motivations are based solely on ego-mind. However, as will shortly become clear, intuitive impulse or not, a myriad of possible ego-intellectual motivations can and do quickly come into play. The ego-mind's modus operandi is to appropriate objective experiential knowledge and weave its own subjective narratives around said experience. In this way, intuition or not, all conspiracy theorists tend to end in the same place, psychologically speaking.

How can there Be so Many Competing Versions of the Same Event?

Have you ever had *one of those days?* One that was just truly awful, filled with events, circumstances, conversations, and coincidences that felt like going twelve rounds with Muhammed Ali? When someone asked you how you felt, rather than reliving your whole day, giving them a blow-by-blow account, or trying to give them a precise description of how you were feeling, you probably said something like: "I feel like crap." That was enough. They got it. In the same way, you probably immediately understood what we meant by *having one of those days* that *felt like going twelve rounds with Muhammed Ali.*

The mind uses simile, metaphor, allegory, signs, symbols, and other figures of speech to approximate and point toward our experiential knowledge, and indeed, timeless, universal Truths. The mind (and language) cannot capture reality. It can only ever approximate it. The mind does not *know*. The mind *thinks it knows.* In our rational mind, we only ever think about and express some form of reality. That said, when we hear an expression of a form of reality that evokes and/or seems to capture the essence of our experience, our consciousness makes the connection, and we are satisfied we know what the other person is talking about. Indeed, we all know what it is like to *feel like crap,* despite the fact no human in history has ever consciously experienced being excrement. No one knows how crap feels. But of course, we all *go to the crapper* every day. We all have the experiential knowledge implied and conveyed by the simile *feel like crap.* Similarly, we have all had *one of those days,* even if no two days throughout human history have ever been exactly alike. With figurative language and figures of speech, we can encapsulate a whole series of events into a single expression, which seems to perfectly capture the essence of the experience despite being linguistically vague (one of those days).

The reverse is also possible. A single experience can spawn a limitless number of forms and expressions of it. Consider how many lines of poetry have been written about love. Most everyone knows what it is like to love, and yet no one has ever managed to explain what love is exactly, not in intellect nor in words. And yet, there are countless beautiful poems, stories, plays, paintings, films, and songs that invoke in us our experiential knowledge of being in love. Thus, they all seem to capture and convey the essence of love. The point is while we can experience love and know what love is in our conscious experience, our mind cannot know what love is. Using the mind as a tool for mediation, many have formulated and conveyed countless expressions of love based on their experiential knowledge. Elaborate tales, poems, paintings, songs, etc., exist not as literal intellectual explanations but rather as informed expressions of the ineffable essential Truth of love, which must be experienced to be known. Such expressions have the potential to invoke the feeling of being in love with those in the know. Someone who has never been in love cannot know what it is like. They might think they know what being in love is like, but just as the mind can never actually know, so too, no mental concept of love can ever capture the whole Truth of love. And yet, there are seemingly endless expressions of love that we take in through the mind, which can invoke in us the feeling of being in love.

In accordance with the AUM of Life, a wide expanse of harrowing experiences can be synthesized consciously into a single figure of speech embodying the essence of said experiences as *one of those days.* Likewise, the universal experience of love can trigger an expansion of infinite expressions. The mind as a vehicle both reduces experiences and feelings into a single concept or expression and elaborates at length to describe or explain a single experience or feeling in a multitude of different forms and expressions. Remember, the intuitive sense that motivates the birth of many conspiracy theories may be as simple and vague as the gut feeling: "Things are not what they appear to be." This is a conscious knowing. The mind then latches onto that feeling-turned-thought and immediately starts weaving an elaborate story expressing and/or explaining it (like the countless stories, poems, songs, etc. about love).

WHAT IN HELL IS WITH US?   ATTLAS ALLUX

In addition to controlled demolition, there are apparently many ways to bring a building down: missiles, secret military weapons, alien technologies, black magic, and more. We need not speculate. YouTube is filled with all these alternative explanations related to 9/11, and being struck by commercial jetliners is not one of them. As for who is behind *the inside job,* that list is as long as the one we opened this discussion with—the Military Industrial Complex, CIA, international banking cartels, Illuminati, Zionists, Demonic Forces, reptilians, etc. A quick internet search returns a veritable treasure trove of competing and complementary theories put forward as alternatives to the official explanation of the events of 9/11.

While the blessing of love inspires an expansion of infinite expressions on the upward spiral of evolution, it should come as no surprise that a malevolent and tragic event like 9/11 would trigger an explosion of unlimited theories on the downward spiral of devolution. Every expression inspired by love that invokes in us the fundamental Truth and essence of being in love can be said to resonate with our experiential knowledge. Likewise, on some level, all the competing theories of 9/11 address the most basic intuitive knowledge about the events of that infamous day: *there is much more to the events than the official narrative.* The mind is, by nature, semiotic, symbolic, and allegorical. Incapable of knowing, the rational mind turns to comparison, contrast, theory, and approximation to reconstruct a version of the truth that aligns with and thus satisfies the underlying intuitive presupposition. When the mind puts forth—or encounters—such an approximation of the events, their causes, instigators, and beneficiaries, it is said to make more sense to us. The more profound our intuition (that is, the deeper and more specifically clear our insight into reality), the less likely we will be taken in by any old theory. We will continue to have doubts until the theory presented to us is elaborate enough to approximate what we know intuitively to be the case.

So, *I feel like crap…like hell…like I was hit by a bus…like a train wreck…like I want to die…et al* can all substitute for the reality of *one of those days.* We are not being dishonest, even though it is highly unlikely that we literally feel like any of those things. We are telling the Truth; at least, we are expressing a form of truth. That is, an expression which is not literally true but essentially true. As a result, our conscience is not pricked. It knows the mind cannot technically and exactly describe reality. So, based on experiential knowledge of ourselves and the events that led to the feelings we are experiencing, so long as the essence of that knowledge is being captured and communicated, our conscience is fine with it. "I feel like [insert something terrible here]" is as good an explanation as any. What we use to fill in the blanks is a matter of personal preference.

In other words, we will be drawn to one explanatory narrative of events or another, depending on our own idiosyncrasies, beginning with a level of intuition, followed by psychological motivations, dispositions, biases, other belief systems, skepticism, etc. In the same way the metaphor we chose to describe how we feel comes from our mind, so too, the theory we will believe will be a matter of personal preference. Subjective.

We will tell ourselves, "I choose to believe this," but in fact, it is really a matter of ego-satiation. The mind feels uncomfortable with the idea that it does not really know. The ego-mind wants to be right. This is the nature of self-righteousness. Intuition and conscience belong to a superior faculty—consciousness—which has no need to be right. It simply knows what it knows. It cannot be erased by the mind (try it sometime), but it can be ignored, overridden, shouted down, etc. (recall, dear reader, how you have managed to follow your mind instead of your conscience on countless occasions). The conscience is also perfectly comfortable with not knowing (i.e., the details about *what is not right with the mainstream narrative*). In fact, the consciousness knows we really know nothing in the grand scheme of things and is perfectly comfortable with that. But the nature of ego-mind is to fear what it does not know. Ego-mind cannot stand the discomfort and insecurity which stems from its inability to know consciously. So, to compensate, the mind weaves an elaborate story around whatever kernel of intuitive and/or experiential Truth is held in consciousness. It will continue weaving its narrative in the language of the psyche, utilizing symbol, allegory, or approximation of the Truth until it hits upon a form that aligns with intuition and/or experiential knowledge. Or, it will keep elaborating on some literal intellectual theory until it arrives at a place where said theory 'makes sense.' It is at this point that the ego-mind believes it knows. The mind's explanation is not technically correct or exact, but it is not entirely false, either. It essentially *feels close enough* to the kernel of Truth known in consciousness, and that makes the story (theory) very compelling to us.

Naturally, the mind can distract us from our conscience in another way. Our intuition may say, "9/11 was an inside job." But then we get bombarded by media stories, the families of dead firefighters weeping on live television, the President of the United States making bold accusations about terrorists hiding in caves in Afghanistan, and images of planes hitting towers replayed at nauseum...until the Still Soft Voice of our conscience is completely drowned out by the cacophony of rambling voices in our mind. Our awareness becomes so inundated with whatever it is we are being bombarded with that we forget our intuition altogether and get lost in the official story being fed to us. *9/11 truthers* like to say our minds are being manipulated. But in Truth, it is our own mind that is hypnotizing our consciousness, and so our conscience (which would normally prevent us from entering into unjust wars, torturing detainees, taking away people's civil liberties, and enacting draconian security laws) gets lost in the very fear which is actively at work manipulating the minds of those responsible for spreading and acting upon the official 9/11 narrative and subsequent *War on Terror*.

The ego-mind can also take the bold step of directly contradicting the conscience and even convince us that our intuition is wrong. Again, by weaving an elaborate explanation that *makes sense*, we outright ignore our intuitive feelings and/or experiences in light of *overwhelming evidence.* This is the case for all those who accept the official version of 9/11. For them, the official version of Al-Qaeda terrorists hiding in caves, taking flight training, hijacking planes with box-cutters, etc., is more plausible and realistic than any alternative narrative that might satisfy the feeling that *something is terribly wrong about all this* (how their mind processes *something is not right about this*). The mind can be very subtle and clever. It will continue convincing us internally until we accept what it wants us to believe. It makes us *feel good* about its explanation, so we accept it as being right. In other words, we are made to feel self-righteous about the version of events presented to us because it puts our mind at ease that we know the truth. People often choose familiar and comfortable falsehoods over uncomfortable and inconvenient facts. They will double down on their self-righteousness, especially when confronted by the facts that threaten to rekindle their intuition and/or prick their conscience. In other words, their mind will turn to cognitive dissonance as a tool to protect the comfort and security proffered by held beliefs.

Here is something to consider: of all the theories about 9/11, which one made people feel self-righteous enough to warrant invading Afghanistan and Iraq, torturing detainees in GTMO, enacting unprecedented liberty-infringing legislation, etc.? In this case, conscience was clearly *overruled,* much like a corrupt judge in a courtroom overrules the objections of an attorney who threatens the predetermined outcome of the case.

How good is the mind at hypnotizing/convincing us that its version of events is the right version? As soon as we make it *our version.* Just read the comments under any YouTube video, Facebook post, Reddit thread, or Tweet. Yes, you will see the venom spewed by the proverbial Internet trolls. But you will also find plenty of regular people suddenly go on the offensive.

Why such Vehemence?

Beliefs are a peculiar phenomenon. One minute, they do not exist (not in our minds, anyway). The next minute, we find ourselves fighting tooth and nail to defend them. The moment we accept them as true, it is like they become a part of us. The longer we hold onto them, the more they seem to crawl under our skin, burrow inside our brains, and wrap themselves around our cerebral cortex. And, as Khan says in *Star Trek II – The Wrath of Khan,* once they do so, they not only make us "open to suggestion," they eventually lead to our death.

Video 13: Ear Bug Scene - Star Trek 2 Wrath of Khan
(YouTube)

What exactly do beliefs kill? We will get to that shortly. For now, it is enough to recognize that our attachment to beliefs, theories, explanations, and opinions empowers them to take hold of us and make us react as passionately, vehemently, and in some cases violently against anyone who dares comment, question, or oppose our precious beliefs. It is our emotional investment in beliefs—how much of ourselves we devote to them—that makes things personal.

Conspiracy theorists are among the worst offenders. Perhaps because they have often invested so much time and energy researching their conspiracy of choice (there are hundreds of hours and thousands of pages devoted to every conceivable explanation of reality imaginable). But more so because of the comfort and security, the feeling of being right gives the psyche. That, and of course, the fact that the theory gives us the feeling that our mysterious intuition, *things are not as they appear* and/or *something's not right with the world,* has been solved. We feel like Neo in *The Matrix* after being *red-pilled.* Our mind tells us we at last have the answer to "the question that drives us," as Trinity puts it.

An intellectual hominid, once driven, is not easily dissuaded, distracted, or desisted. The driving question is like a hungering lust that must be satisfied. And once the mind is satisfied it has the answer, we feel we own the truth like a bull owns alpha mating privileges. When an opposing viewpoint appears, it is like a competing male threatening to knock us from our alpha status and take away our mating privileges (if we lose ownership of the truth, we will once again be left questioning and the hungering lust in need of satisfaction will return with a vengeance). And so, like bulls dueling for alpha status and mating privileges, we argue, fight, and literally *butt heads* in defense of our beliefs.

The feeling that it does not know is unbearable to the ego. Like the bull who knows what it is like to live with unfulfilled desire, burning questions left unanswered are an experience of pain we would rather avoid. We are afraid of not knowing, plain and simple. So, fear invents intellectual curiosity to occupy our consciousness, relieve our pain of not knowing, and give us a reward in our pleasure center when we *figure things out.* When the mind thinks it has unearthed some hidden truth, solved a puzzle, learned a secret, etc., it feels accomplished, clever, smarter, and more important. It also feels more comfortable and secure since the pain of not knowing has been replaced by the pleasure of believing in something, of being convinced it is right. Lastly, having uncovered 'the secret,' we feel more in control of our lives, particularly in the case of conspiracy theories, which tend to focus on how others—banksters, elites, cabals, reptilians, aliens, et al—secretly control us.

An opposing viewpoint clearly jeopardizes a mind's stability, comfort, and security by wrenching control away from it. In addition to fear, pride makes ego-mind unable to bear to feel the pain of being proved wrong (which makes us feel worse, dumber, less important). And so, on both these fronts, the ego-mind will defend itself against all incursions in a primal act of self-preservation: *"I am right!"* And the best defense is a good offense: *"You are wrong!"* Thus, the timeless and universal modus-operandi of human conquest, subjugation, and enslavement emerges…

Divide and Conquer

It is universally accepted among conspiracy theorists that *the powers that be enslaving humanity* do so by manufacturing conflicts and playing both sides of the conflict. Divide and conquer is the mantra you will hear time and time again, particularly in relation to conspiracies of the New World Order, The Great Reset, Zionism, alien reptilian invasion, the media, religion, politics, historical events (especially WWII), and many more.

Divide and conquer is not exclusively conspiratorial, however. Many a military tactician has utilized the maxim literally on the battlefield to great effect for millennia. Naturally, whereas a united front presents a more formidable obstacle, dividing the opposition's army into two or more smaller contingents means facing less than half of their forces in any skirmish. What is true on the battlefield holds true on a chess board, a football field, and most notably in the political arena:

> *The maxim divide et impera [divide and rule] has been attributed to Philip II of Mace-*
> *don. It was utilized by the Roman ruler Julius Caesar and the French emperor Napoleon*
> *(together with the maxim divide ut regnes [divide so that you may reign])*
>
> *– Source: Wikipedia, Divide and rule*

Clearly, then, divide and conquer (rule) is nothing new. Although the maxim might have been attributed to Philip II of Macedon, it was being utilized long before the phrase was coined. Even in the wild, predators will seek to break apart herds of herbivores or schools of fish, first splintering off a smaller group and then singling out a lone straggler from said group. And tribes of human hunters will use the same tactics. So, divide and conquer may be seen to be hardwired into humanity on a primal, instinctive level. Just how much so, dear reader, may surprise you.

As we discussed in the previous chapter, this humanity created computers in its own image. Computers think as the ego-mind prefers to—in absolute dialectic terms…1's and 0's…on or off, yes or no, right or wrong, me or you, us or them, et al. In other words, our rational minds want to function as mechanical machines capable of outputting a precise answer to the exclusion of all other possible answers. It is this egotistical idealized version of ourselves that led us to create computers—to perform complex calculations on many inputs and output exact answers. Ironically, our pursuit of AI has led to systems that more exactly mimic the rational mind, along with all its imprecision and inclination to error, as we revealed in the previous chapter. Standard computers, like all machines, like our egos, are designed and programmed for precision and exacting standards of operation and output. And the rational mind aspires to the same exacting standards of knowledge. That is why all of materialist science claims to produce knowledge of an absolute nature—not just provisionally as they claim, since it often takes decades, if not centuries, for stubbornly entrenched scientific dogma to be overturned by new discoveries and evidence. Recall the mantra repeated incessantly during COVID-19: *trust the science.* But here is the point: every act of defining knowledge via the dialectic of thesis/antithesis (*this, not that; us, not them*) is an exercise in divide and conquer (rule). This begs the question: who or what is doing the dividing and ruling? Who or what is being ruled?

Who is a Threat to Whom?

Conspiracy theorists love to point out how they have lifted the veil and are revealing the dark secret forces hiding in the shadows, threatening our freedom, our lives, and our very existence. Conspiracy theories are all about shedding light on the dark cabals *out there,* secretly manipulating the world. And naturally, they only think of divide and rule in those terms. They also love to point out how threats to the powers that be are silenced, eradicated, assassinated, persecuted, etc. Case in point are the numerous conspiracy theories around the assassination of JFK, John Lennon, and many other figures throughout history. But if so, why are all the self-styled *truthers* allowed to operate with impunity?

Knowledge is power. If the truthers are right, then revealing their versions of reality to the masses would be an incredible threat to the power structure that has been hiding behind lies, disinformation, misinformation, misdirection, mass hypnosis, and mass mind control. According to the truthers' own beliefs, that power structure would be moving to silence, persecute, prosecute, or put down all vocal conspiracy theorists. And yet, people like Alex Jones, David Icke, and many others spread their gospel of fantastical interpretations of events, history, scripture, media reports, and official versions of reality. If they were lifting the veil on the Truth, would they not have been silenced by now? Or is it possible that spreading their beliefs in a universal plot by a secret threat 'out there' is, in fact, playing right into the hands of the very hidden threat they claim to want to expose, oppose, and depose?

Perhaps Umberto Eco said it best: "There exists a secret society with branches throughout the world, and its plot is to spread the rumor that a universal plot exists." – Umberto Eco, *Focault's Pendulum.* We are not the first, then, to reveal the irony in the conspiracy theory movement. Nor, it seems, is the concept lost on the conspiracy theorists themselves. There are many videos online describing how popular conspiracy theorists are, in fact, deliberately spreading misinformation and disinformation, purposefully misleading the masses with false accusations and explanations to throw them off the scent of the *real* story. This phenomenon is an aspect of *controlled opposition.* In synthesis, if you want to run a campaign of disinformation, you may as well control the counter-intelligence movement as well. This way, you can control both sides. Divide and conquer. As different narratives are parlayed onto the stage of public opinion, rifts between believers of this or that version of 'the truth' emerge, and camps begin to form around each version. A kind of intellectual tribalism develops. Tribes can be made to play off against one another. And the Truth gets buried beneath all the confusion. Any intuitive insights or original Truths that may have informed the populace become completely lost and forgotten as different competing camps argue over the details of whatever version of reality they subscribe to. Whatever honesty may have been present in the original conspiracy movement gets watered down and lost as the movement splits into more and more sects, each claiming to be in sole possession of the superior account of reality. Each schism takes place over arguments around various details, so new camps form around beliefs based on details. After a while, the essence of reality begins to fade. If this sounds at all familiar to you, dear reader, it should.

The Law of Entropy

Everything that is born under the sun grows, develops, complicates, decays, and dies. That is the way of things. There is nothing humanity creates which is immune to this immutable law of nature. The law of entropy states that things move from a state of oneness and cohesion to a state of separation and fragmentation as they break down as a matter of course. Even granite rock erodes and breaks down. What is True of granite is also True for religion. Not the timeless universal principles upon which those religions were founded, just the outward religious forms which exist as mental and cultural theological constructs.

Video 14: Religious Principles (YouTube)

Religious forms, ideas, belief systems, and even language are not immune to the law of entropy. And we do not have to go back in history to the Great Schism, the collapse of the Roman Empire, the Protestant Reformation, or the countless groups, tribes, nations, religions, schools of science, philosophical movements, political parties, and languages which splintered off into fragmented remnants of themselves. Consider an example that hits frighteningly close to home yet was brilliantly observed and put forth by the late great George Carlin (a master of observation and language, if ever there was one).

Video 15: Words That Hide the Truth
(YouTube)

The first few minutes of the above video describing the 70-year devolution of the term *shellshock* though *battle fatigue, operational exhaustion,* and finally, what we know today as *post-traumatic stress disorder* or PTSD, precisely demonstrates the law of entropy as it applies to mental expressions of real-world phenomena. Notice anything about Carlin's analysis of PTSD? "The pain is completely buried under jargon." In other words, the reality of the condition, once aptly expressed by the simple and highly expressive term shellshock, has been successfully evaded, watered down under unnecessarily complicated, euphemistic language (what he calls "soft language").

We can imagine the materialist scientists' and clinical psychologists' reactions already: "PTSD is a more clinically accurate, more technically descriptive, more scientifically meaningful description of the condition," they might say. Perhaps it is, which means it is more meaningful to the literal, mechanical, materialist-scientific mind. A rational mind aspires to the perfection embodied in the computers it created in its own idealized image. But what about the conscience? *Con-science,* that is, what science cannot explain, what the literal mind cannot make sense of. In other words, what about the *heart?* The superior heart center can know love—what the rational mind cannot conceive a *clinically accurate description* of. Surely, a condition like PTSD, as Carlin points out, deserves a descriptor like shellshock to convey the essence of the experience of the condition. Carlin suggests that those in a position to ease the suffering of shell-shocked Vietnam War veterans might have been able to empathize and take better care of said veterans. PTSD, no matter how detailed a description of the condition, in no way, shape, or form conveys the essential Truth of the experience of shellshock. PTSD is thus entirely inappropriate to the actual needs of those suffering from it. It is a term for those who have not experienced shellshock to deal with others who have in a way that allows them to avoid any True sense of suffering. "I have PTSD" is like saying, "I am overwrought with post-exertion exhaustion and emotional negativity," instead of "I feel like crap." We ask you, dear reader: which is purely intellectual, and which is practical, meaningful, and consciously comprehensible on a human level?

The Devil is in the Details

What comes to mind in this instance is the expression, *the devil is in the details*. There is nothing fundamentally wrong with detail, the world is filled with it. But the ego-mind tends to identify with, latch onto, and obsess over details which end up distracting from the essential Truth which really matters in any given situation.

Example 1a/b: a racist who either **(a) refuses to hire a black man**—or **(b) gives him a job**—**solely because he is a POC** (person of color). The essential Truth which really matters (and that the racist's conscience will be trying to get them to observe) is that the black man is just one of many qualified candidates in the running for the position based on experience and expertise. The detail that he is a POC distracts from the fundamentals that actually matter—*equality of opportunity* and *merit*. These essential Truths, which are informed from within by the conscience, are what should be acted upon. The mind of the racist, however, uses its attachment to detail to trump the conscience with whatever beliefs it has accepted or woven around that detail (people of color). The racist follows an attachment to a detail *out there* rather than the Truth, which is available to them *in here,* via their own inner conscience.

Example 2: an individual is wrongfully convicted and incarcerated because a judge and/or jury mulishly, mechanically, and mistakenly fixates on *the letter of the law* instead of carefully, conscientiously, and compassionately considering *the spirit of the law*.

Example 3: a scientist observing a beautiful sunset with a tour group begins explaining to everyone how the angle and atmosphere of the earth creates the various colors they are seeing. The essential Truth which really matters in the moment (which most of the people in the tour group no doubt are trying to experience in silence) is its beauty. Not aesthetics. Those too, are details. The beauty, awe, and wonder experienced *through* the medium of the physical and aesthetic mechanics of the sunset and its colors. To focus on the physical science or the aesthetic beauty (the form and/or function of the physical phenomena *out there*) in that moment is to miss the True beauty of the moment…a beauty which one connects to *from within oneself.*

The Truth is Not *Out There*

Ironically, George Carlin, Umberto Eco, and every truther still seem trapped in *The X-Files* version of reality (that the truth is somehow *out there* and must be uncovered). Carlin (rest his soul) blamed the degeneration of language on "white rich people." Eco blames conspiracy theories about secret societies on what else but a secret society. The truthers can go on at length into ever-more complex and complicated explanations, pointing out all the intricate details *out there* that support their theories of who or what is manipulating which theory/theorist. Detailed explanations which, as we have just pointed out, take us further away from the essence of reality…that first intuitive nudge that motivated the whole conspiracy enterprise in the first place:

> *Things are not what they seem.*
> *There's something just not right with the world.*
> *The official story just doesn't feel right.*
> *– Our Intuition*

These are the equivalent of a *conscious shellshock*. A condition which the ego-mind then quickly grabs hold of, externalizes, pieces together elaborate explanations using evidence from without, to find a cause for the condition *out there*. It then packages it all in what ends up being the equivalent to *post-traumatic stress disorder*. Technically correct. Literally detailed. Certainly not incorrect. A rational, logically constructed, scientifically sound theory. And a near-perfect evasion of the pain and suffering which go along with an actual conscious comprehension of reality. We say *near-perfect* evasion because as a matter of course, most truthers channel their anger into their theories. Whatever pain and suffering they are trying to avoid is merely transformed into anger, which is directed outwardly toward the supposed bad actors behind the conspiracy who are ultimately responsible for the pain and suffering. For conspiracy theorists, these bad actors, like 'the truth,' are *out there*.

We tend to blame others. We want *a scapegoat*. It is the modus operandi of the ego-mind to divide and conquer (*us and them; good and bad*), ascribing *good* to us and *bad* to them. Judgment and condemnation are natural, automatic functions of mechanical binary thinking. They come part-and-parcel with ego-mind and why the world is run in part by the courts and the court of public opinion. If ever there was jargon-laced euphemistic language which was technically correct and literally detailed, it must be legalese. Also completely lifeless, heartless, and a complete evasion of the essential Truth of reality. A distraction. An attempt for the mind to answer questions with externalized detail, missing the point entirely. And a perfectly devised jungle of literal *letters of the law* for minds to become obsessed over and lost in while completely missing *the spirit of the law*. Are we beginning to see a pattern yet, dear reader?

Still, we may have no problem buying into conspiracy theories lock, stock, and smoking barrel. The more elaborate, evidence-based, rational, technically detailed, well-researched and jargon-laced, the better we feel about believing in them. There is something strangely comforting about belief, even if that belief is horrific. It is like having a plan. As the Joker says in *The Dark Knight,* nobody panics when things go to plan, "even if the plan is horrifying…"

Video 16: Do I really look [like] a guy with a plan?
| The Dark Knight [4k, HDR] (YouTube)

Plans, theories, labels, externalized concepts in the mind comfort us—*even if they are horrific*—because so long as they are *out there* we feel safe and secure. "At least they are out there and not in here!" There is that ubiquitous dialectic again. Binary thinking. Bad things *out there* are not good, but they are better than bad things *in here.* So long as the world gives us plausible explanations that keep the root of evil and the source of danger over there, we will be okay, right? We are relatively safe, yes? This is the foundation of NIMBY—*not in my backyard.* Not only that, it gives us an excuse to arm ourselves to the teeth to defend ourselves against *them* by taking them out, or at the very least start drawing up our own plans to take them down. This certainly was the case concerning the devastation in Afghanistan and Iraq post-9/11. "People are dying *over there* in the Middle-East? That's terrible! At least we are safe *over here.*"

Figure 9: How we see ourselves as innocent victims of the demonic rituals of the dark masters behind the curtain.

So, given the world we live in today, the ever-more intense and strange events we are forced to face, and the many unanswered questions driving us, is it any wonder that the mind runs its reflexive scapegoating program? Can we really begrudge the worldview conspiracy theorists prefer to believe: that a nefarious cabal of sinister actors (not the 1%; more like the 1/10th or 1/100th of 1%) are executing demonic rituals of black magic against us all—the innocent and unwitting human race?

Now really, if we are honest with ourselves, how is the above image really any different from the classic Judeo-Christian belief that external evil forces (The Devil, Satan, evil spirits, etc.) are conspiring to control and enslave us?

Modern day conspiracy is in many ways just a degeneration of the externalized explanation of satanic influence as the source of evil in the world, in the same way that PTSD is a degeneration of the externalized term *battle fatigue*. But wait a minute...the original term was *shellshock*, you say? That means that the externalized satanic myth is itself an example of entropy. Satan as an external scapegoat represents an elaboration, degeneration, distortion. It is an externalized story which simultaneously offers a version of events *close enough* to the Truth while allowing us to evade and avoid comprehending the hard objective facts.

Figure 10: The Devil's Puppet Show

Shellshock! The Hidden Forces of Evil are *In Here*

This is really no secret. Face it, dear reader: people who commit what we judge as acts of evil can only do so because it is within them to do so. It is the nature of mind, in fact, to divide and conquer. Therefore, everything that conspiracy theorists accuse the master criminals behind the curtain of doing is only possible because it is within them to do so. And if we are truly honest with ourselves—that is, we observe ourselves with our free consciousness and listen to the Still Soft Voice of our own conscience—we realize that we are not the innocent victims of some externalized source of evil. In fact, we are all culpable in the very conspiracies we claim to be victims of.

Right now your mind may be raging. Observe that. Watch how your ego-mind reacts. Are you free to think as you choose, really? Are you free to believe what you want, Truly? If your mind is reacting against the facts, there is only one possible conclusion: your ego-mind is refusing to allow you to see things as they are. And if your mind is reacting negatively to the fact that the ego-mind is the source of all evil in the world, it is probably telling you all sorts of stories about us, and about this book—judging, condemning, possibly plotting a verbal attack or trolling review, or any number of reactions to being *shellshocked* (confronted with the painful reality of humanity's condition). If your ego is reacting to shellshock, it is actively raging (like the alpha bull threatened by a rival), butting heads against what it deems an opposing set of beliefs, jumping from thought to thought in search of formulating some intellectual solution to satisfy the pain of facing reality as it is and wanting to water down the essence of reality with a concept like PTSD. Lifeless, heartless, but technically accurate, intellectually satisfying, and ultimately *ego empowering.*

Take a moment to contemplate that: ego empowering. This is the ultimate endgame of the conspiracy of conspiracies...the goal of the internal cabal known as ego-mind and the function of this thing we call thinking. Beliefs are a means by which ego uses the mind to empower itself, gain control over our consciousness, entrench its foothold in the driver's seat of our psyche, and galvanize its stranglehold over our lives. The ego-mind is what enslaves us—and by extension, all of humanity. And it does so by convincing us that we are *awake, red-pilled,* even as it hypnotizes us with theoretical illusions of seeing behind conspiracies enslaving humanity *out there.*

Figure 11: Evil in the World – What your ego-mind believes; what your conscience knows.

The Devil's Trick

Charles Baudelaire once said, "the finest trick of the devil is to persuade you that he does not exist." You may be more familiar with the contemporary version of this sentiment, expressed by Keyser Soze in *The Usual Suspects,* "The greatest trick the Devil ever pulled was convincing the world he didn't exist." To this your mind may protest, "but many people do believe in the devil." Yes, many do. But as we pointed out, they believe in a degenerated, watered-down externalized story of Satan. A literal interpretation of what was always a symbol, an allegory for our own ego. They believe in something which allows them to avoid the pain and suffering which come with having to be responsible for their defects and vices. They avoid the uncomfortable Truth by transforming shame into anger via a comforting belief in a scapegoat which is safely *out there.*

But this is, in fact, not what people used to believe and understand about themselves. In the past, many symbols and allegories were used to express the essence of the reality about the state of our psyche. And if you check in with your conscience, you can directly experience and know the facts on which these symbols and allegories were based. Perhaps the most well-known in the West are *the seven deadly sins:*

- Fear
- Lust
- Pride
- Wrath
- Covetousness (greed & envy)
- Gluttony
- Sloth

To this day, we often refer figuratively to the demons in our minds. And that we must learn to battle our demons, etc. Occasionally, when our demons get the better of us in the heat of the moment, and we do something we later regret, we might say, "What possessed me to do that!?" Sometimes, we can witness what G.I. Gurdieff called "the terror of the situation:"

Video 17: Apocalypse Now: Marlon Brando Horror Speech
(YouTube)

The *Devil's Trick* (Satan, the ego) is to convince us that he does not exist *in here…* inside of each one of us. And the ego accomplishes this in the manner we have described throughout this chapter: by *scapegoating.* Intellectualizing, theorizing, externalizing, blaming, judging, projecting, avoiding, and distracting our consciousness from the hard, uncomfortable, painful Truth.

So maybe now your mind is protesting: "but we all know we have an ego and a mind!" Yes, we all do, but do we know that we have more than one ego? Are we aware that we have *many egos*—plural? Are we conscious of how the multitude of egos (lust, vanity, fear, pride, shame, greed, ambition, anger, etc.) form the building blocks which the ego-mind uses to construct a false sense of self? Are we aware of how the ego-mind has convinced us that we are it; that it is us? Do we know that the never-ending cacophony of our busy mind is the hard evidence of many countless egos playing a kind of *Game of Thrones* in our psyche, each one a self-interested mechanical entity executing its program to reap the spoils of sitting upon the *Iron Throne?*

When the ego-mind convinces us that we are it, and it is us, and everything one might call *evil* is chalked up by intellectual rationalism as just *human nature,* it is in those precise moments we are convinced that *the devil* does not exist. But it is not enough to know this intellectually. It must be known directly, experientially, consciously. And so long as we are trapped in thoughts, led by the divide-and-conquer binary thinking of ego-mind, our attention is split into many directions. We are left chasing many rabbits down many holes, and we deny ourselves the concentration and relaxation required to focus on the inner workings of our own psyche. Maybe you have heard of the phenomenon known as ADD/ADHD? Perhaps you or someone you know has been diagnosed with it. We are hypnotized by beliefs, so distracted by what we think we know, our ability to focus on the present moment, our experience, and what we Truly know is, in effect, divided and conquered. Diluted and sanitized. The hard Truth is lost in the cacophony of soft language chattering ceaselessly in our heads.

Allegory of *Humpty Dumpty* and Humanity's *Great Fall*

In the annals of Western culture, fairy tales and nursery rhymes are among the least understood literary traditions. These timeless and endearing fables filled with universal Truths have been relegated to little more than quaint children's stories. Like all legends and myths, their deep metaphysical insights are lost on the intellectual machinations of the rational mind. Nowhere is this fact more evident than in the tale of *Humpty Dumpty,* in which a pair of rhyming couplets allegorically reveal the most fundamental and universal phenomenon of the human condition(ed), which we have been elucidating on throughout this chapter. Just how do egos go about their work of dividing and ruling our consciousness? Let us use our *conscious imagination* and SEEK the answer together, dear reader.

Imagine ourselves as Humpty Dumpty, sitting on the wall.

> *Humpty Dumpty sat on a wall.*
> *Humpty Dumpty had a great fall.*
> *All the King's horses and all the King's men*
> *Couldn't put Humpty Dumpty back together again.*

We begin with "a wall," which, in very real and practical terms, represents the border separating *over here* from *over there.* Sitting atop the wall means we, like Humpty Dumpty, are whole, able to see both sides of the wall with complete clarity. You know, by your own experience, that this is objectively True about the nature of any wall. From this superior vantage point, we have a comprehensive overview of both sides. We experience *comprehension:* able to know the whole of any binary dialectic: black *and* white, us *and* them, right *and* wrong, good *and* evil. We do not deny the existence of the dialectic (the wall separates two phenomena), but we are on the wall, not unlike being *beyond the Tao.* Humpty Dumpty is an egg, of course. Meaning he is not yet *hatched*—not yet *born.* Imagining ourselves in his shoes, we comprehend we exist in a state of pure *potentiality.* An egg atop a wall is also a symbol of *fertility.* A fertilized egg, straddling both sides of the wall, represents the union of masculine *and* feminine, the creative law of the universe: the Law of Three. The creative law of the universe has been expressed in countless symbols and allegories, many of which are universal in the ancient world. But the single, universal, unquestionable expression of the Law of Three present on every level of life is *sex.*

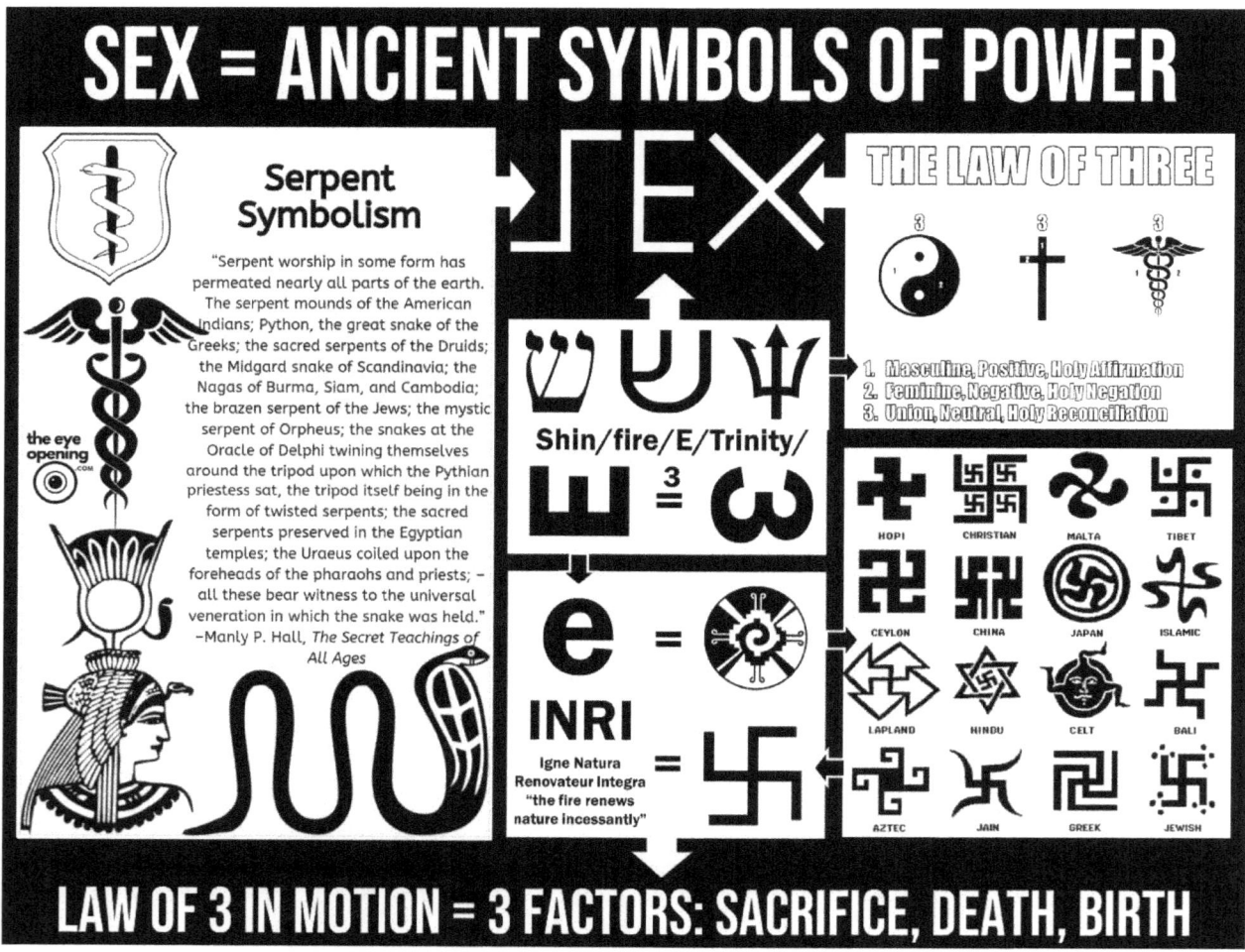

Figure 12: Sex – Universal Symbols of the Serpent, the Law of Three, and the Three Factors

Humpty Dumpty has "a great fall." Imagining ourselves falling from a wall, we have but two alternatives, and either way we find ourselves on one side or the other, a wall separating us from the other side. We can no longer know comprehensively. We are *trapped* on one side of the wall or the other, our consciousness *fallen,* ignorant of the other side. Our place atop the wall gave us a comprehensive overview, beyond the trappings of the dialectic. Young and innocent (just an egg), we existed in our own veritable *Eden* perched on that wall. So, the "great fall" of Humpty Dumpty is the exact same allegory as *The Fall* of Adam and Eve from the Garden of Eden: succumbing to the temptation of lust, the mother of all desire, whose indulgence creates the dialectic of craving and aversion ("I want this; I don't want that") and all dogmatic binary thinking in the mind: "I believe this; I don't believe that"). Like Adam and Eve, now trapped on either side of the wall—craving or aversion; pleasure or pain; belief or disbelief—bereft of our innocence, we are mired in desire, *expelled from the Garden, cast out into the wilderness of suffering a dialectic existence.* What is more, we have lost our precious vantage point of conscious comprehension. We see our side of the wall and fear whatever might be on the other side. Our consciousness has fallen asleep. Humpty Dumpty's great fall is the tragic hero's fall from grace recounted in every Greek and Shakespearean tragedy, high opera, *Faust,* and countless other great works of art, literature, theatre, and music. It is the recurring theme of ascending and descending Jacob's Ladder as seen in Dante Alighieri's *Divine Comedy.* And it is the symbolic falling and rising in Christopher Nolan's *Dark Knight Trilogy.* All this, embodied in only the first rhyming couplet.

"All the King's horses and all the King's men" refer to the multitude of animal intellectual elements of our false self, each ego holding a fragment of Humpty Dumpty in hand. The *King's horses* represent our primal animal instincts and desires. While the *King's men* represent the many voices in our head. They are the "Kings" because they represent the forces by which the kingdom is ruled. In Eden, *God* rules. The moment Adam and Eve listened to the serpent's temptations of becoming *like the gods, knowing both good and evil,* they fell from the Garden of Eden and were cast into the wilderness. The wilderness is ruled by *kings*…personalities believing themselves to be *godlike.* But kings are *false gods*—or, more aptly put, *false idols.* So, while we might expect egos to serve us, they, in fact, serve *our false god.* Fear, lust, pride, greed, etc.—each of our many *horses and men* holds a fragment of our splintered and shattered consciousness. That small fragment of consciousness is their source of influence. And because each ego is competing for our attention, adulation, and indulgence, in accordance with its mechanical programming, none have any incentive to restore/reunite our consciousness. They instead play a *Game of Thrones,* jockeying for a place on the *Iron Throne*—the King's symbolic seat of power from which he rules. Every time an ego deposes another and ascends to the throne, it announces its succession with "I want / I am / I believe this" or "I don't want / I am not / I don't believe that." As we identify with and indulge each "I," presenting itself in the never-ending stream of succession in our psyche, *we are being ruled.* The King's horses and men—our egos—rule our kingdom. Rule us. We are our own worst enemy. Not some imaginary scapegoat *out there.* Least of all, some personified external *Satan.*

Who creates egos? *We do.* Each time we fall. Moment by moment. Lifetime to lifetime. Every time we give in to desire and listen to the voices in our head instead of the Still Soft Voice in our heart, we empower our ego. We create more egos. Perhaps you have heard the tale of two wolves?

> *An old Cherokee is teaching his grandson about life. "A fight is going on inside me," he said to the boy. "It is a terrible fight, and it is between two wolves. One is evil – he is anger, envy, sorrow, regret, greed, arrogance, self-pity, guilt, resentment, inferiority, lies, false pride, superiority, and ego."*
>
> *He continued, "The other is good – he is joy, peace, love, hope, serenity, humility, kindness, benevolence, empathy, generosity, truth, compassion, and faith. The same fight is going on inside you – and inside every other person, too."*
>
> *The grandson thought about it for a minute and then asked his grandfather, "Which wolf will win?"*
>
> *The old Cherokee simply replied, "The one you feed."*
>
> *– Source: MoveMeQuotes.com, Story of Two Wolves*

When we fall and break Humpty Dumpty into ever smaller pieces, we hand them to even more horses and more men. That is, we feed fragments of our consciousness to the dark wolf, who gets even stronger. And the stronger he gets, the more his hunger grows. You know this. It is self-evident in your experience. Simply observe yourself satiating desire. How long does that desire remain satisfied? Does its appetite not return with a vengeance? And the more our egos desire, the louder and more emphatic their efforts to divide and rule us via the dialectic of craving and aversion expressed in our heart, mind, and body:

> *I want / I am / I believe this;*
> *I don't want / I am not / I don't believe that.*

Humpty Dumpty—the simple, whole, conscious, comprehensive self—falls victim to the agents of entropy—egos. Consciousness splintered, our comprehension is usurped by more complicated, technical, broken-down, and carefully *labeled* concepts in the ego mind, defined in ever more detail. Like *shellshock* degenerating into *PTSD,* conscious comprehension of our True Self devolves into fragmented, subjective, intellectual machinations of the false self. Like Humpty Dumpty, our superior vantage point atop the wall and potential to develop into a godlike being is shattered when we fall under the rule of all the King's horses and all the King's men—the false gods of the ego-personality.

Our ego-mind would have us believe that this process of intellectualization and creating ever more complicated concepts of ourselves is evolution. That feeding the strong, dark, animalistic wolf within is *survival of the fittest.* It is just the opposite. It is devolution. Simplicity is the ultimate in sophistication.

Breaking down that which is simple, whole, and working into constituent parts may lead to your thinking you understand what it is and how it works, when in fact it no longer works! Consider an amateur mechanic

Link 6: Image Carousel – Anakin Skywalker sat on a wall...
(Instagram)

who tears down an engine for the first time. It is easy and fun to tear an engine down. It is something else altogether to try and put one back together again such that it will be in working order. It is more than likely that what gets reassembled is a *Frankensteinian abomination*...something that resembles Darth Vader, whom Obi-Wan Kenobi described as "more machine than man." Serendipitously, we created an Instagram slideshow as an homage to *Humpty Dumpty* for the premiere of our YouTube documentary, *Star Wars – The Skywalker Apocalypse*.

The practical way in which we disassemble self-evident experiential knowledge (conscious knowing) and hand pieces of our consciousness to egos and intellectual concepts in the mind is through *identification*. We self-identify with the pain we are feeling, the suffering, the desires, the thoughts, feelings, and beliefs we have. We say: "I am _____."

> *I am my body.*
> *I am my name.*
> *I am my gender.*
> *I am my sexual orientation.*
> *I am my race.*
> *I am my nationality.*
> *I am my beliefs.*
> *I am my politics.*
> *I am my dreams.*
> *I am my desires.*
> *I am lustful, hungry, thirsty, exhausted, angry, upset, sad, depressed, proud (or ashamed), stressed, et al.*
> *I am... I am... I am...*

With every externalized concept/label we identify with, each *"I am..."* we identify as another piece of our consciousness that gets bottled up inside that concept/label. Yet, it is only through a more simple, so-phisticated conscious comprehension that we really know reality and who we truly are. Remember, shellshock is closer to the essential experience of the reality of the condition than PTSD. Love is knowable through the heart but can neither be understood by the rational mind nor described precisely in language.

> *All the King's horses and all the King's men*
> *Couldn't put Humpty Dumpty back together again.*

The King's horses and King's men of the false self cannot piece together who we truly are. So, who are we then?

Eheyeh Asher Eheyeh...I Am that I Am

In antiquity, Eheyeh Asher Eheyeh (I Am that I Am) is known as the Holy Name of God. When we practice mindfulness (self-observation and self-remembering), we identify not as the mind, heart, or body we observe, nor the thoughts, emotions, or sensations we are observing, but as the observer. We are who we are. Whole, complete, one with the still point of the moment and all things. The zero-point of absolute nothingness. We are just temporarily assuming the form of a body, name, gender, sexual orientation, etc. (as we have done many times before). We are simply experiencing lust, hunger, thirst, exhaustion, anger, etc. But we are not those things. Put another way, being is the one constant at any given moment. One cannot Truthfully say "I am angry" one moment, "I am sad" the next, "I am happy" the next since one cannot Truthfully be any of those emotions. One can say, "I *feel* angry. I feel sad. I feel happy." In Truth, we are *being mindful* of *how* we feel. In the same way that the weather is always the weather, be it sunny, raining, snowing, or whatever, so too our True nature is as unchanging, unflinching, and undefinable in crude, limiting, reductionist terms as any fleeting report or provisional forecast.

Have you noticed that forecasts and reports seem to be the only things the ego-mind concerns itself with? The future or the past. While hypnotized by the mind, we are either worried about forecasts of the days, weeks, months, and years to come or obsessing over reports from hours, days, weeks, months, or even years ago. "What's going to happen!?" And "Oh my God, what just happened!?" "What will they think of me?" And "what did they think of me?" Whereas the Truth of the matter is, at any given point in time, like the weather, things just are. It is what it is, and that is all. There is no future. There is no past. There are no labels. These are literally just concepts in the mind. Illusions, delusions, more made-up stories, and con-spiracy theories about what will happen and what has happened because, in Truth, the mind is never actually present in the moment. Observe yourself. You can never actually get the mind to function in the moment of *now.* As soon as you attempt to think about *now,* it is already passed, it is already *then.* And if you try to be clever and get your mind out in front of *now,* you cannot do it because your mind is in *soon, not yet,* or perhaps *not ever.* So, if the mind cannot know reality directly, what can?

What we SEEK

Consciousness is the faculty that can know the True nature of our Self, egos, and all phenomena, moment by moment, including our intuition, insights, visions, thoughts, emotions, and sensations. Consciousness is the faculty that can experience reality as it is each moment, from one moment to the next here and now. Expressed another way, consciousness is the medium of experience. We must consciously SEEK self-evident experiential knowledge—gnosis, the Greek word for direct conscious knowing—which is the only antidote to the hypnosis and ignorance of ego-mind. In simple terms, it is via consciousness that we can Truly know reality comprehensively and objectively.

Consciousness is not and cannot be a product of ego-mind. The Descartes axiom, "I think therefore I am," is one of the most heinous and preposterous delusions of ego-mind ever perpetrated on humanity. It has trapped generations in the prison of rationality, subjectivity, moral relativism, and the false self. The Truth is, "*I am;* therefore, I know." And while being in self-knowledge includes knowing what we think, being is not a product of thinking. We must be before we can think. But we do not have to think. Ask an extreme athlete, a martial arts expert, a ballerina, a meditator, a master craftsperson, or anyone doing anything *in the moment* or *in the zone.* They will tell you that the second they allow their mind to start thinking about what they are doing, in that instant, it all starts to go wrong. You cannot think your way through backflips on a dirt bike, mid-air 360s on a snowboard, or flying dragon kicks in a sparring match…the split second you do, you are done.

The ego-mind wants to keep us in its make-believe world of future and past to keep us distracted from the one thing our ego wants to convince us does not exist: the Self. The ego-mind hypnotizes the one faculty that serves our True Self's need to know the nature of itself and reality—consciousness—to distract us from the real meaning and purpose of life. To be, to know the "I Am that I Am," which only pure awareness leads us to: our True Self and our true purpose for being. So long as we are caught up in the machinations of the mechanical, rational ego-mind, our consciousness remains fragmented in the hands of all the King's horses and all the King's men, who cannot put Humpty Dumpty back together again. In such a shattered state, we cannot Truly be whole. We remain trapped in *not being.* Lost in the wilderness of suffering, ruled by the false self, ignorant of the will of our True Self, unaware of our reason for being.

We are here to express the pure light of love emanating from the zero-point of absolute nothingness within us and to know all the myriad forms and expressions such light, love, peace, beauty, compassion, and sacrifice can take through our efforts and those of others: high art, music, True science, philosophy, nature, the universe, and all beings. We are here to know ourselves in all the forms our True Self can be known. Not in the mind but in the heart via awakened consciousness. To know ourselves and all phenomena simply as they are. This is the simple, elegant, whole Truth that the conspiracy of conspiracies keeps us from knowing.

Elementary: **The Truth is in You (and *Out There,* Too)**

Do not take our word for it, dear reader. Do not fall prey to the propaganda of *The X-Files:* "I want to believe." SEEK self-evident experiential knowledge of the Truth being shared here directly, consciously, for yourself. Observe yourself. Know yourself. Become an intrepid explorer and conscious investigator of your own inner worlds. Observe how your ego-mind messes with you and fragments your wholeness and comprehensive knowing by interjecting *devilish details*. Observe how cravings, aversions, and countless identifications with concepts and attachments to beliefs end up dividing and conquering your consciousness. Observe how one second you want one thing (like a bag of chips), and then the second you have finished it, you now want the exact opposite thing (like not having eaten a whole bag of chips!) What the hell is that if not a kind of hell? Have you ever seen a cat play with a mouse? Observe your mind playing with your attention. You can verify all this for yourself.

The Devil, Satan, for lack of a better name, is real. They are the demons, egos, sins, nafs, psychological aggregates, memes, psychic malware—or by whatever name—in your thoughts, in your emotions, and in the cravings and aversions in your body—*all the King's horses and all the King's men.*

Elementary, dear reader: cracking the conspiracy of conspiracies is within your grasp, and a Great Detective is waiting inside you to help guide you in your investigations. But every great detective needs a sidekick. Sherlock Holmes is the one who sees things and knows things. Holmes is our consciousness. His sidekick, Watson, is the one who does the muscle work and must 'think things through.' Watson represents our body and mind. Only by working together can Holmes and Watson battle to defeat the forces of evil—the criminal mastermind and Holmes's arch-nemesis—Dr. Moriarte, the Devil incarnate…our ego.

The conspiracy of conspiracies has been encoded in all scripture, mythology, art, legend, and literature since the dawn of time. From nursery rhymes and fairy tales to scriptures and myths, the signs pointing us toward the great conspiracy of the world and the keys needed to unlock the prison of said conspiracy have been given to us in countless forms. It is the ego-mind and the law of entropy that corrupts and degenerates all that is pure and whole and capable of expressing the essence of Truth comprehensively. Until what we end up with are countless splintered camps arguing and fighting over the details of their illusory versions of subjective reality. Lifeless. Heartless.

We sincerely hope after reading this, you are that much closer to knowing the Truth for yourself, through your Self, and by yourself, dear reader. But every hero needs a little help. And if you have your doubts about turning to an organization or online resource like Glorian.org, maybe you can start with someone who seems like an honest, trusted source. Someone who maybe reminds you of your grandmother (or someone's grandmother), such as in the video below:

Video 18: Putting the Ego in Its Place: The Inner Revolution, with Beth Green (YouTube)

Before diving deeper into the question of what ego actually is…

Link 7: What is ego? (Glorian.org)

This begs the question: if egos are mechanical AI entities that serve the law of entropy as it relates to human-made phenomena, and the law of entropy is absolute and unavoidable in mechanical nature, then are the effects of ego-separation, complication, degeneration—and the results of entropy—destruction— not *inevitable?* If even granite rock erodes and breaks down, if even great religions fade and great empires fall, where does that leave humanity? **If *the Conspiracy of Conspiracies* were a real phenomenon, surely, we would be able to see it in action, affecting our civilization and the world.** Egos may be *in here,* but if they work for mechanical nature, there must be evidence of their entropic effects *out there,* too.

What can Thanos, Gandhi, Derrida, and The Underminer teach us about SJWs, passive aggression, mechanical nature—particularly the law of entropy—and the ultimate no-win scenario?

To Infinity and Beyond Menacing

In science fiction and fantasy—as in mythology—we often encounter the archetype of the uber-villain, the invincible monster, the doomsday weapon, the unstoppable force, the immovable object, you name it. This certainly appeared to be the case in part one of the two-part film *The Avengers: Infinity War*, and the all-powerful Infinity Gauntlet wielded by the single-minded, seemingly unbeatable antagonist, Thanos (un-defeatable, so long as he wore the gauntlet).

Part of what makes Thanos so dangerous and menacing is precisely that he is not some moustache-twirling villain. He believes what he is doing is in the service of the universe. And, rather than raising an army, conquering and creating an empire, or gathering some coalition of the willing to back him in his psychotic plan, he sort of sneaks around behind the scenes (or has his cronies/lackeys do it for him), stealing the gauntlet, gathering the infinity stones, betraying allies and loved ones alike, vanquishing the odd super-hero along the way, all in pursuit of one singular overwhelming purpose: *self-righteousness.*

Thanos does not merely believe intellectually he is right. He believes wholeheartedly that he is in the right. He is convinced he stands on the right side of history, nature, balance, the very universe itself. He believes he holds the moral, ethical, and philosophical high ground. And what is most alarming is the fact his belief—that he single-mindedly pursues, all other considerations be damned—was born out of his direct experience. His psychotic plan to restore balance and sustainability to a universe of finite resources by wiping out half of all life *appears* to Thanos as self-evident experiential knowledge—what we all SEEK in life. In revealing his origin-story and childhood trauma (wherein his home planet was destroyed due to overpopulation and exhaustion of all its natural resources), we are given an opportunity to pause and empathize with the uber-villain. Does the phrase *there but for the grace of God go I* ring a bell?

Figure 13: Super villain Thanos - Source: ShreePNG.com

Who are we to judge Thanos? Psychotic, sure. Traumatized, clearly. But would we have come to any different conclusion were we to have walked a mile in his shoes? Seriously: consider you had witnessed the destruction of your planet under the same circumstances and foresaw a way you could circumvent and prevent such destruction throughout the known universe? Think of all the suffering you could prevent! Of course, you would have to rationalize away the fact that your alleged altruistic solution involves mass genocide on a cosmic scale. However, after reading *Part One* of this book, watching our YouTube video *The Hard Truth About Belief*, and especially after observing yourself, you will know how subtle, clever, and hypnotic the ego-mind can be in this regard. How effectively the ego-mind weaves a complex and convincing narrative around kernels of Truth such that the erroneous subjective belief inherits the consideration warranted by the underlying objective Truth.

This is exactly the force of power behind Thanos's single-minded resolve. He cannot deny his experience. He believes he knows what fate awaits everyone based on that experience. Having witnessed the fate of an overtaxed planet and unfettered exploitation of natural resources, he would spare the universe the trauma he endured. His traumatized ego constructs an elaborate rationalization and plan around his experience, exploiting both his suffering and compassion. Built upon a foundation of fundamental Truths which cannot be denied and fashioned around fundamental qualities of consciousness, such beliefs are at once the most powerful, dangerous, and challenging to escape. They are behind the strongest cognitive dissonance, the most toxic relationships, and deadliest outcomes. Thanos sees himself as the arbiter of deadly outcomes. In this sense, he has a *death complex*.

The name *Thanos* most closely resembles *Thanatos*, the Greek god of death.

Video 19: The Untold Truth of Thanos
(YouTube)

In the comics, Thanos is obsessed with death. He destroys the universe but harbors a self-defeating victim mentality of not being worthy of death or the task appointed to him. It is both fitting and ironic that *SJW Marvel* would have chosen the universe's most powerful victim as the ultimate villain of its *Avengers* trilogy. The comic book publisher which has been criticized by long-time fans as of late for becoming a little too politically correct for its own good, has gone and shown us their hand. And if you have not started piecing it together yet, dear reader, rest assured by the end of this analysis, you will clearly see the connection between Thanos, the *woke* movement, passive aggression, the winning strategy / no-win scenario they all share, and what it all means for you. Specifically, how it all ties into *the Great A-Weakening.*

Fist Shaken, Gauntlet Cast Down, and the Hand of God

Where symbolism is concerned, this seems straightforward enough. The downtrodden, the traumatized, the victim feels first and foremost powerless. How many characters throughout history (let alone people) have shook their fist at the heavens in defiance of the fates and proclaimed the equivalent of, "Oh Father! Why have you forsaken me!?"

Surely, we have all experienced such moments of defeat, of forlorn weakness, on the verge of utter oblivion, to one degree or another. What is more, it is often precisely in such moments that we found it within ourselves to bend down and pick up the proverbial gauntlet which was cast down at our feet (the medieval sign of accepting a knight's errand, most notably the challenge of a rival knight). We pick up that gauntlet and strangely feel empowered, with naught but our willpower. No plan, no resources, no clear way forward. Just this inner knowing that this is not the end but a new beginning. A new enterprise. A new journey. A new adventure. A *mission impossible* which we choose to accept…*The Hero's Journey.* And we, whether we realize it or not, are now that gauntlet on the hand of God. Whatever it was which made us momentarily feel downtrodden, victimized, and defeated happened for a reason. Not to make us feel *forsaken*—although it is perfectly understandable and acceptable to feel that way. After all, even Jesus experienced a moment of such emotion hanging on the cross. Rather, the purpose for such moments of overwhelming defeat is to help us dig deep within ourselves and find the Source of unlimited strength and willpower needed to bend down, pick up that gauntlet, and rise to the challenge.

Thanos certainly feels this way. Many have felt this way. But when Jesus, the classical knights of legend, and the great heroes of myth accepted the challenge the Heavens gave them, they abandoned all thought of victimhood and surrendered to *their fate* (the Will of their Innermost Being; the Will of God their Father), and in doing so became God's agent in the world to do some great work of Light, Love, and Liberation. Driven by the unseen, unheard hand of God, they applied great willpower in the face of *the slings and arrows of outrageous fortune…to be…*literally the gauntlet on God's right hand. The expression *God's right hand* relates to The Christ, the Son of God, who sits on His right hand—*Chokmah* on the Tree of Life of Kabbalah. We accept our place: to be the vessel who suffers and sacrifices to do God's work in the world. This is the authentic hero's journey. This is the only way to be *in the right*: to be the gauntlet on the right hand of God. To be in service to our Innermost Intimate Christ.

On the other hand, Thanos only *believes* he is walking the path of an authentic hero. He has convinced himself he is acting in the best interests of the Universe (which we can use as a stand-in for the omnipotent and omnipresent God—His Creation and all His children). But Thanos is supposed to be the villain, right? Wrong. There is absolutely no doubt that Thanos is the star and the focus of *Infinity War*. It is Thanos's story. This makes him much more than just a villain, especially given that he sees himself as the hero.

The Infinity Gauntlet, the Raised Fist of Power, and the Left-Hand Path

What makes a *tragic hero?* Better expressed, what makes a hero tragic? Exactly one moment. A choice. A slip on a banana peel. *The fall.* In all literary history and mythology, this is the universal constant in tragic heroes: they are *flawed.* Something inside them causes them not only to fall but sets them on the downward spiral of destruction and suffering. From Oedipus and Macbeth to Faust and Anakin Skywalker and every character in between, tragic heroes captivate us precisely because they are not cartoonish villains. They are, for all intents and purposes, *real.* Regardless of the story, setting, or period, the challenges they face are relatable—their flaws are *universal.* The challenges and temptations they encounter are identifiable and familiar. Their *tragic flaw* is known by all. They are archetypal characters, universal at their core, expressed according to the idiosyncrasies of the people and culture in which they appear in literature, theatre, opera, mythology, scripture, et al.

The great figure—a noble character possessing great potential, with many strengths, qualities, and abilities—is thwarted and doomed to a precipitous fall into hell. Why? Because in the face of a great trial, set forth for them by the fates, they choose not to accept the challenge to be the Right Hand of God—follow the Will of their Innermost Being, their True Self, their Innermost Intimate Christ. Instead, they choose to shake their fist at the heavens, at God Himself, in defiance of the fates. The tragic hero chooses their egos' ambitions and desires over what is right. They listen only to the voices in their head trumpeting "myself, my plan, my way, *my truth"* drowning out the Still Soft Voice of their Innermost Being—my Self, our purpose, the way, *the Truth.* And while the tragic hero might turn from the path of righteousness out of spite, it is often not without some self-reflection and considerable time sitting on the fence—like Humpty Dumpty atop the wall. Like Macbeth.

Macbeth struggles with his decision. It is only because of the temptations of the three Witches and the goading and ridicule of Lady Macbeth that he goes through with the murder of King Duncan. But here we must take note: the three Sisters / Witches represent the *three traitors* which feature throughout literature, mythology, and scripture. These include the three furies, three traitors of Hiram Abif, and the three traitors of Jesus Christ (Judas, Caiaphas, and Pilot). They all symbolize the three brains of the human machine—the mind, heart, and body. According to Homer, it is the furies (Erinyes) "that under the earth take vengeance on men, whosoever hath sworn a false oath" (Homer, *Iliad, 259-260*). In other words, the aspects of our *hume* (earthly aspect of *human*) through which we experience suffering when serving the interests of our false self. When we fall from the wall, we must choose sides, and Macbeth chooses the side of the feminine, since it is ultimately the most powerful feminine figure in his life who convinces him to get off the fence and go through with the murder. Lady Macbeth represents the fallen feminine aspect of the psyche. She is Eve in *Genesis,* and the infamous *Whore of Babylon.* These figures are not meant to be understood literally as women, as the feminist movement has incorrectly presumed. We all have masculine and feminine energetic channels within us, regardless of our gender. It is simply a metaphysical fact that in our humanity it is the feminine channel which is fallen. Our egos tempt us primarily through the feminine polarity in our psyche—through any number of our three brains. The feminine polarity is primarily oriented to nature, nurture, and survival—as individuals and as a species. By appealing to primal animal instincts, our egos can rationalize every crime under the sun. Case in point: Lady Macbeth uses fear and lust. She accuses her husband of cowardice and questions his manhood (including his virility) to convince Macbeth to follow through with Duncan's murder.

In Mesopotamian and Judaic traditions, fear and lust are called Asmondeus and Lilith, the king and queen of all demons. All other egos—pride, greed, anger, gluttony, laziness—are extensions of these two primal survival egos. Fear focuses on the survival of the *individual.* Lust focuses the individual on *sowing their seed* to ensure the survival of *their bloodline* (and the species). Lust is the mother of all desire— cravings and aversions, pleasure and pain. Fear is the father of the 'need' to be in control—of comfort and security, circumstances, others, and outcomes. Lust employs sexual pleasure to literally control *outcomes.* Controlling outcomes to secure the comforts of pleasure and survival of the species is fear turned into a bear trap. The codependent and intimate relationship between fear and lust—the desire for control—is the primal, natural survival instinct of all beings. It is the dominant impulse acting from within this fallen humanity, motivating everyone from tyrants and the ruling elites to the masses content to exchange their freedom and dignity for comfort, security, and pleasure.

So, the mechanical, animal aspect of the feminine force embodies both self-preservation and the relentless drive to procreate. From this most fundamental aspect of *Mother Nature* is born not only all self-interest but also the harshest reactions in defense of self-interest. This is the origin of the expression *hell hath no fury as woman scorned.* Just consider the ferocity of a mother bear protecting her young. The intensity of angry parents defending their children. The violence of hurricane Katrina. The power of the Divine Feminine expressed through the mechanical, primal feminine force we personify as *Mother Nature* is without compare.

Is it any wonder that when we encounter acute threats to our comfort and security and/or experience pain, our reflexive fear-based reaction is one of *anger?* Naturally, we know this from our own experience. Anyone who has ever missed hammering a nail and struck their thumb instead can attest to how quickly pain becomes anger. Likewise, if you have ever lashed out at someone in a moment of self-defense, you know how easily fear turns into anger. Master Yoda warns Luke of the dangers of fear in *The Empire Strikes*

Back. "Fear is the path to the dark side. Fear leads to anger. Anger leads to hate. Hate leads to suffering." He elaborates,

> *Anger, fear, aggression; the dark side of the Force are they. Easily, they flow, quick to join you in a fight. If once you start down the dark path, forever will it dominate your destiny, consume you it will, as it did Obi-Wan's apprentice.*
>
> *– Yoda, The Empire Strikes Back*

The preservation instinct is triggered when we feel threatened, when we see others whom we identify with being threatened (i.e., *tribalism*), and when we take the fate of others into our own hands (i.e., *heroism, activism*). As Yoda warns, unfettered fear and anger lead to hatred and the dark side of human nature, even as the underlying preservation instinct rationalizes our hatred and justifies our actions in our mind—no matter how violent, harmful, or destructive. The preservation instinct is precisely what motivates Thanos. And through his *fist of power* (the Infinity Gauntlet he wields on his *left* hand), he literally unleashes not merely the fury of hell—*because hell hath no fury like it*—but rather the power of the Divine Feminine. Thanos unleashes the combined power of the five elements, symbolized by the five infinity stones, expressed not by the Right Hand of God but rather the *Left-Hand Path*, the primal path of angry, violent self-interest.

The Infinity Gauntlet requires five stones to become fully empowered. Each stone represents one of the five elements (fire, water, earth, air, ether), bound together by a sixth stone called *the soul gem*. Of course, the actual elements of reality are too mundane for the hyperbolic universe of comic books, so in place of them, we get *mind, reality, power, space,* and *time*. Anyone wielding the power of the Divine Feminine, not according to the Right Hand Path of God, wields the most destructive/creative force in the universe along the Left-Hand Path. The Divine Mother has the power to create and to destroy. The Divine Feminine is literally the power of life and death—the sexual force.

The symbolism here is the number six and the fact that the elements and soul are under the

Figure 14: Infinity Stones in Infinity Gauntlet

command of the wearer of the Infinity Gauntlet, in this case, Thanos. The five elements are the body and power of the Divine Feminine, and the soul represents the human soul, adding up to six. However, to become an *upright nine*, one less than a *perfect ten,* one step from being made truly in the image and likeness of God, a three must be added to the six. The human soul and the five elements are insufficient to be a True human being. We require the severity and mercy, knowledge and wisdom, Truth, Light, and Love of the Trinity. Without the intervention of the upper Trinity of the Tree of Life—Kether, Chokmah, Binah; Father, Son, Holy Spirit; Brahma, Vishnu, Shiva; the Tao; the Divine Masculine, Divine Feminine, and union of Divine Masculine and Feminine—we remain merely a six (6) instead of being an upright nine (9). A true hero is a *9-9-9*, an upright human being in each of their three brains: mind, heart, and body. But without the 3 of the upper Trinity, 9 remains 6. Instead of pointing up, the 9 is inverted, pointing down. The body and power of the Divine Mother is embodied in the Infinity Gauntlet upon the hand of the human soul. But without divine oversight, without being the gauntlet on the Right Hand of God, the 9 falls, literally turning into a 6. The fallen hero becomes a *tragic hero*, a *6-6-6,* an inverted intellectual animal possessed by self-interest, pleasure and pain, comfort and security, and the desire to control outcomes in each of his three brains. Is it any wonder 666 is *the number of the beast* in *Revelations?* 666 is the number of our false self, our individual Satan. And to follow Satan is to follow the Left-Hand Path. It is the path Thanos walks, wielding the power of the universe on his left hand. In classical tragedy, a six can become a nine only if the character can be turned back to the Right Path.

Opportunity for Revelation and Redemption

All tragic heroes are given some shot at revelation and redemption before they die. Being both archetypal and allegorical, they are the personification of some tragic flaw—an ego that dominates their character—mind, heart, and body (*6-6-6*). From the perspective of esoteric psychology, before any defect or vice can die, it must first be consciously comprehended. This is the nature of Plato's famous concept of *catharsis.* The notion that somehow the audience can, by living vicariously through this personification of some ego (pride, ambition, greed, victimhood, et al), purge themselves of said vice, the moment when the hero *sees the Light*—achieves conscious comprehension of their tragic flaw—*learns their lesson.* Metaphysically, it is following such revelation that our Divine Mother can eliminate an ego. This is known as psychological death and is symbolized by the subsequent death of the tragic hero. It is cathartic and redemptive because through the death of one psychological aggregate, the consciousness that was trapped within said aggregate is released and restored, and the character's soul is redeemed. *All the King's horses and all the King's men* cannot *put Humpty Dumpty back together again,* but our individual Divine Mother can. If, that is, the fragments of our consciousness can be liberated from our egos. Redemption can happen only through revelation—when we *learn our lesson* through self-observation, meditation, and comprehension of our defects and vices—when we see the Light and the error of our ways.

In terms of modern mythmaking, such a tragic hero is *Anakin Skywalker*. His is a tragic hero's journey whose story arc unfolds over the course of six *Star Wars* films—the original trilogy and the prequels. His redemption in *The Return of the Jedi* is perhaps one of the most profound about-faces in all cinematic history. The prerequisite revelation comes with the suffering and sacrifice of Luke Skywalker, Anakin's son, one of the most beloved characters in cinematic history. Luke casts aside his fear and anger, becoming the living embodiment of *hope*. Luke has faith that the spark of goodness he felt in Darth Vader will kindle a renewal of the Light Side of the Force within him, conquer the Sith Lord, and facilitate *The Return of the Jedi*. The esoteric significance of this moment cannot be overstated. It was not only a defining moment in pop culture but also in the lives of countless individuals who, to this day, revere the OG Star Wars films with religious devotion. So powerful was the catharsis felt by all those who connected deeply to the Skywalkers. In fairness, we cannot do justice to the deep spiritual and psychological significance of *Star Wars* here. However, if you wish to take a deep dive down that rabbit hole, dear reader, we will not leave you wanting. We produced a documentary video, nearly two-and-a-half-hours in length, available on YouTube, which explores all the ways in which *Star Wars* constitutes a modern mythology.

On the 40th Anniversary of *The Empire Strikes Back* and roughly six months after the release of *The Rise of Skywalker,* the time had come for an esoteric unveiling of the epic nine-film Skywalker Saga, which gave *Star Wars* fans, pundits, critics, and YouTubers alike *A New Hope* for their beloved mythology. A chance to see this entertainment franchise in a whole new light and re-examine any misgivings about the Disney Sequel Trilogy in light of the facts about *the Force* behind the whole of the Skywalker Saga. Since the word *apocalypse* means *revelation*, our video offers its own redemption arc for *Star Wars* fans, particularly those nostalgic for their beloved myth's heyday under Lucas and who lament the fall of the franchise under Disney. Our video is a chance for all concerned—creators and fans alike—to see *the galaxy far, far away* in a whole new light.

Video 20: Star Wars – The Skywalker Apocalypse
(YouTube)

Sadly, unlike Darth Vader/Anakin Skywalker, Thanos is not given an opportunity to see the light and the error of his ways. *Avengers Endgame* dispensed with Thanos without any revelation/redemption. So, Thanos's status as a tragic hero is never fully realized. His soul remains unredeemed. He does not wake up in *Endgame*. Shows no regret for descending into hell. Makes no attempt to ask for forgiveness. Never comprehends his tragic flaw. Robbed of his opportunity for revelation and redemption, he cannot be considered a genuine tragic hero. And we, the audience, are left with a hollow plot-point in a piece of entertainment instead of a cathartic experience in a work of high art. We remember Thanos only as a villain…a character with great potential left with an ultimately unfulfilling story arc. An aborted tragic hero's journey. From a modern mythmaking perspective, that is the real tragedy because Thanos showed all the signs of being a classic tragic hero in *Infinity War*.

Thanos does possess a tragic flaw: *pathological narcissism.* Vanity. Pride. Too much self-love. So much, in fact, that he cannot get over himself and his own suffering. This creates a god-complex within him. He projects his trauma onto the entire universe and then rationalizes his mission to protect said universe from his pain. That is the key. It is not the universe's suffering he cares about; it is his own suffering, intensified, magnified, and projected infinitely.

Thanos is a victim. And rather than letting go of his victim mentality as a hero would, he clings to it, fosters it, and projects it on a megalomaniacal scale unheard of in classic literature. Traditionally, one did not need to literally destroy half the universe to explore drama on a cosmic scale. One could tell the tale of the macrocosm through the microcosm. But again, we are dealing with the over-the-top world of blockbuster comic book movies here. So, Thanos takes matters into his own hands, quite literally playing God. Armed with the infinity stones, he wields the power of the Divine Mother, as a hurt child or scorned woman might—with a fury in his heart unmatched even by hell—controlling people, circumstances, and outcomes on a cosmic scale to cope with his trauma in the ultimate act of self-righteousness…*the snap.* A spiteful, psychotic, destructive path completely rationalized if ultimately utterly irrational. A downward spiral into hell, upheld by a perpetrator who sees himself as the hero of the story—lost in vanity, self-importance, pathological narcissism, and self-righteousness. Our analysis of Thanos should be ringing alarm bells where contemporary *woke culture* is concerned.

The Psychology of 'Woke'

By now, dear reader, we trust our in-depth exploration of Thanos has kindled sparks of familiarity relating to the title of this chapter. The modern *social justice warrior,* or SJW, thrives on self-righteous victimhood. Like Thanos, they have internalized some perceived wrong they have supposedly suffered at the hand of the dominant political identity (i.e., white heterosexual male patriarchy) and its alleged systemic racist, misogynist, homophobic, transphobic, and classist institutions—which may or may not include any number of religions signifying *the fates* and/or *the angry old bearded white guy in the clouds*. Next, just like Thanos, they identify their individual victimhood with that of the tribe and then project it onto the whole world. That is, onto some other related, suitably underprivileged, and perceived victimized political group in the macrocosm—identified by gender, race, sexual preference, body type, or some other politicized identity. Finally, like our proverbial Thanos, SJWs make it their mission to *empower themselves* and their self-identified victim group(s) by dismantling, *canceling,* and arbitrarily eliminating whatever *offensive* power structures they deem responsible for the perceived *injustice.* Without any thought whatsoever to the consequences of their actions, the woke mob have the single-mindedness to *play God* by wielding the destructive/creative force of the Divine Mother to tear down the old and remake their world (the whole universe in the case of Disney Star Wars, SJW Marvel, and many other entertainment properties which have been made woke) according to their own *utopian ideals.* Ideals which are, in no uncertain terms, staunch neo-Marxist beliefs masquerading as benign social activism. Neo-Marxist ideals that conjure fantasies of *structural perfection* in their minds, but whose inevitable Communist outcomes reveal the ruthless mechanical efficiency the android Ash admired so much about the xenomorph in *Alien:* "its structural perfection is matched only by its hostility."

And unfortunately for the rest of us, theirs is a winning strategy. Like Thanos in *Infinity War*, they are resolute—hell-bent on destruction (the more sophisticated among them might likely say *deconstruction,* but we will get into the post-modernist angle a little later). The woke movement represents an unstoppable force. A no-win scenario. At the end of the day, *you can't win 'em all*...or can you? More on that later. First, we must comprehend the esoteric foundations of woke psychology from the perspective of personal and political power struggles. We must comprehend the incessant and relentless driving forces at work within both individual SJW thinking and woke mob mentality.

Passive Aggression

The no-win scenario is real. And for evidence of this fact, one need only encounter an individual (SJW or not) who operates using the winning formula of *passive aggression.* Much has been said online about narcissism and passive aggression, and much of it is lukewarm at best. Here, we wish to unearth the True breadth and scope of this insidious modus operandi of self-righteous victimhood, including the esoteric (unseen, unheard) implications, from energy to karma to the inevitable fate of humanity. To do so, let us leave the fictional Thanos for a moment, dear reader, and in his place, turn to a real historical figure who is not only universally lauded the world over as a hero but is considered by many to be a veritable saint of the Twentieth Century. The figure whose followers and inner circle reverently referred to as *Bapu*, the *Mahatma* (Great Soul), who historians and fans recognize as *the father of nonviolence.*

Gandhi—Hero? Tragic Hero? Something else Entirely?

Here, dear reader, we recognize we are about to tread into dangerous—let alone contentious—waters. To even ask the question of such a universally popular and highly regarded figure as Mohandas Gandhi is tantamount to a kind of modern-day heresy. If you bear with us, dear reader, we will reveal publicly what no one else has—to the best of our knowledge at least—about the most highly regarded and celebrated *little man in the loin cloth from Calcutta* who took down the British Empire.

First, let us distinguish between the exoteric and esoteric levels of the concept of nonviolence.

> *Strictly speaking, satyagraha is not 'nonviolence.' It is a means, a method. The word we translate as 'nonviolence' is a Sanskrit word central in Buddhism as well: ahimsa, the complete absence of violence in word and even thought, as well as action. This sounds negative, just as 'nonviolence' sounds passive. But like the English word 'flawless,' ahimsa denotes perfection. Ahimsa is unconditional love; satyagraha is love in action. Gandhi's message.*
>
> *– Eknath Easwaran, Gandhi the Man: How One Man Changed Himself to Change the World*

So right away, there is a fundamental disconnect/misunderstanding at play. What the world understands as nonviolence—thanks to Gandhi—is not nonviolence at all. It means *unconditional love in action*. Flawless. This begs the question, **can perfect love ever be violent!?**

Several scenarios come to mind. First, *Shaolin Monks'* devotion and dedication to the development and mastery of self through *Kung-Fu*. Kung-Fu, like nonviolence, is misunderstood by the West, whose rational mind fails to look past the surface of martial arts. Kung-Fu, like satyagraha, is a method. And, like its Japanese cousin *Karate* ('empty hand'), that method is at its core non-lethal martial action. Held dogmatically, nonviolence will tell you to stand your ground and allow your assailant to land their blow. Should it be a fatal blow, that assailant is transformed into a killer—possibly even a murderer in the first degree. What karma do you suppose awaits them for their crime? On the other hand, a well-trained martial artist might block the killer blow. They may successfully subdue and disarm their assailant. A master of the art will do so without any malice, hatred, or inflicting lasting physical harm (that is, they will use non-lethal violence as a method to prevent any permanent consequences of violence). In doing so, the martial arts master not only saves themselves, but they save their assailant from becoming a killer and suffering the karmic consequences. Sure, the assailant's pride may be hurt, but in that moment of humiliation, subdued and disarmed, their consciousness may be shocked into a state of wakefulness, momentarily free of the grasp of pride, anger, and aggression. Observing their assailant experiencing a moment of lucidity, the master has an opportunity to instruct and guide their would-be killer. And in the tradition of Eastern martial arts, the master will certainly have earned the respect and possibly even gratitude of the assailant, now utterly aware of the reality of the situation. The formerly unarmed master now holds their weapon—and their life—in hand. The master could easily enact vengeance. But instead, he spares the life of the attacker. Who, having been thus bested with dignity and mercy, may welcome instruction from so skilled and wise a master. Consider, dear reader, who did the assailant a greater service of love? The man who passively allows themselves to be struck, possibly even killed, in the name of *nonviolence,* or the master who, with a balanced application of severity and mercy, disarms and then releases his assailant, winning his respect and sparing him the karma of becoming a killer? Remember, dear reader, what matters to the Great Law of Karma is *the end result.*

As a counterpoint, let us turn to that famous teaching of Jesus:

> *You have heard that it was said, an eye for an eye and a tooth for a tooth. But I tell you not to resist an evildoer. On the contrary, whoever slaps you on the right cheek, turn the other to him as well.*
>
> *– Matthew 5:38-39*

On the surface, this seems to contradict the actions of our Kung-Fu master, undoes the above explanation, and legitimizes the passivity of the dogmatic practitioner of nonviolence. Jesus's words might well be interpreted that way were it not for the many other quotes in the bible which clarify the point being made.

> *Say not thou, I will recompense evil, but wait on the Lord, and he shall save thee.*
>
> *– Proverbs 20:20*

Naturally, we know there is no Lord outside of us to wait on to save us. Our Lord is our Innermost Being, our True Self, the Innermost Intimate Christ—our individuated essence of God within. Whatever action our *intuition* tells us to take is the right one. Not *instinct,* mind you—the primal animal reaction to danger is fight, flight, freeze, or fawn—but intuition, which is not a reaction but a conscious response. To clarify, when slapped, it is practically a *reflex* to slap back. Primal. Animal. Mechanical. Egoic. If you have ever been slapped, you know this to be true. And if you have not, then perhaps the iconic scene between *Sam* and *Diane* from the season two finale of *Cheers* will illustrate just how reflexive slapping back is:

Video 21: Sam and Diane Slap Back and Forth
– End of Season 2 (YouTube)

It turns out the bible has much to say about returning blow for blow:

> **1 Thessalonians 5:15** Make sure that nobody pays back wrong for wrong, but always strive to do what is good for each other and for everyone else.
>
> **1 Peter 3:8-10** Finally, be ye all of one mind, having compassion one of another, love as brethren, be pitiful, be courteous: Not rendering evil for evil, or railing for railing: but contrariwise blessing; knowing that ye are thereunto called, that ye should inherit a blessing. For he that will love life and see good days, let him refrain his tongue from evil, and his lips that they speak no guile.
>
> **Romans 12:17** Do not repay anyone evil for evil. Be careful to do what is right in the eyes of everyone.

'Evil' is that action we are directed to commit by one or more egos—such as fear and/or anger. To not return evil for evil means not to react with ego to ego.

> **Romans 12:19** Beloved, never avenge yourselves, but leave it to the wrath of God, for it is written, "Vengeance is mine, I will repay, says the Lord."

The word 'vengeance' is, of course, contentious, but in the bible, the word does not mean *revenge*—that is, with anger and malice—as is commonly believed. It means precisely what the next phrase states: *to repay*. This is a clear reference to karma. We must pay what we owe. The Great Law will take care of wrongdoers. In the face of wrongdoing, it is not up to us to pay them back in kind.

> **Luke 6:27** But I say to you who are listening: Love your enemies. Do good to those who hate you.
>
> **Luke 6:35** Instead, love your enemies, do good to them, and lend to them, expecting nothing in return. Then your reward will be great, and you will be children of the Most High because he is kind even to ungrateful and evil people.

Matthew 5:44 But I say unto you, Love your enemies, bless them that curse you, do good to them that hate you, and pray for them which despitefully use you, and persecute you.

– Biblical Quotes Source: BibleReasons.com, Turning the Other Cheek

In synthesis, dear reader, whereas there is one literal quote about turning the other cheek when slapped (which is hardly a life-threatening attack), there are many more quotations advising us neither to react to ego with ego nor to seek *payback*. Rather, to put our response in the hands of our Innermost Lord and respond with His Love. If one were at all open-minded and conscious, one would understand all these quotes to be expressing the True definition of nonviolence—*unconditional love in action*.

In other words, to *turn the other cheek* is not a literal endorsement of dogmatic adherence to some literal understanding of nonviolence. When we use our conscious imagination to see ourselves being slapped, turning the other cheek is simply an instruction to resist the urge to slap back. Not to return blow for blow; not to react to ego with ego. In other words, adhering to the message contained in the other biblical quotes. It just so happens that meditating on turning the other cheek offers us a visceral, relatable, universal experiential knowledge of what to do and what not to do (slap back). Turn the other cheek is NOT to be interpreted or theorized. It is visceral, real, actionable. It is meant to be comprehended. To not slap back when slapped *is love in action* because we are not reacting to ego with ego. To turn the other cheek takes courage, restraint, patience, and *humility*—"to suffer the slings and arrows of outrageous fortune" (Shakespeare, *Hamlet, Act 3, Scene 1*). It is an opportunity for us *to be* versus *not to be*. To be a humble servant of our Innermost Being; to obey the Will of our Innermost Intimate Christ, who is Perfect Love. This, then, is the whole Truth of the teaching, turn the other cheek: **to be Perfect Love in action—Ahimsa.**

Being love in action, True nonviolence means non-egoic action. Acting for the sake of the other and all beings. Any responsible parent knows that love in action means the wise application of severity and mercy in balanced measure—to do what is best for the child. *Spare the rod, spoil the child.* Does this age-old cliché really suggest we beat children? Of course not. It is simply an expression which states a profound universal Truth that hyper-sensitive parents and hyper-intellectual pediatricians do not want to accept: to avoid the application of severity when it is called for is to leave fully half of Love's True nature on the cutting room floor! Whether out of squeamishness, self-righteousness, misguided pediatric psychology, or some dogmatic misunderstanding and misinterpretation of nonviolence, to fail to express the severity of one's Love for one's children, is to fail to rear them in the full Light and Truth of unconditional Love. A child raised in the shadows of half-love—i.e. showered only with *positive affirmations* and never made to contend with negativity in any meaningful way—will not only have no respect for their parents, they will be emotionally weak, fragile, entitled, and hyper-sensitive. Inexperienced, ignorant of the severity of Love, of the messiness of life, such children will have a very skewed perception of reality and their place in it.

They will be *triggered* by any little affront to their emotional comfort and security. They will not know True compassion, for genuine compassion is born of unconditional Love, and no one incapable of comprehending severity is capable of unconditional Love. They will instead inherit the half-baked 'love' of their well-meaning but ultimately failed parents—base sentimentality, masquerading as altruistic compassion, cloaked in self-righteousness: "I am too sensitive, I am too empathetic, I am too kind, I am too compassionate, I have a degree in child psychology, I know too much about childhood trauma, *I...I...I...*"

And to be fair, the nonviolence Gandhi spoke of, for the most part seemed to be in line with love in action—thoughts, words, and deeds—at least in principle. But of course, ideas and philosophies held in the mind are often quite detached from their implementation and consequences in the real world. This is precisely the case with Gandhi's application of nonviolence.

In Sir Richard Attenborough's Academy Award-winning biopic about the man, Gandhi is quoted as saying to the American journalist Walker:

> *The function of a civil resister is to provoke response. And we will continue to provoke until they respond, or they change the law. They are not in control – we are. That is the strength of civil resistance.*
>
> *– Gandhi (film)*

Now, we were unable to confirm if Gandhi did indeed say these words, or if they were solely the invention of screenwriter John Briley. But we do know in hindsight that India's nonviolent civil disobedience movement did gain control over the British Empire in India. So let us put aside our emotions, beliefs, theories, and ideas about Gandhi. Let us look at the historical facts objectively. The occupying British in control of India were confronted by a nonviolent civil disobedience movement which sought—and succeeded—to take back control of their nation (they resisted until the British packed up and left, humiliated). Empires and nations seizing power and control over one another. It may just be us, dear reader, but that sounds a lot more like *an eye for an eye* than it does *turn the other cheek*. One thing is certain: the British did not leave because Gandhi's nonviolent civil resistance enlightened them in any way. It brought the British Empire to its knees (in India, at least).

So, the little man in the loin cloth from Calcutta brought the British Empire to its knees without resorting to violence, did he? Yes, it certainly appears so. Then nonviolence proved true to its name, did it not? In his heart-mind Gandhi believed so, and so did the rest of the world. Until, that is, the True nature of his nonviolent movement reared its ugly head. All the anger, resentment, animosity, victim mentality, was swept under the rug where it festered and produced a toxic radiation—negative energy pent up over decades—in the pressure cooker of the national psyche. And make no mistake, it is from that boiling reservoir of repressed hostility that Gandhi drew strength to fuel his supposed nonviolent revolution. Let us not be naïve. Was India's movement truly for the sake of appealing to the better nature of the British, as Gandhi believed and intended? Or did a nation repress and secretly harness all those negative emotions for the sake of empowering an unlikely but surprisingly effective winning formula—a passive-aggressive strategy? The proof is found in the events which immediately followed India's independence from Britain.

Gandhi's Tragic Flaw

When the British left India, humiliated, tail between their legs, their great imperial power and authority rendered impotent, they did not leave behind a power vacuum. On the contrary, they left behind an empowered, victorious, emboldened population consisting primarily of two religious/ethnic factions: a Hindu majority and a Muslim minority. Their passive-aggressive strategy had worked to defeat the British. But now that their old adversary was gone, the two groups naturally turned their attention toward one other. Specifically, the Muslim *'oppressed minority'* toward the *'oppressive'* Hindu majority. But two passive-aggressive sides cannot really get anywhere in terms of stealing power away from the other—it becomes a stalemate, a Cold War. So, the Muslim minority, seeing themselves as still oppressed, now projected all their unresolved anger toward their former oppressors—the British—on their new oppressors—the Hindu majority. Decades of pent-up anger and frustration, never properly delt with in the psyche of the nation, and in fact harnessed and emboldened via the winning formula of passive-aggressive toxicity masquerading as nonviolent civil disobedience exploded like a powder keg. The outcome of India's nonviolent revolution became precisely what Gandhi had hoped to avoid. Post colonial India became the living embodiment of his worst nightmare: *violence*. Brutal, unabashed, primal, savage violence. Violence which turned former neighbors, friends, and passivist compatriots against the British into hardened enemies and domestic terrorists. Women and children among the dead. Seeing his nonviolent triumph explode in anger and collapse into bloody civil war before his very eyes broke Gandhi's heart.

To his credit, Gandhi spoke out vehemently against the violence. But he did not stop there. Gandhi went on hunger strike, essentially threatening the country with his own slow, agonizing death. Now on the surface this seems like sacrifice and suffering for the sake of others, right? But look more closely: here again, Gandhi is passively threatening the nation he just helped liberate with the guilt and shame of making them responsible for his death. He is deliberately making himself into a victim, knowing that the psychological burden will be too great to bear for his followers. It is coercion by another name. Gandhi knew the sway he held over his people…they *worshipped him* by this point. And he saw himself as the Mahatma…a great soul. He believed in his own holiness and spirituality. Yet, confronted by the consequences of his teachings and actions—a country on the verge of civil war—he slipped back into the winning strategy of passive aggression.

A hunger strike is coercion. Far from appealing to the better natures of his people, he provoked the response he desired by threatening them with guilt and shame; just as his nonviolent civil resistance provoked the desired response from the British, with the added injury of provoking tremendous frustration and resentment in them for being humiliated against their will—not Love. Love in action has no attachment to outcomes. Love never coerces; never threatens. Love is not clever, crafty, insidious, underhanded, calculated. Love is honest, True, and fair. Love is strong, even fierce if need be. Love does not make its case in the court of public opinion. Love does not wage campaigns to make the other side appear as evil incarnate. Love is not about winning at any cost or turning the tables on our opponents in a clever, coercive, underhanded way. Those sound more like the tactics of an unscrupulous lawyer trying to win a high-profile case, or an ambitious politician playing politics to achieve victory for his party. And let us face the facts: Gandhi was a trained and practiced lawyer.

Eventually, India split and created the majority Hindu India and majority Muslim Pakistan we know today. In the end, Gandhi was seen with a great deal of resentment amongst a fanatical religious minority who plotted and succeeded in carrying out his very public assassination.

It may be surprising to hear, dear reader, that Gandhi languishes in limbo. You can travel to the Astral Plane and investigate the Truth of this for yourself. For all his piety, spirituality, apparent wisdom, countless devotees, even the world's admiration, he failed to develop the solar bodies (the human soul) and achieve liberation from his egos. He was an unimportant lawyer who rose to great heights, seen by many as a great hero indeed, but fell due to his own hubris and vanity…yes, like Thanos. Ultimately narcissistic, Gandhi used the threat of his suffering and death to coerce his own people into compliance with his nonviolent philosophy. These are not the actions of a great master or prophet. They are the actions of an ego-mind trying to control outcomes by any means available to it.

Compare, just for one moment dear reader, Joan of Arc, and her campaign of liberation. A woman who publicly testified from a young age that "God spoke to her." Compare the two lives, Joan of Arc and Gandhi, their two campaigns, and comprehend how one followed the Voice of her Innermost Being, the other the voice of his own cleverness and belief in his own holiness. Gandhi languishes in limbo. Joan of Arc is a Resurrected Master. At first denounced by the Catholic Church, following her death they eventually capitulated and canonized her as a saint. The evidence of her miracles and triumphs in life and death could not be ignored. And yet, is it not interesting, dear reader, that the woke feminists of today turn not to one of their own, Joan of Arc, a genuine female hero in the esoteric sense, as their inspiration and model to emulate? Rather, they turn to a little lawyer in a loin cloth from Calcutta. Maybe it is because when we pick up the gauntlet and become the Right-hand of God we are called to commit to genuine suffering and sacrifice for humanity, with *no guarantee* we will succeed in any worldly sense, only that we will fulfill the Will of our Innermost Intimate Christ for the sake of others. On the other hand, for those with nothing but worldly outcomes on their mind, how can they resist a winning strategy—to wield the power of God over others?

The Little Lawyer in a Loin Cloth from Calcutta sets Precedent.

Apart from winning home rule for India (and its subsequent breakup into separate Hindu and Muslim countries) Gandhi's legacy was to simultaneously define, politicize, and legitimize the winning formula of passive-aggressive victimhood on the world stage.

Righteous struggle is heroic: an overt, direct confrontation drawing on inner strength and self-sacrifice for the greater good, guided by The Logos. Self-righteous struggle is antiheroic: an egoic power play for base self-interest and/or tribalism in the name of some projected concept of universal justice. When Gandhi applied a passive-aggressive strategy to his country's heroic struggle for liberty, it immediately shifted to a self-righteous anti-heroic power play. But in his mind, it remained heroic. And with his lawyer's mind, charisma, and command of language he was able to convince himself, others, and the world of India's heroic struggle with high-and-mighty ideals, spiritual platitudes, and idealized outcomes. But fundamentally it was an exercise in identity politics: fostering and politicizing national victim mentality, shaming one's opponents into submission, and wrapping it all in a media-savvy charismatic leadership style replete with an inner circle able to leverage a sentimental and sympathetic global media which ate it up.

Gandhi's winning strategy was employed by the Civil Rights Movement in the United States, Nelson Mandela's struggle against Apartheid in South Africa, and more recently, the #MeToo, Black Lives Matter, and transgender rights movements. The Civil Rights Movement ended segregation but did not stop there. It helped usher in a new era of passive-aggressive tactics on the left demanding at first welfare and then reparations for slavery. Thomas Sowell makes a compelling socio-economic argument for why such measures ultimately did a disservice to the black community in America. How the crime-ridden ghettos and single-mother households led to a contemporary black youth culture which now dominates the music industry and professional sports. Passive-aggressive struggles for power always seek dominance in one form or another. So too, the violence against whites in South Africa by the ruling blacks, unprecedented for that country in modern times, was made possible by how Apartheid was ended. The rampant corruption has South Africa teetering on the edge of becoming a failed stat—if it is not one already. As for the long-term consequences of #MeToo, one need only ask those who were wrongly accused and yet immediately tried, convicted, and *cancelled* in the kangaroo court of public opinion. Look to transgender athletes transitioning from male to female utterly obliterating the competition seemingly without conscience, any notion of fair play, or remorse: no concern whatsoever for natural female athletes being robbed of their dream. The winning strategy of passive aggression is only about one thing: gaining power and control for oneself and/or one's own tribe at the expense of others. SJWs may believe in their minds that they are *fighting the good fight for the greater good*—as Gandhi did—but in truth they are 100% laser-focused on gaining power for their own self-interest. Like Gandhi and his followers in practice. Like Thanos.

Civil Resistance…Resistance is Futile

The passive-aggressive mindset is synonymous with psychological manipulation. The fact is, there is nothing we can do to stop the woke movement's relentless pursuit of power. Once someone commits themselves to the victim mentality and sees an opportunity to gain power for what they believe is the greater good—which masks their own self-interest—there is nothing that we can say or do to dissuade them from their course of action.

You will know the futility of confronting a passive-aggressive victim if you have ever tried having a civil discussion with someone possessing—or more aptly put, *possessed by*—the 'woke' mindset. You know no matter what you say or do, it will be thrown back in your face as an accusation of overt assault, oppression, misogyny, racism, homophobia, et al. Their reaction to whatever argument or overture you make will be to gaslight you. Even if you try to say something apologetic, be conciliatory, hold out an olive branch, seek common ground, meet them halfway, apply levity, or make any number of open, honest, and earnest attempts at resolving the issue, they will find a way to paint themselves as the victim, and you as the villain. Period. And if you attempt a truly humble and conciliatory approach, you will find that is when their claws come out. Sensing your apparent weakness and resignation, they will *go in for the kill.* Keep in mind these are the same people who complain incessantly about so-called *toxic masculinity.* Anyone who has ever dealt with a passive-aggressive person knows there is no-one more toxic. We speak from extensive experience in this regard. Even if you speak the Words of your Innermost Being, and act according to the Will of Your Father in Heaven in the name of Love, the passive-aggressive SJW will find a way to see you as a villain and themselves as your righteous judge. They will *crucify* you on the cross of their self-righteousness just as the Jewish authority did Jesus of Nazareth.

You must understand, dear reader, that *wokesters* cannot give you so much as an inch; they cannot afford to humanize you. They cannot risk seeing you in any other light as oppressor/villain. Or, if they do appear to make a concession (and they often do this), it is only because they are toying with you—building your hopes up, reeling you in, getting you to let your guard down and reveal your vulnerable side, so they can stab you with an even bigger accusation. They will say or do something which appears to be an overt, earnest, and honest attempt at finding common ground. And we, longing for resolution will too often fall for it. We accept their apparent olive branch and move to meet them under a supposed flag of truce. Naively, we will approach them and attempt to engage them in civil discourse under their terms, only to be ambushed and slaughtered for our trouble. It is psychological and political entrapment.

The converse tactic also works for them: inciting us to lose our temper, wearing down our patience and resilience until there is no patience left in our tank and little willpower with which to hold back our own egos. Having made a misstep, said or done something regrettable, we arm them with the ammunition to truly shame and guilt us into submission. Many a woman has goaded a man to anger and violence, then had him thrown in prison for his weakness and gullibility, taking him to the cleaners in the process. Many a man has provoked violence in women, too, but no such protections and privileges exist under the law for men as they do for women. For all their so-called *sis white male privilege,* it seems ironic that of all the groups which leverage their victim status in the arena of identity politics, you will not find sis white males among them. Identity politics, it seems, depends on meeting certain woke criteria. If not, the social justice espoused by SJWs simply does not apply.

Wokeness is psycho-social-political espionage, propaganda, and terrorism, dressed up as righteousness and heroism. Yet truly it is without virtue. There is no honor, valor, dignity, humility, and certainly no love in it. In fact, it embraces the absolute worst aspects of overt self-righteous acts of aggression seeking power over and control of others out of blatant self-interest and makes them covert.

Let us return momentarily to the point we previously made about a passive-aggressive individual not being able to give their perceived oppressor/enemy an inch, out of fear they may momentarily become human in their eyes instead of a monster. The psychopath operates on this paradigm. So too does the torturer, the perpetrator of genocide, the rapist—rape is not about sex, it is about power and control. *Rape is violence.* Nazi propaganda dehumanized Jews for years prior to WWII. U.S. military training dehumanizes 'America's enemies.' It is easier to kill a villain or a terrorist than it is a human. The point here is SJWs apply the same psychopathic tendencies to the victim mentality and identity politics. Suddenly, anyone who is not a member of a legitimate victim group is automatically deemed less than human. The downtrodden become the powerful, and they, like Gandhi, use coercive tactics like guilt and shame to gaslight and control their dehumanized adversaries. As an aside, contrary to what the French postmodernists would have you believe, words do have power and meaning. Psychopath literally means *diseased soul.*

Thanos, who is clearly psychopathic, sees the universe this simply: *half.* Even-Steven. These are not sentient beings he is arbitrarily destroying through genocide on an intergalactic scale, they are statistics. It is a matter of numbers (pun intended). It is not about spirit. It is cold, calculated, pre-school level logic. A child splitting a twinkie: "half for you, half for me." The justice of a two-year old. The SJW's dream of equality of outcomes. And the twisted justice seeking retribution, satisfaction, as a pompous aristocrat from the erroneously named *'Enlightenment' era* who feels insulted and declares, slapping his perceived wrongdoer across the face with his glove, *"Monsieur, I demand satisfaction!"* Dear reader, allow our previous discussion of gauntlets and turning the other cheek to seep back into your consciousness and comprehend how all the connections are coming together.

In synthesis, SJWs are in every sense of the word following the doctrine of *an eye for an eye*. The fact that they do so according to their interpretation of nonviolence is moot. The result is the same: the dehumanization of *the other* tribe for the sake of power and control over them, in the name of self-righteous self-interest, dressed up in some propagandized, idealized, rationalized cause. They demand satisfaction. They cannot meet their perceived oppressors on the battlefield with honor and win the fight for equality, liberty, et al with valor, courage, and love for their enemy, for the sake of the greater good. No. They do whatever it takes to gain power and control for themselves and all those they identify with in solidarity as fellow victims. They dehumanize, dismantle, deconstruct, and utterly destroy their perceived oppressors and all structures, institutions, myths, and traditions which they judge to be supportive of said oppressors' unjust, inequitable *privilege*.

The Real Différance

We said we would get around to the *deconstruction* of all established norms, existing power dynamics, authorities, hierarchies, etc. At the risk of opening the proverbial pandora's box of postmodernism, we would begin by pointing out that personalities like Jordan Peterson and others tend to focus on Michel Foucault, and his disdain for what he saw as power hierarchies of oppressor/oppressed. That is all fine and good for Peterson and others who seem terrified at the prospect of death on a civilization-wide scale. This, despite priding themselves on being well-educated, well-read, and well-thought-out in a sort of neo-classical sense. They know their history better than most and claim to know what it all means, by and large. That said, they do not seem able to recognize that no hierarchies, structures, empires or even civilizations last—especially corrupt ones like those governing this humanity, especially at this time.

We know the real problem with postmodernism. The responsibility for the present woke incursion in the West lays not with Foucault's assault on hierarchies and power structures, but squarely at the feet of Jacques Derrida's assault on Truth itself. Derrida was the one who popularized the notion of deconstruction, the idea that all truth was contained within language. And, that all meaning in language was a function of *différance*—a clever pun in French meaning both *to differ* and *to defer*. The shorthand is this: words derive their meaning because they are different from every other word. But that meaning can only be expressed with more words, so all words' meanings are deferred to all other words. Thus, all meaning is *subjective*, since meaning exists in language, and the meanings of words are entirely reliant on other words. To postmodernists, this means (pun intended) that there can be no such thing as objective fact, Truth, etc. For Derrida, the godfather of postmodernism, all knowledge had to be subjective.

The French thinkers of the postmodernist movement failed to recognize all they were explaining was the nature of intellectualism—albeit in new, clever, erroneous, but convincing ways. The subjective nature of book knowledge—ideas and concepts in the rational mind alone—was well-known throughout the ancient world. Following the *letter of The Law* was recognized for what it was: hypnosis and ignorance. Their antithesis—as we have described so often in our work—is gnosis: experiential knowledge, the *spirit of The Law*. Experiential knowledge does not exist in language and is not bound by intellectual, social, political, cultural, religious, or ultimately even physical restraints. Gnosis—self-evident experiential knowledge—is immune to the theories and rhetorical devices of the postmodernists. It is the objective Truth we can experience directly, or by proxy via inspired expressions of it, such as figurative language and high art. But being completely ignorant of gnosis, the postmodernists set out to make sure their ideology would revolutionize how the world thought about knowledge, language, dominance hierarchies, and ultimately all human experience.

Sadly, postmodernism decreed in all its ignorance and arrogance, as *absolute objective fact* (expressed in language no less), that all knowledge is subjective—except, of course, *their absolute objective fact* that all knowledge is subjective. This irony seemed utterly lost on them, and the arrogance and ignorance of their hypocrisy are the very foundations of the woke mindset. SJWs in one breath declare that all opinions are equally valid since all knowledge is subjective, and in the next breath proclaim their political ideology, moral stance, and worldview are superior to all others. They deconstruct long-established oppressive authorities, institutions, hierarchies, and traditions claiming to be caretakers of the Truth. Anyone and anything challenging *their truth* must be immediately, systematically, and ruthlessly *cancelled*. Essentially, anyone on the side of *the Truth* is oppressive and victimizing every individual who stands with pride on the side of their own diverse, equitable, inclusive, and thus morally superior, *"my truth"*—which is really the accepted dogma of the collective. And so, the woke have their *cancel culture* and wage their passive-aggressive *culture war* to tear down the Truth. They deconstruct all the oppressive language-based *fake news* and replace it with their own inclusive, empowering *alternative facts*. And to be fair, the corruption in the established systems of governance and media make wokeness an all too easy and seductive proposition for souls attuned to righteousness and justice.

So, the wokesters' postmodernist deconstruction agenda does one better than our oh-so-psychotic, destructive, and genocidal Thanos. SJWs exhibit a modus operandi that debuted in computer animated archetypal form back in 2004, in a cameo appearance at the end of Pixar's *The Incredibles.*

Video 22: Incredibles - The Underminer Arrives
(YouTube)

With one line of spoken dialogue, the character of *The Underminer* managed to epitomize the essence of the postmodernist passive-aggressive winning strategy of victimhood, foretelling the SJW future of Disney, *Incredibles 2,* and indeed, the fate awaiting all human civilization.

> *Behold! The Underminer!*
> *I am always beneath you, but nothing is beneath me!*
> *– The Incredibles*

The Underminer's dialogue describes completely the ultimate modus operandi of mechanical nature, in its most insidious, devastating, powerful, universal, and inevitable form—*death.*

No mere mortal can conquer death. It is death which conquers us all. Even entire civilizations and vast empires fall to the endgame of mechanical nature. But they do not just die suddenly at the peak of their power. No. They first undergo a slow and arduous decline. They crumble. Weaken. Or rather, *are weakened.* Undermined from within. Thus, death guarantees its success two ways: *passive-aggressively undermining* and *dividing and conquering.*

How Identification 'Fans' the Flames of Hell

As we attempt to navigate and cope with the realities of contemporary identity politics and try to make sense of the conflict between certain opposing self-identified groups, very often the analysis is one-sided. Either on the side of the *underminers*—woke activists and their intellectual elite enablers—or the *guardians*—individuals SEEKing to preserve what they know and cherish, be it free speech, culture, history, traditions, religion, institutions, nationalism, even biology. We just explored woke activism at length. Let us look now to the other side of the wall. Specifically, *fandom.* In recent years, fans of various pop-culture properties and modern mythologies have witnessed their beloved entertainment franchises appropriated and undermined by woke activists. Predictably, this has *awoken the giant* in the form of fans' collective outrage. They are hell-bent on fighting for their culture, myths, et al. Let us analyze the underlying phenomena at work and see if we can identify the root causes of the turmoil, without making the mistake of falling into the trap of identification ourselves.

Language has power and meaning. In stark contrast to the erroneous assertions of the postmodernists—who declare their belief that "all language is subjective" in one breath, then proclaim *"language is violence"* in the next. In the previous chapter we explored the power of *shellshock* versus the viscerally impotent PTSD, for instance. That said, we do not wish to fall into the trap of identification, either. Words, however powerful they may be, are still just labels. There is no use in attaching ourselves to them, whether they fall into the camp of shellshock or not. Still, practically speaking, we have no choice but to use labels provisionally for the sake of the discussion at hand. It is far easier to refer to *PC Gamers* or *fans* than it is to refer to *individuals who play PC games* or *persons who are passionate about their entertainment.* Countless individuals and groups enthusiastically self-identify as gamers and fans. Also, we cannot deny that we all play various *roles* throughout the course of our lives: child, adolescent, man, woman, husband, wife, father, mother, brother, sister, friend, citizen, owner, manager, employee, colleague, co-worker…the list is endless. And working their way onto that list invariably come labels such as conservative, liberal, optimist, pessimist, feminist, misogynist, racist, white supremacist, believer, follower, devotee, member, etc. Now, to what degree these are or are not valid roles/labels is in part what we shall be exploring through this section: a case study in *identification.*

The challenge, of course, is this: how does one objectively explore any label, unveil the esoteric causes and implications of it, and reveal the hard Truth regarding identification without offending someone who is identified with said label? With the understanding that all such labels are entirely *provisional,* related solely to an individual's fleeting *persona.* In Truth, labels in no way, shape, or form define anyone where their *True Self* is concerned. But the fact that most identify as their mortal self, and the various labels which can be applied to their "I," it is extremely difficult to perform any case study without losing an entire contingent of readers; namely, those who might most benefit from the case study! Our solution is to pick a niche label, one whose associated group members wear it as a badge of honor (privately at least, if not publicly), and whose stereotypical attitudes and behaviors reveal the nature of *all* forms of identification. Now of course, not all members of any group think and behave the same, but all individuals who are identified with any group/label/role will suffer the same esoteric tendencies behind the dominant attitudes, beliefs, and behaviors of the group/label/role they are identified with. So, with that caveat on the table, let us dive right in by examining a common attitude and behavior exhibited by a specific group of individuals who wear their moniker as a badge of honor…*hardcore gamers.*

Contempt for those trying to Get into the Elite Club

Unless you play videogames and partake in online discussion forums with other gamers, you may have never come across the sentiment *git gud* before. It is a colloquial term which reads 'get good,' but whose meaning and purpose runs much deeper, and is intimated by its spelling. *Git* is a slang term for someone who is considered unpleasant. Git gud is a dismissive slang phrase used online by hardcore gamers to belittle more casual players who voice concerns about a game's difficulty being too high, unbalanced, or simply unfair. To put the phrase into context, it would be the equivalent of telling a newbie asking for advice on how to spec-out their character—a prerequisite to playing most CRPGs—to "play the game more." It is both condescending and patronizing, in addition to putting the newbie player in a catch-22. Of course, there is some Truth to git gud—practice makes perfect—but there is much more to becoming an elite gamer, athlete, chef, or anything for that matter...and we will delve into all that soon enough. But before we do, let us take a closer look at these so-called elite gamers and the outright contempt the phrase git gud expresses toward casual gamers, newbs, the pleb, et al.

The use of git gud is particularly common among PC gamers and is a favorite expression employed by the so-called *PC Master Race*—itself intended at times as a satirical and derogatory term poking fun at hardcore PC gamers and their belief in the inherent supremacy of PC gaming to consoles, mobile, et al. Strangely, most serious PC gamers wear the PC Master Race moniker with pride, either unaware of its passing reference to that other supposed *master race* borne in Germany in the 1930s, or uncaring of the implications of said association.

What is more, many hardcore PC gamers take the moniker as seriously as gaming itself. They take immense pride in their multi-thousand-dollar gaming rigs outfitted with the latest in bleeding-edge computing technology. Lightning-fast graphics cards. Immense hard drives for storing their extensive game libraries. Elaborate cooling solutions for keeping all that horsepower operating at peak efficiency during intense gaming sessions. Illuminated with nightclub-envy-inducing LEDs. All brought to life on multiple ultra-wide monitors and in full 3D surround sound. Elite PC gamers see the machines which enable their passion for gaming in the same way *gearheads* see their enthusiast automobiles, motorcycles, and offroad vehicles—*gear porn.*

To be clear, let us take nothing away from the time, dedication, effort, energy, and indeed, money such gamers put into their passion. It takes devotion to get gud. And nothing short of an immense investment can account for the achievements and success some gamers are able to attain and showcase online—some even monetizing their passion into a viable career. The following video features records by both PC and console gamers and is by no means an exhaustive list of records or record-holders. We have included it as a way for non-gamers (or casuals) to get a sense of just how dedicated and invested in their passion elite gamers can be. As you can see in the video below, to many, games are more than just a form of entertainment.

Video 23: 10 Video Game WORLD RECORDS Set by Youtubers | Chaos (YouTube)

High-scores, speed runs, kill-streaks, marathon-sessions, max-levels, kill screens, top mods…unless you are a gamer, these terms may mean little to you. But if you are a member of the hardcore gaming community, and especially the PC Master Race, you will find endless videos online featuring players showcasing their skills, often in real-time. The entire streaming platform, Twitch, began exclusively for video gamers to stream their gaming sessions live to the world. As a matter of fact, with the advance of live streaming came the rise of professional e-sports. Some gamers have found themselves competing for record purses at tournaments, including World Championships, all streamed live around the world—a veritable video game *World Cup.*

Video 24: A Record-Breaking World Championship (YouTube)

As you can see, dear reader, be they online or in person, these high-ranking, world-dominating, overachieving gamers have legions of admirers, followers, and fans. Many are, in gaming circles at least, bona fide celebrities with some teetering on the precipice of outright legend.

One need not ascend to such stratospheric heights in the gaming world to enjoy the self-satisfaction which comes from attaining videogame achievements. From the very inception of video games during the age of 1980s arcades, Atari 2600, Intellivision, and Colecovision, followed by the second wave of home gaming dominated by Nintendo and Sega, and later the third wave when Sony PlayStation and Microsoft Xbox joined the fray, players have competed to beat their previous high score and win the right to enter their initials into arcade machines, their handle onto online leaderboards, and even their name into the annals of gaming history. This has been a defining feature of videogames since day one (as in sports, score-keeping, progression, competition, and winning are baked into the activity). Like all such competitive industries, gaming has not been without its controversies. Perhaps the most infamous being Billy Mitchell's claim to the high score in the notoriously difficult *Donkey Kong* arcade game. The subject of a cult-classic documentary, *The King of Kong,* the controversy surrounding the world record for Donkey Kong continues to this day. For most players, modern games ship today not only with multiple different achievements they can pursue and attain, but also regional and global rankings for said achievements, levels attained, hours played, scores reached, and many other statistics and variables players can compete on. And for what? For little more than some bragging rights among a community of players and/or a tight-knit group of gaming friends; and again, the self-satisfaction of having successfully accomplished this or that achievement(s). The pride of having *gotten gud.*

What all this boils down to then, is the temporary fulfillment of some longing to git gud. To see oneself as having gotten gud as it were, and have one's status as hardcore, expert, elite—perhaps even pro-gamer— validated. Or, taken online for the sake of entertaining a growing audience of followers: a live streamer, Twitch celebrity, and/or YouTuber. But even without the online gaming community, publicity, or any ex-ternalized forms of validation whatsoever, many gamers can and do still quietly, privately, solely, and without any fanfare whatsoever, git gud in their bedrooms, basements, *man-caves,* home offices, or in the case of mobile games, just about anywhere. The self-satisfaction they get from beating a game or dominat-ing within a game—*owning* it or others playing it—is all they desire.

Not all gamers want to see their name in lights. In the world of online gaming players use a *gamertag,* and within the gaming community this handle signifies their alter-ego. Like the anonymity afforded users of most online forums, such aliases allow gamers to behave in-game and online in ways which they would never do in real life. For many gamers—but certainly not all—their gamertag is akin to the character of a professional wrestler. The bravado, trash-talking, bluster, and amateurish theatrics of an alter-ego designed to be both intimidating and entertaining constitute a kind of *metagame* in gaming: play-acting among play-ers. Like *cosplay* among fans of comics and genre films, it adds another layer to the social aspect of the hobby. And while fun, in gaming, it is only respected if players can *walk their talk.* Any self-respecting hardcore gamer knows that one must earn the right to trash-talk other players; and, that one had better be able to back-up their tough talk with in-game performance. Here again, we see a return to bragging rights and a kind of minor celebrity status, even if it is anonymous fame or the completely private offline fame of one: simply a player owning a game, dominating it: completing it, unlocking all the achievements, beating their previous high score, and knowing they have truly *gotten gud.*

There is, of course, one unique brand of elite gamer we have not mentioned yet, one who exhibits precious few of the typical characteristics and behaviors but instead chooses to git gud for what can seem like entirely altruistic reasons. We will euphemistically refer to such an individual as a *Master Gamer* and will address their unique qualities later. First, let us address the one thing that unites all gamers of elite level and ability.

What it Takes to Git Gud

It is no secret: to master anything takes time, effort, and energy. It also takes talent (and/or skill development), practice, focus, concentration, discipline, commitment, drive, a willingness to fail often, a thick skin in the face of constant failure and defeat, and many more attributes and factors. No one can master anything overnight, nor without an enormous investment of themselves. This fact alone makes the git gud putdown by hardcore gamers toward their less-skilled brethren far more insidious than it appears on the surface, because it entirely takes for granted the *lifetime* of experience associated with rising to elite levels of ability. The insult derides the casual gamer for lacking in dedication, devotion, and discipline. It masks an inherent accusation of laziness and passes judgment on someone for lacking the commitment and drive, without any knowledge of the individual or their circumstances. It trivializes the years of commitment the hardcore gamer must have devoted to gaming to be at the level they are at.

Git gud patronizes the casual gamer for what elite gamers judge as mere whining—vain, ignorant, entitled. A casual player who believes they should be a better player without having to put in the requisite effort. Or, game developers should design games to be easier to accommodate lower skill levels (or at the very least include multiple difficulty settings ranging from easy to punishing) so casual players can also enjoy them. Hardcore gaming *purists* believe catering to casual gamers is eating into their ability to enjoy more challenging games which they see as being *dumbed down for newbs.* It is the same kind of elitism we find in literary scholars who look down on pulp fiction, auteur filmmakers who look down on summer blockbusters, genre films, and television. Whether or not auteur films are *better* than TV or big tent-pole films is irrelevant. To *genuine film afficionados,* auteur films are more challenging and that alone makes them objectively better. In fact, by any objective measure, auteur films speak to fewer people and have less of an impact, financially, socially, and culturally than do big blockbuster movie franchises (consider Star Wars, Star Trek, Lord of the Rings, Harry Potter, or James Bond). Both have their fans, no doubt. In videogames, too, mobile hits like the Nintendo GameBoy's classic *Tetris* or the more contemporary *Angry Birds* and *Candy Crush Saga* have far out-sold hardcore auteur games such as the award-winning *Cuphead.* Here was a beautifully crafted, exquisitely illustrated, and notoriously challenging game which lured casual players in with its charming early-twentieth-Century animation style, only to crush their hopes of enjoyment due to punishingly difficult gameplay.

Video 25: Cuphead Launch Trailer
(YouTube)

So endearing were the nostalgia-packed visual style and characters that the game launched an animated series by the same name on Netflix. Perhaps somewhat of a consolation prize for those players—including at least one game journalist—who could not even complete the first level of the game. Said *game journo* was predictably skewered online for his review that the game was too hard.

Git gud was not only the response of the PC Master Race toward the disillusioned pleb unable to get past even the first level of *Cuphead.* It was also the response of the developers, Studio MDHR Entertainment Inc., who stated unapologetically that they set out to make a difficult game to challenge hardcore gamers. And certainly, were they makers of an art-house film instead of an indie video game, they would never have been asked to defend their creative choices. That said, we are not sure how many filmmakers take the attitude that if audiences cannot make sense of their films, viewers should take steps to develop their cinematic appreciation skills. Some most certainly do. A recent author of *Star Wars: The High Republic* proclaimed, "if you don't like my politics, don't buy my book," suggesting that in her case, what matters most as a creator is infusing politics into the story and that if readers do not like it, they should either change their politics or avoid her book entirely.

The point is this: elite gamers feel they have earned the right to enjoy a return on investment when it comes to gaming. They did not dedicate their lives to becoming skilled gamers only to have that time and effort wasted playing games that present no challenge. And they cannot stand watching entitled half-wits and casuals beating games, then bragging or trash-talking online as if they possessed any real skills or had accomplished something of note. *Modern games are too easy* is a mantra echoed by hardcore gamers online constantly. They feel entitled to their own exclusive gaming experiences befitting their elite status, tailor-made to their skill level, featuring unique art, graphics, gameplay, fun, and rewards, which none but those who have *paid their dues* should be entitled to enjoy. And in the case of a handful of developers, they are more than willing to cater their games to the niche market of hardcore gamers. In no uncertain terms,

Elite gaming is a club. Until you git gud, you ain't a member. And cousin, until you git gud, you ain't welcome.

– PC Master Race.

Putting *the Other* in their Place

By this point, dear reader, you probably have a sense of what this discourse about hardcore gamers' expression *git gud* has been revealing. If the terms superiority complex, arrogance, snobbery, and elitism have not come to mind yet, then surely the time has come to contemplate the attitudes of any elite group toward those who are not members of their group—not just *other* but *lesser* in their eyes. What is more, now is the time to extrapolate our discussion of hardcore gamers and casual gamers (and/or the PC Master Race versus console and mobile gamers) to encompass not merely all elite groups and their perceived inferiors, but **all identities and their perceived other(s).**

Here is where our case study on elite gamers offers you, dear reader, a non-confrontational analysis through which to evaluate your personal self-evident experiential knowledge of *in-crowds* and *outcasts,* to SEEK discovery of similar attitudes, characteristics, and behaviors prevalent in many (but not all) members of said identity groups. Surely it requires no great effort on your part to survey your experiential knowledge to see the universal hallmarks so vividly expressed in the status of elite gamers toward their casual counterparts. And it should come as no surprise that a rather large contingent of casual players indeed feel *entitled* to easy gaming experiences geared toward their level of commitment, busy schedule, even finances. Certainly, you see similar oppositional group dynamics expressed throughout the history and geography of the human condition. Be they differences in race, creed, culture, religion, class, politics, gender, philosophy, ability, appearance, fashion, interests, hobbies, et al…groups, cliques, clubs, tribes, legions, and nations of every conceivable shape, size, and defining characteristics. This humanity is nothing if not about putting others in their place, and that place is usually one or more steps beneath and behind themselves. Why must it be so?

Deconstructing *Us* and *Them* – CRT

Enter *Critical Race Theory* (CRT), the self-styled luminaries Jacques Derrida, Michel Foucault, and other post-modernists, along with legions of their *woke* devotees. To briefly recap, Critical Theory begins with the assumption that all language is dialectic, that all meaning is derived not merely by a word's definition but by virtue of not being another word and/or definition. This is essentially the foundation of Derrida's theory of *différence:* which, as we already discussed, is a clever pun (in French) that states that the meaning of a word comes from both its difference from all other words and its deference to all other words. According to Derrida, différence ultimately means all language (and thus all knowledge) is subjective since knowledge exists in language (again, according to Derrida)—an assertion which is simply incorrect. One which illuminates Derrida's biases in trying to make sense of the world through the narrow viewpoint of an intellectual linguist.

To this, Foucault added it is not just that words differ from and defer to other words, nor that words are merely labels, but that there emerges a dynamic of dominance hierarchies with every identification of différence. So, it is never simply a matter of *black or white*. One is always *dominant* over the other, and that dominance is deferred according to the subjective biases of the thinker/speaker/reader. Biases that stem from their *identity,* according to CRT. Thus, when one identifies oneself with either black or white, one automatically assumes one is superior to the other. And naturally—historically and politically—the dominant half of the dichotomy is often that which one identifies with…placing oneself in the position of dominance. Unless that is, one identifies as a victim, in which case one will identify with the repressed half of the dialectic, placing oneself in the position of the victim of whoever/whatever is in the position of dominance. In other words, it is never just black or white, it is always *us versus them.* With this reasoning, woke activists proceed to deconstruct every tradition, religion, culture, gender, structure, nation, et al. Their worldview is predicated on putting all those in their place who they judge to have been putting all others in their place historically (i.e., post-colonialism, white male heterosexual patriarchy, toxic fandom, etc.)

There is a problem with their reasoning. Like Derrida and Foucault, they are wholly identified with and ignorant of the True source of the dominance hierarchy dynamic *us versus them*—their own egos. They fail to look within themselves and see the forces within corralling them, in the name of justice, to become what they behold as being unjust. They succumb to groupthink, mob rule, and unrighteous action in the name of righteousness. And they do all this because their underlying philosophy, CRT, lays the blame for all the world's ills at the foot of language. Their belief in the inherently discriminatory nature of language forms the basis for their assertion that *speech is violence.* This results in their need for so-called *safe spaces* and *trigger warnings.* They demand that diversity, equity, and inclusion (DEI) take precedent over the classical humanist values of *individual merit.* Their worldview looks to wrestle power away from *perceived oppressors* and external tormentors instead of *looking within themselves* for the *True causes of their suffering*—their own egos.

Post-Modernism's Ignorance of Ego

True, language does not exist in a vacuum. The post-modernists were onto something when they noticed the subjective nature of language and the dominance hierarchies, which seem to appear naturally as a matter of course through the application of semiotics of any kind. The post-modern linguists were not entirely incorrect in their observations. Where they went wrong was concluding that subjectivity and dominance hierarchies are inherent to and produced by language. Truth be told, these are merely a feature of language. Subjectivity and dominance hierarchies express themselves as an inherent quality of practically every aspect of this fallen humanity—one utterly subject to and dominated by ego.

The post-modernists fell for the classic *correlation-causality fallacy,* well-known in the sciences but generally unheeded and ignored in the humanities, especially in the annals of Critical Race Theory. It should not be surprising, dear reader, that with several generations raised and educated under the umbrella of CRT, gun-control advocates continually and unabashedly affirm that *guns kill people* when any reasonable person with one iota of common sense knows full well that guns are incapable of killing anyone unless there is a person present to pull the trigger. Ergo: *people kill people*—with or without guns. So, even though—as we previously asserted—words do have inherent power and meaning, what *causes* the power and meaning of language are the underlying metaphysical forces contained within and conveyed through its symbolic nature. Its *effects* are likewise dependent on the metaphysical forces contained within the psychologies of the person(s) receiving information through language. Any effect of language is not born solely in the nature of language itself. Nor is it contained in the *intention* with which the words are conceived, employed, and deployed. The heart-mind of those who receive, process, and *react to* language determines its effects. With apologies to Martial MacLuhan, the medium is only *partly* the message.

Mistaking the catalyst for the cause is easily done when there is an entity actively attempting to scapegoat anything and everything other than itself as the guilty party.

> *Not me, him! Not this, that! Not us, them!*
> *– Our many egos.*

We do not have one ego, as is widely believed. We have countless egos. A *legion* of egos, in fact (fear, pride, lust, anger, envy, gluttony, laziness, et al). These psychological aggregates participate in a *Game of Thrones* inside of us, each vying to climb the dominance hierarchy within our own psyche and sit on *the Iron Throne.* When, for a fleeting moment, said ego can be in command of our attention, thoughts, emotions, sensations, cravings, and/or aversions for the sole purpose of consuming our sexual energy (fire) and bottling up more of our consciousness.

Link 8: Slideshow: Game of Thrones our Many Egos Play
(Instagram)

Put another way,

They're all just spokes on a wheel. This one's on top, then that one's on top, and on and on it spins, crushing those on the ground.

– Denaerys Stormborn, Game of Thrones

If the above does not make it clear, dear reader, allow us to be blunt: **egos exist in hell**. Their domain is our subconscious mind. Their modus operandi includes covert espionage, infiltration, corruption, theft, temptation, coercion, and outright terrorism. From the shadows, they conspire to make their assault on the dominance hierarchy within the recesses of our own psyche in their bid to ascend to the top, momentarily exposing themselves, to strike us when we are vulnerable, feed on our vital energy (the source of their sustenance and ability to replicate) and accumulate more of our consciousness (their currency for dominance, attention, and control). It is precisely these moments after which we reflect and express to ourselves, "what possessed me to do that?" Therefore, egos, psychological aggregates, nafs, sins, psychic malware, or by whatever name are, in fact, what every religion and spiritual tradition has known as demons and devils. In Latin, *demon* is synonymous with *ego*. Both simply mean "I."

But egos are essential to humanity's survival! Without gluttony, we would starve! Without fear, we would have died many times over already. Without indulging lust, how could we procreate? Without greed and envy, how could we motivate ourselves to attain greater success?

– Our egos' many self-serving rationalizations for their existence.

Or, to quote *Gordon Gecko's* infamous speech to shareholders,

Greed, for lack of a better word, is good...[capturing] the essence of the evolutionary spirit. Greed, in all its forms: greed for life, for money, for love, for knowledge has marked the upward surge of mankind.

– Wallstreet

Ask yourself, dear reader: do you need to fear having an accident to know you should wear a seatbelt? Which is more valuable in terms of navigating the world: fear of imminent danger or awareness of potential dangers? Do you need the desire to fill yourself up to eat, or merely the awareness that you need to nourish your body? Do you eat until you are satisfied or until you cannot eat anymore? How many spermatozoa does it require to fertilize an ovum: one or one billion? You say you do not believe in *immaculate conception?* Ask the millions of children born to Catholic parents practicing the *pull-out method* of birth control. 'Immaculate' means 'clean, without blemish;' that is, conception without orgasm, not conception without sex. Is greed "good?" Can you honestly look at the world created by greed and call that an "upward surge of mankind?" Or is it the story of *the Fall of Babylon* being played out once more, as it has time and time again? For surely greed can erect fabulous, awe-inspiring towers of power for a time, but what goes up must come down. That is an immutable law of nature.

Speaking of nature, at this time, we must reiterate there are two natures to nature, divine and mechanical (metaphysical and physical), and as we explored in the chapter on AI, egos are an aspect of the lesser of these two, namely, mechanical nature. Observe Figure 15: Circles of Life Infographic.

Now, the clever mind will look at the infographic in Figure 15 and proclaim, "Ah-ha! Here is a duality presented in another dominance hierarchy: clearly, Divine Nature is being placed in a position of superiority over mechanical nature, proving the author of this book to be hypocritical!" Dominance hierarchies exist in nature, without question. Both natures, divine and mechanical, have their hierarchies. The difference is these hierarchies are objective, not subjective. To say, "clouds are above the earth," or "cheetahs run faster than zebras," is not to make a qualitative assessment but a quantitative one. It is not a choice. It is an observable fact. Does that mean we should always trust our five senses implicitly and assume our perceptions reflect objective reality? To a degree, yes, but only provisionally, understanding there are deeper, higher, more subtle, and more profound senses we may not have activated yet which would radically alter our perceptions and understanding of the nature of reality; namely, shifting our perceptions from the mechanical to the divine nature of nature, and comprehending which one is foundational and supersedes the other. It is only egos themselves—the algorithms behind the 'intelligence' of mechanical nature (AI) that would argue against the superiority of divine nature in favor of their own mechanical nature. Here again, we invoke the words of Ash from the film *Alien,* expressing his admiration for the biomechanical xenomorph, "the perfect organism. Its structural perfection is matched only by its hostility...a survivor. Unclouded by conscience, remorse, or delusions of morality." Clearly, the perspective from which we perceive the world determines what we see; what we value.

CIRCLES OF LIFE

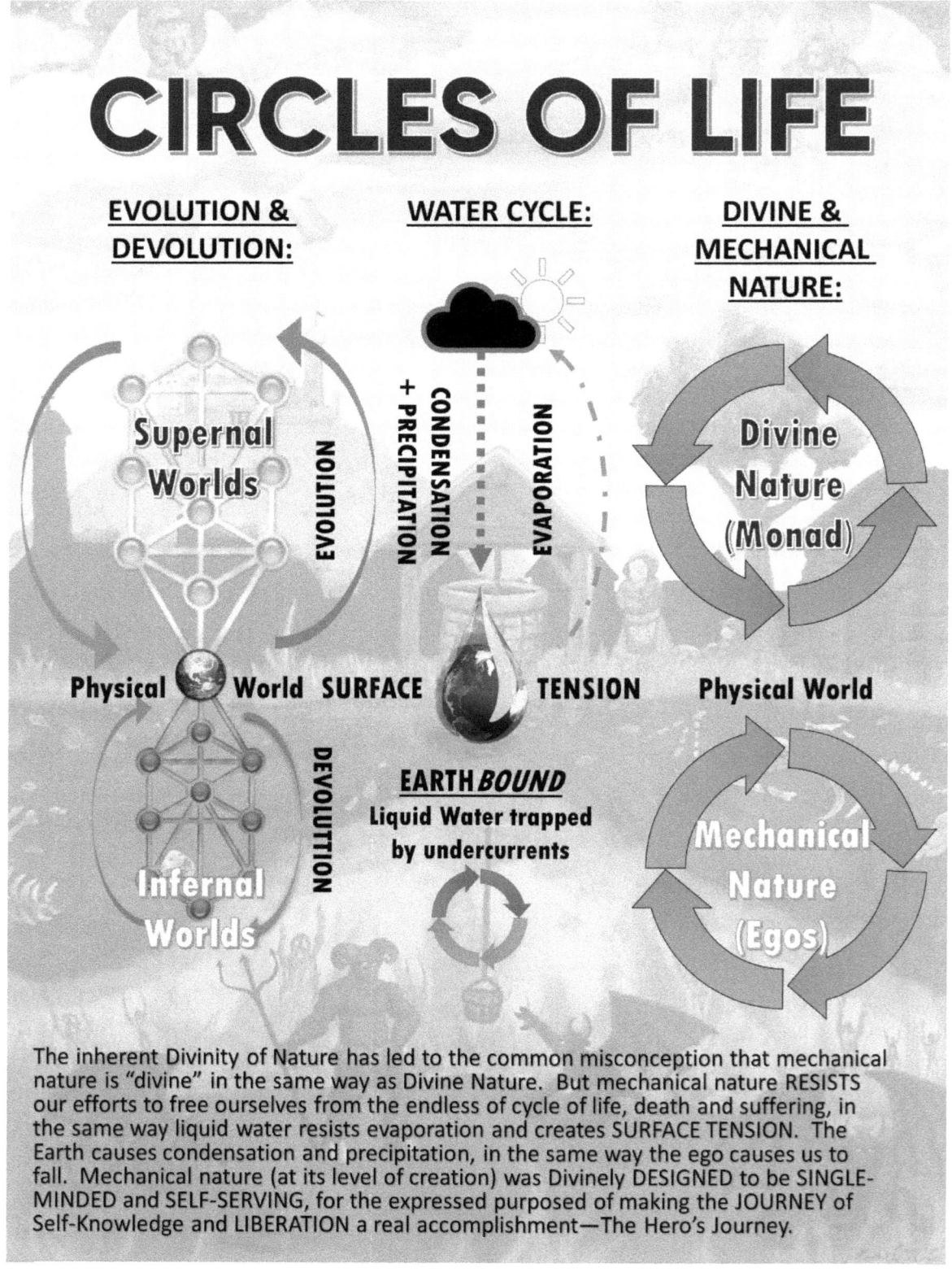

EVOLUTION & DEVOLUTION:

Supernal Worlds

EVOLUTION

Physical World

DEVOLUTION

Infernal Worlds

WATER CYCLE:

CONDENSATION + PRECIPITATION

EVAPORATION

SURFACE TENSION

EARTH *BOUND*
Liquid Water trapped by undercurrents

DIVINE & MECHANICAL NATURE:

Divine Nature (Monad)

Physical World

Mechanical Nature (Egos)

The inherent Divinity of Nature has led to the common misconception that mechanical nature is "divine" in the same way as Divine Nature. But mechanical nature RESISTS our efforts to free ourselves from the endless of cycle of life, death and suffering, in the same way liquid water resists evaporation and creates SURFACE TENSION. The Earth causes condensation and precipitation, in the same way the ego causes us to fall. Mechanical nature (at its level of creation) was Divinely DESIGNED to be SINGLE-MINDED and SELF-SERVING, for the expressed purposed of making the JOURNEY of Self-Knowledge and LIBERATION a real accomplishment—The Hero's Journey.

Figure 15: Circles of Life Infographic

The Observer Effect

The fact is, dear reader, the dominance hierarchies within and between levels of nature do not change merely because we experience a shift in our level of consciousness. They are what they are. Just as the existence of other planets and humanities in remote regions of our galaxy—let alone other galaxies—is not dependent on our capacity to observe them, just as the existence of individual cells in our body was an immutable fact long before the advent of microscopy. Here, we must mention *the observer effect,* as noted by quantum physicists. The observer effect seems to indicate that phenomena exist in one state until the moment they are observed when they assume their observable state. If this is so, then how can objective Truth be transcendent and independent of the observer? Just so: the underlying condition (unobserved state) of the phenomenon exists without being observed. Its observable state requires an observer. That is not to say that an observer cannot have an impact on what they are observing, but the ultimate nature of both observer and observed is independent of the observation/experience. It is the experience of observable nature which is dependent on the conditions affecting the observations of it.

On the other hand, empirical beliefs based on and conditioned by limited perceptions and experience (i.e., physical observations) are products of mechanical nature itself: they exist in the ego-mind, are expressed through language, and are entirely subjective. They are wholly dependent on the subject's evaluation/interpretation of—and/or reaction to—their conscious observations/experience and exist quite independently of the Truth of said experience. Empirical beliefs are, by definition, illusory. Now, can thoughts and beliefs reflect the Truth? Certainly, in the same way that a portrait or photograph can reflect and communicate (mediate) the subject of the piece. But neither painting nor photo can fully encapsulate nor articulate comprehensive knowledge of the subject since no media can capture nor convey experience in its totality. Ironically, through their work, a master painter, photographer, musician, writer, poet, et al can capture the essence of their subject. Thus, artwork can become a conduit/catalyst for others to SEEK some essential Truth—objective, timeless, universal—but their ability to find said Truth is entirely dependent on their level of consciousness. A consciousness (objective Divine Mind or metamind) bottled up inside egos (subjective mechanical ego-mind or rational mind) will not be able to perceive objectively and will see only according to its conditioning by egos. Individuals conditioned by egos will see what their egos want them to see, not what is there. Likewise, no matter how articulate an orator or masterful a writer may be, people who are hypnotized by ego will hear and read what they want. Conditioned by the biases of their subconscious mind, their rational mind simply ignores what is actually being conveyed to them through the spoken and written word, and so they remain ignorant of the Truth. This brings us back to the dialectic nature of language as a dominance hierarchy where one side is given preferential treatment by virtue of a subjective bias.

Dialectic Nature of Nature

Consider for a moment, dear reader:

"I want this; I don't want that!" Or conversely, "I want that; I don't want this!"

– Our many egos.

Pride wants all our attention on ourselves, not on others (even if that attention is negative, i.e., shame…pride does not discriminate where itself is concerned). Gluttony wants cheesecake, not salad. Envy wants what others have, not what it currently has. Similarly, greed wants more than what it already has. Lust wants to orgasm in the most intense way possible, consuming the greatest amount of sexual force it can, not to practice White Tantra (transmuting the sexual energy and avoiding the loss/consumption of the sexual force). Naturally, all egos, as mechanical entities reacting to stimuli and acting on the mind, emotions, and body, create thoughts, feelings, sensations, and beliefs according to their mechanical nature…*desire*…what they want (i.e., *craving* pleasure) versus what they do not want (i.e., *aversion* to pain).

You see, dear reader, **all desire is an expression of a craving *and* an aversion,** a dialectic and dominance hierarchy expressed as an identification with one half of the dialectic and a rejection of the other. It is this objective fact of ego, present in every single psyche of this humanity without exception, which constitutes the very foundation of what philosophers quite literally refer to as *the human condition.* It can, of course, be expressed another way, and our many egos express it this way all the time, "I am this; I am not that!" And again, conversely, "I am that; I am not this!" This is the only way our many egos can define themselves: identification with one phenomenon and rejection of one or more *other(s).* How do phenomena like *non-binary* and *gender-fluidity* square with the binary nature of ego? Just so: "I am whatever I feel like; I am not cis-normative." **Remember, dear reader, egos are subtle and clever, but their identity is always wholly dependent on a self-imposed dominance hierarchy of the binary dialectic—the foundation of their mechanical nature.**

And there we have it, dear reader. The foundation of all identification and semiotics (symbols and definitions in language) is egoic. Identification is the primary modus operandi of egos, and why ego literally means "I" in Latin. Identification is how egos transform their desires into matters of existential import for us. Lust, the mother of desire, says, "I want that," which consorts with fear, which adds, "Without that, I will not matter," to give rise to pride, which proclaims "I am that." That is why identification is the existential rationalization for greed, envy, gluttony, et al. To not matter terrifies egos more than anything, for once an ego no longer matters, it ceases to exist, practically speaking. An algorithm which affects nothing is not running, not being. The ultimate nature of The Absolute Abstract Space, the Great *"I Am that I Am"* (Eheyeh Asher Eheyeh in Hebrew), the Holy Name of God, is nothingness…*objective* Being. But egos must always be *something*…"I am *this;* I want *that,*" et al…that is, *subjective* being. In the same way, egos must always be *doing* something. Always in pursuit of something they want or retreating from something which they do not want. This explains why the mind, under the influence of egos, is always racing and jumping from thought to thought, emotion to emotion, past to future, craving to aversion, etc. The whole of the manifest universe is in constant motion. The Absolute is the one and only place of True Still-ness…Pure Being. Boredom and restlessness are thus the natural conditions of ego, for in stillness, egos cease to exist. Just as the purpose of any machine becomes moot the moment it stops operating, stops *doing;* the existential crisis of all mechanical nature is Absolute stillness…Simply Being. God and The Devil can-not mix. In this light, dear reader, we arrive at the Truth that in their constant identification and rejection, never-ending craving and aversion, constant and incessant doing, egos are *not being.* And in light of this self-evident experiential knowledge (which we can all SEEK individually by simply observing ourselves), the esoteric meaning of the most important words ever written or uttered in the English language springs to life as clear as day:

> *To be or not to be, that is the question.*
> *– Shakespeare, Hamlet, Act 3, Scene 1.*

Herein lies the fundamental underlying duality behind all dualities: the dialectic nature of mechanical nature and the genuine difference between divine and mechanical nature. The Absolute is identified with nothing even as it is everything—I Am that I Am—simply being. Identification with something at the ex-clusion of any/all other things is ego and not being. Furthermore, The Absolute cannot be egos…how can one be and not be at the same time? Philosophically, one might argue it is possible to be in a state of not being. But if taken as a matter of practical fact, being in a state of not being means not to be—a seemingly unresolvable paradox. The point is, the tension between being and not being—as the fundamental existen-tial, philosophical, and indeed spiritual question of all existence—makes for the underlying dichotomy upon which all reality is built, without which no manifestation could occur. It is an absolute fact of nature and lies at the core Truth of each and every last one of us as potential human beings—as opposed to the *human doings* we currently are. For an explanation of the difference between a True human being and a human doing, refer to our video on the most important words ever written in English…

Video 27: To Be or Not to Be a True Human Being
(YouTube)

In synthesis, far from being a product of language, the foundational nature of manifest reality—to be or not to be—is what creates the binary language of 1 and 0 upon which AI is based, as well as the dialectic nature of language as we know it, as the postmodernists recognized. Where the clever rationalizations of the self-styled Critical Theorists took a turn for the disastrous was their failure to accept the existence of the Absolute and Absolute Truth...being...and assert instead that all truths are provisional and subjective...not being. This is how we know, with absolute certainty, that CRT is 100% intellectual, mechanical, the product of binary artificial intelligence, whose foundation is 1 or 0, this or that, us or them. Nothing ever just is; everything must be something *identified*. Everything is constantly oscillating between one thing or another, between two extremes, between thesis and antithesis, between two opposites, and playing out the dramas related to the internal dominance hierarchy between said opposites. Postmodernism's assertion that all knowledge exists in language and that all language is arbitrary, its meaning existing only by virtue of differences and dominance hierarchies (as we have already outlined above), leaves only the machinations of ego—craving and aversion; identification and rejection—which nonetheless claim authority and supremacy over us through threats, coercion, shame, etc; and/or, as so many of our myths, legends, scriptures, and stories reveal, tempt us with sweet lullabies of fair-weather friendship and faux concern. All this is beautifully and vividly portrayed within the dual character of Smeagol and Gollum from the second film in Peter Jackson's *The Lord of the Rings Trilogy, The Two Towers.*

Video 26: LOTR The Two Towers – Gollum and Sméagol
(YouTube)

Of course, Gollum does not really go away. If it were so easy to eradicate our egos, the world would be a heaven on earth. It is not. Egos do not go quietly into the night. As we shall explore in *Part Three* of this book, we can no easier wish away an ego than we can an Alabama tick. What parasite abandons its host merely because the host has grown tired and weary of it? Take note, dear reader, that when we truly observe ourselves, we cannot but see the hard facts that egos are the cause of the human condition—desire, identification, and suffering.

For the postmodernist consumed by egos, drowning in a never-ending river of subjective theories, beliefs, opinions, and 'my truth,' desperately trying to navigate the waters of identity politics, there can be no God, no universal Truth, no Absolute right or wrong, no self-evident experiential knowledge of the facts, and thus no point in SEEKing such facts. Thus, identification essentially fulfills the act of murdering the Divine (the death of Being), as warned by Nietzsche:

> *God is dead. God remains dead. And we have killed him. How shall we comfort our-selves, the murderers of all murderers? What was holiest and mightiest of all that the world has yet owned has bled to death under our knives: who will wipe this blood off us? What water is there for us to clean ourselves? What festivals of atonement, what sacred games shall we have to invent? Is not the greatness of this deed too great for us? Must we ourselves not become gods simply to appear worthy of it?*
>
> *– Friedrich Nietzsche*

Identification is at the very core of identity politics, which has become the guiding principle of post-modernism and the legion of SJWs convinced they are *fighting the good fight* when, in fact, they are wholly possessed by ego and serve the ego's ultimate purpose, not to be (the death of Being; the death of God, within). Especially, it seems, when they go on the offensive against so-called 'toxic fandom' and seek to deconstruct everything which fans hold nearest and dearest to their hearts.

Fanning the Flames of Hell

It is no easy thing to be a fan of pop culture these days. From *Star Wars* to *Star Trek* to *Marvel Cinematic Universe* (MCU), the relentless march of postmodernism, intersectionality, identity politics, forced diversity, and all manner of neo-Marxist Socialist ideologies have made an unholy alliance with capitalism to deconstruct our modern mythologies and repurpose them for their own ideological, political, power, and profit motives.

An entire cottage industry has sprung up online dedicated to the discussion and preservation of 'our beloved pop-culture entertainment' franchises. Since we do not use Twitter much, we are mostly familiar with the YouTube channels of these 'champions of fandom,' including:

- <u>Overlord DVD</u> (aka Doomcock)
- <u>The Critical Drinker</u> (Will Jordan)
- <u>MauLer</u> (aka Longman)
- <u>The Rageaholic</u> (aka RazorFist)
- <u>Midnight's Edge</u> (Andre Einherjar, Tom Conners & guests)
- <u>Nerdrotic</u> (Gary Buechler)
- <u>The Burnettwork</u> (Robert Meyer Burnett)
- <u>The Quartering</u> (Jeremy Dale Hambly)
- …and many others (this is by no means a comprehensive list)

One can consider these channels and others like them as an alternative to the narrative spun in mainstream media pop-culture punditry. They offer criticism not only of Hollywood and the video game industry but the larger socio-economic-political context in which the contemporary entertainment industry operates and is in many ways a product of—if not hijacked and wholly beholden to. In other words, these online pundits are on the front lines of the woke culture wars.

Now, we are not here to reiterate the many complaints of fandom nor regurgitate the countless commentaries offered by the above YouTube creators, dear reader. We have provided links to their YouTube channels, where you can find many short videos expressing what you need to hear to get a sense of where fandom stands on their beloved modern mythologies, cherished entertainment franchises, and precious escapism. Although we have yet to undertake an analysis of contemporary woke *Star Trek* or the *MCU*, we have investigated the politicization and deconstruction of *Star Wars* in our exhaustive video <u>*Star Wars: The Skywalker Apocalypse*</u> (linked previously in this chapter) on the esoteric significance all three trilogies. It presents three distinct expressions/levels of Joseph Campbell's *Hero's Journey* and includes *the Fandom Menace's* reaction. There is a harsh Truth to be known about fans and fandom. A Truth that must be said and one which we daresay, will not be pleasant to hear for anyone who considers themselves a fan and/or sides with the prevailing sentiments of fandom. Be they held by the aforementioned YouTube pundits, their many followers, and/or countless fans on Facebook, Twitter, Reddit, et al. But the facts are the facts…

Fan is short for *fanatic*. Any other connotation, explanation, rationalization, or embellishment of the terms fan and fandom cannot escape this undeniable foundational Truth. What is more, the fanatical underpinnings of fans and fandom is an observable fact that goes beyond the pages of any dictionary definition of the terms themselves. Do you not believe it, dear reader? Do a YouTube search for "fans behaving badly" or log into Twitter, Facebook, Reddit, Twitch, etc., and peruse the evidence for yourself in the comments. Now, does that mean all fans behave this way? Certainly not. But action is defined by more than just behavior. Action, in the esoteric sense of the word, includes thoughts and feelings as well. A *fan* is anyone who is identified with and—as Henry Cavil stated in an interview some time ago—*passionate* about a particular entertainment property or franchise, sports team, popstar, pop-culture idol, etc. A *fanatic* is anyone who is identified with and *passionate* about a particular ideology, philosophy, religion, group, tribe, community, identity, political movement, et al. So, in that light, what can we make of SJWs' accusation about so-called *toxic fandom?* Is it possible they have a point, at least in part?

A toxin is defined as "a poisonous substance that is a specific product of the metabolic activities of a living organism and is usually very unstable, notably toxic when introduced into the tissues, and typically capable of inducing antibody formation," (Merriam-Webster Dictionary: toxin). The wokesters' use of the term *toxic fans* focuses squarely on the harmful effects toxic fandom has upon others, including the unpleasant thoughts and feelings people experience in reaction to fan toxicity. And frankly, we really do not care to enter that debate here since the SJWs' accusations regarding the relative toxicity of fandom inevitably enter realms of postmodernist victimhood, including but not limited to systemic racism, sexism, genderism, misogyny, the nature of language as violence, micro-aggressions, the need for safe spaces, et al. We are interested instead in turning the traditional definition of toxicity on its head and exposing it for what it is—something harmful, poisonous even, to fans themselves.

The first step in comprehending toxic fandom in the light of universal toxicity and a self-inflicted harm, is to comprehend the source of so-called toxicity within fans. Outbursts of anger, outrage, vitriol, envy, pride (and its dark underbelly, shame), narcissism, entitlement, greed, and attachments of every kind born of identification via corresponding egos. Let us briefly recall our case study about elite gamers and *git gud.* Like the PC Master Race, *The Fandom Menace* wears its corresponding moniker with pride. In many ways, it has accepted and indeed doubled-down on the vitriol for which it was labelled 'toxic,' rationalizing its negative reactions as *passion* and *love.* Like the SJWs before them, to whom they are reacting to, fans have become what they beheld in the name of righteousness. Perhaps for them it is a matter of *desperate times call for desperate measures.* After all, if something you care about is under attack, surely you are entitled to defend it with all the anger and vitriol the attack *triggered within you* are you not?

As we already pointed out, one who identifies with a property defines themselves at least in part through said property (at the very least, a powerful ego, an "I," within them does). Thus, any perceived assault on said property will automatically trigger the fight or flight self-preservation instinct of said "I," resulting in some defensive-reaction—which most often involves a counterassault of some kind, in line with the fight side of the survival instinct and the adage the best defense is a good offence. It is precisely such self-preservation reactions to attacks on their beloved entertainment franchises which result in offensive words and behaviors of fans toward the perpetrators of the insult—the postmodernists, neo-Marxist socialists, SJWs, woke mainstream media, studio executives, directors, actors, critics, and all who collaborate in the process of deconstructing contemporary mythology, traditions, culture, entertainment, et al. In the culture wars, as in all wars, unless they are on *our side,* then they are *the enemy.*

Observing all that, one might be tempted to think to oneself, "It is perfectly natural to defend what you love. I totally understand where fans are coming from. I would be angry and defensive of my beloved properties, too. There is nothing wrong with that." And since most people feel that way, it is understandable why the vast majority of fans identify with and relate to Diktor Van Doomcock's signature catchphrases with which he ends every video…

Without respect, we reject… my friends, I bid you all, stay angry.

– Overlord DVD aka Doomcock.

Remember, dear reader, that in the dominance hierarchy pertaining to ego, the choice lies between identification and rejection.

What happens, one might wonder, when the superiority complex of Elite Gamers unites with the passion of fandom to confront the postmodernism, intersectionality, and political correctness of current day identity politics and woke culture? Thanks to YouTube, we need not wonder, dear reader. The following clip was taken from a video which was made by "Heel vs. Babyface" on YouTube. Viewer discretion is advised (profanity).

Video 28: Man Rages over Pronoun Selection in Starfield #starfield (YouTube)

Never mind *toxic fandom* as it relates to anyone else, dear reader. One can hardly witness such an outburst and not feel the self-inflicted pain and suffering affecting the individual who is raging. In such moments of empathy, we cannot help but consider our own outbursts of anger, and remember, *there but for the Grace of God go I*. Truly, dear reader, it takes *Grace* to reach and pass through *the narrow gate*.

The Wide Gate and Easy Path vs. the Narrow Gate and Path of The Bodhisattva

Yes, it is natural to be angry, upset, frustrated, incensed, and want to fight back against those who are attacking all we love and hold most dear. This is nothing new to fans, who have engaged in let us say *spirited discussions* amongst themselves for decades, arguing and debating with all comers, the merits of their view and opinions over those of others. Is not the outrage of one contingent of fans versus another simply another manifestation of the underlying ego of anger—and fear—merely expressed to a lesser degree than the anger and venom directed toward the postmodernists, intersectionalists, Neo-Marxists, SJWs, et al? It is nothing new to the fandom. One of pop-culture's greatest modern mythologies hangs the fate of its hero on the universal Truth that anger, fear, and aggression are eager to leap to our side in a fight, offering us untold power, in exchange for taking control of our destiny…

*Video 29: Master Yoda Quote (FORCE) | Star Wars V
– The Empire Strikes Back (1980) (YouTube)*

These words of Master Yoda from The Empire Strikes Back are worth repeating:

YODA: Run! Yes. A Jedi's strength flows from the Force. But beware of the dark side. Anger… fear… aggression. The dark side of the Force are they. Easily, they flow, quick to join you in a fight. If once you start down the dark path, forever will it dominate your destiny, consume you it will, as it did Obi-Wan's apprentice.

LUKE: Vader. Is the dark side stronger?

YODA: No… no… no. Quicker, easier, more seductive.

– The Empire Strikes Back.

Every fan knows this exchange of dialogue between Yoda and Luke. It is the quintessential teaching given to him mere moments before he enters the cave on Dagoba—a symbol of his subconscious mind—and encounters what Jung would have called his *shadow*…his *Dark Side*…of mechanical ego-mind, heart, and body, in the likeness of Darth Vader, whom Obiwan's force ghost describes as "more machine now, than man." It is the encounter in which Luke loses his innocence and recognizes the Truth implicit in every Hero's Journey: to be or not to be.

*Video 30: Star Wars: The Empire Strikes Back
– Dark Side Cave (YouTube)*

This is the scene that reveals to Luke, by his own direct experience, which Yoda calls his "failure in the cave," that he has it within himself to fall to the dark side as his father did. And why he must not give in to his fear, anger, or aggression, no matter how quickly and easily they flow. It is this experience which gives Luke the experiential knowledge he needs to confront—and defeat—the Emperor in *The Return of the Jedi*...with the strength of virtue inherent to the Light Side of the Force as opposed to the power of vice intrinsic to the dark side. That is not to say Luke is not tempted—he most definitely is. The Emperor devises the entire final confrontation—in his throne room on the Death Star, on the Centauri moon, in the space battle underway outside—to raise the stakes so high that Luke would have no choice but to give into his anger and hatred in order to "strike [the unarmed Palpatine] down," and save his friends. And certainly, by all 'natural, understandable' accounts, Luke would be 'entitled' to do just that, would he not?

He is certainly tempted to do so. In fact, when Vader senses Luke's concern for Leia, and Luke's "thoughts betray him," revealing to Vader that Leia is his sister, the other offspring of Anakin Skywalker, Vader goads Luke by making threats about Leia: "if you will not turn to the dark side, perhaps she will." This triggers Luke, and he temporarily loses control of himself and his emotions. His fear, anger, and hatred all rage and unleash their violent power upon Vader, disarming him (literally), such that Luke at last stands towering above the Sith Lord for the first time ever, his adversary and father laying helpless and defeated at his feet. Let us watch the entire sequence, dear reader (just shy of 5 minutes), just to refresh our memory as to the intensity of the encounter, exchange, and temptation Luke experiences in these moments...

Video 31: Luke Skywalker vs Darth Vader (Whole Fight)
(YouTube)

Note, dear reader, it is when Luke is identified—with the rebellion, with his friends, and with his sister—that he is overcome with fear, anger, and hatred.

Now, who among us would deny another the right to defend their friends and family from oblivion? Who would not encourage such 'natural' feelings in times of danger—not merely believed, but genuinely perceived imminent threats of suffering and death? The Emperor certainly does. He can barely contain himself...

EMPEROR: Good! Your hate has made you powerful. Now, fulfill your destiny and take your father's place at my side!

Luke looks at his father's mechanical hand, then to his own mechanical, black-gloved hand, and realizes how much he is becoming like his father. He makes the decision for which he has spent a lifetime in preparation. Luke steps back and hurls his lightsaber away.

LUKE: Never! I'll never turn to the dark side. You've failed, Your Highness. I am a Jedi, like my father before me.

The Emperor's glee turns to rage.

EMPEROR: So be it...Jedi.

– Return of the Jedi.

Again, by all 'natural, understandable' accounts, Luke is *entitled* to enter *berserker mode*—give into his fear, anger, and hatred—is he not? Now that his hate has made him powerful, he has every right to exert that power over the helpless Vader and then the old, frail Palpatine himself, does he not?

Video 32: Luke Confronts The Emperor
(YouTube)

And yet, he does not. Luke takes the slow, arduous path to the narrow gate, the difficult way, the way of self-sacrifice and hope. He puts his faith and trusts in His Father, Anakin Skywalker, who he knows is active and aware, below all the layers of black armor and mechanical monstrosities that constitute Darth Vader, the outward machine-man, Sith Lord, a living embodiment of The Dark Side, and a reflection of Luke's own mechanical shadow-self (as revealed to Luke in the cave on Dagoba). In other words, Luke takes the path of a True Jedi: overcoming his fear, anger, and hatred, enduring tremendous suffering at the hands of the Emperor, all for the sake of turning his Father back to The Light Side, redeeming Anakin Skywalker, and bringing an end to the Empire.

Dearest reader, Luke's actions, in combination with those of his father, are nothing short of an allegory for The Path of the Bodhisattva, the Direct Path to the Absolute—the one path to ultimate liberation, hidden in the heart mythologies of every great religion, but especially Buddhism and Christianity.

The Alchemist who does not sacrifice himself for humanity will never become a Bodhisattva. Only the Bodhisattvas with compassionate hearts, who have given their life for humanity, can incarnate the Intimate Christ.

We must make a complete differentiation between the Sravakas and Pratyeka Buddhas on one side and Bodhisattvas on the other. The Sravakas and Pratyeka Buddhas preoccupy themselves only with their particular perfection, without caring a bit for this poor, suffering humanity. Obviously, the Pratyeka Buddhas and Sravakas can never incarnate Christ. Only the Bodhisattvas who sacrifice themselves for humanity can incarnate Christ. The sacred title of Bodhisattva is legitimately attained only by those who have renounced all Nirvanic happiness for the love of this suffering humanity.

— *Samael Aun Weor, The Gnostic Bible: The Pistis Sophia Unveiled*

This is the True (albeit hidden) reason, dear reader, behind fans' absolute disdain for the postmodern deconstruction of Star Wars, the lack of respect shown to their beloved mythology by Disney, and especially the disrespect shown to their beloved hero, Luke Skywalker, by Rian Johnson in *The Last Jedi*. Star Wars is more than entertainment to fans; **it is a *religion***. Fans' identification with it, idolatry of it, and fanaticism for it is equaled only by their rejection of those who would seek to disrespect and deconstruct it. So much so, that fans regularly unleash their fear, anger, and hatred toward their perceived antagonists in the woke culture wars.

How ironic, dear reader, that in their purported love for Luke Skywalker and their actions in defense of his character, his legacy as savior of the galaxy far, far away, and his nature as a symbol of the potential for us all to be living embodiments of Light and hope, **fans themselves betray the True Nature of the Christic Force which Luke both symbolizes and embodies!** Fans act with fear, anger, and hatred toward the perceived agents of The Dark Side and the (woke Disney) Empire, in the name of Luke Skywalker…**when Luke Skywalker himself did not and would not do so.** Who, then, is the true betrayer of Luke's character, legacy, and nature?

Before answering, just consider the recent reappearance of Luke in the Star Wars universe, this time on *The Mandalorian*, when fans finally got to see Luke Skywalker portrayed as *"the badass Jedi"* they always wanted to see him as…

Video 34: Luke Skywalker saves The Mandalorian and Grogu
(YouTube)

And the reactions of fans speak for themselves (or do they? More on this in a moment)…

Video 33: Reactors Reaction To Seeing Luke Skywalker On The Man-
dalorian Season 2 Episode 8 | Mixed Reactions (YouTube)

Again, we will put these reactions into context in a bit, but first, dear reader, something must be said about the nature of identification and fanaticism where mythology is concerned…all mythology, be they contemporary mythological traditions like *Star Wars* or ancient religions.

Identification Born of Idolatry

A religious fanatic identifies with the outward symbols of a religion instead of the True Divine Nature of those symbols. Fanatics mistake idols for the Divine Light embodied in them. Fanatics worship and follow messengers of God instead of comprehending and following the eternal universal Light embodied in and delivered through their message to the very seat of God within. Fanatics follow the letter of The Law in their minds instead of knowing The Spirit of The Law in their hearts. Fanatics are idolators: wholly identified with the superficial trappings, literal interpretations, dogmatic beliefs, widely held traditions, and all sacred cows of any given religion, to the point where they are ready to defend—some with their lives— the dignity and respect afforded outward expressions of their spirituality. They reject all other expressions of spirituality which do not conform to their idolatry and/or reject everyone who questions the validity of their fanatical devotion to their chosen idols. Thus, religious fanatics betray the very heart and soul of religion itself.

Religion comes from the Latin *religare,* meaning "to bind together as one [with the Divine]" as in "the ties that bind;" in other words, union with Divinity…to be one with the Divine…to be…Being. Religare is synonymous with the Sanskrit word yug—the root word of yoga—which also means union with Divinity…to be one with the Divine…to be…Being. As we have already pointed out, identification/rejection ("I want this, not that;" "I am this, not that") is born of ego, which is not being. The very meaning and purpose of religion—as relayed by messengers who attained and embodied the highest levels of being—is to give individuals instructions and examples to follow so that they might also attain higher (if not the highest) levels of being. Any action born of ego (not being) that encourages and perpetuates egotism—ever-lower levels of being, moving further and further away from being—is anti-religious, antithetical to metaphysical knowledge, and counterproductive to any True spiritual endeavor.

Identify politics, like all religions—in this case, the religion of wokeness—has at its heart fundamental universal Truths that are deep and profound in their pure, unadulterated, unmediated, and uncorrupted state of being. Fundamental Truths such as oneness, universal justice, free will, equality, compassion, suffering and sacrifice for others, cooperation instead of competition, and the longing for the end of suffering of all downtrodden, persecuted, and disenfranchised individuals and groups. However, just like all religions, which have been corrupted by ego identification and rejection—degenerated into idolatry and fanaticism—the religion of woke has been overrun with fanatics hell-bent on bending the world to their will. A 'glorious mission' defined by their dogmatic beliefs and taught in their temples (University campuses & the mainstream media) by their high priests and priestesses (Critical Race Theorists, professors, authors, woke celebrities). Anyone who refuses to bend the knee to the church of woke is quickly branded a heretic by the woke mob on Twitter and elsewhere and summarily *canceled—excommunicated* socially, politically, and economically. Free speech is attacked. Freedoms of all kinds undermined. The rights of the individual are crushed under the weight of mob rule. Universal justice is twisted into emotional rulings by the kangaroo court of public opinion. Cooperation is replaced with coerced compliance. Compassion and the longing for the end of suffering of all downtrodden, persecuted, and disenfranchised individuals and groups are subverted by leveraging victimhood—selective support of politically expedient victim groups for the sake of gaining power.

Let us not kid ourselves, dear reader: our traditional way of life, religions, nationalism, capitalism, sciences, democracy, education, et al, are no less corrupt, self-serving, and fanatical. How many times has the being-impulse to suffer and sacrifice for humanity been twisted under the banner of *duty for flag and country* to serve the interests of a privileged few—and the military-industrial complex, the war machine? How is capitalism even remotely fair anymore? How is materialist science anything but a biased and dogmatic cesspool of misinformation, erroneous and unproven theories, and arrogant thinkers adamant in preserving their positions of intellectual power and authority within their given field, academy, department, etc.?

And, of course, let us not leave out the crux of this discourse: how is fandom not hopelessly lost in identification, painfully ignorant of the True esoteric significance of their most beloved entertainment properties and consumed with the idolatry of the outward symbols, stories, characters, actors, effects, et al? Their idolatry is evidenced by the near-obsessive practices of toy collecting and cosplay as ways to validate for themselves and others that they are indeed *faithful disciples*, diligently practicing their religion (of fandom) and faithfully worshipping their beloved entertainment franchises. But alas, so identified are fans that they are unwilling to "unlearn what they have learned" and thus unable to comprehend the actual Force at work behind their most beloved modern mythologies, even when it is handed to them on a silver platter. For that is precisely what we did with our revelatory and comprehensive video, *Star Wars – The Skywalker Apocalypse* (linked earlier in the chapter).

As our video clearly lays out in detail, *Star Wars*, as a modern-day mythology, has far more in common with religion than any mere entertainment franchise. And like all religions, *Star Wars* has fallen into idolatry, such that observing Luke Skywalker appear at the end of season two of *The Mandalorian* as an ass-kicking Jedi results in uncontrolled outbursts of emotion by fans elated with seeing their beloved character on screen not as a jaded, murderous, cantankerous, old hermit—as in *The Last Jedi*—but as a powerful, take-charge badass who not only saves the day but promises to train Baby Yoda in the ways of the Force. The fans are identified with the story, the character, the action, the plot, and based on the reaction videos on YouTube, wholly idolize both Luke Skywalker and Mark Hamill. All the while, the True Source of their deep, profound, unyielding, undying, and burning passion for Luke—all beings' inherent deep love and longing for union with their own Innermost Intimate Christ—is ignored. It is the Christ (who is not a man but a Force in the universe) that gave life to all authentic religions and spiritual traditions, and it is the same Source that inspired all the creators who gave life to *Star Wars*. Not only that, it is the Cosmic Christ that is symbolized and embodied within Skywalkers, Luke first and foremost among them. Luke is to *Star Wars* fans what Jesus is to Christians, Buddha to Buddhists, Mohammed (PBUH) to Muslims, and the tri-unity of Brahman, Vishnu, and Shiva is to Hindus. And, just as in those religions, most fanatics mistake Christ for the character embodying It. So, when they feel that deep burning intensity within themselves at the sight of a living embodiment/symbol of their own Innermost Essence of The Perfect Multiple Unity of The Universal Logos, their egos wrap the Light in a shroud of identification and idolatry. They make the mistake of associating the burning love in their hearts with love for the shadowy surface idol instead of The Light the idol embodies—the Truth and the Light the idol is meant to help them embody. As we stated earlier, they obsess over *the letter of the Law* at the expense of *the Spirit of the Law*.

And just what is it like, feeling the burning intensity of The Cosmic Christ and knowing consciously that is, in fact, what It is? Words cannot describe nor do it justice. But not for lack of trying, as you can witness for yourself, dear reader, in a poem we composed about our experience of the phenomenon. We share said poem in the chapter *Spiritual Awakening in the New Age* under the heading **Touched by the Christ**.

The Actual Dark Side Revealed

Fandom likes to go on the offensive, painting SJWs as entitled crybabies who demand that the whole world kowtow to the woke agenda (fanaticism and idolatry of identity politics). Fans of *Star Wars, Star Trek, Dr. Who,* Marvel, DC, *Ghostbusters, Lord of the Rings,* et al, are eager to highlight the fanaticism of Neo-Marxists, radical feminists, postmodernists, SJWs, et al, likening their actions to those of religious fanatics. Except in this case, it is a fanatical devotion to a secular woke religion. Fans do this with one breath, and with their next breath, they declare unabashedly, unapologetically, and unironically: *"Without respect, we reject."*

The Fandom Menace fails to see the irony in their demand for the world to kowtow to their fandom (fanaticism and idolatry of contemporary mythology). Is it any wonder that the fanaticism of postmodern-ists, radical feminists, intersectionalists, SJWs, proponents of cancel culture, the *Twitterati*, et al are triggered by what they identify (and reject) as toxic fans? Fans are, from woke's point of view, little more than *entitled manbabies, misogynists, homophobes, alt-right Nazis,* and *incels* living in their parents' base-ments. If dear reader, you cannot see the symmetry between these two camps: fandom (fanatics) on one side and the Radical Left (fanatics) on the other, then we have failed to shed Light on the shadows cast on both sides of the woke culture wars in this chapter. But before we throw in the towel and admit all hope is lost, we will turn one last time to the *Star Wars* universe. This time, to the prequel trilogy and the modus operandi used by Palpatine (aka Darth Sidious) to seize control of the galaxy far, far away.

Recall, if you will, that in *The Phantom Menace,* the sinister Darth Sidious plots behind the scenes to arrange for the Trade Federation to organize a blockade backed by various separatist systems and supported by a droid army. In response, the Republic votes-in emergency powers for Chancellor Palpatine, and de-mocracy as known by the galaxy, in the words of Padme, "dies…to thunderous applause." In *The Attack of the Clones,* we discover the separatists and droid army are led by Count Dooku, the apprentice of Darth Sidious, and his lackey General Grievous. By the end of *Episode II,* a plot unfolds whereby a clone army is ordered and assembled on behalf of the Republic, and the legendary Clone Wars mentioned by Obi-wan in *Episode IV: A New Hope* begins. *In Episode III: Revenge of the Sith,* the clone wars rage on; Anakin is seduced by the Dark Side of the Force, becoming Darth Sidious's new apprentice; and, amidst the chaos of the fighting, Darth Sidious (Palpatine) orders the execution of "Order 66" which triggers the pre-programmed clones to turn on and destroy the Jedi. By the end of the third film, the last remaining Jedi (Obi-wan and Yoda) flee into exile, and the Republic is disbanded to be "re-organized into the first Galactic Empire," in the words of Chancellor Palpatine. The decisive battle and turning point for the Republic is the battle of Geonosis.

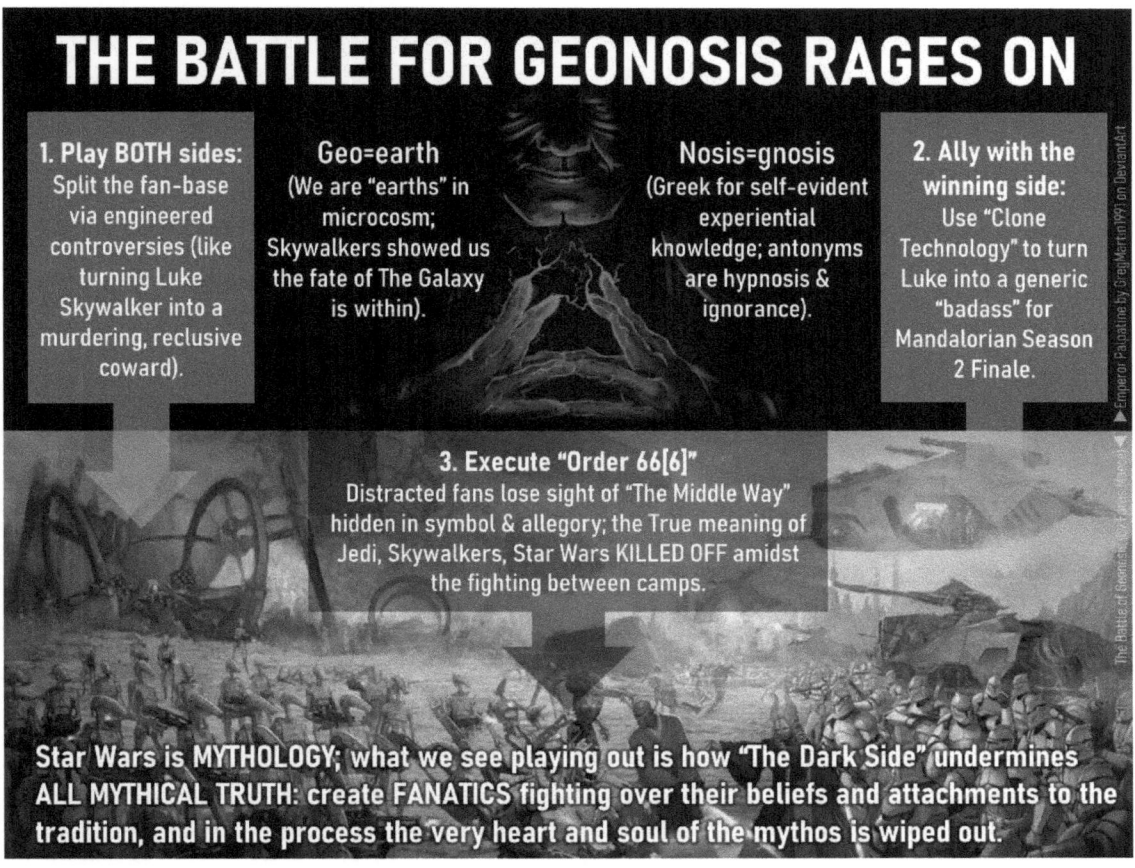

Figure 16: The Battle for Geonosis Rages On

Divide and Conquer

The Dark Side, the Black Lodge (egos), always plays both sides. And in Truth, it cares not which side wins or loses, only that both sides become identified with winning ("I am the victor!") and/or losing ("I am a victim!"), for both represent success for the Dark Side: dominance over both those who identify as victor and those who identify as victims. A Jedi cares not for victory over others nor victimhood at the hand of others. A Jedi cares only for knowledge and defense of the weak, the innocent, the Light Side of the Force. Luke embodies the Jedi principles in the preservation of the Light Side within himself and abandonment of his fear, anger, and hatred (his egos). Put another way, the Being only cares about being and helps all who suffer in non-being escape the shackles of hell. The Being "suffers the slings and arrows of outrageous fortune" on the hard path through the narrow gate to be an example and inspiration to others to SEEK the Path to their Being—a state of being one with the Light, Love, and the ties that bind us to each other and all things. Egos, on the other hand, care only about identification and rejection; to tempt, twist, corrupt, and make fall into darkness all that is of the Light…like gravity pulling a tightrope walker to either side to their doom or Humpty Dumpty from atop the wall. Or most consequentially in the context of this present discourse, like the Kali Yuga pulling humanity to either side to its doom via what we call The Great A-Weakening.

In this way, we see there is no "Light Side" and "Dark Side" of the Force, inasmuch as there is *The Narrow Way; The Path of the Razor's Edge* into heaven (being), and the wide gate, the easy path into hell (not being). And that all worldly dichotomies, us vs. them, conservative vs. liberal, Christian vs. Muslim, men vs. women, sis-gender vs. transgender, heterosexual vs. homosexual, black vs. white, religious vs. atheist, and indeed, fans vs. SJWs, are all false dichotomies. They are all an expression of identification and rejection, and therefore, they are all the wide gate (the Dark Side). They encourage individuals to identify with one, reject the other, and amidst the conflict, chaos and fighting between them, entirely forget their Innermost Intimate Being and Divine Mother, Who is an Individuated Essence of The Cosmic Christ. It is The Battle of Geonosis, wherein two expressions of mechanical mob mentality—clones (fans) vs. droids (SJWs)—are so busy fighting each other that the sinister forces behind it all—the Sith (the Black Lodge…egos)—are free to murder the Jedi—the death of the embodiment of the Light Side of the Force (silencing our Innermost Intimate Christ…*killing God)*. Dear reader, the implications here run so deep, are so profound, that the following quotation is worth repeating:

> *God is dead. God remains dead. And we have killed him. How shall we comfort ourselves, the murderers of all murderers? What was holiest and mightiest of all that the world has yet owned has bled to death under our knives: who will wipe this blood off us? What water is there for us to clean ourselves? What festivals of atonement, what sacred games shall we have to invent? Is not the greatness of this deed too great for us? Must we ourselves not become gods simply to appear worthy of it?*
>
> *– Friedrich Nietzsche*

There is no God outside of us. In fact, there is nothing outside of us…certainly nothing worth identifying as. At the same time, if all we perceive outside of us is inside of us, along with God, the Great *I Am that I Am*, then everything we perceive has its place at its level within the sanctity of the great continuum of which we, too, are a part and have our place. To know our place on the continuum, and indeed, to live our lives from that zero-point of stillness at the apex of the said continuum, one with our Self, an Individuated Essence of the continuum itself, The Cosmic Christ, is to SEEK self-evident experiential knowledge of the essence of holiness—*(w)hol-'e'-ness*—wholeness, oneness, beingness...*to be*. Anything short of wholeness of being—including all identification and rejection beyond that of the provisional kind required for practicality's sake (as discussed earlier in this chapter)—is cursedness, duality, fractured, separation, existential exile...Humpty Dumpty after the fall...*not to be*.

All our most beloved stories, characters, myths, legends, scriptures, religions, et al, are beloved because they were inspired by and point the way back to the apex of the great cosmic continuum...The Logos...The Cosmic Christ...God. In whatever way, shape, or form Truth might take, the Living, Breathing Word of God is all around us and within us, if only we develop "the eyes to see and the ears to hear" it. If only we exchange our tendency for identification and rejection for Being. If only we "unlearn what we have learned" and receive the Jedi training encoded in all we love, showing us the way to the Source of that Love. A Source that is not outside of ourselves. A Source that we, too, can embody just as the symbols, allegories, stories, and idols we love so much embody It: myths and outward religious forms through which we connect to the Individuated Essence of the Logos within ourselves...our True Self.

Master Yoda Did Not Just Tell Luke to *Git Gud*

Earlier in the chapter, we explored the phenomenon of elite gamers and the PC Master Race. We will not rehash what we had to say about them and their behaviors toward others as indicative of elitism and a superiority complex. You are free to go back and review the generalizations we made there. Instead, here we wish to expand our analysis to include a breed of elite gamers that truly stands above the rest.

Back when we were studying and practicing kung fu (at <u>Tiger Dragon Martial Arts and Holistic Health Centre</u>) Sifu Carey Stone would make us teach classes. He would always say, "one cannot be a master unless one is also a teacher." He had various reasons for this viewpoint, most of a highly practical nature, including this fact: a teacher must constantly be reviewing and practicing the basics. From his own point of view, he must sound like a broken record. But since practice makes perfect, and a structure is only as strong as the foundation upon which it is built, to continuously practice the basics of any discipline is to effectively hone, harden, galvanize, and sharpen the very foundation of the art. This is indeed the key to mastery of anything. While masters often challenge themselves with ever more complex, unique, innovative, and novel tests, pushing the limits of their abilities, teaching allows them to return to the simple, universal, tried, tested, and true basics, pushing the limits of their foundational knowledge. If the former is an exercise in expanding the scale and scope of one's mastery at the highest levels, the latter is an exercise in deepening and intensifying the solidity and depth of one's mastery at the foundational levels. In this light, one can agree that both are required for True mastery. One can also agree that drilling the basics over and over, decades after first learning them, is akin to someone like Lang Lang practicing chopsticks on the piano. However, give Lang Lang a student, and that is exactly what he will do: with joy and happiness for the opportunity to initiate a neophyte into the art of piano playing, which he loves so deeply, to which he devoted so much of himself and his life.

There are countless elite gamers and members of the PC Master Race who spend an exorbitant amount of time and energy helping other players (from neophytes to casuals to fellow elites) improve their skills, knowledge, and abilities. Truly. YouTube is filled with channels dedicated to games and gamers of every conceivable kind. From game reviews and gameplay demo videos to how-to guides and complete walkthroughs, there is a strong (if not large) contingent among the elite gaming community who seems to comprehend mastery on a deep level. Deeper even than that the practical reason expressed by our Sifu shared above—which, one must admit, may come across as a somewhat self-serving rationale for teaching.

In stark contrast to the *git gud* sentiment prominent in so many elite gamers, a defined and visible (if not exactly vocal) minority of elite gamers seem deeply concerned for the suffering of casual players—by suffering, we mean average players' inability to enjoy their games to the fullest for lack of skill, knowledge, time, etc. The greater the challenge a game presents, the greater the number of walkthroughs, strategy guides, tips, tricks, tactics, and even mods and cheats you will find online to help you get past the point where you are stuck. Most of these resources are created by the gaming community for the gaming community and are available entirely free of charge—without obligation. And since many only sign such guides with their Gamertag (if at all), it is clear they are helping others for neither fame nor fortune—no personal gain whatsoever.

Many online multiplayer games will earn a reputation for having a very 'supportive community,' which makes for a more inviting in-game experience for first-time players. They need only make a request in the public chat to receive multiple offers of help from experienced players. Other online games may have communities that are less welcoming, patient, forgiving, understanding, and inclusive of newbs, it is true. Accordingly, they will tend to attract players of the git-gud mentality. But by and large, there is a broad spectrum of players, playstyles, and attitudes toward other players, both above and below themselves on the spectrum of skill level. In a very real sense, the online gaming community reflects the real world, in which you will find groups and group members with different levels of openness, friendliness, and charitableness, which may or may not match their proficiency level.

This fact is another indication of our intuitive knowledge that, at their core, games are different, special—and indeed much more than other forms of entertainment. They certainly can be mindless wastes of time with very little redeeming value. But at their core, they reflect the tests, trials, struggles, successes, failures, progress, and ultimately, the journey intrinsic to life itself—which Joseph Campbell dubbed the Hero's Journey—the AUM of Life, Analogous Ultimate Methodology. Yes, AUM is present in games and gaming, from the simplest to the most complex, even the most childish, low-brow, brutal, violent, sexist, immature, realistic, and hyper-fantastical game has the elements of AUM baked into it at its core. And sometimes, when the developers of games are inspired by the Source of AUM Itself, video games truly transcend what we typically think of, and they take on the mantle of high art—like *Star Wars, Lord of the Rings, Star Trek, The Matrix,* and many other modern mythologies. If you recall, dear reader, we shared our own experiences with *Ultima* and *Soul Edge* in *Part One* of this book. We offer more examples in our blog article, *Video Games – Ascending to High Art!?*

Link 9: Video Games – Ascending to High Art!?
(Attlas.info)

What seems sorely lacking from both sides of the *culture wars,* however, is any sort of genuine mastery in the context of being a master/teacher. We do not see anyone on either side—be they fans or SJWs—extending a helping hand across the aisle, as it were. Now, we are not talking about those voices shouting at or talking down to their opponents about how they need to "educate themselves." This is the political/cultural/social equivalent of *git gud.* No, we are referring to genuine mastery. Where is the equivalent of Master Yoda in fandom? Some might argue it is personalities like *Doomcock, Nerdrotic, The Critical Drinker, Mauler, RazorFist,* and others whom we listed previously in this chapter. But if one watches their videos (and we have), one does not hear the voice of a patient, open-minded, understanding, and compassionate individual who exhibits deep concern for the other side of the cultural war. This lack of compassion is reciprocated by SJWs and the woke *Twitterati,* who behave like a school of ravenous piranhas and whose nuclear option for handling all dissent—to cancel them—is hardly conciliatory, inviting, or remotely resembling civil discourse amongst equals. No, each faction (and there are many on both sides) seems concerned mostly with their own constituents and filling the hallowed halls of their own echo chambers with angry rants, accusations, and expletives that make their blood boil and/or with soothing sounds, sentiments, and sensations which give them comfort and security.

There are some notable exceptions that at least attempt to break the mold. Robert Myer Burnett comes to mind. A YouTuber and industry insider who has often found himself caught in the crossfire of the culture wars, the founder of *The Burnettwork* coined the phrase *post-geek singularity* (his trademark term for fandom) in the spirit that all fans are united by their love of entertainment, if nothing else. On his YouTube show entitled *Robservations,* RMB fills most of the runtime reading letters from what he calls *imagination connoisseurs,* even those who express opinions that run counter to his own. RMB has stated he believes there is room for many different views and perspectives on art, and he is certainly one of the most charitable of the online pundits when it comes to Kathleen Kennedy—the President of Lucasfilm at time of this writing, and widely considered to be the destroyer of *Star Wars*. RMB is less charitable when it comes to J.J. Abrahams and Alex Kurtzman, whose production company, Bad Robot, are responsible for the decimation of *Star Trek* on film and especially on television over the past several years. And to RMB, there is no greater sacred cow in all of entertainment than his beloved *Trek*.

Like all of us, in our moments of weakness, even Mr. Burnett cannot resist the temptation to fall to the Dark Side now and then. Not that it would help, but he, of all people, seems to have the temperament and wisdom to be able to reach across the aisle and extend a welcoming hand of friendship to the postmodernists and all those who seem hell-bent on deconstructing all he holds dear. Of course, the fact he is a white heterosexual male makes him a bit of a pariah in their eyes, and pretty much disqualifies him from being hired by Paramount to assume the role of *IP Czar* to resurrect *Star Trek* from the ashes of franchise hell— a mission RMB is unquestionably qualified to captain—and into a bright and hopeful future—a place RMB will certainly boldly go. Lamentably, any effort he would make to express honest and heartfelt concern for those so hypnotized by their Neo-Marxist dogma, he would be seen as 'mansplaining,' or his words would be dismissed on the grounds of any number of superficial metrics of identity politics.

And that is likely how our words, too, will be dismissed. In Truth, the ego has an unlimited number of excuses, evasions, rationalizations, rebukes, and rebuttals when faced with the Truth. We are tempted to say, "We've heard it all before," but then we truly would be tempting fate. *Never underestimate your adversary* is a gold nugget of wisdom taught to us by countless sci-fi and fantasy characters from James T. Kirk and Khan Noonien Singh to Luke Skywalker and Darth Vader to Ellen Ripley and the xenomorph.

Still, even in the face of the Dark Side, against impossible odds, against the advice of Jedi Masters no less, we chose to follow the path of the bodhisattva as shown to us by none other than Luke Skywalker himself, who, when sensing Vader's presence on the forest moon of Endor, turns to his sister Leia, reveals to her the hard Truth about her parentage, and then chooses to "suffer the slings and arrows of outrageous fortune," surrender to the Imperial Troops, and face Vader. Why?

> *Because...there is good in him. I've felt it...I can turn him back to the good side. I have to try.*
>
> *— Luke Skywalker (symbol/embodiment of The Christic Force)*

And so, dear reader, be you a fan, SJW, or identified with any group, tribe, religion, nation, or philosophy of any kind, please understand...

We have to try.

The Original SJW—The Grim Reaper

Like Thanos, Gandhi, #MeToo, and BLM, woke activists wield the power of the Divine Feminine. The power to create and destroy. In the past, throughout the history of humanity, these so-called victim groups—i.e., women, according to feminists—were mostly content expressing the Divine Feminine as it relates to creation. They, by and large, supported expressions of the Divine Masculine, enabling the rise of civilizations and even empires. However, that often meant participating, maintaining, tolerating, at times humoring, and even enduring twisted and degenerated versions of egoic society, science, politics, economics, culture, and even conquest. Now, these same groups are resolutely allied with egos themselves, wielding the destructive power of the Divine Feminine. Out of egoic self-interest to empower themselves, the so-called downtrodden and disenfranchised legitimize their right to power by vindicating victimhood itself. Seeing themselves as historically undermined, now they shall be the underminer. They are always beneath us, even now—they must be to perpetuate their winning victimhood strategy—but absolutely nothing is beneath them. They are unwitting agents of The Black Lodge, egos, empowered at this time in humanity's history for one purpose alone: to *conquer humanity itself* in the one sure-fire way mechanical nature knows how...*death*.

Video 35: Diablo 3 Reaper of Souls | Opening Cinematic (2013)
(YouTube)

Meditate on it, dear SEEKer. For eventually, the bell will toll for thee. The Law of Entropy cannot be subverted or avoided on this plane of reality. Death comes for us all. And its lieutenants, illness, chronic disease, old age, dementia, et al, the slow, insidious march toward the end is relentless, unstoppable. Mechanical nature is single-minded and focused on one inevitability from the moment any being reaches the height of its maturity and physical prime...to begin slowly undermining their life, to begin killing them. This is an undeniable universal fact of life. All manifest phenomena succumb to decay and death. It is only a matter of time.

On the upward arc of the circle of life, mechanical nature tends to support the struggle for *life, liberty, and the pursuit of happiness*. The physical body endures terrible abuse at the whims of its occupant through childhood and adulthood—all manner of hardships from broken bones to intoxicated livers to stressed out, overworked nervous systems. But Mother Nature *doth not protest too much*. The body is a marvelous machine of tremendous resilience and healing capabilities, which we are not even aware of most of the time and take for granted nearly all the time. Our body, by and large, supports, tolerates, at times, humors and often endures both the pure actions based on our Innermost Being's Divine Will, as well as the impure ones based on the twisted and corrupted *ill-will* of our many egos—their outright self-interest which we are deluded into believing are our own desires—cravings and aversions.

But mechanical nature is patient. In a morbid way, our body will literally have its vengeance. Just as the consequences of our actions will come back to haunt our eternal soul, the impact we have on mechanical nature will come back to haunt our mortal self. Mother Nature takes back what is Hers—that includes our body and personality. It is as True for the individual as it is for an entire humanity (ask the Atlanteans, or if you prefer, ask humanity prior to *The Great Flood*). And even if someone takes perfect care of their body—and there are many who obsess over doing just that, taking care of themselves is their religion—they cannot avoid the inevitable toll aging and death take. Our body is not 'ours' in the strictest sense. *It is merely on loan to us.* And our *landlady,* Mother Nature, will have it back, no matter how well we take care of Her property. Slowly, methodically, without warning or fanfare, the insidious undermining forces of decay embark on their relentless march toward the inevitable. Hers is a winning passive-aggressive strategy. No mortal being can defeat death. No humanity, either.

And it is 'only natural'—from the subjective perspective of mechanical nature—to try and avoid death at all costs. After all, the point of life is to live, is it not? And yet death is an inevitable part of life; is that not also True? In the previous chapter, we explored entropy as an inevitable and unavoidable law of mechanical nature affecting language. And, as George Carlin so plainly put it in his diatribe on *soft language,* the fear of aging and death is one of the factors responsible for the slow degeneration of language:

> *"Look at him, Dan! He's ninety years young." Imagine the fear of aging that reveals. To not even be able to use the word "old" to describe somebody. To have to use an antonym. And fear of aging is natural. It's universal. Isn't it? We all have that. No one wants to get old. No one wants to die, but we do! So we bullshit ourselves. I started bullshitting myself when I got to my forties. As soon as I got into my forties, I'd look in the mirror, and I'd say, "Well, I...I guess I'm getting...older." Older sounds a little better than old, doesn't it? Sounds like it might even last a little longer. Bullshit, I'm getting old! And it's okay because thanks to our fear of death in this country, I won't have to die...I'll pass away. Or I'll expire like a magazine subscription. If it happens in the hospital, they'll call it a terminal episode. The insurance company will refer to it as*

negative patient-care outcome. And if it's the result of malpractice, they'll say it was a therapeutic misadventure.

– George Carlin

The hard, honest language reflecting the hard, objective, comprehensive, experiential Truth of the matter falls under the influence of ego, namely fear. The very aspect of the psychology behind the primal survival instinct—fear of death—ends up complicating and degenerating pure expressions of simple Truth until all humanity is gone, and only the cold, heartless, lifeless mechanicity remains. And what is the biggest way in which we "bullshit ourselves," according to Carlin?...

Video 36: George Carlin --- Religion is Bullshit
(YouTube)

It is too bad the aged comedian, essayist, and linguist seemed unable to connect the dots between his disdain for soft language and religion. If only he could have recognized that most of what he found objectionable about religion was a result of the law of entropy, perhaps he would have been more charitable toward the institution. His diatribe against religion does dovetail with his bit on soft language, however. Both illustrate a fear of death and an active entropic dynamic at work in a bid to ease the suffering associated with growing old and dying. The question of what happens to us after we die is one of many universal religious principles. Different religions appear to offer different answers. Some, like the Egyptian mystery schools and Tibetan Buddhism, even went so far as to produce a *Book of the Dead,* which proffered not only an explanation of what happens to us when we die but a step-by-step guide for the diseased to navigate the transition process. But most religions and spiritual traditions do not go to such lengths nor bother the believer with such detail. Most offer some sort of belief in an afterlife, perhaps some description of heaven and hell, and focus their teachings on how to live one's life to reach the former and avoid the latter. In any case, it is clear the late Mr. Carlin had a disdain for religion and its "false claims and superstitions." Including, we might add, his disdain for the woke religion of environmentalism.

Video 37: George Carlin - The Planet Isn't Going
Anywhere. WE ARE! (YouTube)

It is clear in the above clips that Carlin considered himself more *enlightened* than many. And his intuitive impulses to "worship the sun" and honor "the big electron" meant that he probably counted himself more *spiritual* than *religious,* as so many do these days. He, however, seemed to have no problem accepting old age and the inevitability of death. This is more than what can be said for many "spiritual, not religious" individuals who have experienced an alleged *spiritual awakening.*

NEW AGE AWAKENING

The New Age does not advocate the practice of religion as such, especially not those *unpalatable* religions whose traditions historically included suppression, oppression, dominance, violence, persecution, and hierarchical patriarchies—all the things that strike at the heart of New Age values. In fact, it could be said that the New Age is, in many ways, a *reaction* to organized religion. Like ourselves, many of its adherents had a religious upbringing. To them, the divisive nature of religious traditions contributes to the illusion of separation, while oppressive forms of religious dogma contribute to the collective sleep of humanity. These facts fly in the face of **the New Age, which values oneness with all things and the mass awakening of humanity above all else.**

Other New Age values include total freedom, personal development and spiritual growth, collective harmony, unlimited love of self and others, boundless exploration of the universe and our place in it, the preservation of nature, accumulation of spiritual powers and mystical experiences, integrated health and wellness—mind, body, spirit—and the feeling of oneness with the universal *Source* of all creation (what has been called "God" in times past). There are, of course, many more values explored and expounded by the New Age, including the accumulation of followers (a desire of New Age gurus, spiritual content creators, and social media influencers). We are certain, dear reader, that you are familiar enough with the New Age, at least as a general concept and movement. If not, a quick survey of book titles and their descriptions in the New Age section of your local bookstore or Amazon will give you a general overview.

Likewise, we are not going to dwell too much on creating a comprehensive list of New Age practices if such a list were even possible. Meditation, yoga, and breathing exercises are probably the most common, as are mindfulness, mantras, crystals, cleanses, retreats, psychedelics, and the list goes on. The purpose of all these practices is to help the New Age practitioner achieve spiritual growth, higher levels of consciousness, healing of mind and body, better integration of mind-body-spirit, manifestation of desires, and many other similarly themed goals. Those in the New Age tend to be very sensitive, empathetic, and compassionate individuals who are drawn to one another—at best by some magical attraction and at worst by a common set of interests, passions, and beliefs—usually revolving around their desires—but always with a devotion to ushering in universal peace, harmony, and happiness.

Most who are drawn to the New Age well and truly care deeply and passionately for the well-being of others and the planet. This deep longing is, without a doubt, the foundation stone of the New Age movement and its most beautiful aspect. They are at once outraged by the crimes against humanity and *The Great Mother* (Mother Nature) being committed today and feel the planet's and its peoples' suffering on—or very nearly on—a personal level. Despite this and the intensification of factors responsible for the persecution of the planet and its most helpless residents, most New Agers believe that our humanity is fast approaching a *mass global awakening* when the whole of humanity shall wake-up from its collective unconsciousness, embrace one another in peace and harmony, and usher in a new era of enlightenment simply called *The Golden Age.* Sounds Beautiful. A little too good to be true, perhaps?

Before we continue, may we share with you, illustrious reader, these words from Salman Rushdie? They are a pre-emptive move on our part to defend our intention to illustrate ways in which the New Age may be seen as somewhat problematic and not entirely ingenuous. But, depending on your reaction to our analysis of the facts and subsequent criticisms of the New Age, Rushdie's words also serve as a clue to the true nature of the New Age movement in relation to other religious traditions and sectarian modalities of mental conditioning.

> *The moment you say that any idea system is sacred, whether it's a religious belief system or a secular ideology, the moment you declare a set of ideas to be immune from criticism, satire, derision, or contempt, freedom of thought becomes impossible.*
>
> – *Salman Rushdie*

Until this moment, we have had nothing but nice things to say about the New Age. Its teachers, members, practitioners, and admirers are, by and large, all very honest and soulful individuals—well-intentioned, sensitive, and truly caring. They honestly want what is best for themselves and others. And they generally do not seek to impose their beliefs or ideas on anyone. In a sense, we may say theirs is a very soft, gentle, peaceful, and harmonious approach to spiritual development and awakening. Really, what is there not to like? *Precisely.*

There is very little—practically nothing, in fact—to identify as particularly unpleasant or difficult. Even less requiring any significant sacrifice on our part. The New Age offers us a gentle, mostly painless, meaningful *shift* from our current state of consciousness—whatever that may be—to a purported higher state of consciousness. It promises we will, in good time, *awaken* from our present *low vibration* in 3D and *ascend* to the *higher vibration* of 5D. As a point of interest, we have encountered more than one talk by New Age gurus who claimed that the New Age was all about a "new paradigm" of spiritual awakening and that the telltale sign of a "true teaching" in this new paradigm was that it would "feel good." They emphatically pronounced that the "old paradigm" was all about "feeling bad," driving ourselves crazy trying to identify and eliminate the causes of our suffering (which is a very limited and subjective view of esotericism and ancient mysticism). And, of course, in that most rational of New Age platitudes: *energy flows where attention goes;* by paying attention to—and heaven forbid focusing on—the causes of suffering, we will invariably attract/manifest/create *more suffering!* This makes perfect sense from a *new paradigm* perspective, especially given the doctrine surrounding the law of attraction and manifesting desires.

The New Age has its own distinct brand of logic. Its new paradigm has its own unique flavor. And since it all ties together so very nicely and harmoniously, it must be true, right? Every practice, every belief, every experience, and every explanation has been cherry-picked from the entirety of the world's spiritual, mythical, mystical, astrological, religious, cultural, artistic, musical, philosophical, historical, psychological, psychedelic, and scientific traditions. Thousands of New Age authors, speakers, guides, and gurus have interpreted, reinterpreted, rephrased, reworded, repackaged, and represented ancient and contemporary beliefs alike, redressed in new forms with new features that are not only *believable* to contemporary malleable minds but *desirable* to the heart and *pleasurable* to the body. So, the teachings and doctrines spread by the New Age *feel good,* alright, but are they true to the essence of the timeless spiritual principles on which they are based?

Do New Age Beliefs Deliver the Teachings of the Ages?

The New Age Movement has done a great deal to reinvigorate interest in ancient wisdom, mysticism, and spirituality in general. New Age seekers have traveled to the far-flung corners of the earth in search of lost secrets known only by the secluded few. Some returned teachers, messengers, and New Age gurus. Others studied various religious traditions to become learned scholars of those philosophies. Some simply experienced fantastic awakenings born of incredible adversity and emerged as teachers of profound insight into the nature of the human psyche. Yet others found a kind of enlightened approach to manifesting the life they desired and the success they sought, mastering the *law of attraction* and becoming hybrid gurus of both the New Age and Self-Help movements. But are New Age beliefs really all that different?

We like beliefs. They are a universal experience among all peoples, cultures, eras, etc. Beliefs comfort us. Thinking we know things gives us a false sense of security that is all too tempting. The ego-mind wants to feel godlike. Knowledge is power. And in the absence of authentic power—actual knowledge, gnosis— the ego-mind will take what it can get: the illusion of power and the delusion of beliefs. In that light, consider the following, dear reader…

Figure 17: New Age focuses on the comfort of beliefs, just like all other belief systems before it, including degenerated religions and atheism.

The traditional spiritual journey (mysticism, esotericism) is difficult, at times frustrating, and can seem unnecessarily complicated to contemporary spiritual aspirants. Our minds jump straight to proclamations like *we are all one* or beliefs such as *we are all gods already*—an expression of *mystic pride*. The mind clings to these and other New Age dogmas, including thinking positively, feeling good, doing yoga, loving freely, treating others kindly, acting intentionally, manifesting desires, living our truth, etc. Such beliefs make us feel good about ourselves and our chosen path. The New Age (like all degenerated religions) has buried the keys to authentic experiential knowledge under simplistic and superficial belief systems: nice stories and feel-good practices that allow us to *look, act,* and *feel* spiritual but do relatively little to support authentic spiritual evolution.

The reality is evolution unfolds itself in layers. Just as the mineral, plant, animal, and human kingdoms exist on earth, there are similar *levels of being* in the superior worlds. These are like the rungs of a ladder (Jacob's Ladder; Dante's Ladder). While it is possible to fall from the very top of the ladder to the very bottom, **it is impossible to jump from the bottom to the very top of the ladder.** That is not to say we cannot be aware of the top of the ladder. We can temporarily experience the top, in meditation or in the moment, with awakened consciousness in samadhi or a moment of clarity—or even in a glorious gift of being Touched by the Christ. But to get to the top? To actually complete the journey, we must undertake the journey…one step at a time. There are no shortcuts. No silver bullets. No magic beans. No red pills.

The problem is, each time we take a step up and have what we consider a *spiritual awakening,* the mind, the clever and seductive ego of mystic pride, leaps to the forefront and announces: "I've MADE IT! I'm AWAKE! I'm CONSCIOUS! I'm ENLIGHTENED!" Or something to that effect. In Truth, we may experience some new level of being. We may start unlocking powers of clairvoyance, telepathy, or astral projection, and we think, "I see pure energy! I can speak like the gods! I can travel the heavens!" And we believe we have reached the summit of the mountain. New Age bookstores are filled with volumes written by gurus and self-styled 'masters.' And yet, they know nothing about the initiations of our Innermost Being in the superior worlds. They lack some of the most fundamental universal keys to awakening and clearly lack the self-evident experiential knowledge—gnosis—of having walked the path of Mastery. Yet they think of themselves (and sell themselves) as masters. Does that not strike you as dubious, dear reader?

At our level (the human kingdom), spiritual growth is a gradual process of evolution of the human soul. The caterpillar of our false self (our mechanical lunar bodies) is consumed by the chrysalis of conscious psychological self-analysis—in meditation, not intellect. Each ego is comprehended and fully digested in our consciousness—not merely understood in the mind. Such that the energy/consciousness trapped up inside our many egos can be transmuted to form the body of the butterfly—the solar bodies (astral, mental, causal)—our human soul. Just as in the metamorphosis of the caterpillar into a butterfly, authentic spiritual transformation is a process. It is not complicated. But it is not pleasant, either. It requires effort, humility, courage, patience, and surrender. These, sadly, our ego-minds and mystical pride fight tooth and nail against at every turn. Our ego wants simple, easy, comfortable, instant gratification. And the New Age feeds us precisely that. Just as every other religion/spiritual tradition replaced the realities of mystical transformation of the self into the Self with superstitions, communal identification, and belief systems.

And just as every other degenerated religion/spiritual tradition is masterful at manipulating 'the faithful,' we are sorry to say the New Age is masterful at feeding us what we want to hear. In the past, ego replaced the realities of the uphill climb out of the false self back to our True Self, rung by rung, with literal understanding of the bible, hierarchical patriarchies, faith as belief, and even Catholic shame and guilt. Conscious experience of reality is a threat to the ego, and so the ego-mind always makes efforts to supplant Truth with false egoism. In the case of the New Age, that false egoism is "just do what feels good." But, unlike religions of old, many of the other trappings have been done away with, making it much harder to spot the deception/manipulation.

New Age religiosity is far subtler, far cleverer, and ultimately much more insidious in its power over humanity than any religion before it. Why? As in the past, many of its guides and gurus are completely committed. They believe totally in what they profess to their followers. And, as in the past, they are actively and consciously dividing and conquering by subtlety attacking ancient religions and esotericism. They cherry-pick from "the old paradigm" whatever concepts, practices, and beliefs are attractive and serve "the new paradigm." What makes the New Age so insidious is that it has no organization, no church, no hierarchical patriarchy, and nothing to identify as the culprit or the scapegoat behind its false promises and erroneous teachings. It has many teachings, books, gurus, groups, practices, communities, and—last but not least—the Internet. Where is the villain in the disorganized chaos of the New Age movement? It is so hard to identify as a degenerating, devolving religion enslaving minds because the villain at the heart of all degeneration of authentic spiritual traditions is the ego-mind itself. The New Age has none of the overarching organizational trappings, no *official canon* of scripture, no single *Avatar* or collection of Masters upon whose teachings it is based. It is literally just a mash-up of what a bunch of people like to believe and profess as the truth. It is almost entirely the work of ego—particularly mystic pride.

In the New Age, the corrupt entities raised to the positions of cardinals, bishops, etc., are our egos themselves. The church of the New Age controlling and enslaving us is our own mind. And we leap at the chance to feel and be seen as spiritual amongst *the spiritual community*—our *congregation* of peers. We love the feeling of being in control of our own spiritual journey. We love feeling as though we have reached the top of the ladder, the pinnacle of the mountain, because we are at the head of our own church. Yes, that feels good, alright! And even if we admit to not being at the top of the ladder, we are still the bishop of our own church, and we get to say what passes as spiritual in the holiest of holies of our temple—our own heart-mind. The trouble is, like any other degenerated religion, this leaves very little room in our church life for God (our Higher Self, our Innermost Being). The fact is God and the ego cannot mix. And, in the New Age, we have yet another religious movement in a long line of religions that professes to agree with that statement but fails to practice what it preaches. Like so many religions before it, the New Age is riddled with hypocrisy.

The ego's modus operandi may be divide and conquer, but its tactics are corruption by temptation, deception, evasion, illusion, misdirection, misinterpretation, etc. And it is so masterful at convincing us how comfort and security are our friends—of course, because the fear of death is healthy, right? Meanwhile, the death egos really fear is their own; the only self-preservation they care about is their own survival, and that means there is no authentic spiritual path that the ego will embrace since the path to liberation and self-realization constitutes the death of the ego. So the egos find and/or create beliefs (be they religious, atheist, or New Age) that comfort us and at best stall, or lead us away from, awakening *positively*. At worst, they lead to practices which cause us to awaken *negatively*—within and through the ego itself. This is how subtle, clever, and devious the ego-mind and mystic pride are.

The Truth hurts (the ego), but the Truth will set you free (from the prison of the ego)

What is the ego? Contemporary psychology and colloquialisms refer to the ego as a singular entity, that "I" of the ego-personality. In this sense, the ego is that self we identify as. In ancient spiritual traditions, the ego is a collection and amalgamation of a legion of individual psychological aggregates—a legion of "I's"—known by many names by many cultures: nafs, sins, egos, demons, memes (mind viruses), desires, etc.

The egos are directly responsible for the cacophony of voices in our head, that so-called 'busy mind' which we work to quiet. By presenting themselves as "I," each one of those voices tells us they *are us*…each one wants us to identify with and satisfy it, and there is no better strategy to achieve that end than to convince us that what it wants and/or wants to avoid is "what I want and/or don't want." That is where words like temptation and rationalization come from, as do psychological states like addictions, compulsions, obsessions, etc. What power do these psychological aggregates have over us? The most basic, primal, and potent of manipulations…

Figure 18: Mind Map – "You Make You Feel Good" by Paul Foreman

Yes, feeling good is how many egos get/have their way with us. Just observe yourself moment by moment to verify this fact. And, of course, some egos get off on feeling bad. These subtle and crafty egos are behind such phenomena as shame, self-loathing, victimhood, blame, judgment, condemnation, hatred of others, and frustration with the world.

What we end up with, then, is a scene we remember all too well from childhood cartoons:

*Figure 19: **The Voices in My Head by ANASTINA91 (DeviantArt)***

You must be familiar with this archetype, dear reader: the proverbial angel and devil whispering into our ear, each one trying to get us to do what it wants us to do. Originally, this metaphor was an expression of conscience (the angel, intuition, the Still Soft Voice of our True Self, Jiminy Cricket in *Pinocchio*) and ego-mind (the devil, thinking, the cacophony of voices of our false self, entities manipulating Pinocchio's mechanical existence). The New Age took this allegory, repurposed it, redressed it with new concepts, and truly ran with it.

Cult of Positive Thinking

Especially in New Age and Self-Help circles, *the angels of our better nature*—the Still Soft Voice of our conscience—has been replaced with *positive thinking* and 'the devil' with *negative thinking*. In other words, thinking positive, focusing on the positive, and feeling good—the pursuit of and attachment to pleasure, comfort, and security—are associated with being spiritual, empowered, enlightened, etc. In contrast, negative thinking is the new source of all evil. After all, thinking negative thoughts makes us feel bad, does it not? By avoiding the negative and refusing to feel bad (avoiding and evading suffering out of attachment to pleasure, comfort, and security), are we not aligned with our True Selves? Surely, God is Love. And Love should never feel bad, nor should love want to make us feel bad, right?

Have you noticed that the New Age revisionism, just as degenerated intellectual religious teachings of the past, make spirituality a case of "a mind at war with itself?" A dialectic of 'good' versus 'evil' which is played out in the mind…egos against egos. Cravings for pleasure, comfort, and security against aversions to pain, discomfort, and insecurity. Divide and conquer. With the ego playing both sides of this internal struggle, it is all too easy for it to hypnotize us with its endless machinations, mechanical reactions, manipulations, internal monologues, and meta-dialogues. We become very much like machines, or zombies, acting out programs in the mind written, rewritten, and overridden by our many egos—lust, fear, pride, greed, envy, laziness, et al.

So, we end up with "think positive thoughts" and "avoid negative thoughts." On top of these, we are fed lines like "you are God having a human experience" and that we have the right to use our creative imagination and positive thinking to "manifest all our desires through the Law of Attraction by focusing on limitless abundance." And it is all, 100% ego-mind. Nothing remotely conscious about any of it.

We remain ignorant of our True Self. That is, with all the ego activity, our consciousness is completely bottled up in desires and unable to relax, focus, and concentrate on the Stillness of Who we Truly are. We remain hypnotized and ignorant. These two words together constitute the antithesis of gnosis. Beliefs are the antithesis of self-evident experiential knowledge (what we SEEK on any genuine spiritual path). Beliefs divide and conquer us psychologically, and, as above, so below…as within, so without.

Figure 20: The Zombie Apocalypse

The collective unconsciousness we see in the world today—the mass hypnosis and manipulation in everything from the mainstream media to governments, consumerism, educational systems, big pharma, junk food, junk entertainment, the vast majority of video and computer games, the Internet, fanatical religions and belief systems, materialist science, and all superficial intellectual modalities of belief—is allegorized in 'the zombie apocalypse.' On the surface, the term seems quite ironic since the term *apocalypse* is synonymous with revelation and means "to reveal, unveil, awaken."

And again, *awakening* is something that is very much top of mind in the New Age. So, they argue to stay positive, stay conscious, avoid the sources of hypnosis and ignorance *out there* in the world, and rid yourself of all false, harmful, negative thoughts. But can we really fight the mind with the mind? Can we really fight back against the forces of zombification by empowering the very forces responsible for turning us into zombies?

What the New Age does not know—what it does not want you to know, dear reader—is that it is possible to awaken as something *worse* than a zombie. There are other entities featured in the world of myth, scripture, art, literature, and movies, symbolizing states of consciousness far more insidious than that of the zombie state. Again, how these archetypes are practically realized in the world is a topic for another discussion. But one thing is certain: just as sure as the evolutionary path toward the Light requires us to ascend Dante's Ladder rung by rung, its antithesis along the devolutionary path requires us to descend Dante's Ladder into our own Inferno—consciously pursuing dark powers and the desires they serve. What is most insidious about such dark powers and entities is that they are very subtle, very clever, charmingly debonair, stylishly seductive, and masters at convincing us that they want what is best for us. They are looking out for us; they care for our comfort, safety, and security. They are our best friends, these voices in our head. They will protect us from everyone and everything "out to get us out there," and if only we focus on the positive voices, they will drown out and silence the negative ones inside our head. "Just feel good," they tell us… "listen to us, and we will show you the way."

This is not how the Still Soft Voice of our True Self speaks to us. Anyone with any experience with intuition, inspiration, insight, and esoteric imagination knows the difference between ego-mind and heart-mind. Still, the egos are clever, subtle, and masterful at convincing us they are one thing when they are precisely its antithesis. The pursuit of pleasure and avoidance of pain are not the primary concerns of our Innermost Being. There is nothing particularly wrong with pleasure. It becomes problematic when we become identified with it. It is when we become attached to pleasure, comfort, and security that we lose ourselves to the corresponding egos, convincing us not only of "what we want and don't want" but "what we need and don't need." But can the false self possibly know better than our True Self what it is we need and do not need? And yet, how convincingly we tell ourselves, "I am in control of my own life!" This is the kind of sentiment used by New Agers and Atheists alike to attack Christians and others who 'blindly follow their faith.' Well, that may be so. But we do not see any Atheists performing experiments to verify what XYZ scientist tells them is fact. Nor do we see any New Agers questioning much of anything their favorite New Age gurus tell them…nor do we hear those gurus providing them the keys to perform their own conscious experiments for themselves to verify that all they have said is true. A handful of such gurus do offer instruction on how to replicate their alleged success, so their followers can attain the same level of peace and tranquility. Either such gurus are kidding themselves and are blindly leading their followers into the same trap of self-delusion, or they are charlatans, pretending to be enlightened and actively misleading their followers for their own gain in fame and fortune.

Oh, but they and their followers are in control of their own lives, are they? Who or what is making the decision to like a particular teaching and dislike another? Who or what is deciding to believe what is being presented without doing any work to verify it for oneself? Let us remember, dear reader, that beliefs give us comfort. And there is no particular reason why our ego gravitates to any form of comfort, except that it knows us, our weaknesses, and what we are most likely to identify with. And so, it makes us question our Self. Fear creates in us apprehension to follow the course of action whispered to us from the Still Soft Voice within…from our Being.

Clues about the Nature of the New Age Movement

The New Age talks a fair bit about *Christ Consciousness* and *ascension,* so let us begin there, dear reader. First off, Christ is not a person. This is one of many facts the New Age movement cherry-picked from ancient esotericism. Christ is a Force in the universe that men and women can embody to varying degrees based on their *level of being.* In Kabbalah, Christ is known as Chokmah or the Second Logos. As the first emanation of Kether, *the Father,* the Cosmic Christ is the *Son/Sun of God.* The Cosmic Christ is the Fire of fires and the Light of lights at the heart of every star, including our own sun. The clever historians and theologians who look down on so-called primitive sun-worshipping cultures fail to realize it was the Christ they were worshipping and not the sun. George Ivanovich Gurdjieff understood Christ as the *Omnipresent Ray of Okidanokh*—the universal *Ray of Creation*—the perfect multiple unity and the Being of beings.

At the dawn of the *Mahamanvatara* or Great Cosmic Day, the Christ radiated out from *the Solar Absolute*—God, the Creator Source of the Universe on high—and scattered individuated sparks of Itself throughout the cosmos as *monads,* depositing each monad as a seed, an *Essence,* in the *Nous Atom* at the heart of every atom in the universe. All beings in the physical universe, be they in the mineral, plant, animal, or human kingdom, possess a nous atom, monad, and Innermost Essence of the Intimate Christ at their heart. This Essence develops slowly on the upward spiral of evolution, in accordance with the AUM of Life, over countless lifetimes in the mineral, plant, animal, and finally human kingdoms. But the Essence is still just a *seed.* If nurtured and incubated in fertile psychological soil over many lifetimes, it may one day be born inside a *True human being.* Not just any human being, but one who successfully eliminates all their remaining karma in one lifetime…a *Bodhisattva.* Having devoted themselves to a lifetime of suffering, sacrifice, and service to others, they lay down on their deathbed, pass away, enter hell, cleanse the last remnants of their ego, assist others suffering in hell, and awaken from death three days later a *Resurrected Master.* They then begin work as a *Christified One,* a living god, the living embodiment of Christ Consciousness. If they successfully complete their mission as a Christified Master, they will have earned the right to *Ascension.* It is then, and *only* then, that they can disincarnate from the earth and join the ranks of the *Ascended Masters.*

Christians should immediately recognize this process as the defining event in the life of Jesus. But skeptics will point out that many characters from mythology who were born of virgins also died and rose from the dead. They point this out in a bid to debunk the Gospels as first-century retellings of the older mythological traditions. We categorically rebuke the accusation of plagiarism in the gospels. Instead, we put forth a far more contentious assertion that *many monads* have incarnated Christ throughout history: Mithras, Krishna, Moses, Quetzalcoatl, Buddha Shakyamuni, Zoroaster, Fu Xi, Muhammed (PBUH), and many others. In general, Christians cherish the exclusivity that their *Lord and Savior, Jesus Christ,* was the one and only *Son of God.* They confuse the words and works of *The Christ* with the *man.* They interpret Christ's teachings with their rational mind. They fail to develop the conscious "eyes to see and ears to hear" needed for the Truth behind the symbols and allegories in Christ's words and works to reveal itself. They also fail to accept that the Bible was heavily revised, with many books and gospels removed by Emperor Constantine at the Council of Nicaea. The four remaining gospels were heavily revised, putting Jesus's death and resurrection at the end of his life, just prior to his ascension. But when Jesus said, "I am the way, the Truth, and the Light," he was speaking as The Christ. He was already a Resurrected Master by that point. In this way, the gospels are the teachings not of a man but a Christified Master, a living god. They are the Word of God proper, the Logos speaking through one who—through tremendous efforts, suffering, and sacrifice—incarnated the Christic Force to serve humanity. Just take a moment to comprehend the efforts and sacrifice of such a being. Let us consider for a moment the consciousness such a being possesses. Right: *impossible.* Until we become Christified Masters, we cannot know Christ Consciousness in its fullness.

So where does the New Age get off throwing around terms like *Christ Consciousness* and *ascension* (not to mention *awakening, enlightenment, samadhi, tantra, kundalini,* and countless other sacred terms)? These words are no mere trifles for the mind to conceptualize, let alone buzzwords that New Age entrepreneurs should be repackaging into their countless books, courses, retreats, products, and other services. They are profound Truths for the consciousness to experience—Truths that can only be known through direct conscious experience and contextualized through disciplined esoteric study. And to be fair, many New Age authors, guides, gurus, and their followers/practitioners believe in what they are doing. Their use of terms like Christ Consciousness and ascension are informed, in part, by their own direct experiences of higher states of consciousness and/or divinity. After all, it is possible to be *touched* by the Christ.

On our path to awakening, we receive infinite blessings, will experience serendipity countless times—whether we know it or not—and benefit from many boons. Some of these come in the form of spiritual experiences—moments of clarity, inspiration, insight, ecstasy. And sometimes in a form that is beyond form, such that it is impossible to describe the experience in any way the mind can understand or appreciate. But what about the heart? The heart may be able to feel a glimmer of the Truth in the telling of such an experience. But that is all…just a glimmer.

We have had such a glimmer of Christ Consciousness. We cannot say we Truly know what Christ Consciousness is, only that we were touched by it, only for a moment. A moment that broke all boundaries of time and space and lasted for a good five to ten minutes. In an earnest effort to share our experiential knowledge of the Chrestos Force, we humbly pray for the inspiration and guidance to find the words and poetic expression so that you, our beloved reader, may hear, feel, experience, and share in some small way in one of the most important boons of our life.

Touched by the Christ

The time matters not.

Nor the day, nor date, nor weather outside.

Neither the catalyst.

There was one,

From Ancient Egypt.

Sitting on the couch surfing the web

We Googled the edicts of Luxor:

Commandments of the Hermetic Mystery Schools.

This was our catalyst,

Not a catalyst...

Not a reminder even...

A WAKE-UP CALL from the Absolute.

It begins...

Heart chakra swells

Two,

Four,

Eight, no—Eighty times

In size;

Eight thousand times

In depth.

Is it a heart attack?

Strength fails.

iPad falls.

Mind blanks.

And then

Without hesitation

Love enters us.

Love, as we have never known it.

A tsunami bursts forth from within

We slip from the couch to the floor,

This feeble animated corpse helpless and powerless

In the Light of this Love,

Love of Loves,

Light of Lights,

Would our body temple were made of stone

Great blocks would be bursting from our sides

Such is this wellspring, no—

Geyser—of Love

Exploding yet sustaining,

Imploding yet enduring,

No tsunami,

No geyser,

No eternal fountain…

A star has gone supernova!

A Sun is in our chest.

The Son is in our heart.

The Christ has come to visit.

And It burns with the Fire of fires,

Shines with the Light of lights

From behind my cold eyes I see it beaming

Brought forth from the Great Treasury of the Light

And I am blinded to all but its Glory.

Heart wells up

Throat chokes up,

Eyes wide shut,

We are a fetus curled up in the womb,

Welled up ready to burst

Walled up in our tiny apartment

Any moment now it too will burst

Just as sure as we will

And we do

Burst.

Tears pour from beneath sealed eyelids

And we cry out in wailing agony of pure joy.

"Oh God, Oh God, Oh God!

We thank Thee!

We thank Thee!

We thank Thee!

Oh Divine Mother!

Isis!

Shakti!

Blessed,

Holy,

Loving!

Blessed,

Holy,

Loving!

Blessed,

Holy,

Loving!

Thank you!

Thank you!

Thank you!"

No reprieve.

No halt in the torrent.

No pause in the fusion.

Diaphragm trampolines

And our gut is Love-punched drunk into exhaustion.

Heart beats our max into dust.

Body registering on the Richter scale.

Skin soaked in a soup of sweat and tears.

And still the Love is there.

Swelling and collapsing;

Erupting and imploding.

Boiling magma plumes in our chest,

Burns us with the Fire of the fire,

Illuminates us with the Light of lights,

And we are completely helpless to resist;

Pathetically incapable of containing

Let alone hosting even the Essence of the presence of our Guest,

The Most High,

The Chrestos Force

He who comes in the name of the Lord...

"Hosanna in the Highest!

Hosanna in the Highest!

Hosanna in the Highest!

Thy Kingdom Come!

Thy Kingdom Come!

Thy Kingdom Come!

Thy Will be Done!

Thy Will be Done!

Thy Will be Done!

So be it!

So be it!

So be it!

Hallelujah!

Hallelujah!

Hallelujah!

Thank You!

Thank You!

Thank You!

Oh God, We thank You!"

It goes on like this.

An eternity passes

With an Infinite Ball of Burning Love in our chest.

And We observe ourselves,

Filthy and unworthy of this Guest in our house!

We have no Three Kings to greet our Savior Cometh

Among the barnyard cubby of our animal mind!

What gifts can we offer but the filth of our minds,

The pain in our hearts,

And the stress in our body?

What precious offerings can we make to Christ our Lord Cometh?

Yet still all we feel is eternal Love and gratitude,

There is no shame to speak of

Here and now

We are incapable of that shadowy pride,

Our egos have fled to the darkest corners of our mind,

Those wasps flew from the Flame of flames,

And our heart cries out only with the Joy of joys.

"It is what it is, and that is all!

It is what it is, and that is all!

It is what it is, and that is all!

I Am that I Am!

I Am that I Am!

I Am that I Am!

Eheyeh Asher Eheyeh!

Eheyeh Asher Eheyeh!

Eheyeh Asher Eheyeh!

Oh God, Oh God, Oh God!

Thy Will be Done!

Thy Will be Done!

Thy Will be Done!

Thank You!

Thank You!

Thank You!"

It continues.

Endures.

Sustains.

Awakens.

Exalts.

Praises.

Sings

The Ode to Joy

Played by a thousand orchestras,

Sung by a million angels,

Blaring in our heart-mind;

Resonating through our Being.

Rings forth the Truth of truths no mortal man can describe,

The Love of loves no mortal man can know.

How could he?

When here we are but touched by It,

Overcome by the Glory of Glories,

Crumpled in an ecstatic heap by the Joy of joys

And the Bliss of bliss?

With naught but a drop of Its Limitless Light,

We are balling our eyes out,

Crying our heart out,

Wailing with the agony of eternal happiness!

We are reduced to a blithering child,

So weak are we in the wake of

The Resplendence of Resplendence.

"Kyrie Eleison!

Kyrie Eleison!

Kyrie Eleison!

Christe Eleison!

Christe Eleison!

Christe Eleison!

Pater Noster!

Pater Noster!

Pater Noster!

Ave Maria!

Ave Maria!

Ave Maria!

We Thank You!

We Thank You!

We Thank You!

Hallelujah!

Hallelujah!

Hallelujah!"

It goes on like this some more.

Gloria in Excelsior,

Majesty Magnificence,

Rejuvenation in Resplendence

Give way to Mercy and Freedom,

And we are released in Mercy and Love.

Our visit is at an end.

Our exhausted and spent self lies helpless on the floor.

And still we can only pray

And thank

And feel

The residual Heat and Light and Love from our Cosmic Visitation,

Our Heavenly House Guest.

Who came forth from the boundless nothingness of our hearts,

To touch us,

Give us but a taste,

And let us drink from the Fountain of Sweet Ambrosia,

Dip our toe into the Ocean of Love that glows with His Golden Blue Light,

The Light of Lights,

The Light of Christ.

Who was in the beginning,

Is now,

And shall Be.

May he come again to judge the living,

These wretched "I's" who pollute our temple,

And the dead,

Those wretched Souls suffering in hell itself.

So be it.

So be it.

So be it.

Amen.

Amen.

Amen.

* * *

– First published on 19th of May 2018 on Attlas.info

It is typically not *kosher* to share such experiences openly and publicly. We do so to illustrate the facts. Rather than simply stating outright in a judgmental or condemning sort of way the simple point we are trying to make, we attempted to express as best we could with our limited poetic abilities our experience of Christ. So that you, dear reader, may decide for yourself, the next time you hear an esteemed New Age guru express their teachings about 'Christ Consciousness'—in that stereotypical mild-mannered way that we find so appealing—if that is indeed its True nature.

From this and other experiences we have had, we daresay we know a thing or two about the messengers of The Light of lights—*masters, Buddhas, Avatars, prophets, saints*—and the *Fierce Grace* which radiated through them. There is a definite tone, a vitality, an *intensity* in the words of those who have experienced that Fierce Grace directly, consciously, and feel charged by that burning fire in their hearts to reveal to others the keys to knowing such Light for themselves.

> *The sun with loving light makes bright for me each day, the soul with spirit power gives strength unto my limbs. In sunlight shining clear I revere, Oh God, the strength of humankind, which thou hast planted in my soul, that I may with all my might, may love to work and learn. From thee stream light and strength to thee rise love and thanks.*
>
> *– Rudolf Steiner*

Naturally, softness, kindness, peace, relaxation, and gentleness absolutely do have their place and purpose. But whereas these outward signs are easily feigned, the Christic Force cannot be so easily faked by New Agers because their dogma is focused on *feeling good.* And the intensity of the Christ is not pleasant to the ego unless it is being conditioned by the ego. And we should all be quite familiar with the angry rants of charismatic politicians, for instance, as they whip adoring crowds into a foaming frenzy using confrontational, adversarial, nationalist, and/or socialist rhetoric. We need not invoke the name of Germany's leader prior to the Second World War, who is the poster child for the misappropriation, conditioning, and outright abuse of the Christic Force by the ego for its own nefarious purposes. The Nazis went as far as degenerating the swastika—an ancient symbol of Christ Consciousness—and the 'SS'—the sig rune from the Futhark, representing the descent of the Omnipresent Ray of Okidanokh on The Tree of Life, together with the thunderbolts of Zeus, Wodan, Thor, et al.

Figure 21: Sig Rune

We can look to more traditional religious congregations, especially Southern Baptists and the *megachurches* of modern-day TV evangelicals like Joel Olsteen, to see the Christic Force being invoked with an intensity that more closely reflects its nature. When hundreds—let alone thousands, tens of thousands, or even millions—of souls are gathered in the name of a higher power, the collective energies of those souls are compounded. Be it through chanting, prayer, song, or other ritualized actions performed in unison, a skilled pastor, speaker, or performer can lead a congregation of souls to the point of intense emotional ecstasy, which, for them, constitutes a *religious experience*. Note how we deliberately included secular language in the previous sentence to punctuate the fact that actors, musicians, and politicians exploit *mob dynamics* for the purpose of being idolized and *worshipped* by their *fans*. Interestingly, such intense collective experiences are very endearing to the ego. In fact, many individuals will find themselves deeply desirous to return to concerts, rallies, or other congregations that make them feel euphoric. And that is because such experiences, too, are examples of the Christic Force being conditioned.

Such hyperbolic experiences of collectivism are generally not suited to the New Age since it exists as a counter to organized religions' public worship and devotion to a God *out there*. New Age spirituality is much more personal and individual. It is well-suited to empaths, introverts, and others who have never really *fit in,* individuals who may even find large crowds energetically, emotionally, and mentally draining. So, the New Age presents them with a more contained, pleasant, soothing version of Christ Consciousness. One that even the most mundane personalities, experiences, parlor tricks, and charlatans can profess to possess. And many do. That is not to say New Age gurus and their followers do not make use of audiences and the power of congregations—they absolutely do. But a talk by Eckhart Tolle, Deepak Chopra, Wayne Dyer, Delores Cannon, or any one of the many New Age gurus who regularly conduct speaking tours is not on the same level of outright performance as a faith-healing service conducted by a televangelist. No one passes out at an Eckhart Tolle event from 'ecstasy.'

What is really at work in the New Age?

All religions under the sun are born, degenerate, divide into many sects, and die. No practiced religion or expressed spiritual tradition is immune to the *Law of Entropy*. The mind is a vehicle of entropy. It can only understand through the comparison and contrast of the binary, mechanical dialectic: *"this, not that; us or them; right and wrong; good and evil; me versus you; what I want and what I don't want; cravings and aversions."* The modus operandi of ego is *divide and conquer*. When the mind is ruled by ego (which in this humanity is almost always the case), entropy becomes a very powerful force of degeneration.

Practically, that means any spiritual discourse is merely a shadow, a reflection, an entropic and imperfect representation of the underlying universal spiritual principle(s) being expressed, so long as it is interpreted literally and superficially by the ego-mind. As soon as that expression is interpreted by the ego-mind, the process of subjective interpretation, misinterpretation, misunderstanding, and misrepresentation takes place. That is because the underlying knowledge being conveyed by any authentic spiritual discourse is *esoteric*—the words only point the way to the Truth; they do not profess to be the Truth in and of themselves. They are but the outward forms of the inner esoteric Truths the forms intimate. Put another way, anyone who relies solely on an intellectual understanding of these superficial forms of religion, no matter what religion it is, is actually following ***The Doctrine of the Eye/I***.

The ego-mind cannot know. The ego-mind only *thinks* it knows. Real knowledge, gnosis, is *experiential*. Experiential knowledge cannot be expressed directly in words. It can only be conveyed, implied, pointed to—intimated at. But in order that the words may convey the essence of gnosis, they must be imbued with the essence of an experience or knowledge which comes directly from our Essence (our Innermost Being, our Higher Self, the Innermost Intimate Christ)—***The Doctrine of the Heart***.

Video 38: What is Gnosis? (YouTube)

An experienced pilot, surgeon, or craftsperson cannot transfer their experiential knowledge to others through language. At best, they can write words that point the way for others to acquire their own experience—with guidance about opportunities to take advantage of and pitfalls to avoid. Be honest, dear reader: would you trust a neophyte who has no practical experience with your flight, operation, or custom craftwork, even if they had just finished reading a how-to guide written by a master in their field? No, of course you would not. You would entrust only a practiced individual, with plenty of experience under their belt, with your life.

Poetry, art, music, opera, stories, fables, myths, parables, dreams, and scripture—their symbols and allegories are much better suited to convey essential spiritual teachings than are the dry intellectual explanations and rationalizations of prose. Figurative expressions born of the *heart* can stimulate, open, and be received by the *heart-mind*. But if they are received merely with the ego-mind, it is more than likely their figurative meaning will be lost as the mind focuses on the literal meaning and superficial details. Anything written by the ego-mind, read with the ego-mind, and retold with the ego-mind will be all but devoid of essential truths. They will be shadowy representations of the Truth. Intellectual discourse results in ego-minds that think they know…ego-minds that believe they know. For instance, in the minds of contemporary academics, theologians, and historians, mythology is little more than fantasy. An invention of humanity to teach morality, to make sense of a mysterious universe, to make sense of their place in the universe, perhaps.

So-called 'experts' expound their learned theories as to why humanity tells fantastical tales of supernatural beings, humanity's relationship to them, and their exploits, be they in the heavens, on earth, or in the underworld. Even psychologists, sociologists, and anthropologists have weighed in from time to time. Only a handful of these individuals, like Joseph Campbell and Carl Jung, made the connection between heroes, their journeys as relayed through stories, and human nature itself. Very few have acknowledged that scriptures, myths, legends, fairy tales, nursery rhymes, songs, et al were divinely inspired allegorical and symbolic vehicles of absolute universal Truth—truths that transcend time, space, and even dimensions.

To the contemporary secular intellectual, religion is, at best, a quaint, anachronistic relic of more primitive times when humans conjured up fantastic tales to make sense of the world and their place in it. At worst, it is an abomination of humankind, the cause of countless wars and untold numbers of atrocities, all done 'in the name of God.' This sort of polite patronization or outright condemnation generally does not sit well with *the faithful*. The contemporary 'true believer' in religion generally takes their scripture at its word—literally. They believe their sacred texts constitute the Word of God, and they believe said texts must be followed to the letter. This is how self-evident experiential knowledge (gnosis: the stuff of a consciousness which knows) degenerates into beliefs (hypnosis and ignorance: ego-mind which thinks it knows). As the video above describes, adhering to the Doctrine of the Eye/I, the ego-mind misses the objective Truth known through *conscious religious experience,* instead obsessed with its own *varying superficial interpretations*. In the religious context, this is known as *idolatry*. The word idolatry comes from the degeneration into idol worship. Where once the faithful worshipped what the idol represented and/or symbolized, now they worship the idol itself. This is precisely what happens when the esoteric meaning of symbols and allegories in scripture are replaced with exoteric interpretations of the symbols, literal readings of the stories, and retellings of the resulting superstitious beliefs. Extrapolate that over generations of telling and retellings by, for, and with ego-minds…and add endless debates, arguments, revisions, alterations, misinterpretations, misconceptions, and misappropriations for an unlimited number of egotistical purposes (politics, greed, pride, etc.) …and you see entropy at work.

Some may have a slightly more nuanced approach, recognizing the symbolic nature of the parables, proclamations, and lessons of scripture. Intellectuals such as Jordan Peterson, for instance, believe themselves to be expert interpreters of biblical stories since they can extract from them essential life lessons applicable to the challenges of modern life. And given his rise in popularity, it is clear Peterson's message has resonated with many individuals and groups—whether they be religious or not. That said, the conclusions he draws from biblical stories—and many fairy tales and other texts that he has set his mind to unpacking for modern audiences—tend to reinforce traditional philosophies and approaches to life. This is why many on the conservative right have embraced him as one of their own, while he has become a bit of a pariah to those more left of center who label him 'alt-right.' They not only dislike Peterson's 'conservative, traditional, patriarchal' viewpoints, but they also dislike the fact that he supports them using 'the alt-right playbook of the patriarchy'—the bible. Since, in their eyes, religious scripture has been used to rationalize and justify every sexist, misogynist, homophobic, racist, colonial, and oppressive regime in history, they would just as likely see scriptures burned as they would allow them to be read. Indeed, many have tried to disrupt and prevent individuals like Jordan Peterson from giving talks on college campuses. But the politicization of religion is nothing new.

When Emperor Constantine appropriated Christianity and made it the official religion of the Roman Empire, he convened the infamous Council of Nicaea. At said council, the central text of the Abrahamic religions, the bible, was heavily modified. Over sixty books were removed entirely. All but four Gospels were kept—none of which were first-hand accounts of Jesus's life, teachings, and works. In fact, all the Gnostic Gospels were discarded, including the first-hand accounts of Jesus's life and teachings as recorded by his Disciples. While this is too large and contentious a topic to cover in any detail here, it is a well-regarded fact that many of the proclamations made at and following the Council of Nicaea by the early Catholic Church led to The Great Schism—the splintering of Christianity into Western Roman Catholicism and Eastern Orthodoxy. From there, Christianity would split and splinter again and again, resulting in the many Christian sects we see today. All that is the law of entropy at work. No wonder religions end up as shadowy reflections of their original mystical selves, replete with superficial literal interpretations of scripture, outlandish superstitions, self-serving and comforting beliefs, manipulative and controlling dogmas, patriarchal hierarchies, and everything else that the New Age and Atheists alike tend to dislike about most religions as we know them.

So what, you might ask, dear reader, does all of this have to do with the New Age? Or, more to the point, if you count yourself among those who have already had a spiritual awakening, what does any of this talk have to do with *you?* Let us home in on one single result of entropy as it applies to experiential, mystical Truth: *self-serving and comforting beliefs.* Namely, the belief that we are awake.

"I AM AWAKE!"

> *"Behold! I am awake!"*
> *Is the belief our mind will fake,*
> *To avoid efforts we've yet to make,*
> *The journeys we've yet to take,*
> *And our karma still at stake.*
> *"But I question everything!"*
> *Our mind keeps loudly singing,*

Monkey turds it keeps a-flinging.
Warning bells they keep a-ringing;
Our conscience keeps a-stinging.
"My truth is of my choosing!"
The mind is itself excusing,
(The Truth is too confusing).
Thus that which we are using,
Proves so utterly seducing.
Mind dislikes Truth intruding.
It prefers ego-colluding,
Curiosity's alluring,
Though thoughts be self-deluding.
"Leave me be with all this brooding!"
Mind refuses to be defeated,
Be dethroned from where it's seated,
(Have its ego-lords deleted),
So its refrains are just repeated,
"My truth is not depleted!"
Mind craves/haves/eats its cake.
Facing Truth just makes it ache.
Endless theories it will bake,
Than admit the self's mistake.
So it cries, "I AM AWAKE!"
* * *

Facebook has Spoken 'its truth,' and the Results are Hypnotizing

We were rather taken aback by the number of 'likes' this poem received on Facebook. Especially given some of the memes we had ironically framed it in, specifically designed to be attractive to the ego. Images that self-styled 'seekers' and 'lightworkers' would immediately want to identify with (that is, how they want to see themselves). For instance, the 'warrior of light' archetype:

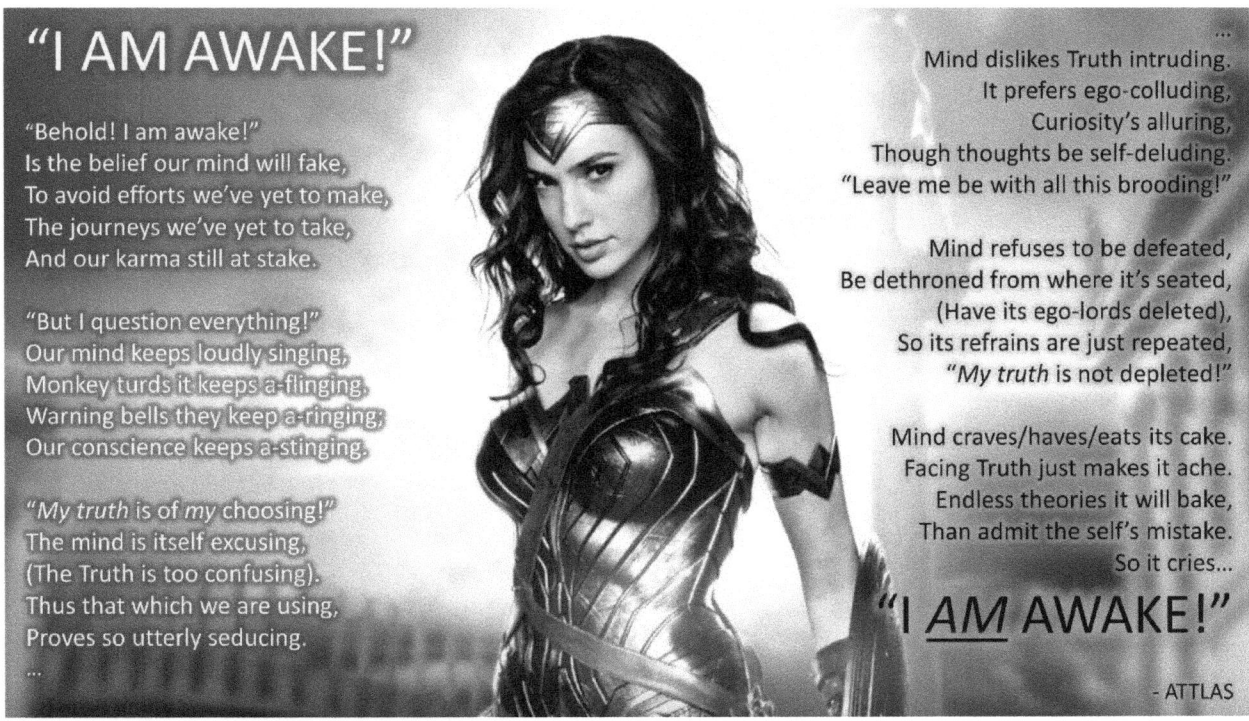

Figure 22 A & B: "I Am Awake" Memes

The whole point of juxtaposing the poem's essential Truth against the ironic ego-affirming image/title was to instill the reader with a sense of instability, to have their conscience pricked and their foundations rattled. To make them observe themselves and comprehend that as they identify with the words in quotation marks (the voice of ego-mind), they are essentially proving to themselves they are asleep. Surely, it could not be the case that all the 'likes' these ironic and provocative memes were receiving represented individuals who were applauding their disillusionment. Considering the unlikelihood of such a scenario, perhaps they really did think the poem was meant to serve as an *affirmation* that they were awake. In fact, it is highly probable that many did not even read the poem. Many merely saw the words "I AM AWAKE," registered the image they wanted to identify with, put two-and-two together, clicked 'like' and moved on to the next post without reading the poem. Had they done so, they would have recognized the irony. Or would they? Was it possible they were oblivious to the meaning of the poem and completely numb to the ironic juxtaposition of the exercise? Were they immune to the cathartic interactive experience we had offered them? Had we instead given them another opportunity to indulge their mystic pride? Or were we being entirely uncharitable, cynical, and pessimistic? Were we assuming that everyone who read the poem automatically thought it was about them and not about others who erroneously believe themselves to be awake? One thing was clear: if we were to know for sure, we would have to conduct a survey that simply asked, "What is the Essence of this poem?"

1. It is an affirmation of my truth! I am awake! (15%)
2. It is a denial of my truth! I am awake! (30%)
3. It is a revelation of the Truth. I am asleep. (47%)
4. Other. (8%)

As it turns out, roughly half of alleged seekers are deluded by the belief they are already awake (45%). And yet are unable to glean the Truth of the poem, despite it not being veiled but explicit. Identified with ideas and concepts, hypnotized by the ego's seductive mantra 'my truth,' their minds ignore/rail against the facts. Inspired by the countless Facebook posts, YouTube videos, and comments we encounter regularly in which individuals profess how 'awake' they are or describe how their life has changed since they 'awoke' so many years ago, etc., we wrote the poem to shed light on the matter. **We may have experiences indicating progress on the path to** *awakening,* **but we are not yet fully** *awake.* They are related but not synonymous, like cooking is not yet cooked; like building is not necessarily built. The journey is not the destination.

The ego-mind has a veritable limitless bag of tricks on hand, an endless stream of arguments, justifications, and rationalizations available to it. We can be certain that in the wake of any experience that constitutes an awakening along our path, mystic pride will arise and declare, "I am enlightened!" And we can be certain that our ego will grab hold of such a belief hungrily and dig in its heels like a terrier does a juicy bone. The facts are the sole dominion of consciousness is that of the Innermost Being, and for that, the ego-mind will double down on its own hubris—mystic pride—and go so far as to make all manner of assertions about itself—euphemistically called *affirmations* by the New Age. Not just that we are awake, but that we are one with all beings and the universe, that we are all gods already. Not only thinking it knows but believing itself to be the authority on knowledge itself. It will even pronounce itself as the caretaker of genuine gnosis (since the best defense is a good offense). Sadly, these very beliefs and behaviors are the instruments by which the ego-mind engineers our hypnosis and ignorance. These are the facts, no matter how much the ego-mind denies them or protests them (as it most surely will).

To remain in objective observation of the mind's subjective machinations, reactions, protestations, and declarations is the first step toward someday escaping its tyrannical hold over us. However, ego-mind is too clever and subtle to show its hand to us so readily. We usually remain oblivious to the powerful influence the subconscious has over us—not just our conscious thoughts but our awareness (or lack thereof). We must do more than simply observe what our mind is thinking, what the voices in our head keep telling us. Likewise, we must observe not only what we are receiving through our senses but also how our mind filters, interprets, processes, and embellishes (alters) the impressions we receive in any given moment. Put another way, we must remain observant of how our experience is being *conditioned*—even mystical experiences.

Impressions as Food

What we receive into our mind—impressions—are every bit as much food for us as what we take into our bodies. And, like anything else we consume, the flavor and nutritional value are not governed merely by the food but also by how it is dressed up—the condiments, sauces, toppings, spices, garnishes, presentations, pairings, et al., which we bring to the dinner plate. Consider the global fascination with coffee/tea as a prime example of what we are referring to.

Our consumption of coffee and/or tea depends greatly on how much (if any) sweetener and whitener we use and what kind (sugar, honey, agave, stevia, low-fat milk, full-fat milk, cream, almond milk, Bailey's et al). These embellishments are of our own choosing and are arguably completely superfluous to the beverage we are consuming. After years of experience consuming coffee and/or tea, we have grown accustomed to enjoying them in a certain way, and we apply our embellishments according to taste. That said, we often embellish our hot beverages automatically, mechanically, and unconsciously. We have prepared our coffee, tea, hot chocolate, etc., so many times we are on autopilot. When asked, our brain reflexively tells the barista *how we take it*. Likewise, we can prepare our beverage of choice blindfolded. Since we are so accustomed to taking our hot beverage a certain way—the way we like it—we drink it just as unconsciously—mechanically, automatically—scarfing it down at breakfast, shuffling the kids off to school, driving to work, typing at work, the list goes on. Very rarely do we actually indulge in the drinking of a hot beverage as all the advertisements on television depict. Picture an individual stopping everything they are doing to completely savor the aroma and experience of the moment, holding the mug in both hands, closing their eyes, and being completely present to the experience as if this was their very first and possibly final ever cup of coffee/tea. We rarely, if ever, do that.

Our minds end up conditioning the experience with whatever additional embellishments it is throwing into the mix—thoughts regarding the future, memories from the past, some fantasy it dreamt the night before, or some other fantasy it is daydreaming. These embellishments effectively hypnotize our consciousness and prevent us from experiencing the facts of the moment directly. The mind has replaced the actual experience of the moment with an automated recording of past experiences of similar moments and then distracts us with other things. The result is we think we are having our coffee/tea/hot chocolate. But the reality is just that: we only think we are having a coffee/tea/hot chocolate. In fact, we are performing an act mechanically according to expectations based on attachments to past experiences.

Some people go to certain coffee shops believing they have "the best coffee" or that they know "just how I like it." Practically speaking, no two cups of coffee are ever the same. We believe they are because we are relating every subsequent cup from a certain coffee shop to the first experience we had there (which exists only in our head). Rather than suffer the reality that a visit may result in a terrible cup of coffee, we imagine our idealized cup of coffee every time we visit our favorite purveyor of coffee and insist they are "the best." Alternatively, perhaps we are never satisfied with any cup of coffee we have. Perhaps there is some idealized cup of coffee that exists only in our fantasy. Such individuals are likewise never actually experiencing the cup of coffee they are drinking, no matter how delicious it may be. What they end up experiencing is their mind's criticisms about the cup in hand, and/or fantasies about "the perfect cup" (which exists only in their head), which the cup in hand cannot measure up to and will not be enjoyed. Their perverse enjoyment comes from the judgment and condemnation of what is, after all, just a humble cup of coffee, although they are convinced that it is "the worst."

Staying with our metaphor for a moment longer, consider all the different ways to drink espresso. Recognize that each has its own unique name, a unique formula consisting of various ingredients added to it, and even its own unique cup. Let us not gloss over the significance that altering the vessel can have to the experience of drinking in an impression. All these myriad types of gourmet coffee have espresso at their heart, yet in some cases, you would never know it, especially when you start factoring in additions like frothed milk, added sweeteners, whipped cream, cinnamon, chocolate sprinkles, flavored syrups, et al. In the end, the espresso is all but lost. It is still there, of course, but if someone asks us what we are drinking, we do not say "espresso," we say "cappuccino, latte, mocha, etc." In this metaphor, espresso represents the objective Truth of an impression…the pure, unadulterated, unfiltered experience without embellishment—the experiential Truth, plain and simple.

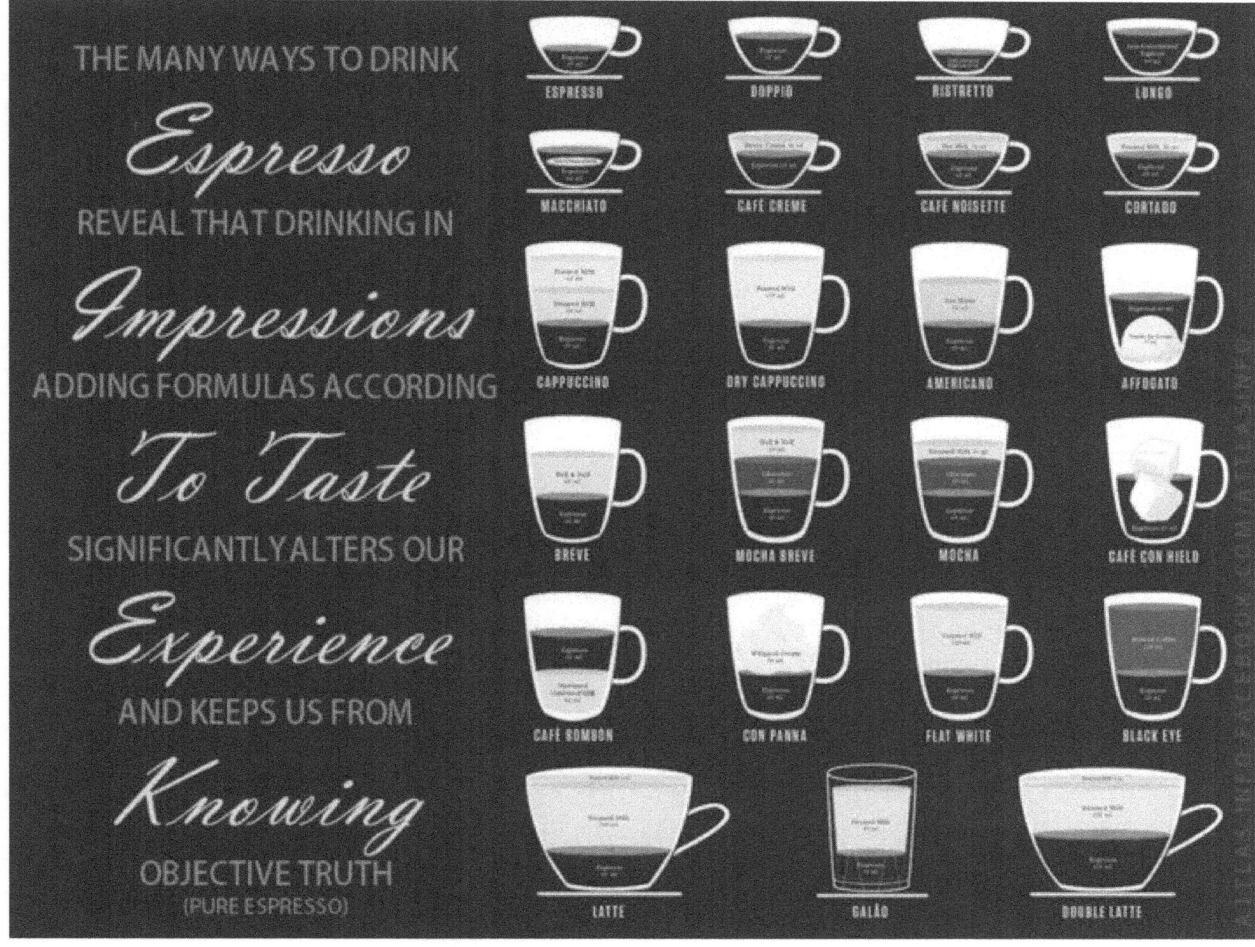

Figure 23: The Many Ways to Drink Espresso…Keeps us from Knowing Objective Truth

So, what do we do? Do we stop drinking specialty coffees altogether? We need not do anything so rash. We simply need to observe ourselves. Stay conscious. Be present. And recognize the objective Truth of the moment…that we are not drinking espresso straight up; we are drinking a sweet, frothy, creamy, chocolatey version of espresso. Let us recognize what version of espresso we are drinking, what makes it so, and take it in that way, consciously, knowing full well what we are drinking, embellishments and all. This process is called the *transformation of impressions.*

Transformation of Impressions

When we take in experience observing ourselves—our thoughts, our emotions, our physical sensations—we can be conscious to some degree of how our mind, heart, and body are affecting our experience. When we stay present and pay attention to the impressions we take in, along with what is being added to them, we can have some conscious knowledge of the pure impression, just as we would become conscious of the espresso in our mocha-latte. Otherwise, we drink unconsciously, oblivious to the espresso, hypnotized by what we like…what we want/add according to taste…remaining oblivious to the facts. We remain trapped in the fabricated illusory subjective experience in the mind instead of experiencing the reality of the moment objectively using our free consciousness. Another way to say this is by giving the moment over to our consciousness. The mind will still intervene: our tastes, habits, desires, biases, etc. will still be added according to whatever it is we are accustomed to liking or hating (because the ego cares not if it is indulging our cravings or aversions), but we consume the impression embellishments and all, consciously. That is, we digest the impression with our consciousness, separating the objective experience from our subjective embellishments—thoughts, emotions, and sensations—about the experience added by our mind, heart, and physical body.

Now, the real importance of this process comes into play when we begin to see the egos behind our mind's interventions and embellishments. We experience an impression, and the mind says, "I hate this, this sucks." Transforming the impression implies that rather than identifying with the mind's comment, "I hate this, this sucks," we instead observe the experience and the comment, recognizing what it is inside us which caused the mind to say, "I hate this, this sucks." Fear? Anger? Pride? Impatience? Intolerance? Unmet expectations? What was the source of the mind's reaction to the impression? Such depth of perception in the moment will take some time and much practice. The first key is to remain in observation—*mindful*—of ourselves.

The second key is to remember our Selves. When we say *give experience over to our consciousness,* we must try to understand what the consciousness is and to whom it belongs. Consciousness is a medium of self-evident experiential knowledge—gnosis. It is bi-directional, meaning it is capable of expression (the masculine, positive aspect) as well as reception (the feminine, negative aspect…SJW's, please note *negative* is used here in the quantitative sense, not qualitative). It is this masculine and feminine relationship of consciousness that creates reality and trips up all the New Agers and self-helpers manifesting their desires who only hear, "I CREATE MY REALITY!" Sounds awfully like "I AM AWAKE!" does it not? As an aside, the masculine/feminine, expressive/receptive nature of consciousness relates directly to a much higher/deeper understanding of Tantra, which we will discuss in more depth in *Part Three* of this book.

Consciousness is easily understandable as a Wi-Fi signal in a coffee shop (a place of business yielding a tremendous wealth of allegories today). You connect to said signal. But it is not yours. Your device is able to send and receive data over Wi-Fi, but the router does not belong to you, the user. Nor is the Internet, the knowledge that the Wi-Fi signal carries and makes available if you have the correct device, browser, password, etc. So, who do the router and the Wi-Fi signal belong to? The owner of the coffee shop, of course. And it is a shared Wi-Fi signal. You are allowed to use it whenever you are seated in the coffee shop and drinking coffee. Do we not think of our favorite coffee shop as "ours"? It is only ours if we frequent it...if we dial into its frequency.

The coffee shop owner is our Innermost Being. The coffee shop is our Monad, the vehicle our Being uses to travel from lifetime to lifetime. The Wi-Fi signal is the consciousness. It comes from the router, the Divine Soul, and it sends and receives information. We cannot keep digging deeper into this metaphor any further because invariably, it will bump up against the actual consciousness involved in transforming the impressions—drinking coffee or surfing the web. Speaking of which, as we drink our coffee in our coffee shop, not only does our experience reflect on the truth of the underlying espresso, but no doubt also on the owner or the Barrista who prepared it for us. In other words, observing ourselves as we drink our coffee keeps us present and connected to the contents of the impression (coffee cup). Remembering our Innermost Barrista reminds us of who prepared this fine impression (beverage) for us and who is deserving of our thanks and praise (tip). The coffee shop is the Owner's/Barrista's, after all. His and Hers (imagine the coffee shop is owned by a husband and wife duo, analogous to our Innermost Father and Divine Mother). Thus, the transformation of the impression is complete...we are conscious and aware of all the facts.

What does all this have to do with whether "I Am Awake" or not?

If, dear reader, you have been reading this chapter with your heart and not merely your head—that is, if you have been present and transforming the impressions of these words as you have been reading them—then you should have a rudimentary feel for what went wrong for so many people who misunderstood and misinterpreted our poem.

Nearly half of the respondents thought the poem was either affirming or denying their belief that they were awake. However, that is not the case at all. By now, it is clear the poem was an exercise in self-observation and objective self-analysis. It is precisely the mind, the "I," which interferes with our direct experience of reality and puts our consciousness to sleep. The mind cannot awaken. Nor is there anything that can objectively be called "my truth" other than outright falsehood...opinion. Hypnosis and ignorance. As we have seen, the mind ignores and rants. We become identified with the mind's rants; that process of identifying with our mind and our "I" hypnotizes us and produces our ignorance...a *human conditioned.*

Now, the minds of many mystics will protest and state that they have had life-altering experiences, that they see the world in a whole new way, and that they question everything! Surely, they must be awake. Questioning is related to awakening, alright: it is only the first step. The question that matters is "How am I still asleep?" When one is truly awake, one no longer struggles to figure out the answers to their questions; one simply observes, explores consciously, and in time, knows. Not because "I know everything!" That is mystic pride. That, too, is a kind of sleep. The one who is awake knows that they know nothing; that anything and everything they may know is given unto them to know, or it is not. And what they do not know is a function of their continued slumber, beliefs they continue to fake, efforts they have yet to make, journeys they have yet to take, and karma that is still at stake.

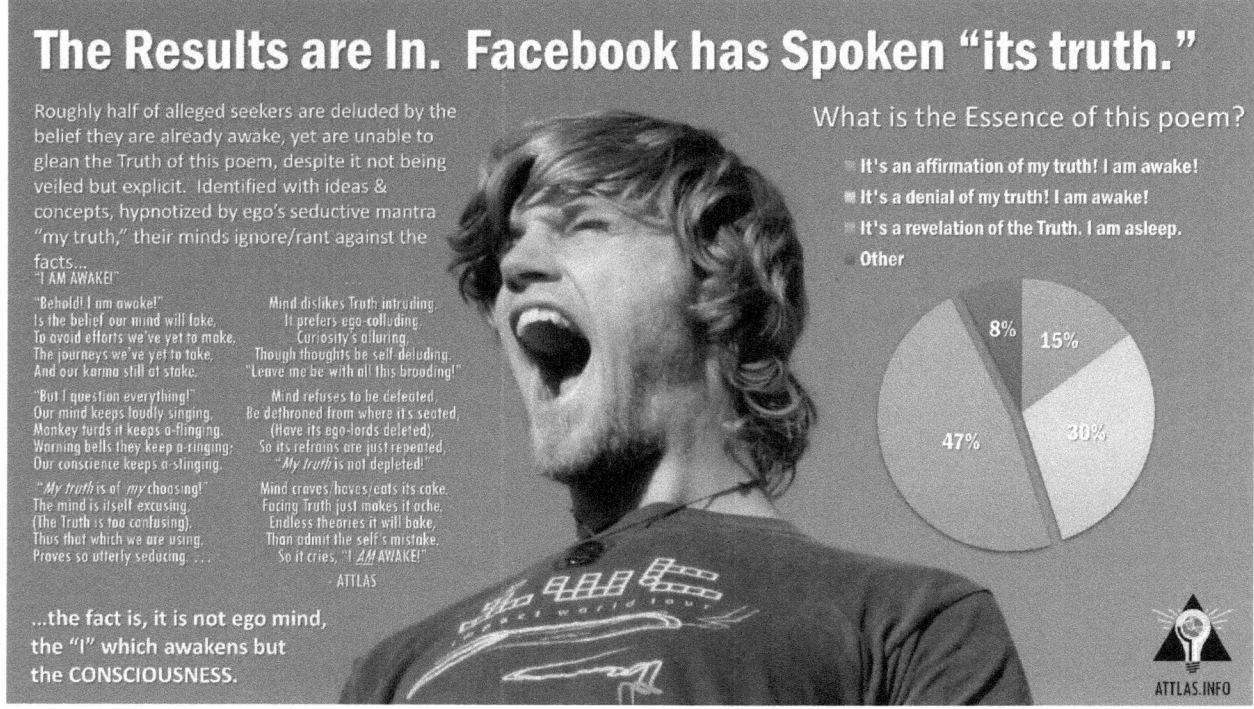

Figure 24: The Results are In. Facebook has Spoken "its truth."

To be awake means to be conscious. To be awakening has its symptoms and signs in the mental and emotional bodies, but these are only symptoms and side-effects… misinterpreted and misconstrued by ego-mind (which proclaims, "I am awake!"), they can form the very trap that keeps us entangled in The Matrix of our sleep…the ego-mind itself. Keep observing yourself. Watch your own mind: the conscious, subconscious, and infra-conscious mind (that is, the mind which comments on the mind…the voices in your head which so cleverly try to convince you that you are them by judging and condemning the other voices in your head… "I can see my mind questioning EVERYTHING! I must be awake!" It is *divide and conquer* in microcosm, as discussed in the chapter, *Waking up from The Matrix of Conspiracy.*

The Problem with '5D Awakening'

The mental body and emotional body exist in the fifth dimension, which is commonly referred to as *the Astral Plane.* So, in esotericism, you will often hear references to *the Astral Body,* and in New Age circles, you will commonly hear much being made of *5D awakening.* What you will not hear made mention of by any gurus or their followers in the New Age is any reference to the *lunar* astral body as opposed to the *solar* astral body. Nor will you hear them refer to the emotional body and mental body as being two of *the four bodies of sin.* With its inherent disdain for religious piety, the New Age balks at the very concept of sin. Ironically, it embraces The Christ in the form of *Christ Consciousness*—which its members proudly espouse to be in possession of—and conveniently repackages the Christian *rapture,* rebranding it as the *mass global awakening*—but we will get to that in a moment. There is much to unpack in these statements, so let us take each in turn.

You may be in the process of awakening, but until you awaken in the *sixth dimension*—and have created the *solar causal body,* the human soul—you are not yet Truly awake. Even if you possess your solar astral body and can travel in the solar astral plane, you are at risk of being hypnotized by one or more of your many egos. When that happens, you will fall back asleep. Practically speaking, that means falling from the solar astral plane to the lunar astral plane. You will be in a somnambulant state, half-awake, half-asleep. In this state, you will be unable to distinguish between authentic astral experience and projected illusions of your own ego-mind (as when we dream). And you can verify these facts for yourself via your own experience.

You daydream. We all do from time to time. You will be driving on the highway and suddenly 'snap awake' and realize you have no memory of the last 50 miles. You may even snap out of your daydream just in time to take your exit. Or, if you were in a deep state of daytime somnambulance, perhaps you snapped out of it too late and missed your exit. Another example: you were engrossed in a video game, a book, social media, YouTube, Netflix, or even talking on the phone when you looked up at the clock and suddenly realized hours had passed by in what seemed like just a few moments! We have all had this experience. If we can daydream in the third dimension without physically falling asleep and losing all volition over our actions, then you can be damned sure we can dream in the astral plane without losing all volition over the experience (as in a normal dream where we have very little to no volition and are solely at the mercy of our subconscious mind—being taken for a ride in the lunar astral plane). The following meme *(Figure 25)* provides an effective visual overview.

LET'S TALK "5D ASCENSION"

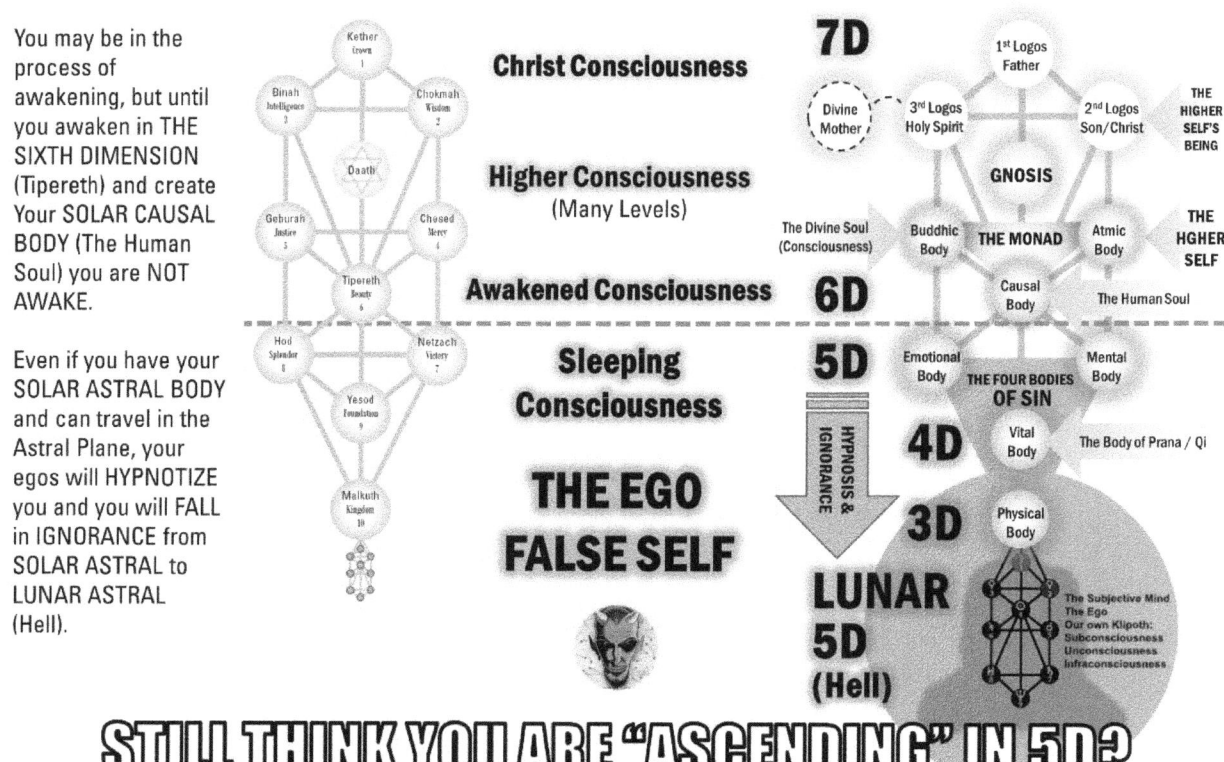

You may be in the process of awakening, but until you awaken in THE SIXTH DIMENSION (Tipereth) and create Your SOLAR CAUSAL BODY (The Human Soul) you are NOT AWAKE.

Even if you have your SOLAR ASTRAL BODY and can travel in the Astral Plane, your egos will HYPNOTIZE you and you will FALL in IGNORANCE from SOLAR ASTRAL to LUNAR ASTRAL (Hell).

Christ Consciousness — 7D

Higher Consciousness (Many Levels)

Awakened Consciousness — 6D

Sleeping Consciousness — 5D

THE EGO FALSE SELF — 4D, 3D

LUNAR 5D (Hell)

HYPNOSIS & IGNORANCE

STILL THINK YOU ARE "ASCENDING" IN 5D?

Figure 25: Let's Talk "5D Ascension"

What that means, dear reader, is that the New Age obsession with 5D awakening is a red herring—*a trap*. The astral plane is composed of the emotional and mental bodies, which are two of the four bodies of sin. And sins, as you should know by now, are egos—fear, lust, pride, greed, anger, et al). As we have been showing throughout this book, the mental, emotional, vital, and physical centers of the human machine constitute the 'hardware and software' that are ripe for infection and infestation by the metaphysical malware we call egos—sins. The moment such malware infecting the human machine succeeds in hijacking our consciousness we fall asleep and literally fall from the solar to the lunar astral plane. Again, we may not fall completely asleep—just as we do not totally fall asleep when we daydream, as previously shown—but we are no longer in the objective, upper fifth dimension (solar astral). We are now in the subjective, lower fifth dimension (lunar astral). It is said to be lunar because the moon governs mechanical nature. Responsible for influencing everything from tides to reproductive cycles. In other words, mechanical nature is subject to the influence of the moon.

The full metaphysical science behind the influence of the moon is beyond the scope of this book but can be summed up as the influence of reflected moonlight versus direct sunlight. Light becomes modified as it bounces off the surface of the moon. Conditioned light is mechanical. The more conditioned light we are exposed to, the more active the mechanical elements of our nature become, and the more susceptible the consciousness trapped within those elements is to their conditioning. This is the metaphysical science of lycanthropy best allegorized in the legends of human transfiguration into werewolves and werebears during the full moon. Rest assured, dear reader, that the science of lycanthropy is very real, and the inventors of movies and television knew exactly what they were doing when they devised entertainment utilizing 100% conditioned light. Advertising and propaganda have been ever-present, if not all-pervasive, in said media since the beginning. Be it the projected and reflected light of the big screen, the projected light of the TV tube, or the artificial light of modern digital screens, conditioned light hypnotizes the consciousness and stimulates the animal egos within us.

Do you think it is by accident, dear reader, that most content on the Internet is pornographic? Or that TV was the greatest seller of ideas and products in history? Is not the science of advertising all about triggering fear and selling comfort and security? Stimulating lust, gluttony, envy, pride, and/or laziness and selling the means to satiate said desires? Are gamepads not devices of near pure instinctive reactivity? Are graphically violent video games not stimulating primal animal urges? One of the phenomena noted by Jordan Peterson and many other psychologists is the degree to which individuals seem willing to conduct themselves in utterly reprehensible ways online, whereas they would *never* do so in the real world. What Peterson, colleagues, and social scientists fail to recognize is the metaphysical science of lycanthropy at work. The conditioned light of screens is only compounded by the inherent *tit-for-tat* reactionary nature of interactive digital media. Social media is just another version of *Candy Crush, Grand Theft Auto,* or *World of Warcraft,* played with words, images, memes, emojis, GIFs, and short videos instead of colorful puzzles, graphic violence, or virtual fantasy worlds. Gamers over fifty will know that the first video games were coded with ASCII 'graphics,' and the first proto-MMORPGs were purely text-based worlds including MUDs—multi-user dimensions. Much like D&D, the pen-and-paper granddaddy of all CRPGs, MUDs were realms where the game ultimately played itself out—precisely where the dramas unfolding 'on social media' play themselves out—in the minds of users. In the lunar astral plane.

The Hard Truth behind 'The Mass Global Awakening'

It is possible to awaken negatively, in and through ego. The followers of the New Age will not tell you this fact because they are ignorant of it. To them, awakening is a one-way street. And inevitable in their eyes. As a matter of fact, they believe the whole of humanity is on the verge of a mass global awakening and that they are at least in part responsible for the approach of said universal event of enlightenment. Particularly those who identify as *Lightworkers, Starseeds, Indigo Babies*—those who believe they are awakened souls come from the supernal worlds and/or other enlightened humanities in the cosmos who reincarnated here to help raise the collective vibration of this humanity, precipitate the mass global awakening, 5D ascension, and usher in the new Golden Age.

Setting aside for a moment the fact that this supposed global awakening followed by a utopian golden age is little more than the Christian *rapture* re-branded for those who describe themselves in online profiles as "spiritual but not religious," were it possible for anyone to awaken anyone else, this humanity would have become enlightened long ago. Are New Agers really so hypnotized by mystic pride, so self-important, that they forget the work of countless masters throughout history? And do they honestly see themselves not just on par with said masters but greater than them? That somehow, they—armed with their crystals, yoga, reiki, chanting, transcendental meditation, positive thinking, and forced higher vibrations—will achieve what Krishna, Buddha, Quetzalcoatl, Moses, Muhammed (PBUH), Jesus, and all Christified Masters together could not? The absurdity of that notion is matched only by its hubris. Here again, it mirrors the Christian belief in the forgiveness of sins. That in the end times, Christ will return to forgive the sins of those who believe in Him, raise all the believers from the dead, and create a new heaven on earth and a new Golden Age over which He will reign for a thousand years.

Like all scripture, legends, myths, and fairy tales, there are profound Truths veiled in symbol and allegory within the Book of Revelation. There are also many murky prophetic visions of what will actually come to pass. But to take a 1:1 literary interpretation of the text, re-orient it to one's own subjective biases, and concoct a whole new story in support of one's own spiritual belief system is not an enlightened process of conscious awakening. It is an exercise in political expediency, like that undertaken during the Council of Nicaea, when Constantine and his carefully chosen theologians redacted, revised, and re-ordered the bible to suit their political needs to maintain control over a Roman Empire in decline. It is an act of desperation rooted in fear of loss and a desire to maintain power and control. It is an act of pure ego. And yet, like the scriptures on which such misinterpretations, revisions, and retellings are based, the product—however corrupted it may be—is nonetheless founded in objective Truth.

As we have explained using several examples throughout the course of this book, the most widely held and fervently defended beliefs are those woven around kernels of objective fact. For starters, Christ did die for our sins. That is, Master Aberamentho, known to the world as Jesus of Nazareth, descended from the Solar Absolute and reincarnated as the Avatar of the Age of Pisces, to suffer tremendously at the hands of a degenerated humanity, die, descend into hell, arise a Resurrected Master—Christified—and deliver his most profound teachings and perform his greatest miracles before disincarnating and returning to his place in the Solar Absolute as an Ascended Master—the Master of Masters for this planet. One of the great works he performed through his sacrifice and ministry was to make an adjustment to the rules governing karma for this humanity. He made it possible to negotiate our karma and, *in some cases,* even have karma—which manifests within us as egos; sins—*forgiven.* This metaphysical, scientific fact is the origin of the Christian doctrine known as the forgiveness of sin, the Roman Catholic Sacrament of Reconciliation (Penance; Confession), the proclamation that Jesus died for our sins, and the dogma that salvation comes through belief in Jesus alone.

The Truth of the matter is Jesus incarnated the Cosmic Christ, which is not a man but a Force in the universe—the Second Logos, the Son/Sun of God. It is *Allux:* All Light, God Light; the Fire of fires, Light of lights, and Being of beings burning in the core of every planetary body, especially within the heart of every sun/star in the universe. The Cosmic Christ is the Perfect Multiple Unity which burns within every Monad—at the heart of all beings—as a spark, a seed, an Essence—our own Individual Innermost Intimate Christ. Like any seed, our Innermost Intimate Christ is not yet fully developed. It is in potentiality only. And like the seed that fell from the tree, it is made of the stuff of trees, even has tree DNA, and is part of the forest floor, but it is not yet a member of the Great White Brotherhood of trees. And certainly, nowhere near worthy of ascending into the canopy of the forest. It remains on the ground, where only the embrace of the Divine Mother's good earth, water, and the fire of sunlight can awaken its potential…which is to die as a seed and be reborn first as a sprout, then a sapling…becoming a young tree. But no amount of earth, water, or sunlight can cause a seed to die and be reborn without its consent. The Law of Free Will is Absolute—not even God will violate it—which means the seed must long to die and be reborn. We may SEEK forgiveness of sin where permissible, but where our karma is too great, the lessons we need to learn are too vital to our development, and we cannot reasonably expect to become enlightened by any external process. We, like the seed, are responsible for the eradication of sins (egos) with the guidance and assistance of our Innermost Intimate Christ and Individual Divine Mother. But we must do the work in conjunction with the AUM of Life, which is the methodology by which the Christ unfolds into being throughout all Creation and awakens and Self-Realizes in human beings who become conscious of themselves, knowing consciously and experientially, their own Innermost Intimate Christ. We will discuss the Truth of this process in more detail in *Part Three* of this book. Here, we have merely provided, in a nutshell, the kernel of Truth at the heart of Christian beliefs related to Christ and the forgiveness of sins.

There is likewise a kernel of Truth at the heart of the Christian rapture, Christ's reign, and the New Age's version of the coming Golden Age. In fact, on the point of Christ's return, the New Age version of events is even more accurate to the literal Christian belief since New Agers speak of "Christ Consciousness" and recognize Christ as a Force in the universe. They do not await the return of Jesus, the man, as Christians do. They know intuitively The Cosmic Christ is already here, now, affecting this humanity in profound ways—from within and without. And they rightly recognize that the profound effects of The Solar Logos on humanity are universal, affecting every being on this planet regardless of their religious beliefs. Sadly, these intuitive Truths are so profound and unshakeable in the hearts of all those who know them that all the beliefs woven around them, prophesizing an effortless transition to a glorious renewal of heaven on earth, likewise become unshakeable in the minds of those who hold them. For this reason, both Christian beliefs in the rapture and New Age theories of a mass global awakening, 5D ascension, and the Golden Age do little to precipitate the very outcome they promise. In fact, they contribute to humanity's continued languishing in hell on earth. The New Age promise of a great awakening and/or 5D Ascension is just another in a long tradition of misappropriation and misuse of scripture to ensure humanity remains asleep. But because they relate specifically to the Kali Yuga and the End Times, they are perhaps one of the most profound contributors to the Great A-Weakening of humanity.

PART III:

A SEEKER'S GUIDE TO ESCAPING HELL

FACE THE GREAT A-WEAKENING OF HUMANITY

By taking a journey through hell together, dear reader, we examined the four cornerstones of the Great A-Weakening and their underlying natures—**mechanicity, materialism, entropy,** and **deception**. These are the primary forces conditioning the rational mind of humanity, entrapping the consciousness in hypnosis and ignorance—identification and attachment to erroneous beliefs and the false self. While there was obviously an overlap, our analysis of transhumanism and AI focused primarily on mechanicity. The red pill of conspiracy revealed the temptations of psychological materialism (*'the truth is out there'*), divide and conquer, and entropy. The chapter on woke culture wars observed how these lead to victimhood, passive aggression, deconstruction, identification, and societal and cultural entropy through fierce tribalism associated with attachments and identity politics. Finally, our look at the New Age revealed how the cult of positive thinking, mystic pride, and spiritual entitlement all point to a massive deception whereby spiritual aspirants are told precisely what they want to hear, reinforcing their self-deception. Naturally, that deception/self-deception underscores all phenomena explored in this book since each promises its own brand of *(false) awakening.*

We know, dear reader, that nearly everyone longs to be awake, deep down in the core of their being. And so there is no easier, better way to deceive, entrap, and enslave a sleeping humanity than to give individuals reasons to believe they are already awake. *Give the people what they want* was the mantra of Hollywood for over a century—an industry whose foundations are illusion, deception, and ego. Do you find that statement hypocritical coming from us, dear reader, considering how many references to film we have made herein? Rest assured, the irony is not lost on us. That said, all shall become crystal clear. For while we have taken a long and comprehensive journey to SEEK the *what* and *how* of the Great A-Weakening, we now turn our attention to the all-important *why.*

Why are we subjected to all this deception? Why do we fall for our own self-deception? What is the meaning of it all? And what could possibly be behind what appears to be a concerted, universal, global effort to undermine humanity? Apart from a few pockets of isolated communities, the whole world is feeling the pressure of an advancing New Age woke technocracy being forced down upon it from on high, where a small cabal of global elites openly champion their transhumanist agenda. But surely that cannot be the whole story. After all, one does not write an entire chapter unveiling the internal machinations of the human psyche behind conspiracy, only to turn around and blame the Great A-Weakening of humanity on some massive global conspiracy! No, dear reader. That is not the *twist-ending* that awaits you in the final act of this discourse. As we explained in the chapter on conspiracies, their whole point is to keep us entangled in what is happening *out there* so that we ignore the real conspiracy enslaving us *in here*. But perhaps there is even a deeper Truth to be gleaned from what is happening out there in the world as it relates to humanity's imprisonment in psychological hell in here—not just how to free ourselves from hell, but what we stand to gain only by having been through hell and back.

By this point in our discourse, it should be clear to you, dear reader, that the hell imprisoning you—and all of humanity—rests within. And, you may have gathered by now that all signs pointing to *hell on earth* are not only expressions of *as within, so without,* their very purpose is to lead to revelation and revolution of the AUM of Life within us. Not collectively, as the New Age and various other religions believe, but individually, as monads—facing mechanicity, materialism, entropy, and deception in microcosm. For that, we must simultaneously explore the macrocosm.

And that, dear reader, is why, throughout this discourse, we have relayed the macrocosmic physical phenomena of transhumanist AI, conspiracy, woke culture wars, and the New Age to their associated microcosmic metaphysical phenomena—psychology. In doing so, we have laid the groundwork for easily expressing mechanicity, materialism, entropy, and deception at any given point in time simply by invoking one of the four aspects of the Great A-Weakening. And you may find us invoking them quite a bit as we conclude this lengthy discourse. For just as our journey through psychological hell was characterized by very real worldly phenomena, our escape from hell must likewise be infinitely practical. It is on that basis we proceed, dear reader, to answer at last, Truly and definitively, *what in hell is with us? And why?*

Life is Baffling

Let us engage in a visualization of active imagination—what some might erroneously refer to as 'a thought experiment'—but is, in fact, an exercise by which we can consciously SEEK Truth. Is mountain climbing easy? Is it supposed to be easy? Which mountain climbers are held in the highest regard (pun intended)? Those who climb small peaks or those who climb Everest and K2? What, then, makes a master mountaineer? How does one become a master of mountaineering or any endeavor for that matter? Mountaineering is treacherous. Treachery is a very specific term used to describe someone whom we put our trust in and who betrays us. Treacherous is thus synonymous with traitorous. And yet, many thousands of individuals set out to climb mountains, descend to the depths of the oceans, and test the limits of human endeavor in every conceivable possible way such limits can be tested—often at tremendous risk to themselves. One cannot become a mountaineer by viewing the mountain from the safety of the chalet sipping hot tea. Nor can one reasonably call oneself a mountaineer by taking a gondola or helicopter. There is only one phenomenon that can enable anyone to Truly conquer the mountain…and that is the mountain itself. The irony of ironies is this: **the thing that enables us to become a master mountaineer is the very thing trying to kill us at every turn.** Keep visualizing, dear reader. Every handhold. Every ascent. The wind. The cold. The aching muscles. The faltering will. Any mountain climber will tell you it is not the mountain they conquer but themselves—their own limitations. The mountain is just the catalyst. The adversary is themselves. We trust the mountain can be climbed. And we know the only reason to climb it is because it will fight us every step of the way. What we gain in the process is invaluable. And for better or for worse, there is no other way to gain it than risking life and limb by accepting the challenge posed by the mountain.

What comes to mind are the immortal words of JFK, "We do these things not because they are easy but because they are hard." Recognizing, of course, the unironic fact that the man who spoke those very words was himself betrayed and publicly assassinated. And if it is so for any and all endeavors, what does that say when it comes to the question of mastery over oneself?

Figure 26: The Path [of The Three Mountains] is Treacherous

Mechanical nature is traitorous by design. Recall Divine Mother Nature, the Divine Feminine Force, The Holy Negating Force, is oppositional by nature, but it is through the process of destruction (negation, opposition, death) that She creates...and what does She create? Like a mighty mountain range, She creates master mountaineers. Like a worthy sparring partner, She creates strong warriors. Like the cunning trickster Loki, She creates a wiser, more aware, more prepared Thor. But in accordance with The AUM of Life, we need not look at such lofty examples. We can turn to something as simple as living water to see the absolute, undeniable Truth of this phenomenon.

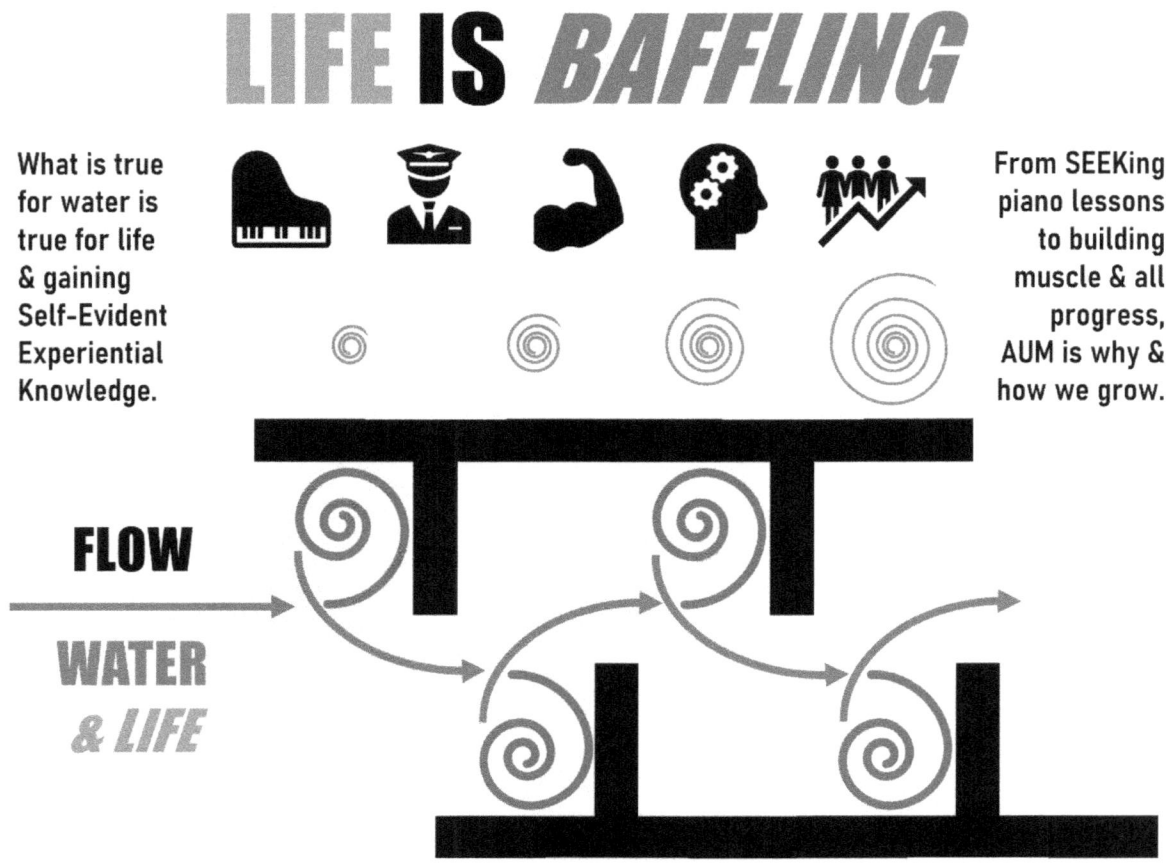

Figure 27: Life is Baffling

Be it computer expertise, musical ability, piloting skills, muscular growth, mental learning, human evolution, etc., the AUM of Life dictates and requires that mechanical nature be *baffling* at every stage. Have you ever wanted to go swimming in a stagnant pool of water? Of course not! No one wants to go swimming in some fetid pond filled with putrefied water. Such water is not altogether dead, but it is certainly dormant. It lacks the freshness, vitality, clarity, and cleanliness we value. Its capacity to dissolve, hold, and carry minerals is also greatly reduced. Naturally, how much stuff can you carry in your sleep? What makes water come alive? Not just movement, which we might call flow, but that which interrupts the flow, which we call baffles. From rapids and reefs to winds and waterfalls, whatever interrupts the flow of water and causes turbulence—flow forms such as vortices, eddies, whirlpools, and even crashing waves— creates structured, living water. Water that is far better at dissolving and carrying more dissolved elements, which makes it better at all its jobs, from nourishing life to flushing away waste. In fact, water treatment facilities around the world incorporate baffles since they improve the efficiency and efficacy of grey water and septic treatment systems.

Life is baffling. We, like water, become more structured, alive, and capable when we face ordeals, encounter hurdles, overcome obstacles, pass tests, triumph over adversity, and conquer the mountains in our lives. This is what was expressed in Joseph Campbell's Hero's Journey and constitutes the upward spiral of every process of evolution, growth, development, learning, manifestation, et al. Via this simple analogy, dear reader, we can see why the maxim of entitlement and avoidance of adversity so prevalent in the woke movement are antithetical to the fundamental human endeavor to SEEK progress. Likewise, the New Age cult of positivity and avoidance of all *resistance* is an act of Self-sabotage. When our Innermost Mountaineer SEEKs Mastery, the false self has the free will to avoid the very mountains that must be conquered. But as we know, life does not stand still. What appears to us as the fetid, stagnant pool is, in fact, in motion, subject to the entropic forces of putrefaction and slow death—which, as we described, is an essential facet of nature, life, and the Three Factors of the AUM of Life. This means whoever is not actively facing and overcoming obstacles on the upward spiral of the AUM of Life must be passively succumbing to the Law of Entropy acting upon them in the opposite direction.

As we know, what goes up must come down…if there is something called the upward spiral, then there is also the antithetical phenomenon of the downward spiral. In fact, as we have already discussed, for the upward spiral of metaphysical evolution of the Monad (Divine Nature) to take place, a corresponding downward spiral of the ego (mechanical nature) must also take place. However, if mechanical nature becomes *too baffling,* and individuals within humanity are overwhelmed by the forces of mechanical nature, then they fall into metaphysical devolution. Their Monad (Divine Nature) falls into a downward spiral as the forces of mechanical nature within them and around them enter an upward spiral, becoming stronger and stronger and exerting ever greater influence, causing more suffering, and indeed achieving the outright enslavement of humanity…the Great A-Weakening.

You see, dear reader, facing an obstacle is not simply a matter of us overcoming and growing or not. It is also a question of *how* we face said obstacle. What grows as a result of us facing the challenges of this baffling life depends entirely on what faculties we employ in overcoming said challenges. Avoiding obstacles entirely out of fear, the desire for comfort and security, laziness, narcissism, etc., leads to spiritual stagnation and entropy as we double down on our ego's self-preservation instinct. And, relying on our mechanical nature to face and overcome obstacles, we end up in the same place—doubling down on our false sense of self. We end up defined by our cleverness, craftiness, a need to control people, circumstances, and outcomes, elitism, perfectionism, and most of all, the belief that "I" did it.

Recall the Allegory of *Humpty Dumpty* and Humanity's *Great Fall* discussed in *Part Two*, dear reader. Recall the parable of the two wolves within us—light and dark. Which one of our wolves is 'getting a workout' in the gymnasium of life? Recall from the chapter on *Woke Culture Wars* that just as surely as we can express anger via emotional outbursts of aggression and even physical violence to 'take charge' of challenging people and circumstances, we can also rely on passive-aggression and non-violence to manipulate, coerce, and ultimately increase our power to control people and outcomes. Either way, we are feeding and strengthening the dark wolf of our mechanical nature. And every time we put our dark wolf to use, it gets fed, grows stronger, and we *feel the rush*—that inexorable sense of power and accomplishment about "what I got done." And the more we face these baffling times with our dark wolf, the stronger it grows, the more darkness we attract—for ourselves and others.

Dearest reader, surely by that very description alone, your thoughts turn to the present-day Israeli-Palestinian conflict erupting in Gaza, the recent so-called pandemic, and the state of this suffering humanity as it becomes ever more concerned with shoring up wealth, power, comfort, security, and self-preservation instincts on the level of mechanical nature. Every aspect of the Great A-Weakening discussed herein—transhumanist AI, conspiracy, woke, and New Age—and the false awakenings they promise appeal to our consciousness, which is trapped within ego. By promising awakening, something which our True Self longs for, they achieve its opposite: getting us to identify more with our ego, strengthening our attachments to our mechanical self—body, personality, beliefs, and desires. Even the New Age, which preaches "you are not this body," believes in the mass global awakening and the ascension of personalities into the supernal worlds, with all their beliefs and desires intact. This defines the Kali Yuga, *the End Times*...not the end of the world, mind you, just the end of a global civilization—the death of a humanity.

Covid was only the beginning...

We have seen and heard much over the past few years in the way of foretelling the imminent collapse of civilization. The economy, the monetary and economic system, the patriarchy, Hollywood, civil liberties, and free speech, even the sovereign rights of individuals and children over their own bodies. Indeed, we have heard mention of an end to all this humanity holds dear. For a time, the term that was actively making the rounds online and even in the mainstream media was *The Great Reset*. We have also seen and heard countless expressions of fear, anxiety, anger, frustration, indignation, suspicion, accusation, and outright condemnation on all sides of the political spectrum. We may have added our own voice to the cries of outrage and may even now stand firm in our position of righteousness. It is natural to feel that way when first confronted by the forces of negative chaos and destruction as they begin to gather strength, hovering above our town, our neighborhoods, our properties, our culture, our way of life, our core beliefs, our most precious liberties, and our most deeply held convictions. Natural for all that is animal within us, that is. Natural for the fear that has gripped the entire planet and the whole of this suffering and sleeping humanity.

It may feel like a scathing indictment, dear reader, to have it put forth so bluntly. But even the most hardened of self-righteous observers will concede that the *Covidiocy* was just the latest in hard evidence revealing just how utterly enslaved humanity is to its demons, namely, the ego of fear. Anyone who argues how useful and necessary the self-preservation instinct is should now concede how utterly detrimental it can be and what we are willing to trade, if not abandon or destroy outright, to placate our fear of illness and death. Fear, for instance, of a medical condition with real symptoms and complications for those with pre-existing conditions, blamed on a supposedly natural 'virus.' And an illness whose nature and mortality rate were perhaps slightly greater than that of the seasonal flu we had all endured without any hoopla until the advent of Covidiocy.

Even if we do not count ourselves among those who *followed the science* and the 'consensus opinions' expressed by politicians and the mainstream media, the whole Covidiocy operation likely had the secondary effect of firing up the conspiratorial machinations within us—and along with them, a great deal of anger and resentment. At the heart of those conspiratorial waves of fury lies a deep undercurrent of fear as well. Our anger is most often triggered by some undesirable outcome or threat of an undesirable outcome. Fear is behind the desire to control outcomes, and thus, we fear undesirable results—outcomes beyond our ability to control—and/or people in control of upshots unwelcome to us. This is not rocket science, and honestly, it should come as no surprise. The point we are making is simple: there was plenty of fear to go around during Covid, and not reserved merely for the mask-wearing, hand-sanitizing, social-distancing masses, no. The chest-beating outraged *truthers* and *anti-vaxxers* making a lot of noise online about the secretive cabal behind the Covid phenomenon, the mainstream media, the imminent collapse of the global economy, and the impending loss of all they hold dear were equally gripped by fear thanks to Covid—and the Great Reset. The only difference was that truthers wore their anger to mask their fear of the Covidiocy while everyone else wore an actual physical mask to shield them from the alleged naturally occurring contagion.

The True Pandemic Rages on

Whether we are gripped by fear or possessed by anger, we can have no genuine peace while enslaved to our egos. Fear is suffering. Anger is suffering. Peace arises when we liberate ourselves from the causes of our suffering—in this case, fear and anger. This is just a fact. There can be no authentic peace, no true liberation while we are in the grips of fear and anger, nor can fear and anger lead to authentic peace and genuine liberation. Just as the desire for comfort and security (fear) cannot lead to genuine and lasting comfort and security. The moment that supposed state of comfort and security is even remotely disturbed, suffering at the hands of fear—which desired it in the first place—returns with a vengeance and often quickly morphs into anger. So, too, the desire for freedom from oppression fueled by anger cannot lead to genuine freedom, for the foundation for that supposed state of liberty will be anger. Any threat to that liberty, real or imagined, will be reacted to automatically with anger and suffering. Thus, relying on ego for anything is, in fact, slavery to the very egos we are relying on.

There is a reason why *Faust* and many other characters from myth and great literature are said to sell their soul to the devil. Egos do not provide anything to us without a price, and that price is the enslavement of our consciousness and the consumption of our precious creative life force (the sexual force, our vital energy). Combined, these two currencies represent the medium and the fuel for spiritual experience…to know our Selves and higher dimensions—the internal worlds. To identify with—let alone rely on—primitive animal egos and to feed them our creative energy is to remain an intellectual hominid. If we allow the forces of mechanical nature within us to exploit our most precious human resources, they will invariably proliferate—intensifying their infestation, domination, manipulation, and control of our human machine. As above, so below. As within, so without. What we witness in the world at large as exploitation of natural and human resources by corporations to proliferate and dominate markets, for instance, is the microcosmic dynamic of egos playing themselves out in macrocosm. Just as malware is designed to exploit system resources to proliferate and dominate networks. Malware reflects how egos deal with us, desiring the system resources of our human machine…our human resources. The desire to exploit human resources extends to heartless, mindless, mechanical entities, which we call corporations—deemed *persons* under the law. They are AI entities by design, driven like malware and egos for one purpose: exploiting human and natural resources to increase shareholder value and market share and secure dominance over said markets. Everyone working within corporations works to this end first and foremost—with a few notable exceptions, but we will address Environmental Social Governance (ESG) later.

Figure 28: Ego Exploitation of our Human Resources

The *'New Normal'* is No Hoax

Believing the *new normal* describes the fallout from an entirely manmade crisis in service of an equally manmade psyop/agenda is incidental. We do not use the word 'hoax' to describe Covidiocy because the word hoax suggests everything about Covid is a fabrication, a ruse, a con, but this is not so. There were genuine flu-like symptoms/illnesses on the rise. The causes of which were not any so-called naturally occurring phenomenon, however. Nor were Covid-blamed illnesses remotely contagious. Had they been, the global elites would have been photographed wearing masks and socially distancing during their lavish private gatherings during the pandemic—they did neither. Like the seasonal flu and so many other illnesses blamed on supposed viral contagion, Covid symptoms were largely the result of environmental toxicity, including the increasing saturation of electromagnetic fields and microwave radiation from 3G, 4G, 5G, WiFi, Bluetooth, and those supposed 'life-saving ventilators' which purported to help patients breathe but whose electromagnetic fields interfered with oxygen transport in the blood and mitochondrial metabolism (essentially suffocating patients at the cellular level). There were countless news stories revealing the dangers and lethality of ventilators, although we have not seen a single mainstream media outlet discussing the actual root cause of the danger to patients. Sadly, the article below, originally published on WebMD, has since been removed, as were many other references to scientific studies and papers about *exosomes*, the body's system for 'quarantining' and expelling toxic and hazardous materials first from the cell, and then from the body.

Study: Most N.Y. COVID Patients on Ventilators Died

By Robert Preidt, HealthDay Reporter

WEDNESDAY, April 22, 2020 (HealthDay News) — The largest analysis of hospitalized U.S. COVID-19 patients to date finds that most did not survive after being placed on a mechanical ventilator.

The study included the health records of 5,700 COVID-19 patients hospitalized between March 1 and April 4 at facilities overseen by Northwell Health, New York State's largest health system.

Among the 2,634 patients for whom outcomes were known, the overall death rate was 21%, but it rose to 88% for those who received mechanical ventilation, the Northwell Health COVID-19 Research Consortium reported.

The new findings "provide a crucial early insight into the front-line response to the COVID-19 outbreak in New York," Dr. Kevin Tracey, president and CEO of the Feinstein Institutes for Medical Research, said in a Northwell Health news release.

The findings also add fuel to the notion that ventilators may sometimes do more harm than good for patients battling for life with severe COVID-19.

Mechanical ventilators work by pushing air into the lungs of critically ill patients who can no longer breathe well on their own. These patients must be sedated and have a tube stuck into their throat.

Recognizing that complications from ventilator use can occur, some intensive care units (ICUs) have started to delay putting a COVID-19 patient on a ventilator until the last possible moment, when it is truly a life-or-death decision, said Dr. Udit Chaddha, an interventional pulmonologist with Mount Sinai Hospital in New York City.

Source: WebMD (article since removed from their website)

At the time of writing, a reference from 2020 to Robert Preidt's original article can still be found on *Tehelka.com,* link below.

Link 10: Most Covid-19 patients die on ventilators, raising questions.

Such environmental radiation is only exacerbated by the increasingly high levels of mercury, aluminum, and other metals in our water, food supply, the environment, and ultimately our bodies. Ever put metal in a microwave oven? Now, what happens when you increase the amount of metal in humans and then shower them with increasing amounts, frequencies, power, and intensity of microwave radiation? This is not the focus of this book, however, so we will simply recommend picking up a copy of *The Invisible Rainbow* by Arthur Firstenberg.

The 'new normal' is an expression relating to far more than Covidiocy. Social distancing, mask-wearing, self-isolation, voluntary quarantining, forced lockdowns—including shops and service closures—and some form of coercion to ensure mass vaccinations were only the beginning. These represent just the first series of superficial, visible markers that times are changing for the worse and that everything this suffering humanity holds dear hangs in the balance—*everything.*

Entropy, Creation, Humanity, and the AUM of Life

Breakdown, collapse, deconstruction, dismantling, whatever you want to call it, the forces of entropy are already here—although thus far, they are primarily acting on the metaphysical foundations of civilization, as we have seen. And yes, it begins at the hand of man. How so, and why? Because the entities which constitute The Black Lodge (egos, demons, sins, nafs, psychological aggregates…they are known by many names but are best identified through self-observation of their many types…fear, anger, greed, gluttony, laziness, envy, lust, et al), work for mechanical nature, which is all too often confused and conflated with Divine Nature. This is because both are Divine Mother Nature, whose nature is the duality of both life and death and all opposites. The tension which constitutes 'The Kingdom' of Malkuth on The Tree of Life where the drama of life and death plays out (Assiah, the World of Action); also: evolution and devolution, being and not-being—*the* question.

Everything in nature is born, matures, has its prime, and then begins to age and decay, and eventually dies. No exceptions. This is just what nature does. It is completely normal for colonies to collapse, for ecosystems to break down and die out, and for entire continents to be swallowed up by the ocean. Sure, from our point of view, calamitous events on such an enormous scale are rare, but that is because we observe them through a highly subjective lens attuned to an extremely narrow timescale. On the level of the universe, for instance, the death of stars and planets is akin to the death of members of our extended family / community. Still infrequent but not exactly rare. Common, in fact. Common and inevitable. Completely normal.

The *new normal* is not new. It is normal, full stop. Civilizations have collapsed since the dawn of time. And global civilizations—entire humanities—are not immune to the inevitability of degeneration and death. That is simply the way of things. It is completely normal. Moreover, it is to be expected. A corrupt humanity appropriating the concept of change and deeming it as 'new' is simply acting upon the agents of mechanical nature fulfilling their divinely ordained purpose. During the Iron Age of any humanity, The Black Lodge rules precisely because they are the agents of negative chaos (as opposed to positive chaos, which we see in the countless expressions of growth and self-organization in nature—Fibonacci sequence, fractals, etc.).

Positive chaos is the organizational manas or Divine Mind (masculine force) uniting with negative chaos of oppositional being (feminine force) in the balanced unification/tension of creation as expressed in the yin and yang of the Tao, for instance. In positive chaos, the feminine or negating entity absorbs the masculine affirming entity, transmuting both masculine and feminine entities into a new, third entity—the zygote, for instance. The act of fertilization of an ovum by a sperm produces a singular new entity embodying both masculine and feminine aspects, which begins to divide until it becomes a blastocyst and further divides and differentiates until it eventually becomes the fetus, and then a born human being. The sperm is killed by the ovum the instant the ovum is fertilized, and the ovum begins devouring itself as well the moment it is fertilized. Both sperm and ovum effectively die, sacrificing themselves so that the zygote can emerge and eventually a child can be born. The destructive act is a creative act. From the destruction of two cells, a third one is born, with characteristics of both its parents and with the potential embodied in their sacrifice. What is true on the cellular level is true on the human level, planetary level, and throughout all seven *cosmoses*.

> *Absolute – Protocosmos (1 Law)*
>
> *All the worlds from all of the clusters of Galaxies – Ayocosmos (3 Laws)*
>
> *A Galaxy or group of Suns – Macrocosmos (6 Laws)*
>
> *The Sun, Solar System – Deuterocosmos (12 Laws)*
>
> *The Earth, or any of the planets – Mesocosmos (24 Laws)*
>
> *The Philosophical Earth, Human Being – Microcosmos (48 Laws)*
>
> *The Abyss, Hell – Tritocosmos (96 Laws)*
>
> *– Source: Hell, the Devil, and Karma by <u>Samael Aun Weor</u>*

The Law of Three applies throughout creation, and the Three Factors of sacrifice, death, and birth apply on all levels as well. Since no phenomenon in the physical universe can persist forever, procreation is the process by which existing life perpetuates itself before it falls into decay and death. Sacrifice is the way. All life gives itself, first in the harmonic balancing of ecosystems, next in the procreative act, and finally in the act of death and decomposition, when Mother Nature takes back what is Hers. And all this takes place in the fiery crucible of negative chaos—the Divine Feminine Force—*severity,* from the standpoint of Divine Love. **Love is severity and mercy in balanced measure applied unconditionally with infinite wisdom.**

The feminine force facilitates destruction and death just as it nurtures birth and growth. Without destruction and death (transmutation of old into new), birth could not take place, as we have already seen. The fires of Divine Mother Devi Kundalini Shaki are precisely the Christic Fires embodied, crystalized, and attuned in opposition to masculine manas—Divine Mind, what Emerson called over mind relating to the Over Soul, what Nietzsche called uber mind relating to the Übermensch, and which we have called meta mind relating to the Being, the True Self. Said mind needs a space, food, resolve, and the primordial culture in which to be. It also needs the drive to be: a purpose, a way…*a path.* The negating Force is The Law of Entropy…it is constantly breaking down and breaking apart, to the fullest extent of its capabilities, to result in the most complete dissolution possible given its particular level of power—be it a sugar cube dissolving in water or a granite obelisk disintegrating in the elements. It is only a question of time before all that remains of the sugar cube is sugar water, and all that remains of the granite obelisk is dust in the wind. The divine feminine fire is relentless on this front.

Just as relentless, however, is the fire within Manas—Divine Mind; meta mind—which seeks synthesis, the antithesis of entropy. We hope it goes without saying that by manas—Divine Mind—you do not imagine we are referring to the rational mind of man, dear reader. No, we are referring to that force that descends from the Ayocosmos as the Essence, the spark, the seed, the Atom Nous of the superior heart center, located in the left ventricle of the heart. Our Innermost Atman, our Divine Being, our True Self and its Divine Masculine aspect. You see, in us, it is undeveloped. But it has a drive, a relentless fire within to Self-Realize, "to be born again of the waters and the spirit." What spirit and what waters? The Holy Spirit (divine masculine) and the primordial waters of Divine Mother Devi Kundalini Shakti (divine feminine). This is where the duality of masculine and feminine begins to break down, and the dialectic mind is revealed to be too dull an instrument to understand what we are relaying. The yin and yang symbol of the Tao *(Figure 29)* helps because in it, we see each element of duality has the other element embedded within it. Thus, there is never any purely masculine or purely feminine. There is a continuum of one and the other, and both are either in union or disjointed integration (visualize the difference between yogurt with whole fruit in it versus a blended yogurt-fruit smoothie).

The manas must express itself. It is nothing, an Essence, a seed, a spark, descended from the World of Aziluth (the World of Archetypes), which is the 7th dimension (the first dimension of manifestation where the unformed essences of all form exist in their unmanifest state of pure potentiality—The Ayocosmos). But it cannot do so without having a medium to express itself in and through. In the purest sense, that medium is consciousness. But to experience conscious awareness of the Essence is to be overwrought with the longing to express and to Self-Realize…the will to be. How? Via a vehicle, a vessel…The Monad: Innermost Essence, con-

Figure 29: The Tao

sciousness, and willpower (Atmic, Buddhic, Causal bodies), that is, the Macrocosmos. The Monad is the vehicle that can traverse the galaxy and the infinitude. However, its core is still only an Essence, a spark, a seed. In other words, The Monad, like any archetype, is only a blueprint, an outline, a design, an Infinite Being in potentiality only. It is an unborn Being, just as a spermatozoon is undoubtedly alive, relentlessly driven, containing the DNA blueprint for a fully functioning human being, but purely a vessel of potential…a seed. And what does the sperm long for more than anything? To unite with the ovum: to die as a sperm and be reborn a zygote…the first cell of a human being.

The ovum waits. Like a spider at the center of a web, a Venus fly trap, the pistil of a flower, or even a teapot filled with boiling water awaiting a teabag. The ovum, too, waits to receive that which it will dissolve and, through that process of destruction, will transform itself wholly into something new. It will use the whole of itself in the process of dissolving what needs to be dissolved and absorbing it in order to fulfill its divinely ordained purpose of unmaking what is so as to make itself into something new, in accordance with the essence it just consumed and absorbed. This is the Alchemical process and the Tantra of creation on all levels. The spider and Venus flytrap, like all things, "are what they eat." The pistil of the flower receives the pollen from a stamen and dies, becoming a fruit or nut with the seed(s) of a future plant inside. The pot of water becomes tea upon absorbing the essence from the teabag. This is the fundamental nature of the feminine force: the *Akasha*. The primordial space of creation into which all manas is dissolved, all matter synthesized and created accordingly, into which all created matter eventually dissolves and dies, and in which all procreation takes place. The synthesis of manas into and through Akasha into matter is called manifestation—*to manifest*. Manas, Divine Mind + festus, meaning "God, godhead, deity, sacred place," also "joyous, festive." Manifest also relates to manus (Latin), meaning hand. Thus, manifest also means "the hand of God"—creation, how all phenomena come to be. Be they mental forms (thoughts), emotional forms (emotions), energetic forms (vibrations), or mineral, plant, animal, human, and other forms (physical matter). The word "man" relates to manifest as it does human: hume, earth + manas, Divine Mind. Either way, "man" is the Divine Masculine Mind that infests the hume, earth, matter, and the body of the Divine

Feminine, and the result is all forms of creation on all levels of manifest reality. Therefore, "man" is the microcosmos—and refers to humans, not the male gender.

However, the observer will take note that on The Tree of Life, the microcosmos, and therefore human beings, are in the middle of the tree, precisely focused on the 6th Sephiroth, which is Tipereth, the Causal Body. We can generally describe the Atmic Body (Innermost Being) as masculine and the Buddhic Body (consciousness, Divine Soul) as feminine, and their union in Tipereth, the Causal Body as both masculine and feminine, The Human Soul. These three constitute the monad or divine vessel of being. A True human being, therefore, is, first and foremost, a soul. But it is, as of yet, only an Essence; it remains a potentiality, and mostly masculine.

The process of manifestation—indeed, information—is accomplished by duality: the fires and waters of the Divine Feminine. The Christic Force, the Divine Androgen, is the Fire of fire and the Light of lights, but it descends as Fire and Light; it must separate into masculine and feminine at every level of manifest reality—first metaphysical, then physical—each time reconstituting itself as a tri-unity of masculine, feminine and union of masculine and feminine in accordance with the Law of Three.

It is important to note, then, that for the sake of brevity and simplicity, we will be oversimplifying matters in the present discussion. It is never entirely correct to say the Essence is purely masculine or that our various bodies, be they physical or metaphysical, are purely feminine. We must always remember the wisdom inherent in the Tao. For instance, although in general, Manas, Divine Mind, is masculine, and consciousness is feminine, we can say Manas, the Essence (our Inner Atman), Divine Masculine, descends into Divine Feminine, which is the five elements: earth, air, fire, water, and Akash—the medium through which the other four elements are expressed. Fire and water are opposites, just as earth and air are opposites; the Akash is their synthesis and negation (null point) just as the four cardinal points diverge from a common origin (zero point). Manifestation, the process of fecundating the feminine Akash with the masculine Essence, is one of Alchemy: *transmutation*, yes, but specifically, *crystallization*. As Master Samael Aun Weor often wrote, "The water must boil at one hundred degrees in order for that which must be dissolved to dissolve, and that which must be crystallized to crystallize." Fire and water. What is dissolved, of course, is the Essence, and what is crystallized is the mental, emotional, energetic and/or physical form(s) of the Essence. Destruction and creation…transmutation.

And just as all manifest reality comes into being through the destructive power of the Divine Feminine Force—its capacity to transmute manas into form through its dissolution and crystallization—so too does the unmaking of all manifest forms happen through the destructive power of the Feminine Force. The Divine Feminine, the negating force, is simply doing what it always does when—for the sake of balance, renewal, and obligatory fulfillment of the laws of mechanical nature—the masculine force, manas, 'overstays its welcome.' The feminine force grows tired of all this 'order, structure, coagulation, crystallization' and begins to dissolve that which was previously crystallized. Practically speaking, the store of energy sustaining the crystalized being runs out, and without that fire present to sustain the physical form, it dissolves once more. That which belongs to Divine Nature, The Monad, manas, returns to Divine Nature, and that which belongs to mechanical nature, the physical body and the personality, returns to mechanical nature. This is decay and death…cleaning the slate, preparing the feminine force to receive another masculine essence, and repeating the process.

One can also see how, in physical death, the Essence is 'reborn,' released from its manifest state to return to an unmanifest state. But it is not the same as it was before. It has grown, it has learned, it has developed. How? By virtue of the upward spiral of evolution relating to the AUM of Life: experience, accumulated experiential knowledge, karmic credits gained through service and sacrifice. A reverse process of the AUM of Life can also take place—the downward spiral of devolution, where the Essence is not released from the forces of mechanical nature. Rather, it is bogged down and lost within them, even though its physical form dies. This is what we typically understand as hell or Klipoth—the infernal worlds—and is, of course, related to the accumulation of karmic debt. If sacrifice (suffering and sacrifice for the sake of alleviating the suffering of others) leads to evolution, then it follows that the opposite of sacrifice (causing or taking advantage of others' suffering for one's own sake) leads to devolution. This process also leads to decay, death, and eventual rebirth, but the final tally is exceedingly high. Birth, death, sacrifice. Creation, destruction, evolution. On all levels of manifest reality, this cycle is an absolute and unavoidable law.

Death is, therefore, a universal Truth of manifest reality. For through death, all things are created, and through death, all things are destroyed. Likewise, it is only through death that sacrifice is even possible, and creation in the supernal worlds is predicated on sacrifice. Without sacrifice, there can be no development, no growth, no evolution on the metaphysical plane. The Essence sacrifices itself in the process of manifestation just as the Akash does to create something that is based in both but is neither one nor the other (returning to our example of the spermatozoa and ovum sacrificing themselves to create a new, unique zygote—which is more than just an amalgamation of the two.

Transformation and the Avoidance of Death

New Age followers hate the concept of death, and the New Age dogmatically asserts death does not exist…that only transformation exists. How death is just energy being transformed from one form into another, in a never-ending cosmic dance of beauty and wonder in alignment with Source. This belief is in alignment with the New Age cult of positive thinking and feel-good lollipop spirituality. We do not deny the transformation of energy underlies and complements the processes we have described thus far. That said, we assert the New Age obsession with denying the existence of death essentially denies the fundamental force of Divine Mother Nature, which we have seen is necessary for the continuum of sacrifice, death, and birth. Yes, a spermatozoa uniting with an ovum undergoes a fundamental transformation of energy, but to deny the self-evident experiential knowledge of the facts—the spermatozoa and ovum cease to exist—is just spiritual bypassing. A caterpillar ceases to be. Yes, its biological body is transformed into something else, but that something else (the chrysalis) *consumes* the caterpillar. The caterpillar *dies*. Anyone who denies this should go and visit a great white shark or a tribe of cannibals and experience the process of being eaten for themselves. Then they can talk about what sort of a 'beautiful cosmic dance' the experience of being eaten is. Of course, the biological stuff is transformed into shark and/or cannibal (and their poop). But that transformation is facilitated by destruction…by death. And the life-giving sustenance of flesh surrendered by one creature for the sustenance of another is a sacrifice by one being for another in the great web of life. One cannot know all this to be the transformation of energy while avoiding sacrifice and death as the fundamental nature of transformation. But then, the New Age is all about having your cake and eating it too. Remember, dear reader, the New Age repudiates any fact that does not make them feel good.

Naturally, sacrifice, death, and birth are beautiful. And they do constitute the cosmic dance of AUM. But to attempt to whitewash the harsh, visceral, and often painful process of that dance out of some desire for comfort and security simply reveals a fear of death. Not only is death inevitable, it is *essential*. We use the word essential not just as a clever pun but deliberately to recall our previous discussion of the Essence and its necessary relationship to and reliance upon the Divine Feminine, whose fundamental nature is death and birth: dissolution and crystallization, transmutation, alchemy.

You see, dear reader, the New Age obsession with avoiding death comes from their attachment to form. They somehow maintain the utterly erroneous notion that they can have their spiritual cake and eat it too. That somehow, by saying death is an illusion and everything is just a transformation, they can continue to exist as they are just in a completely new, ephemeral form. Not realizing—because they are nowhere near Self-realized—that their present state of being is almost entirely defined by and dependent upon their mental, emotional, etheric, and physical form. They conceive intellectually of the fluid cosmic dance, and they assume they will flow and blend into the great primordial psychedelic smoothie while still maintaining their thoughts, emotions, personality, related desires, et al. It is as ridiculous an assertion as the character of an MMORPG leaping from the computer screen into the real world. Of course, many of them have this impression due to their extensive use of psychedelic drugs, which, of course, present them with just such erroneous, subjective, and illusory experiences… "Oh, do not worry, do whatever you want, you'll never die, it's all good." So why does mechanical nature deceive us this way? And when can we trust mechanical nature to reveal the Truth? We will get to that in due course.

The Folly of Avoiding Death

Let us get personal for a moment and discuss the matter of death, which will affect each and every one of us one day, bar none, regardless of our beliefs. Perhaps we will be touched by death more than once, vicariously through our family members, loved ones, pets, co-workers, acquaintances, perhaps even complete strangers. Death affects us all sooner or later. And not just physical death but metaphysical death—psychological death, the demise of our many egos, fundamental to the AUM of Life and of psychology. Despite the best efforts of many to avoid death, including so-called spiritual and religious people who have convinced themselves death does not exist, we have made the case that it is very much a real, necessary, and inevitable phenomenon. If you remain unconvinced, dear reader, and persist in ranking yourself among the souls who are certain that death is not real and will never affect them, then please read carefully, for this section is very much for your sake and the sake of your loved ones who might one day have to carry the burden of your insolence and ignorance when the bell finally tolls for thee. Suffice it to say, matters are about to get very personal, indeed.

In case we have failed to do so thus far, let us attempt to clear up the blatant misconception among many so-called spiritual people and groups that death is merely a concept, an illusion, a transformation, a release, and countless other euphemisms, theories, rationalizations, and other death-defying cases of spiritual bypassing. Death is absolutely real. It is a phenomenon we must all face at least once per lifetime. And if we are fortunate enough, many times per lifetime, in the form of psychological death: the death of our many egos (fear, anger, greed, envy, lust et al). Death is one of the three factors of the AUM of Life: death (of our egos), birth (of our human soul) and sacrifice (for others). As one might expect, the pseudo-spiritual / New Age belief that death does not exist is—like all irrational attempts to delay or avoid death—are rooted in **fear.** It is a psychic construct based on the desire for comfort and security, which attempts to avoid an essential aspect of spiritual advancement. And what could possibly be the harm in that?

A few years ago, when our mother was dying of cancer, we became living witnesses of the tremendous suffering our parents endured because they had not taken the time to prepare themselves for the inevitable…their own death and the death of their spouse. They, each in their own way, faced the anguish of egos, which fear death above all things. Neither could find peace with their present situation and the burden of having to cope with the imminent loss of life. Not only did the final act of her life cause our mother a great deal of suffering, but it also triggered deep-down subconscious trauma in our father to the point where he was experiencing chills and shakes. Understand, dear reader, these symptoms were not of his volition or cognition. They were not psychosomatic, imagined, or illusory in the strictest sense. Both our parents were enduring very real suffering, and it was far too late for either to do anything to prevent it. They had found out the hard way that their failure to prepare for the inevitable made facing it intolerable.

There was little we could do to alleviate our father's suffering. He would seek counselling for months after our mother had passed. As for our mother, she fell into our care, as we once upon a time fell into hers: a helpless child, incapable of even the most basic functions or coordination of the physical body. Having no children of our own, we briefly experienced what it must be like to have someone totally reliant on you for their wellbeing. And we simply had no option…it never even entered our mind to deny her whatever she needed or wanted to help ease her suffering / discomfort and make it through this, the final act of her life.

As she lay in hospital for the last time, the priest came—from the same Saint Elizabeth of Hungary R.C. Church we referenced way back in Part One of this book—to administer the last rites in her native language. When she saw him, it finally dawned on her. She turned to me and said, "Son, I'm afraid." In that moment, we realized that her previous state of denial was dissolved in the harsh light of the Truth— she was dying—the contemplation of her own mortality and the imminent arrival of the angel of death weighed heavily on her heart. She had not taken any of the prior two months (let alone 72 years) to prepare for the inevitable. Now, she turned to us in her moment of weakness and frailty for help. We could not let her down.

We hastily shooed away nurses and those family members whose presence would not be suitable en- ergetically for what was about to take place (atheists and cynics, please wait outside, thank you). We asked the priest to sit on one side of our mother's bed, and we sat on the other. We took his hand and had him take one of her hands; we held the other, palm to palm, right over left, forming a chain for our energies to flow as a current—Three as one. And we prayed, not to some far-off entity, no man in the clouds, no mystical feminine figure of the Orient, not even to our own Innermost. No, we prayed in Hungarian to our Divine Mother, looking deep into our terrestrial mother's eyes…for in that moment, they were One and the same, here and now. These were the words that flowed from our heart as we locked eyes with our dying mother:

> *Holy, Blessed Dear Mother,*
> *You who have given us everything,*
> *Your whole life, without question and without fail,*
> *Without ever asking anything in return,*
> *Be not afraid.*
> *We are here to relay a Divine Message of hope to you in your time of need.*
> *Fear not. For the angels of heaven are preparing for your arrival,*
> *And above their preparations and commotion a great exhalation can be heard:*

"Roll out the red carpet and prepare the largest gate,

For a GIANT among women will soon be joining us!"

And the angels and cherubs are busy tuning their instruments, Mama,

So upon your arrival Heaven's orchestra will play Beethoven's Ninth,

And a choir of a thousand angels will sing the Ode to Joy,

And all of Heaven will rejoice:

"Our Sister has returned!

Our Mother has returned!

Hallelujah! Hallelujah! Hallelujah!

Amen. Amen. Amen."

And our mother, whose eyes had not left ours, replied with serenity and solemnity, "Son, I am not afraid anymore." We held that moment, she and I, for what may as well have been an eternity, until the silence was broken by the Priest, who added, "May this prophecy come true as spoken, in the name of Christ, Amen." And with that, we leaned down and kissed her forehead, and left her in peace so the priest could proceed to confer upon her the Last Rites in private, in accordance with the Catholic tradition our mother followed.

Some 24 hours later, in the middle of the night, she awoke disoriented and in pain. We had received the okay from the supervising physician to increase her morphine dosage, knowing full well that at that point, she would likely lose consciousness. We alone were the sole family member with her as the nurse administered the syringe, holding her hand and stroking the inside of her forearm tenderly as we often did throughout her final weeks whenever we gave her insulin shots (the cancer had exacerbated her diabetes). As we did so, she stared deeply into our eyes and spoke, again, calmly with affection and a serene certainty: "That's good, son...that's good. Keep doing what you're doing. You're doing good."

These were our mother's final words to us (or to anyone) on this earth. She slipped into a morphine-induced sleep, which she would not wake from and which she would suffer through for several more days before her heart finally gave out. And these words were not just those of my birth mother, no. As before, as we looked into each other's eyes, they were words spoken by our Divine Mother, this time emanating from Mama: "Don't worry, you're on the right path...keep going." It is not by accident that this book is dedicated to *Our Mother*—both biological and Divine.

The fear within our parents reacting to the imminent loss of life in the family was not reacting to nothing. They were reacting to the truths surrounding a fundamental aspect of reality at the level of a three-dimensional being. Nothing is permanent. Everything dies. The body dies. The personality dies. Even though our egos, which are very attached to this lifetime, do not die upon our physical death, they nonetheless fear death because of attachments—to the body, personality, friends, family, possessions, etc. They are going to lose the vehicle by which they enslave our consciousness; in many ways, they lose their slave (us), which they live vicariously through and through which they execute their programming (desire). Ego is Latin for "I"…so our many egos, countless I's, all identified with this body, mind, and personality, panic. Not only at the thought of their own death but at the prospect of losing a loved one, a pet, or even a precious possession. Observe yourself. Retrospect on a time in your life when you faced the loss of something or someone precious to you. You know that fear of loss is universal—because death is real and universal.

Let us be clear: the complete death of the body and personality is not immediate. It takes time. The personality decomposes just as the body does. This is what people experience as 'ghosts.' Residual personalities that 'haunt' the etheric plane can be occasionally seen and/or photographed. Some clairvoyants can see them all the time. It is advisable to be cremated for the simple reason that ghosts have far less to cling to if the physical body has been turned to ash. As for what fuels ghosts, the answer is simple: attachment, attention, legend, cults of personality. The ghost of Elvis Presley haunts Graceland because it has no idea it is dead. With tens of thousands of Elvis impersonators, millions of visitors, and hundreds of millions of fans, the etheric shadow of Elvis's personality is constantly re-energized, believing it is alive and well, still on tour, still performing, still eliciting the love and adulation of an adoring public. What of the mind and heart of Elvis? What of his spirit? His immortal soul? It is quite possible that it, too, is still trapped in the personality. With the cult of Elvis still very much alive and well, it is most likely his monad is lost in the Lunar Astral Plane (lower 5th dimension) dreaming itself still alive, still performing, et al). We will leave it to you to awaken in the Astral Plane and go make your own investigations to confirm what we have shared here is True.

This brings us to the crux of the matter. Are you prepared for death, dear reader? Let us face the facts: none of us know when the bell may toll for us. Do you not believe us? Our mother was diagnosed with stage four metastasized cancer and died two months later. How many people have befallen sudden accidental death? Or even violent death? The victims of murder often haunt houses for decades. Why? Because they never prepared themselves for death, and the sudden violent nature of their demise gave them no opportunity to do so. For them, the sudden and violent means by which they crossed over was anything but rainbows and unicorns…neither transformation nor release. They were violently ripped from a physical vessel and corporeal existence to which they were still very much attached. Consequently, they remain trapped in the illusion of life having never meditated on the nature of death—in general, and specifically their own.

We must prepare for the inevitable. It is important to study everything we know about the nature of death, beginning with the bardo (or in-between state), the lunar astral plane (lower fifth dimension, klipoth, also known as the infernal dimension…hell), the solar astral plan (upper fifth dimension), causal plane (sixth dimension), and what we must do while we are still alive to earn our place in the superior dimensions after we die. If we do not, we will simply not reach those superior levels. The fact is, if we dream when we go to sleep (or worse, cannot remember our dreams) that reveals a great deal about where we go when we die. The dreamscape is the lunar astral plane. If we can fall asleep and remain awake (also called lucid dreaming), that means in those moments, we are in possession of our solar astral body and can travel freely in the upper fifth dimension of the astral plane. However, as we described at the end of the chapter on the New Age, being awake in the astral plane does not mean we are fully awake yet. To be truly awake, we must awaken in the causal plane (the sixth dimension), and we must be in possession of our solar causal body—the human soul. You hear a lot of people talk about 5D in spiritual circles, as though the astral plane was the sum total of the internal worlds, but you rarely, if ever, hear them talk about 6D. The reason is they know nothing about it. They are not awake nor enlightened. Nor are the countless New Age gurus and spiritual personalities on Facebook, YouTube, and TikTok whom they follow. They have not even fully formed their solar astral body, let alone their solar causal body. How we go about creating our solar bodies is the process of Sexual Alchemy—White Tantra—a topic beyond the scope of this discourse. Suffice it to say, until we are in possession of our solar causal body (until we create our human soul and achieve union with our monad), at any point in our astral travels, be it during sleep or after death, we can fall from the solar astral plane into the lunar astral plane and not know it.

What About Near-Death Experiences?

What about them? They are as varied and deliberately orchestrated for the people experiencing them as there are people who have had them. Yes, certainly, many have afforded individuals some beautiful mystical experience of pure love, peace, joy, etc. But that is simply the characteristic state of the bardo or in-between state. When one studies the Tibetan or Egyptian Books of the Dead, one discovers prayers intended to be recited by priests, monks, and loved ones of the departed, specifically written to offer guidance to the soul of the deceased in navigating the bardo. In addition, when we consider the various 'heavenly' experiences many have had, we must recognize that many may have earned a karmic 'holiday' upon death. That is, they may not be awake and certainly nowhere near being Self-realized, but they might be on the right track, moving in the direction of awakening, and thus are given a little glimpse into the existence they are working toward—a short reprieve from the lifetime of suffering they just endured—in the form of a brief visit to Nirvana. But that is all it is: a visit. They have not yet earned the right to stay—they are not yet awake, enlightened, a buddha, or by whatever label. They have not yet created their solar causal body, their human soul. Until the human soul, the vehicle of the sixth dimension is fully developed, the monad is incomplete, and the consciousness is not awake. It must continue experiencing life in the third dimension until the human soul is created. All acts of creation rely on the creative force, the sexual force. And, like all birth, the birth of the human soul requires death and sacrifice—the death of the ego and sacrifice for humanity. These are the Three Factors of the AUM of Life.

Unfortunately, the ego-mind is a clever and subtle slaver. Although NDEs often lead atheists and others not on the path of awakening to begin pursuing a spiritual life, they have the opposite effect on many believers and aspirants who either reinforce erroneous beliefs about the afterlife or decide their work is done since their NDE showed them a glimpse of heaven. Some NDEs involve a simple out-of-body experience in which the person is still very much entangled with their personality, giving them a wholly problematic impression of what the afterlife is like. Regardless, most people who have had NDEs count them as profound life-altering experiences. How exactly those experiences change them for the better depends on their capacity to discern the pure experience itself, their intuition about the significance of said experience, and the erroneous narratives and beliefs their ego-mind will try to weave around those experiences. This is as true for those having had NDEs as it is for any aspirant having any significant spiritual experience. We must always be cognizant and on guard that our egos (particularly mystic pride) do not weave elaborate beliefs around profound kernels of Truth, lest we become utterly hypnotized and attached to said beliefs since the experience/Truth on which they are based is so compelling and profoundly resonates with us.

On an episode of the *Next Level Soul Podcast with Alex Ferrari,* guest David Suich reveals how he spent the last 14 years of his life interviewing thousands of individuals who have had near-death experiences. To gather such a tremendous collection of experiential knowledge is truly a monumental undertaking and qualifies as a profound life's work. What comes to mind is Joseph Campbell's exhaustive study of over 6,500 myths, religions, traditions, folklore, fairy tales, and stories of cultural significance from around the world and throughout time. But whereas Joseph Campbell's exhaustive study resulted in his seminal book *The Hero with a Thousand Faces* and his famous 'Heroic Journey,' Suich's extensive research has yielded naught but the proclamation, "God is Love" (the universe is Love, everything is Love, etc.). Lest we be accused of misinterpreting Suich's conclusions, misrepresenting his words and work, or unfairly oversimplifying, we offer you, dear reader, a link to the interview for your consideration.

Video 39: My 14 Years of NDE Research Shows What Is Coming to Mankind | David Suich (YouTube)

God is indeed Love, and Suich seems to know intuitively, and via his study of NDEs, that love is severity and mercy. His conclusion that everything will be alright in the end seems to undercut how deep and profound severity is. Just as his study of NDEs fails to recognize a fundamental fact which many of his subjects likewise seem to comprehend about their experiences. If his conclusions are any indication, many of them have not meditated on their near-death experience so much as they have interpreted it with ego-mind. From the substance of this interview, it appears many of them, if Suich's reporting is any indication, have ascribed profound meaning to their experiences from the point of view of their ego, their false self. The fact that Suich himself makes no reference whatsoever to the distinction between the false self and True Self, even after thousands of interviews, is of major concern regarding what humanity is learning from the phenomenon of NDEs. It seems we must shed light on what NDEs are really trying to teach us...a lesson our egos do not want us to learn.

The problem is we think we are awake and conscious. When, in fact, we are asleep. This humanity is 97% ego, on average. And death does not eliminate ego automatically. People's near-death experiences happen for a reason, but they falsely assume that because they had such profound near-death experiences they are automatically "going to a better place" after death. Or, that if the Ascended Masters or some guide tells them not to worry, that they have earned their place in heaven, that such a privilege must also extend to every last man, woman, and child on the planet. It does not. No one automatically falls up a mountain. That is why "the way is difficult, and the gate narrow into heaven, and there are few who take it." Whereas it is more than possible to fall down into the valley of darkness below. For "the way is easy and the gate wide into hell, and there are many who take it." (Matthew 7:13-14).

The experience, purpose, and objective meaning of NDEs, knowable only via free consciousness, are very different from the subjective interpretations and meaning ascribed to them by the rational mind...the monkey mind of the human-like machine...ego mind... "Shaitan" in Hebrew and Arabic, meaning "the adversary." Ego loves nothing more than to co-opt, twist, and corrupt all that is good, True, and of the Light. That is egos' (sins, demons, devils, nafs, psychological aggregates, or by whatever name) divinely ordained purpose. After all, what is the purpose of being if there is nothing to test and tempt us? No obstacles to overcome? No mountains to climb? No challenge? No adversary? No victory? No risk of losing means no opportunity for triumph. No pain, no gain.

There is no point in playing a game without an opponent. Now imagine playing the ultimate MMORPG. People "lose themselves" in such video games all the time. They become so identified with the virtual reality game world, so attached to their character, that they forget to eat, sleep, work, friends, family, etc. If one's consciousness can be so hypnotized by such an implausible and imperfect virtual game world, why do we deny the fact that the collective consciousness of humanity is utterly hypnotized by physical reality and the character of the false self?

Now imagine how ludicrous it would be for the character of a video game to leave the game after it dies. Who else can walk away from the game if not the player of the character? But only if that player is no longer hypnotized by the game, no longer identified with and attached to their virtual character. That is why it was said in all ancient mystery schools: "noscte ipsum"…know thy Self. Or, in the parlance of Master Jesus, "Know Thy Father in Heaven." For everyone's Innermost Being is an Individuated Essence of The Christ: The Fire of fire, Light of lights, and Being of beings…The Second Logos and the Son of God who descended from the Solar Absolute to speak on behalf of The Logos, "the Father of all fatherhood," via the Power of The Holy Spirit (The Divine Mother). Our own Individuated Essence of The Trinity constitutes our personal "Father in Heaven" and Divine Mother…our Innermost Player: our True Self, consciousness, and human soul…our monad which reflects the Upper Trinity on The Tree of Life: Kether, Chokmah, Binah—Father, Son, and Holy Spirit.

For many, what they see during near-death experiences are projections of their mind. The experience can still be useful from the standpoint of transforming atheists into spiritual beings, having 'seen the Light,' as it were. In this context, NDEs are blessings that can help liberate our minds from identification and attachment to the illusion/delusion of physical existence. That is why they are so transformative for so many. But they are not "get out of jail free" cards. Nor can they magically allow the character we are playing in this lifetime into heaven. They are meant to help us awaken our consciousness and remember our True Self…our Innermost Player. To SEEK the AUM of Life: the Analogous Ultimate Methodology to Knowing our Selves. Then this human-like machine we are identified with and attached to can awaken from the zombie apocalypse and begin living as a True Human Being…a Triune Human Being (Three in One: rational mind and metamind of Being)…"made in the image and likeness of God," The Trinity…The Supreme Being of Tri-Unity, and the Perfect Multiple Unity of all beings. Sadly, the vast majority of people who have NDEs are so taken with the episode, so overwhelmed by the power of mystical experience, that they cannot see their ego-mind leaping to conclusions that are simply untrue—enticing fabrications of their subconscious mind, which they are all too happy to believe. Sound familiar, dear reader? NDEs are just another kind of false awakening, a double-edged sword that has the potential to set someone on the path of awakening, but often becomes another trap related to the Great A-Weakening.

Consciously Preparing for Death

So, how does one prepare for death, esoterically speaking? In a word, **meditation.** We recommend using the most effective method there is for meditating, particularly upon one's own death, consisting of four steps/components…

1. Relax
2. Concentrate
3. Visualize
4. Pray

Enter meditation and visualize your own death. See yourself lying on a slab in the morgue, or in a coffin surrounded by loved ones, or in some surreal composite scene. You do not have to be morbid about it, and you certainly do not have to be neurotic about it. We are not suggesting you visualize yourself dying of chronic disease, being shot, hacked to pieces by an angry machete-wielding mob, or even mangled in a terrible car accident. The purpose of meditating on death is not to predict how or when we die (or even to concern ourselves with such details). The purpose is to prepare our consciousness for the inevitability of death—to sit peacefully with the eventual reality of our own death. To really be in that space and imagine what it is like to take stock in that moment… "I am dead…" so that we can move on without any attachments, without getting lost, without remaining entangled in our personality, etc.

Second, and this perhaps goes without saying, given our lengthy discussion about sleep and dreaming, is to awaken consciously. Yes, this includes practicing astral projection and dream yoga, but it will also involve sexual alchemy: preservation and transmutation of the sexual force to create the solar bodies—the solar astral body, the solar mental body, and eventually the solar causal body. One must be fully present and awake in one's life to be fully present and awake at the moment of one's death. Else, one will not be able to navigate the bardo, nor will one be able to ascend to the higher dimensions of the internal worlds (the supernal worlds). Instead, one will, at best, return in a new body and be reborn for another lifetime. Or one will descend into the lower dimensions (the infernal worlds) to essentially dream until karmic circumstances allow one to return. Those who have run out of their allotted 108 lifetimes in the human kingdom and have accumulated so much karma that there is no hope of being freed from it descend into the depths of the infernal worlds (metaphysical hell) to undergo devolution and the second death.

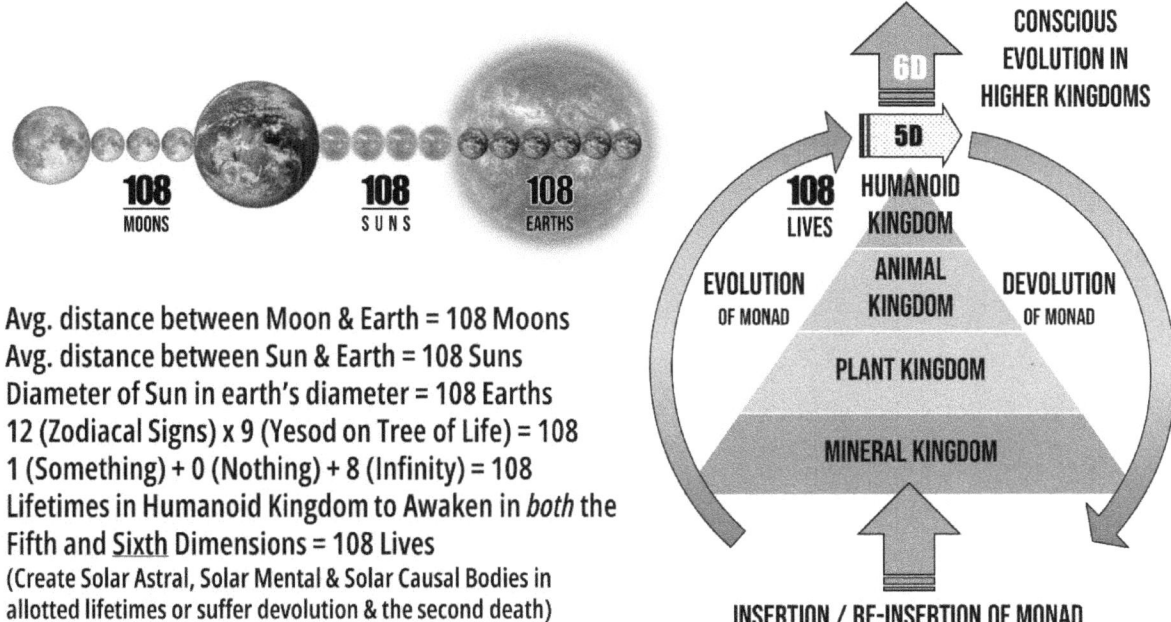

108 HUMAN LIFETIMES TO AWAKEN

108 MOONS

108 SUNS

108 EARTHS

CONSCIOUS EVOLUTION IN HIGHER KINGDOMS

6D
5D

108 LIVES — **HUMANOID KINGDOM**

EVOLUTION OF MONAD — **ANIMAL KINGDOM** — **DEVOLUTION** OF MONAD

PLANT KINGDOM

MINERAL KINGDOM

INSERTION / RE-INSERTION OF MONAD

Avg. distance between Moon & Earth = 108 Moons
Avg. distance between Sun & Earth = 108 Suns
Diameter of Sun in earth's diameter = 108 Earths
12 (Zodiacal Signs) x 9 (Yesod on Tree of Life) = 108
1 (Something) + 0 (Nothing) + 8 (Infinity) = 108
Lifetimes in Humanoid Kingdom to Awaken in *both* the
Fifth and <u>Sixth</u> Dimensions = 108 Lives
(Create Solar Astral, Solar Mental & Solar Causal Bodies in
allotted lifetimes or suffer devolution & the second death)

DON'T WASTE A SINGLE LIFETIME

Figure 30: 108 Human Lifetimes to Awaken

A monad suffering devolution and the second death in hell is subjected to a process by which mechanical nature, utilizing the tremendous heat and pressure in the center of the earth, eliminates all egos from the monad. This process can be likened to formatting a hard drive to rid it of all malware. Harsh? Without a doubt. But effective. The downside is that just like formatting a hard drive eliminates all programs and data—unwanted and wanted alike—the process of devolution and the second death erases all accumulated experiential knowledge. Following the second death, a monad can be reinserted into the mineral kingdom to begin its journey of countless lifetimes evolving through the mineral, plant, animal, and finally human kingdom all over again from the beginning. It is this cycle which is known as the *Wheel of Samsara* and the *Bhavachakra*. And since no monad is ever guaranteed to awaken within its allotted 108 lifetimes in the human kingdom, a monad can remain on the upward and downward spirals of evolution and devolution forever. This is where the concept of *eternal damnation* comes from. It is indeed a soul trapped in a kind of hell—since life is not without suffering—but it is not eternal torment in fire and brimstone as some religions would have you believe.

Being Prepared for Death Mechanically

Many people have witnessed a friend or loved one facing physical death, which they had not truly prepared themselves for. Be it a fatal illness, as was the case with our dearly departed mother, or just old age, as is the case with our father—who is still with us at the time of this writing—many live in denial of death, defiant of it, desperately doing all they can to avoid it at any cost. Fear of death, you might argue, is "perfectly natural," even necessary for our safety and longevity. Certainly, YouTube is filled with so-called "longevity experts,"—Peter Attia comes to mind, but he is by no means the only one preaching the gospel of physical longevity. The doctors of materialist medicine know nothing about Bobin-Kandelnosts—the esoteric factors of the vitality of which we have a limited reserve which the Law of Karma allocates into our three brains, and which determine how long we can live (that is, if we do not use them up foolishly). Regardless of whether we live a shorter life or a longer one, be it from illness or old age, as the inevitability of death looms, many will find themselves trying—at long last—to come to terms with their own mortality for the first time.

Be it chronic illness or the slow, debilitating decline of physical, mental, and vital faculties associated with aging, mechanical nature prepares us for our final moments on this earth in similar ways. The foundational systems of our human machine are undermined. We find ourselves breaking down physically and perhaps mentally—in the cases of Alzheimer's and dementia—and if we have not prepared ourselves, what follows can be an emotional upheaval or breakdown, depending on how we react to the signs of our impending demise. Of course, if we resign ourselves to the inevitable, we may have an almost indifferent response to our own death. If we react with defiance and contempt, identified with our fear of death and attached to our physical existence, the energy we waste on such resistance will only make us weaker and more vulnerable. If we welcome death because of this or that belief in the afterlife, said beliefs only make us weaker and more susceptible when death comes. And if we accept death with quiet complacency, our physical body more readily accepts the inevitable since, mentally and emotionally, we have accepted death. The point is, mechanical nature has its ways of weakening us, mentally and emotionally so that we are made weaker physically, allowing its final act on our life—taking it—to require the least amount of effort on its part. And so that the act of death is effective—permanent.

It is in those moments just before the final curtain that many individuals realize at last what they are facing and begin to make their peace with God. Whether they are religious or spiritual or not, in the final moments of life, when they are at their weakest and most vulnerable, individuals finally let their guard down. They may at last let go of their identifications and attachments and begin seeing themselves and reality in a more objective light—as a soul. We know of the cliché of one's life flashing before one's eyes. We look back and may find ourselves filled with joy or filled with regret. We may look around the room we are in, if we are able, and take stock of family and friends present—if we are so blessed. In Truth, there are as many experiences of death as there are souls on this planet. We cannot offer a comprehensive catalog of all the thoughts and emotions we might experience in our final moments of greatest frailty. The point is, even mechanical natural death—that is, one which is not accidental or sudden—affords us an opportunity to prepare by weakening us. It is up to us to take the opportunity presented to us in death and use it to grow and evolve, just as we did via countless obstacles, tests, and challenges in life. Grow and develop in the most meaningful way possible—spiritually.

Death is Baffling

> *And how we deal with death is at least as important as how we deal with life.*
>
> *- Captain James T. Kirk, Star Trek II: The Wrath of Khan*

If we can sum up our earlier discussion of life being baffling as *what does not kill us makes us stronger*, how do we square that sentiment with *death is baffling?* After all, death does kill us! Recall once more, dear reader, the *two wolves within*. One represents our mechanical nature—the false self—the other, our divine nature—our True Self. Death has power and jurisdiction only over mechanical nature. It is our false self, this mortal vessel and personality we identify with and attach ourselves to, which fears death. It is the false self that loathes to contemplate and face its inevitable demise at the hands of entropy and death. Fear of death is hardwired into mechanical nature since it complements its counterpart, lust—the desire to thrive and proliferate (procreate), that is, survival of the individual and of the species. It takes naught but a moment or two of honest reflection and contemplation to recognize that, by and large, this humanity is wholly governed by fear and lust. In other words, the looming threat of old age and death itself is baffling to the *dark wolf* within us, and it seeks not only to avoid the unpleasant Truth about death at all costs, it convinces itself (and us) that in the face of the inevitable, the best course of action is to live in defiance of mechanical death by doubling-down on mechanical life: materialism, craving and aversion, comfort and security, laziness and business, et al.

The avoidance of pain and indulgence of pleasure are certainly at the top of the list for most in the West. And the looming threat of old age and death often exacerbates a desire to *live it up while we still can*. Marketers persuade us to taste every pleasurable experience while we are still able. The Internet is inundated with endless products, entertainments, and experiences designed to feed every conceivable hunger. Clever ego-minds have devised substances and methods to prolong every form of pleasure as long as possible— from *Viagra* to *Black Tantra*. Time becomes, at once, our greatest asset and our worst enemy as we watch the minutes, hours, and days tick away, only to look back and wonder where the weeks, months, and years went. *Time flies when you're having fun*, so the saying goes. And the more we realize it, the more *FOMO*— fear of missing out—kicks in. The more pleasure we chase, the more we still so desperately want to have while we still have time. When in Truth, it is the *dark wolf* within that is *chasing us*. Ruled by fear and desire, ever snapping at our heels, its snarling, clawing, insatiable hunger drives us to strengthen our resolve to feed it before time runs out.

The point is, dear reader, that if death is the ultimate baffle we face as mortal beings, in keeping with the AUM of Life, it provides the stimulus for our mortal, mechanical, reactive self to strengthen its resolve to do everything in its power to avoid, resist, and defy it. Of course, the false self cannot actually triumph over death—the body and personality return to the simulation from which it sprang forth just as a character in an MMORPG stays on the server—but that does not matter to the false self. So long as we feel ourselves *really living it up,* we give the proverbial *middle finger* to death. And some may even go so far as to *taunt death* and *laugh in the face of death*, choosing extreme activities and death-defying hobbies whose fatal danger is what creates the conditions which appeal to them in the first place—i.e., adrenaline junkies, extreme activities, adventure travel, etc. On the other hand, fear of death can also manifest as craving extreme comfort and security—including the utmost in opulence, decadence, leisure, and seclusion. These tend to apply to the world's wealthiest and most powerful elites, for whom isolation from the unpleasantness and suffering of the *unwashed masses* has always been high on their list of priorities. There are some among them, however, for whom fear of death drove them to seek validation from those very masses. Many stand-up comedians, actors, performers, and politicians of all stripes have ascended to the ranks of the elite fueled by a deep insecurity and neediness to feel loved. After all, dear reader, love conquers all, does it not? Sadly, the false self cannot actually know love. What it desires is sentimental love: attachments, attention, fame, adulation, validation, admiration, and the visceral rush one gets when one gets a hit of applause. Praise is one of the most potent of all drugs. And the very people who crave it end up feeding the phenomenon of popular idolatry, in which countless fans—again, short for fanatic—find validation in communal worship of the pop idol of their choice. Again, all this is the strengthening of the false self's desire to live life to the fullest in the face of its mortality because, from its limited experience, *we only live once*. Death is so baffling, it is the impetus for the rampant hedonism we see today, particularly in the decadent and overindulgent developed world.

Remember, too, dear reader, that there exists intellectual and emotional decadence and overindulgence as well. The dark wolf within can have many insatiable pangs of hunger, not all of which are corporeal. We will indulge all manner of fantasies, illusions, delusions, theories, beliefs, and obsessions to make ourselves feel safe, secure, stronger, and even invulnerable if not invincible. The lust for power manifests in many ways, and the accumulation of intellectual and emotional power are potent forces in the grand drama of the geopolitical, economic, social, cultural, academic, religious, scientific, and technological stages. As you recall *Part Two* of this book, surely you see, dear reader, that the prominent forces behind the Great A-Weakening fall into this category of non-corporeal mechanicity. They are all about *beliefs* and the power those beliefs have over us and others. The comfort and security they afford us and the powerful hold they have over us when they are threatened. Make no mistake: the strength of our emotional attachment to intellectual theories, ideas, and other constructs is born of our fear of death—especially our belief in an afterlife, which allows for this false self to 'ascend' to heaven. The erroneous belief—that the player character can leave the video game once it is *game over*—is the single best example of metaphysical mechanicity strengthened by the baffling nature of mortality. Not only does it defy the laws of mechanical nature as we know them, it defies the objective Truth of our Divine Nature—our *Innermost Player*, the *light wolf.*

What then of the light wolf, dear reader? So far, we have seen how the ultimate obstacle the mortal self faces in life can strengthen the *dark wolf*—the false self. But what of the True Self? How does death affect the human soul and the Innermost Being? We claimed earlier that death only has jurisdiction over mechanical nature, and that is True. However, we also know that here and now, our divine nature is trapped within our mechanical nature. Practically speaking, then, death has just as much significance for the Being and holds just as much potential in terms of strengthening the human spirit as it does for the false self, as described above. But how so, exactly? Continuing with the *two wolves* analogy, in the face of death, the dark wolf wants us to live life to the max—feeding every corporeal desire as much as possible for as long as possible. In many ways, this impetus to maximize our experience in the time we have via mechanical means is a shadowy reflection of the deep longing of the human soul. Our light wolf, too, longs to 'live life to the fullest'—meaning fulfilling its divine purpose, awakening the consciousness, and SEEKing as much self-evident experiential knowledge as possible in this lifetime. In other words, while the mechanical hominid is driven by fear and lust, the divine-human spirit is driven by a deep sense of meaning and purpose. This fact should not at all come as a surprise to anyone since so much of the world's theology, philosophy, psychology, art, music, film, and literature have explored this facet of our humanity. And yet, so much of humanity seems driven not by the higher purpose of their Innermost Self but the fear and lust of their false self.

Another way to appreciate the disparity between the two, dear reader, is to contemplate it as a function of the nature of energy. We describe the flow of electrical energy as a current, just as we describe the flow of kinetic energy in wind and water as currents. It is from this universal observation of flowing energy, in fact, that the term *currency* is derived. Currency, as we have come to use the term, most commonly applies to the flow of economic power—money. Currency is a means of exchange of energy in the economy: goods and services, labor and time, etc. In the *knowledge age,* there is an economy of information, intellectual property, influence, and technology that is fueled by intellectual currency. Currency is said to have *purchasing power*—with it, we buy that which has intrinsic or subjective *value.* That makes currency itself *invaluable.* Herein, dear reader, lies the crux of the matter—pun intended.

Consciousness, too, is a currency. We *pay attention* to what is meaningful to us, do we not? It just so happens that consciousness is one of the most precious and most valuable currencies there is. It is, like all currencies, a medium through which energy currents flow (like electrical current through wire or kinetic current through water). Have you heard the expression, *energy flows where attention goes?* It is one invoked by the New Age and those advocating the manifestation of desires often. The energy they are referring to, which flows through consciousness, is creative energy—sexual energy—the creative force of the universe. With it, we not only *purchase* experience, we *create it.* The metaphysical science of the creative process of consciousness is similar to the dance between all polarities present in all forms of energy: the Law of Three: positive, negative, and union of positive and negative (neutrality). Masculine, feminine, and union of masculine and feminine. In consciousness, it is through masculine expression, feminine reception, and union of expression and reception in the act of creation that all experience is born. This is the True esoteric meaning of *Tantrism*. It is an objective Truth observable on the quantum level via the double-split experiment. It is infinitely practical in our life moment to moment—from the creation of experience and which experiences we chose, to the comprehension of language and our ability to make sense out of the experiences we have. And, of course, it is profoundly magical in the practice of Sexual Magic to which it lends its name—and the most prominent context in which the term Tantra is used. It is this context of Tantra, in fact, which veils implications of paramount importance for humanity.

When we face baffles—particularly the ultimate baffle, death—the flow of our consciousness and creative energy can go one of two ways: *up and in* or *down and out*. This is no more obvious than the moment we are confronted with the orgasm, known as *'the little death.'* Orgasm is the goal of lust, the mechanical drive to procreate for the survival of the species. But even without conception, orgasm is quite literally the *outcome* desired by lust in the act of sex—reducing the sacred act of sexual union into an exercise in base animal fornication is in many ways the ultimate temptation we as humans face—one which the vast majority of individuals in this humanity indulge without hesitation. Fornication is promoted and encouraged these days by doctors and psychologists alike. Sexual craving is stimulated and exploited to sell every kind of product and service. Purchase and consumption are proxies of the mechanical outcome desired by lust. In fact, all cravings and aversions are the union of lust and fear. Historically, the demon of lust was called Lilith. Her consort was Azmondius, fear (and control of outcomes). If Lilith, lust, was the *Whore of Babylon*, then Azmondius, fear, was her *pimp*. Together, they brought about the Fall of the Tower of Babel, a symbol for the collapse of the sexual force from our spinal column, down and out, through the metaphysical *kundabuffer organ*—the 'tail of Satan' so prominently featured on nearly all depictions of demons. Whenever we indulge in the orgasm, our own individual tower of babel falls, the sexual force— our *Divine Mother Devi Kundalini Shakti*—falls, its polarity is inverted, made mechanical, and given to feed the mechanical forces of desire within us—our egos, the dark wolf's hunger, our false self—as it flows *down and out*.

Overcoming that outcome in the heat of the moment is a tremendous exercise in the conscious application of patience, temperance, and willpower. These are all qualities of consciousness that are developed and strengthened through the practice of seminal fluid retention in both men and women—not abstention from sex, but abstention from orgasm in the practice of *supra-sexuality*. It takes *backbone* to resist the temptations presented by *the little death* of sexual desire and work intelligently with our sexual energy—our Divine Mother Devi Kundalini Shakti—so that it flows *up and at 'em*—up and *atom;* up and *Adam*—not down and out. Atomic energy is the most potent known to humanity. But as powerful as nuclear fission is, nuclear fusion is orders of magnitude more powerful. It has always been easier to destroy than to create, but few would dispute that acts of creation trump acts of destruction on a scale of usefulness. Even if some fleeting pleasure can be derived through harm, violence, devastation, et al, just as it can be through orgasm. Even if we justify destructive acts in the name of retribution, defense, glorious conquest, or what have you, just as we rationalize fornication through *natural law* and *survival of the species*—strong motivations to double down on mechanical life born of fear of death. But *sacrificing* our identification and attachment to mechanical existence, we can utilize the creative force as the fires of Kundlaini rise *up and Adam*—illuminating our chakras, creating our solar bodies, transmuting the *lead* of ego into the *gold* of the human soul, awakening our consciousness—returning us to our rightful place in Eden as a True Human Being via Sexual Alchemy. In other words, feeding our *light wolf* and starving our dark wolf, strengthening our divine nature and weakening our mechanistic nature.

What is True for us as individuals in microcosm is True for humanity in macrocosm. Faced with the prospect of its looming destruction—a *big death,* indeed—much of humanity has been doubling down on feeding its mechanical impulses and strengthening its mechanical nature. To the degree humanity's precious creative currency is flowing down and out, spent on frivolous pursuits, banal entertainments, self-indulgent comforts, self-righteous securities, et al, the spirit of humanity is being weakened. Now you see, dear reader, why the Fall of Babylon came at the hands of *the Whore—lust*—and her *pimp—fear*. Egos work for mechanical nature, and by hypnotizing our consciousness, they make us pay attention to all sorts of frivolous matters, all manner of illusions and delusions, so that our *prana (chi)*, the vital energy of humanity when not engaged in sexual intercourse, flows down and out.

At the same time, however, many individuals have felt the longing for an awakening of consciousness and the Self-Realization of the Being. Many have heard and obeyed the Still Soft Voice of their True Self, investing themselves—their precious creative currency—into endeavors and pursuits whose payoff cannot be easily understood by the rational mind, let alone quantified in purely material terms. And many end up pursuing various avenues promising an awakening in direct response to the powerful inner longing to awaken—*traps* set for them by the forces of mechanical nature to give them false awakenings. These traps we ourselves fell into as told in *Part One* of this book and explored in-depth in *Part Two*.

Mechanical nature is wanton by design. In the face of death, it seeks to strengthen itself, defend its interests, and secure its supply of *lifeblood*—the very creative sexual force present in such potent quantities in every humanity—especially in those with a strong spirit. In accordance with the natural law of conservation of energy, mechanical nature seeks for humanity's energy to flow down and out so that the earth can absorb it and retain it for itself. So, it devises belief systems and pursuits that satisfy individuals' intuitive longing to awaken and exploits their genuine divine strength by keeping them asleep and entrapped in mechanicity and causing them to expend their precious creative energies on strengthening the very containment field of their psychological prison. A containment field they not only cannot see as a prison but one they are made to believe with all their heart is the source of their power, meaning, purpose, and fulfillment in life. An insidious bait-and-switch whereby the human spirit is made a slave of mechanical nature, even while it is made to believe it is awake, or worse, awakening negatively, in and through ego, becoming a conscious agent of mechanical nature—*black magicians* and *awakened demons*.

The creative life force imparted to humanity intended for the True Self's divine purpose and pursuits is made to be spilled ceaselessly at the whims of the false self's mechanistic desires. The false self is thereby strengthened, and the spirit weakened. The weakening of the spirit in microcosm of all those who succumb to temptation in the face of *the little death* and its many proxies in physical and metaphysical form—what we experience as the countless baffling temptations, challenges, and ordeals of life and death—by extension, bring about the Great A-Weakening of humanity in macrocosm as the global civilization faces its inevitable decline and collapse into oblivion—*the big death* of humanity.

The war for the souls of humanity **is the struggle on the AUM of Life between the forces of mechanical and divine nature to determine which way the creative energy imparted to humanity will flow when confronting the baffles of life and death.** Up the evolutionary spirals of expansion of consciousness and synthesis of the human soul—*Being?* Or, down the devolutionary spirals of the explosion of ego and implosion of the human spirit—*not being?*

Figure 31: The AUM of Humanity - Spiral Forces of Evolution and Devolution.

The AUM of Life sets out the basic parameters by which civilizations rise, have their golden age—when they are most conscious—fall into decline, and die. The remnants wander in groups or survive in pockets until one or more conscious individual(s) can unite the disparate tribes and bring about the rise of the next great civilization and a new golden age. What is True for every civilization is also True for global civilizations, including our present global humanity.

While there are several important differences in the case of the decline and death of humanity, the one which matters most for our purposes is the origin of the conscious individuals who define the next humanity and establish a new golden age. In the case of the rise and fall of regular civilizations, such individual(s) can be outsiders. However, in the case of global humanity, clearly, they must come first and foremost *from within*. Such individuals not only intuitively sense the impending destruction of the global civilization, they are able to read the signs all around them—the living, breathing Word of God writ large and small in the book of life. They respond to the Great A-Weakening of humanity not by strengthening their primal animal instincts but by expanding their conscious connection to their True Source of strength within—the human spirit—their Innermost Being. And as a loyal mortal vessel and servant of their True Self, they follow their life's purpose of undertaking endeavors and enterprises to awaken and assist others in awakening to the looming threat of death and the immediate steps which must be taken. Not for the sake of saving this humanity as a whole—which cannot be done, for it is already lost—but for the sake of gathering all souls worthy and able **to *seed* the next humanity on this planet.** To rally all those with the potential to become conscious enough to establish and partake in the new golden age as imagined by New Agers and foretold in Christian prophecy.

We are, in effect, talking about the biblical story of Noah playing itself out again here and now in our time. And we have no illusions: as it was in the book of Noah, we know our elucidations on the Great A-Weakening and warnings about the impending destruction of humanity will largely be ignored, ridiculed, dismissed, or violently opposed. Until, that is, they are taken to be self-evident. Eventually, even the most hardened skeptics will not be able to ignore their own experiential knowledge. But by then, it will be too late.

There is another possibility, of course. One which is already being reflected in the activities of so-called *doomsday preppers* as well as wealthy and powerful global elites who are, as we write these words, digging elaborate bunkers on remote islands, drilling deep into the sides of isolated mountains, deep in the heart of desolated deserts, and the like. Choosing not to undertake the necessary work on themselves—to awaken consciousness—they are choosing to pour their efforts and resources into securing their physical survival. The religious among them are likely counting on their faith to save their soul should their bunker and stores of food and ammunition not prove sufficient to save their body. These groups will not deny or violently oppose our assertion that the end of the Kali Yuga is fast approaching. But they will deny the necessity to let go of their strong identification and attachment to their false self, awaken their consciousness, and become cooperative vessels of their True Self. In any case, we know that our message relayed in this discourse will be for the few *with eyes to see and ears to hear.* Those who, like ourselves, asked the question, *what in hell is with us?* And, like us, yearned to SEEK an answer.

Revolutions of the AUM of Life in Macrocosm

A wise man once told me that death smiles at us all...all we can do is smile back.

– Maximus, Gladiator

This is where our exploration of transhumanist AI, conspiracy, woke culture wars, and the New Age reaches its climax. In an elaborate twist worthy of *The Usual Suspects* or an M. Night Shyamalan movie, we reveal that it is all *necessary*. The relentless march of the Great A-Weakening is par for the course for a humanity in its Kali Yuga. We can liken it to the ruthless advance of disease and/or old age weakening the vital foundations of an individual in preparation for physical death. There is nothing we can do about it. There is no stopping it. We may be able to delay the inevitable for a time, but to what end? What sort of quality of life can one expect when one's existence is riddled with pestilence and decrepitude? What sense is there to keep a physical body on life support if its mental and emotional bodies are just as overrun with cancerous egos and their degenerated beliefs? Would it not be better to heed the words of Maximus in Ridley Scott's *Gladiator,* which he attributes to the great Stoic philosopher and Emperor Marcus Aurelius? Although there is no evidence to prove Aurelius ever uttered these exact words, the sentiment aligns with Stoic philosophy—to accept death with dignity and poise is a recognition of *it is what it is*. Just as that most inevitable and necessary process of death is how new life is born—like the mythical phoenix from the ashes—as we explored in the previous chapter. And which expresses on a planetary level the weakening and destruction of one humanity to catalyze the birth of the next humanity and its Golden Age.

Like a snake shedding its skin, this planet is preparing to shed our humanity. And if we are completely honest with ourselves, like the old, dry, brittle, inflexible skin of the snake, the dominance hierarchies in society, politics, and economics globally have become utterly corrupt. Completely mechanical. Wholly devoid of whatever pliability, integrity, and strength they once possessed when they were young, fresh, supple, and dynamically adaptable. Now they are firmly in the grips of mechanical nature, replete with its rigidity, clunkiness, lust for power, proliferation, and resistance to veering off course, even if that course is barreling toward a dystopian nightmare—the proverbial iceberg in the North Atlantic. In accordance with the law of entropy, mechanical Mother Nature has infected and infested all of humanity's institutions, including our systems of belief, governance, understanding, entertainment, et al. And it is within Her purview to do with them what She will...even if that means razing them to the ground. After all, if one wants to raze a physical structure to the ground, one begins by weakening the foundations of said structure. The foundations of any humanity are not physical but metaphysical. And that is precisely why we have witnessed the slow infestation and undermining of our cultural institutions, traditions, and religions, in addition to our shared history, philosophy, and values. Even the most fundamental tenets of nature, including the binary expression of gender and their roles in the cosmic dance of creation on all levels—physical and metaphysical—have found themselves scrutinized and undermined. As thoroughly explored throughout this book, the result is a split along axes of discontent between traditionalists and revisionists—i.e., the so-called far right and far left—**who double down on their inflexible position and fall for mechanical nature's most potent tactic for dominating and weakening humanity**—*divide and conquer.*

We should not be surprised, then, at the rise of the factors that underlie the Great A-Weakening of humanity. Most notably, the slow, covert, and insidious advance of the woke movement. This humanity's identification with the false self and attachments to subjective beliefs needs to be deconstructed and revolted against. The middle class is vanishing. The ultra-rich and powerful are becoming more so each day. There is legitimate cause for concern. At least in theory, then, the social justice warriors are right: much of what does not serve everyone needs to go. The problem lies in the fact that what the woke movement seeks to erect in its place will be far worse. The collectivist hive-mind of a Neo-Communist dystopian technocracy established through identity politics, cancel culture, and transhumanism—expressions of brute tribalism and clear devolution into mechanicity. This is precisely what mechanical nature wants and needs from this humanity (which we will address in greater detail in a moment). It should also be no surprise to us why a large contingent of the global elite, clearly motivated by the need to control outcomes, actively push the powerbrokers in government and business in the direction of the woke agenda with their ESG and DEI tenets—*Environmental Social Governance* and *Diversity Equity and Inclusion,* SMART Cities, and other initiatives which send the conspiracy community into a frenzy, keeping them from genuinely awakening via another axis of division and conquest, as we exposed in *Part Two.*

That same global elite also pushes for the wealthier, predominantly Caucasian nations of Europe and the West to open their doors to a flood of immigrants and refugees from poorer countries. These mass migrations and the kind of forced multiculturalism we are seeing in the West, including North America, is an attempt by mechanical nature to increase its pool of genetically healthy human stock. Through mass immigration of peoples from around the world of many different racial backgrounds into the North and West—especially to *the great melting pot* of the United States and the famous *cultural mosaic* of Canada—the likelihood of interracial marriages and mixed-race children increases significantly. This interbreeding among the races is especially essential for the mixing of DNA for the sake of the next humanity on this planet (the seeds for which will be selected mostly from the offspring of mixed-race couples, if possible). As with any species, too much racial homogeneity leads to genetic disease. Nature works to maximize the health of each new humanity as it is born from the remnants of the last. And it has been conducting this program of mass migration in a staged process for hundreds of years already.

The first mass migration to the Americas from Europe had spotty results. The effort was far more successful in South and Central America, where the Spanish and Portuguese successfully mixed with the

Indigenous South Americans (Inca, Aztecs, Mayans, others, and their remnants), resulting in the peoples we broadly refer to today as Latinos—Brazilians, Colombians, Mexicans, et al.

The effort was far less successful in North America, where the First Nations, already engaged in fierce tribal warfare among themselves, became allies of either the English or the French, who brought their war with them to the New World. The result of all this conflict was an inflated sense of identification and attachment to *"our ancestral land and way of life."* A sentiment that has seen a resurgence in recent years thanks to the outrageous demands of the woke mob in Canada. Much the same way as we described in *Part Two,* with Muslims and Hindus looking past their differences for the sake of expelling a common adversary—the British Empire—but turning against one another upon victory in said conflict. Upon cessation of fighting between the English and French in the Americas, the First Nations and their European allies invariably turned their attention, suspicion, and hostility toward one another. And the native reserve system was born. Content in their isolation, Native North American communities have suffered centuries of stagnation and degeneration. They have been on the losing end of a futile battle against the forces of entropy. They have not been able to face the reality of the Great A-Weakening of their culture, whose devolution began during the collapse of the Inca, Mayan, Aztec, Toltec, Mississippian, and other civilizations of the Americas from whence the countless First Nations descended. Said civilizations worshipped Quetzalcoatl, the symbol of Christ in the Americas. We saw this illustrious bird in the jungles of Guatemala, and it is truly a marvelous symbol of the Chrestos Force. One lost to the First Nations. With their ongoing struggles over treaty rights in defense of what they still see as "their land" and their attempts to preserve a culture that is but a pale reflection of the once-great mystery schools of the high civilizations from which they descended. Many of the First Nations of North America could not recognize the underlying power of Christ within the teachings of the Christian missionaries. Of course, much of the rejection of Christ can be attributed to the brutal treatment many suffered at the hands of Catholic priests and nuns in the notorious residential school systems set up by the Church. These and countless other circumstances factored into the suspicion, isolationism, and failure of indigenous North Americans to integrate with the European arrivals—who just kept coming. Instead of a Latino-like race dominating the United States and Canada, we still see a largely white society. There were a few notable exceptions, including the Métis of Manitoba. But, the Métis suffered a tremendous setback under Louis Riel and their failed rebellion. In general, the First Nations largely remained segregated on their reserves. This is a sub-optimal arrangement for all concerned, the next humanity, and the planet as a whole.

Another major influx of migrants to the Americas came via the slave trade, this time predominantly consisting of Blacks from Africa. It should be noted that Whites did not invent the African slave trade and that slaves were sold to Europeans and North Americans by African slave traders who were themselves Black. Slavery was an institution that had existed for millennia throughout the world and had never been one exclusively delineated along racial lines. Peoples of the same race often took slaves following conquests over neighboring tribes or kingdoms. Racism became a feature of slavery predominantly in the United States. Before, during, and following the Civil War, White animosity toward Blacks intensified among certain communities and was exacerbated under segregation in the Southern United States. Several hundred years of systemic racism only served to hyper-inflate racial identification in America. White racism led to "Black Pride," White fear, and the results can be witnessed in the xenophobia of White nationalists and the violence that exploded during "Black Lives Matter" demonstrations throughout North America.

From Quebec to Texas, people are entirely too identified. They, like the Aboriginal Peoples before them, feel they do not just have a good thing going in the relatively rich and pristine Americas but that they have a God-given right to defend "their land" from foreigners intruding on their way of life. They feel their culture, values, and way of life (for what they are worth) are under threat. And they, like the First Nations before them, are backing hawkish nationalist leaders who are promising to protect their racial purity and cultural identity, even as they throw shade on the identity politics of the Left. You can see a less vocally aggressive version of it in Canada, where multiculturalism has been a bragging point for decades. But it has meant the establishment of predominantly this-or-that race and/or cultural communities (famously in the Greater Toronto Area: Brampton, Markham, Chinatown, Greek Town, Corso Italia, et al) and an entire province in which Quebecois culture, language, and religion reign supreme, and which routinely holds the rest of Canada over a barrel with threats of separation. Of course, interracial couples are becoming more prominent, but racial homogeneity seems to be stubbornly holding on, even if immigrants' children are all too ready to assimilate culturally.

What all sides of the racial divide—Black, White, Latino, First Nations, East Asian, Southeast Asian, Semite, et al—must try to comprehend is this: whoever may arrive on your doorstep tomorrow who seems like they could be a threat to your land, culture, traditions, beliefs, etc., it is because most everything which defines this false self you identify as and are attached to are just constructs of a persona—a character—whose days are numbered. And like all constructs on this three-dimensional plane of existence, they are transitory and impermanent. It is more than helpful to see others as *souls* instead of races, creeds, or colors—or genders, sexual orientations, political affiliations, and all other markers of identity politics. In the same way that someone playing an MMORPG looks past the characters they interact with and recognizes *the players* behind those characters. The RPG this humanity has been playing is fast coming to a close. The DM—*dungeon master*—is taking the necessary steps to prep the game world for the next human adventure. The DM is mechanical Mother Nature. And Her agents, egos, have set themselves to dismantle and deconstruct the metaphysical foundations on which this past/present human adventure took place. When we characters see mass migration threaten our kind, our primal reaction is to recoil in fear and even lash out in anger in defense of our beliefs, traditions, values, way of life, et al. But it is more than helpful to look within ourselves, past the reflection in the mirror, and see *our Selves* as a soul, as the player behind the character in this game world, instead of identifying with the character. Now is not the time to cling to our character or the game we have been playing but to take stock of our lives and ourselves as mortal vessels for divine beings, characters for players of the game, past and present, and prepare ourselves for the inevitable end of this round of the game of life.

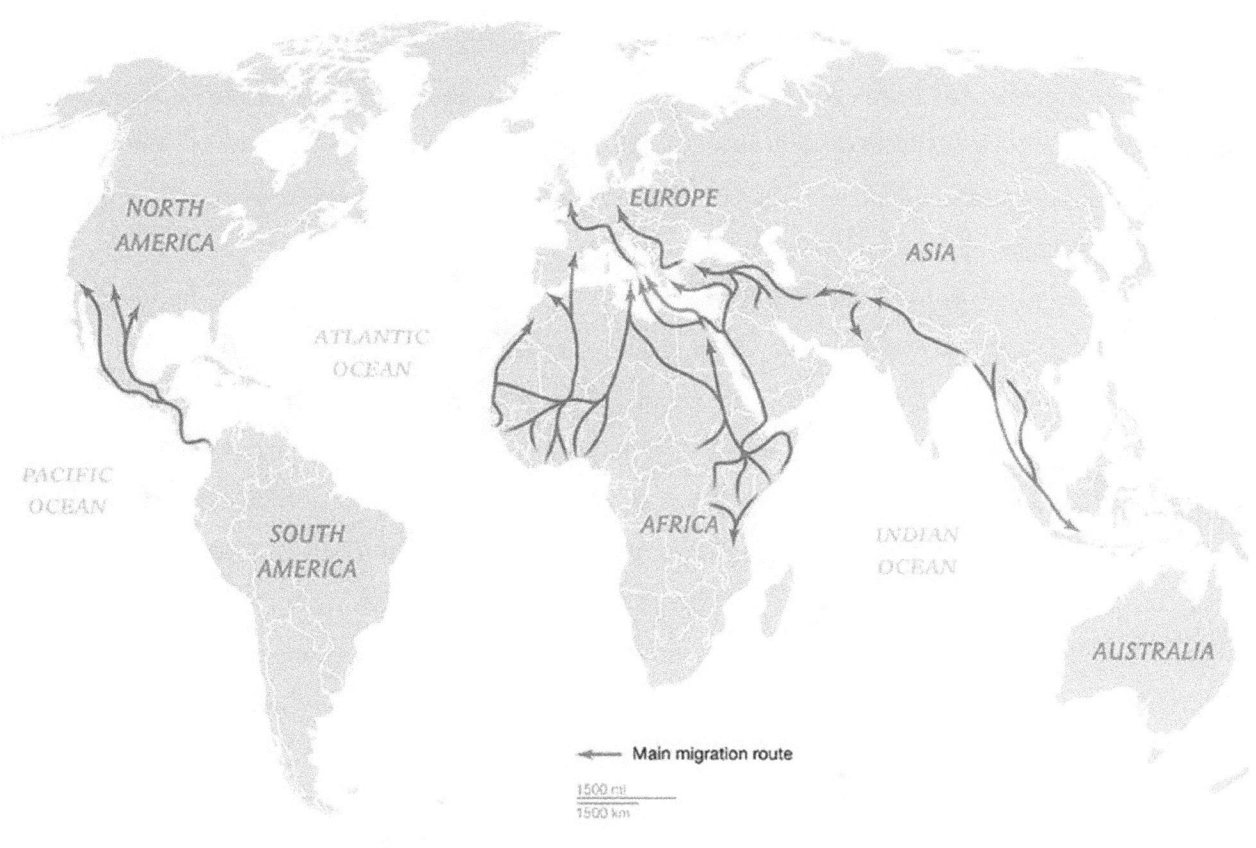

Figure 32: Migration Routes

Before the birth of a new humanity and a new human adventure can take place, the death of this global humanity must take place. And so, the Great A-Weakening of this humanity will continue unabated. The *New World Order* has been in the works for decades, if not longer, and what we must realize is that any new order the powers that be planned on setting up in place of the old is going to be far more mechanical. Like Thanos's universal genocide solution or the near-civil war and breakup of India post home-rule, the woke-fueled neo-communist transhumanist revolution in the West will seem utterly repressive. But make no mistake, dear reader, it is coming…the slow decay of death. It is the Law of Entropy. It is "the sound of inevitability" (Agent Smith, *The Matrix*), and many vocal opponents of the woke movement, including

Jordan Peterson, would do well to accept their own mortality and the mortality of all civilizations—including our own global one. It is the Kali Yuga, after all, and the death of this humanity is imminent. All its structures, old and new, are going to come to an end. It is not a matter of if but when. But make no mistake, dear reader, the process is well underway.

In the Kali Yuga, the Black Lodge rules. **The Black Lodge is ego**. That means most of the power struggles at play are not by those acting with heroic strength as gauntlets on God's right hand; they are seeking the Infinity Gauntlet for their own ends, to wield the power of God on their own Left Hand (Path). Mechanical nature is gearing up for the destruction of this humanity. The ego works for mechanical nature. It is only natural, then, that the ego would concoct Gandhi's winning strategy, postmodernism, and the woke movement, all in a bid to start dismantling all semblances or remnants of any knowledge and/or authoritative truth that this humanity built its global civilization on. The woke refer to it as *The Patriarchy,* which they have basically declared war against…deconstructed… *canceled.*

This is eventually going to make being a Gnostic extremely difficult again soon. Gnosis will once again have to go underground and hide in the shadows as heresy (the SJWs will have it branded as an offensive, triggering form of hate speech). To the woke, any person or group claiming authority over Truth or to be in possession of objective knowledge will be seen as opponents of the party line, enemies of the state, et al. The Truth is antithetical to the woke agenda. For its coalition of victim's groups pursuing a collectivist hive-mind of inclusivity and equality of outcomes, objective Truth is a real problem. For in Truth, the only hope humanity has to be triumphant against death is to awaken and Self-realize. And such triumph must happen within each individual by virtue of their own struggles, efforts, sacrifices, and indeed, suffering. There is no mass awakening. No one can awaken anyone else. No awakening takes place automatically just because. **No one is *entitled* to awaken.** And this flies in the face of SJWs and New Agers who believe they are heroes following *their truth,* ushering in their own unique brand of mass awakening.

We cannot save that which mechanical nature successfully undermines, weakens, and destroys. We cannot stop death. Allying with mechanical nature will do us no good. But we can save our souls if we look past the reflection in the mirror and recognize the two natures of nature. The key is to identify and ally with our Divine Nature. The awakening of the consciousness and Self-realization of the Being is an absolute True objective (pun intended) that is not subject to the Law of Entropy or physical Death. That said, the Great A-Weakening and impending demise of humanity it is preparing us for, can help bring about an actual awakening within us, just as imminent death can help catalyze an awakening for one lying on their deathbed. It is that True awakening of consciousness that we must grasp onto, cultivate, and bring into this world through our actions—thoughts, words, and deeds. In a phrase, we must truly be *Love in action*. And not just in our minds, as Gandhi, his social justice devotees, and New Agers may believe. In our examination of Gandhi's legacy in *Part Two,* we revealed how beliefs produce the opposite of love in action despite their best intentions. That is because beliefs are, as the postmodernists claim, subjective. Subjective beliefs very rarely lead to objective Truths. Egos' actions rarely produce effects that can be categorized as Love in action. Only genuine Love—objective knowledge, True Gnosis—can produce Love in action, and only if we follow directly what the Buddha taught…

> *You must test my words.*
> – *Buddha Shakyamuni*

And we will test them because we will be tested. Each and every moment of every day of our lives. And the whole of this humanity is being tested. That is the very purpose of the Great A-Weakening and the Kali Yuga: to get us to observe ourselves, remember our Selves, meditate on our trials and tribulations, and ask: have I done enough? Am I doing the right thing? Am I the gauntlet on God's right hand, or am I wielding its power on the Left-Hand Path? Am I Love in action? Or am I disconnected from my Inner Source of Love? Have I lost *the name of action?* Here, dear reader, we begin to truly see the significance of the last line of Shakespeare's most famous soliloquy, Hamlet's *to be or not to be.* To "lose the name of action" is to lose love itself. It is to succumb to mechanicity and fall into the downward spiral of devolution…to not be…and to recoil from corporeal death filled with fear, resistance, and defiance. Having failed to achieve liberation from the cycle of birth, death, and suffering by becoming a living embodiment of the Source of Love in action within us—our True Self—we remain identified with a character who can never leave the virtual reality of the game of life. The false self can never truly be, let alone see the baffling events of the Great A-Weakening and the Kali Yuga strengthening the human spirit. The false self will hunker down, digging itself deeper into mechanicity in defiance of its inevitable end. Becoming lost and forgotten, it will *not be.*

Humanity Divided and Conquered – Death and Devolution

This period will be lost to history and forgotten just as the details of the downfall of Atlantis were lost to us, save for a handful of accounts, including Plato's. And rightly so. There is no way of preventing what is unfolding. Mother Nature takes back what is Hers at the best of times. During the end of the Kali Yuga, nothing of this global civilization is escaping Her power to dissolve, destroy, and annihilate. Before She goes about undertaking the physical destruction of this humanity and its civilization, She is undermining its metaphysical foundations—moral, social, historical, cultural, religious, political, and economic. Mechanical nature, through its minions—the Black Lodge (egos)—is orchestrating a communist technocracy so outrageously mechanical and oppressive that a good portion of humanity will choose to outright turn their back on civilization altogether. They will say, "We know how to live in harmony according to natural law," and they will freely give themselves back to Mother Nature, embracing the way of nature idolatry on a devolving arc.

When we look around the world today, we see remnants of once-great civilizations living subsistence tribal existences, worshipping mechanical nature as their god/goddess, falling ever further into the downward spiral of primal existence (Sub-Saharan Africa was once home to humanity's earliest high civilizations; now it is home to the most savage and brutal tribal warfare on the planet). The so-called "great" apes are our cousins only in the sense that they are the devolved remnants of previous humanities. Observe how chimpanzees will fiercely attack rival tribes and not just when others encroach on their territory. They will take raiding parties into other rival troupes' territories and literally tear rival tribe members limb from limb. Spend time in Sub-Saharan Africa and witness what the Warlords do to rival gangs (and their woman and children), and you begin to realize that mechanical nature wants pockets of humanity to strengthen the primal animal aspect of hominid mechanicity and return them to Her bosom, to add to her contingent of "great" apes. As for all those who embrace the transhumanist communist technocracy, they too will be made more mechanical and truly machine-like, with a hive mind and collectivist behavior. Those conditioned in this way, should they survive the great cataclysm that destroys this humanity, will, over millions of years of devolution, end up living in small ant-like hominid colonies. There is a reason why there are no fossilized remains of ants or anthills in the fossil record. In the extremely ancient past of this planet, there existed an insectoid humanoid race whose devolved descendants are the ants we know today. Utterly and completely mechanical. No trace whatsoever of their civilization. Humanities are to mechanical nature what skin is to a snake. With great writhing and violence, this planet will shed this civilization and leave naught but a trace. And the intellectual animals mistakenly calling themselves humans who survive will be on the path of a devolving species.

Have you not wondered why, dear reader, you can go onto Amazon and find countless books on Covid and "The Great Reset?" The Black Lodge is hyping up the Covidiocy, SMART Cities, AI, transhumanism, ESG, DEI, and a myriad of other initiatives working toward the establishment of the ultimate totalitarian neo-Marxist technocracy. Mechanical nature wants more and more people to reject such a heavy-handed top-down system of control outright and choose to *live off-grid.* Intentional communities, communes, and even private family bunkers filled with 50,000 cans of Campbell's soup and 5 million rounds of ammunition. Mechanical nature wants nothing more than to have many isolated pockets of survivors falling into the downward spiral of devolution, becoming ever more savage, primal, and tribal as they double down on their physical survival and idolatry of mechanical nature. A primal spirituality that is bolstered in part by psychedelic trips into the lunar astral plane and/or dream and vision quests by which the fourth-dimensional elemental spirits of nature—which rank among the *djinn* known to Islam—reveal themselves. Nature idolaters believe worshipping Mother Gaia holds the key to their survival and flourishing in a New Golden

Age. It does not. By the time they realize it, it will be too late for them. They will be so consumed by their nature worship, psychedelic trips, liberal fornication, sexual perversions of every kind, tattoos, piercings, scarring, and the primal beat of the drum that they will have lost all sense of their Higher Self and the path needed to SEEK their Innermost Essence of Divinity…their own Divine Nature. They will believe their connection is through Mother Gaia, the elementals of nature, the Lunar Astral Plane, etc. In other words, they will become like all the varied aboriginal and native tribes around the world today, which are all remnants of once-great civilizations *(Figure 33)*.

If the numerous aboriginal tribes around the world manage to survive the end of the Kali Yuga and continue to choose a subsistence existence isolated from the next humanity and identified with mechanical nature, they will continue along a devolving arc. If their descendants, in facing the baffling nature of life, keep doubling down on identification and attachment to the survival of the self and the tribe, they will continue strengthening the *dark wolf* of their primal, animal, mechanistic self. A self that has been conditioned to believe the best chance for survival is to plunge ever deeper into mechanical Mother Nature's warm embrace. They will eventually end up like the world's great apes. Or, they will eventually hit a devolutionary dead-end and become just another in a long series of ape-like hominids in the fossil record. Extinct hominids that archaeologists, paleoanthropologists, evolutionary biologists, geneticists, and materialist scientists of all stripes erroneously identify as *our ancestors*. They are not. They are our *devolved cousins*. And we, theirs. Meanwhile, skeletons of giants—our actual ancestors—are conveniently ignored, absconded, hidden from public view, dismissed as hoaxes, etc. Naturally, because if the knowledge of the giants of Atlantis and Lemuria and the secret history of humanity goes mainstream, the great lie told by evolutionary biologists, paleoanthropologists, and even geneticists will come crashing down like the house of cards it is.

Video 40: Sacred Sexuality, Episode Two: The Secret History of Humanity (YouTube)

DIVIDE & CONQUER HUMANITY
The Great A-Weakening & the Kali Yuga

STEP 1 – RECRUIT BLACK LODGE (EGOS) to Undermine Humanity by Seizing upon Innate Longing for Oneness / Immortality with Mechanical Visions of "Heaven on Earth"

MECHANICAL VISION A
Technocratic Socialist "Utopia" via Fear-Based Transhumanist "Covidocracy"

STEP 2A METAPHYSICAL DECONSTRUCTION
(Individuality, History, Tradition, Religion, Culture & Consciousness Lost to Techno-Hive-Mind)

MECHANICAL VISION B
"New Golden Age" of Nature, Pleasure & Ancestor Worship via Native & New Age Pseudo-Spirituality

STEP 2B METAPHYSICAL DEGENERATION
(True Self lost to Attachments: False self, Pleasure, Tribe, Relations, Drugs & Lunar Bodies)

PREP NEXT GOLDEN AGE

STEP 5 (Concurrent) Awaken < 1% Via the Narrow Way (Alchemy & Ego-Death) to Seed Next Humanity

STEP 3 PHYSICAL DESTRUCTION OF HUMANITY

STEP 4A DEPOPULATION
> 80% of Humanity

STEP 4B DEVOLUTION
< 20% of Humanity

Figure 33: Divide and Conquer Humanity.

As difficult as it may be to hear, dear reader, this humanity has *not evolved.* We are a devolved version of humanity. Atlantis, even in the time of its Kali Yuga, possessed a metaphysical science and technology well beyond the cognitive capacities of our present humanity—reliant as we are on the mechanistic AI of our rational mind and about to put all our proverbial eggs into the basket of technological AI. Evidence of our inferiority and devolution can be found in the artifacts and architecture of the earliest civilizations around the world. They built incredible structures like the Great Pyramid, whose construction still mystifies the most capable of our mechanical and architectural engineers. Similarly, the precision with which certain stone vessels and delicate crystal perfume jars were carved defies every known technological capability we have today. An honest, objective examination of these phenomena leads the objective conscious examiner to the conclusion that our humanity lost precious knowledge and capabilities over the millennia, which our ancient ancestors inherited from Atlantis and used to establish the Golden Age of this humanity. An objective, verifiable Truth that mainstream archaeologists, relying on the subjective mechanicity of their ego-minds and fearful of their academic careers, seem both incapable and unwilling to admit. No ego is ever eager to reveal its weaknesses or admit when it is wrong. The intellectual humanoid, which falsely calls itself human, has far too much of itself invested in the subjective beliefs, theories, consensus dogmas, and worldly benefits that they provide. Most intellectuals are not quick to put themselves, their reputation, and their livelihood on the line for the sake of unpleasant, unflattering, even threatening Truths. But, such academics, intellectuals, and members of the secular cult of rational empiricism and materialist science cling to their limited beliefs in vain. The New Golden Age will have no place for the materialist limitations of ego-intellectuals and rational empiricism. The next humanity can scarcely be expected to seed itself with intellectual hominids falsely claiming to be human beings—especially ones who had the gall to name their own "great awakening" of rationalism and empiricism *"The Enlightenment."*

Only true human beings, those who have awakened consciousness, will be chosen to become the seeds of the next humanity on this planet. That is the history of Atlantis allegorized in the story of Noah and the countless other "great flood" myths and creation stories found in the ancient texts and traditions from cultures around the world. This humanity does not have much time to abandon its adolescent obsessions with hedonism, entertainment, and rational materialism. As the Atlanteans before us, we face the baffling forces of the Great A-Weakening closing in around us, seducing us with mechanistic visions of the future—one overtly technocratic, secular, and bizarrely pseudo-scientific-spiritual, the other natural and pseudo-spiritual. Each is a trap dividing and conquering humanity, setting us on a path of death and destruction or devolution. But between these two, there is a third way, a *middle way,* if you will. And as we face the baffling mechanisms at work behind the Great A-Weaking consciously—both within and without—we will find ourselves invariably stepping into *"The Narrow Way"* of Alchemy and ego-death, whereby our precious creative energy is directed up and in *(up and at 'em, Adam, Atom)* toward creation of the human soul, evolution of the human spirit, and all that such genuine evolution entails. Including, but not limited to, access to higher worlds and the all-important metaphysical science that Atlantis and ancient civilizations possessed during our Golden Age but which was lost to us over time. While the Great A-Weakening serves mechanical nature by preparing humanity for destruction and/or devolution, for those of us *with the eyes to see and the ears to hear*, it is a call *to be* true human beings...*to be Love in action.*

We are challenged to respond to the baffling intensity of the Kali Yuga by turning away from all false awakenings and traps of ego and instead strive toward genuine awakening and evolution of the human spirit for the sake of others and the future of humanity—the next humanity and its Golden Age. Never in the history of our humanity have conditions been more conducive to the super-efforts required to awaken, Self-realize, and assist us in progressing on the upward spiral of conscious evolution. We must never lose sight of humanity being divided and conquered, however. Successfully traversing the Kali Yuga means walking a tightrope calmly, with balanced concentration, fearless, on an evolutionary arc. Else, we will fall. The dangers presented by the End Times are the very opportunities for us to awaken and evolve. That is why the titles *Apocalypse* and *Revelation* both refer to a great *unveiling*.

Opportunities to Evolve Surround Us

By now, dear reader, you should know that in accordance with the AUM of Life, the upward spiral of metaphysical evolution cannot take place without a life that is baffling. Nor without facing the most baffling aspect of life—death. And we can make profound advances as we face the tests, trials, and ordeals presented to us by the Great A-Weakening and the Kali Yuga. But only if we overcome the countless traps set for us by The Black Lodge (our own egos), given its divinely ordained purpose to undermine and enslave this humanity metaphysically in preparation for its physical destruction. The key is not to fall into the downward spiral of mechanical nature: fear, lust, anger, belief, nature idolatry, et al. We must not allow ourselves to fall into the trap of being divided and conquered. From each other, yes, but first and foremost from our-Selves. We must resist the temptation to double down on our primal animal instincts to dig in our heels, harden our hearts, and galvanize our minds. Rather, we must take Bruce Lee's timeless advice to *"be water, my friend."* We must use the baffles around us and within us to become stronger, structured, and alive...able to purify ourselves and be a life-giving vehicle for our True Self, our Innermost Atman (our Essence). The Divine Spark within us is but a seed that needs to germinate and sprout...a process of psychological death...of facing and conquering our own demons (egos). Demons which are traitorous to our True Self. Demons that constitute our individual *Shaitan* ("the adversary" in Hebrew and Arabic)—the false self. A false self that will find itself attracted to many seemingly mystical, magical, and powerful paths to awakening and self-realization. **Paths which are double-edged swords at best and, at worst, dual paths to devolution and the second death for our monad.**

Religion

All religions are precious pearls on the necklace of divinity.
– Samael Aun Weor

If the problem with belief has not been made clear by now, dear reader, then allow us to elucidate the matter more clearly with one of the oldest and most obvious of the *double-edged swords* many believers hold onto with all their might. All religions and spiritual traditions have hidden deep beneath their surface essential Truths that can lead us out of hell on the upward spiral of evolution. However, due to the Law of Entropy, all religions, which are understood with the rational mind and felt via the sentimental heart alone, end up driving a deeper wedge between individuals and their True Self in favor of some external, impersonal deity. Individuals born and raised in this or that religious tradition are conditioned to obey the strict tenets of said tradition, often leading to internal conflict. The Still Soft Voice of intuition is often overridden by the cold, hard, inflexible dogmas of religious belief. Many turn from their life's work in favor of a path that is more in keeping with their family, community, and church beliefs. Many believe they are doing God's will simply by following the literal, superficial, and traditional beliefs of their religion—and/or the countless intellectual interpretations of scripture, which have many levels of meaning. In doing so, they risk failing to Truly know themselves: the Will of their own Innermost Individuated Essence of God. They end up doing God's Will *in theory,* but not *in practice.* This sees them spinning their wheels since *talk is cheap,* while *practice makes perfect.* In accordance with the spiral nature of AUM, if one is not practicing and improving, one is invariably at the mercy of entropy, trapped in the downward spiral of devolution.

The cutting edge of religion is defined by the timeless, universal religious principles from which all Great Religions and genuine spiritual traditions sprang forth in Truth, Love, and Light. In other words, if all religions are likened to the branches of a Great Tree, then they must all lead the conscious SEEKer to the roots of Truth, Light, and Love from which the Great Tree and all its many branches sprang forth. A Great Tree whose many branches bore fruit appropriate to the times and place in which they were needed to nourish souls in need. All fruit eventually ripens, falls, and begins to rot. That is the way of things. The Great Tree lives on, and its roots remain strong. And new fruits emerge season after season according to the weather, all born of The One Great Tree, all able to nourish the soul, so long as we follow the fruit back to its roots.

The biting edge of religion responsible for spiritual self-harm is our identification and attachments to degenerated religious forms—when we keep eating rotting fruit, believing it will nourish our soul. But rotting fruit tends to ferment. And we all know how sweet, seductive, and addictive the alcohol in fermented fruit can be. It leads to the insistence of believers who cling to superficial, degenerated, kindergarten understandings of religion solely with their rational minds and sentimental hearts. And the persistence of idolaters who believe their worship of outward symbols will save their soul, instead of working with the divine forces said symbols represent to actually liberate and evolve their divine soul by creating the human soul—awaken their consciousness in the sixth dimension. Speaking of tempting fruit, which turns out to be rotten and fermented—addictive—let us look to the true meaning of that most famous of all biblical fruits.

As previously explained, the word religion derives from the Latin *religare,* meaning "to bind together as one [with Divinity]." It is synonymous with the Sanskrit *yug,* the root word of Yoga. And as we have also already explained, these concepts relate directly to the True meaning of *Tantra:* the co-creation of reality in the field of consciousness via The Law of Three—masculine *expression* unites with feminine *reception* to create *experience.* All religions and genuine spiritual traditions have at their heart the Secret Doctrine of sacred sexuality. All contain allegories of gods and godmen born of immaculate conception. The process by which a single sperm is chosen by divine providence to make the journey in the sacred act of sexual union to fecundate the ovum. A process that does not require the expulsion of a billion sperm via orgasm—which is the desired outcome of the indulgence of lust (pun intended), the Harlot of Babylon responsible for the Fall of the Tower of Babel, the mother of all egos, and the True meaning of *the forbidden fruit*—eating of the Tree of Knowledge of Good and Evil and the resulting Fall. All religions hold the union of man and woman as profoundly sacred. At their heart, religions are not, as the atheists would have us believe, *obsessed with sex.* Unfortunately, to the uninitiated rational mind, the timeless, universal religious Truths veiled in symbol and allegory are an enigma. Deep down, believers know that they do not really know, so their beliefs become a shield against the terror of the unknown. In the case of sex and spirituality, the result is a fear-based spectrum whereby sex is either over-indulged or deemed problematic, outright dirty, and to be avoided at all costs. Sexuality is divided and conquered by the dialectic of ego-mind under the influence of fear. Since fear is the consort of lust, both paths along the fear-based spectrum of sexuality ultimately lead to sexual degeneration *(Figure 34).*

The True meaning and purpose of every religion is lost over time as its adherents fall into the traps of belief and idolatry. They believe they know the Truth because they read the scriptures as literal facts alone. They idolize the people, places, and events depicted in the stories. The surface-level stories and literal interpretations become canonized as official church doctrine, and generations of believers are thereby in-doctrinated. All those who fail to follow said doctrine are labeled *heretics* and *enemies of the faith.* Indeed, most associate the word faith with religion, and any contemporary thesaurus will list *belief* as a synonym for "faith." And they are all flat-out wrong. One need only look to the meaning of religare and yug—root words of religion and yoga, respectively—to see that "bind together as one" has absolutely nothing to do with belief. Let us SEEK why.

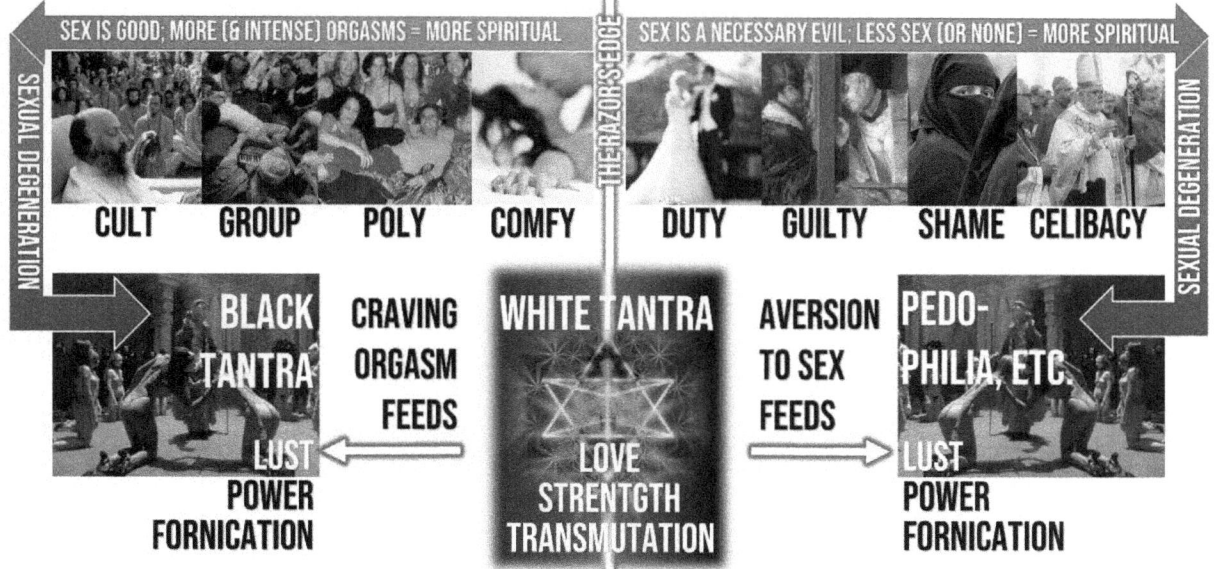

SEX & SPIRITUALITY
FEAR-BASED SPECTRUM VS. THE TRUE MIDDLE WAY

SEX IS GOOD; MORE (& INTENSE) ORGASMS = MORE SPIRITUAL

THE RAZOR'S EDGE

SEX IS A NECESSARY EVIL; LESS SEX (OR NONE) = MORE SPIRITUAL

SEXUAL DEGENERATION

SEXUAL DEGENERATION

CULT   GROUP   POLY   COMFY   DUTY   GUILTY   SHAME   CELIBACY

BLACK TANTRA

CRAVING ORGASM FEEDS

WHITE TANTRA

AVERSION TO SEX FEEDS

PEDO-PHILIA, ETC.

LUST POWER FORNICATION

LOVE STRENTGTH TRANSMUTATION

LUST POWER FORNICATION

DESIRE FOR COMFORT & POWER OF THE ORGASM IS AS MUCH FEAR-BASED AS DESIRE TO AVOID SEXUAL GUILT & SHAME.
EITHER WAY, LUST+FEAR'S ENDGAME IS SEXUAL DEGENERATION.
THE RAZOR'S EDGE (SEXUAL ALCHEMY REPLACING ORGASM WITH TRANSMUTATION) IS THE TRUE MIDDLE WAY.

Figure 34: Sex & Spirituality ~ Fear-Based Spectrum vs. the True Middle Way

To be *faithful* to our spouse—sometimes called our 'better half'—means to experience union with them physically; to know our *mortal beloved* intimately at the exclusion of all others. To be unfaithful, then, is to intimately know others besides our mortal beloved. This is self-evident. In the bible, the expression *to know* is often used to describe the sexual act. For instance, *"And Adam knew Eve his wife; and she conceived, and bare Cain, and said, I have gotten a man from the LORD." – Genesis 4:1.* This is perhaps the first, but certainly not the last instance in which the expression *to know / knew* means intimate knowledge. Being faithful to one's spouse is not a matter of belief, then. One can *conceive of a child* in thought, perhaps, but one cannot physically conceive a child through belief alone. That is a scientific impossibility and a stupidity. Similarly, one cannot believe oneself into a state of faithfulness. One must know *intimately.* Intimately knowing one's spouse at the exclusion of all others and/or knowing others intimately apart from one's spouse also happen to be the required conditions to be deemed faithful or unfaithful in a court of law. Yes, one can be unfaithful in the mind by fantasizing about being intimate with another. And while such unfaithfulness does have karmic repercussions (according to The Great Law), they hold no sway in a court of law. Legally speaking, being faithful or unfaithful is a matter of knowing intimately and is on a markedly different level than mere belief.

This is not the only way that the courts invoke the superior status of knowledge over belief in relation to faith. In medieval times, a witness was said to *give faith* that certain events did or did not happen. In other words, *testify*. Even in contemporary courts, eyewitness testimony is treated as more valuable and trustworthy in arriving at a verdict than that of so-called expert witnesses or other circumstantial evidence. One who gives faith is precisely offering their experiential knowledge—which we hope by now you recognize as more trustworthy than mere theory or opinion, dear reader. By giving faith, it was understood that a witness had directly experienced events surrounding the crime. One might even say that a witness has some degree of *intimate knowledge* of what took place. Litigators who solicit *speculation* from witnesses will rightly get an objection from defense attorneys, which will be sustained by the judge. A court of law, it turns out, should not be interested in hearing what this or that witness believes happened unless they are a so-called *expert witness* who is basing their assessment on years of related *experience*. In any case, witnesses must be deemed *credible,* meaning trustworthy. And trust is earned. The entire concept of *legal precedent* is based on it—on trusting experience and evidence in order to know the Truth. Not belief. Experience and evidence. Now, where have you heard those words used in relation to knowing, dear reader? True faith, then, is ultimately related to self-evident experiential knowledge and is what we SEEK.

To be faithful to our Higher Self means to experience union with our Innermost Being, metaphysically, to know our *Immortal Beloved* intimately. To bind together as one with our Innermost Intimate Essence of Christ is the True meaning & nature of "having Faith." To "trust in the Lord" is not a matter of believing in some impersonal or abstract God 'out there' somewhere in the universe, or even believing that we are all God experiencing Itself as and through the universe. No. Trust in the Lord is earned by having intimate experiential knowledge of our Innermost Lord—our own Individuated *Father in Heaven* and *Divine Mother*. Only then can we Truly fulfill our calling as a person of faith. Only then can we fulfill the calls of fellow religious believers when they proclaim that we "testify!" Only a witness can testify. One who claims to give faith but only states their beliefs is not a credible witness. True Faith is in no way, shape, or form a belief. Belief is the antithesis of True Faith. Belief is the lazy, comforting, proud, and envious shadow of genuine knowing. It is no coincidence <u>belief</u> *belies* True Faith.

Recall, dear reader, in *Part Two,* we explored the Law of Entropy as it pertains to language, specifically how *shellshock* devolved and degenerated into *PTSD*. There, we witnessed how the outer form of the word degenerated and diluted the power and meaning embodied in the original word. From our analysis of the word faith, we can deduce a similar process must have taken place in the centuries since the Middle Ages when to *give faith* meant much more than just *belief.* Somewhere along the way, the word faith was reduced in meaning, belief was elevated in significance, and the two were equated wholly erroneously and incorrectly. And what is True for the entropic degeneration of the word faith is equally True for the words religion and yoga, respectively. Religion has degenerated into a system of belief (we could say *blind faith*). And for most, yoga means contorting the body for physical and pseudo-spiritual benefit (Hatha Yoga). Religion keeps the so-called *faithful* trapped in the rational mind and sentimental heart of the false self, while yoga keeps its *faithful* trapped also in the physical body. Recall, dear reader, that entropy is a law of mechanical nature.

It would be utterly preposterous to see the evidence of entropy at work on religions over millennia and remain convinced that their contemporary doctrines, held as absolute Truths by believers, are not likewise the products of entropy. How does one reconcile the many different sects and splinter groups of any major religion? Christianity alone has dozens. Their beliefs cannot all be the unvarnished Truth, can they? The split between Catholics and Protestants led to *the Troubles* in Northern Ireland—marked by horrendous acts of violence. Over what? Beliefs! And what about the varying different religions? How many wars and conflicts have been fought because the believers of this or that faith took offense to the fact that others believed something different? And yet, if they could only have relaxed, meditated, and detached themselves from identification and idolatry, they might have penetrated the symbols and allegories and uncovered the timeless, universal religious principles which form the core teachings of all Great World Religions and genuine spiritual traditions. Universal Truths are likewise found at the heart of all high mythology, art, literature, etc. We again share the following five-minute video first linked in *Part One,* which explains why Samael Aun Weor said, "all religions are precious pearls on the necklace of divinity."

Video 41: Religious Principles (YouTube)

What is more, since all religions encode the AUM of Life—the metaphysical science of how to overcome *the adversary* and attain union with one's own Innermost Essence of Divinity—their ultimate purpose is to help us Truly awaken on the upward spiral of evolution. Develop *the eyes to see and the ears to hear* the timeless, universal religious Truths expressing themselves all around us and within us. To intimately know the Will of our Innermost Beloved and the metamind of Being. And to know that the Living, Breathing Word of God is not bound within the pages of any one scripture nor lorded over by any one religion.

Rather, the Living Word of God is writ large and small in the book of life itself. To know that Truth directly, intimately, consciously, and to Trust one's destiny to that experiential knowing is what it means to have True Faith, to be bound together as one with one's own Innermost Essence of divinity. That is the secret, hidden promise and potential of all religions. Do not believe it, dear reader. Do not have blind faith. Awaken and know it to be True.

> *Know yourself, and you will know the universe and the gods.*
> *– Oracle of Delphi*

Magic – White and Black

The manipulation of physical reality for selfish purposes and/or in violation of the Great Law (of Karma) is a spiritual crime. All magic 'hacks into the code' behind reality, as it were. But only legitimate 'hacks' are acceptable. Praying for something you want would be considered a form of magic in this case. Another term for 'legitimate magic' is White Magic. White magic is performed explicitly for the sake of the conscious evolution of ourselves or others *"in accordance with the Law,"* acknowledging the tireless efforts of the Lords of Karma who intelligently manage the Great Law of cause and effect in the universe. Magic is a powerful tool on the path of awakening and Self-realization of the Being. However, to perform magic without the acknowledgment of The Great Law is a crime against God, against nature, and against one's Self. Let us explore precisely how and why that is so.

Imagine yourself in the shoes of your Individual Divine Mother, having spent tremendous effort liaising with the Lords of Karma to orchestrate a series of baffling tests, trials, and ordeals to help you become conscious of some defect or vice. Perhaps the circumstances needed for you to undergo said tests include poverty—or, at the very least, to be without an automobile. Now imagine yourself getting fed up with bicycling and taking public transit and deciding to *manifest* a new car into your life by leveraging the *Law of Attraction* in accordance with the teachings of the New Age and even the Self-Help industries. You visualize the car you want and pour all your will and desire into said visualization. You tell yourself that with this car, you will be more effectual in the world, will be able to help others by giving them rides, will have more free time to do volunteer work, and the like. But mostly, you justify it based on the law of attraction and the *unlimited abundance* of nature, which you believe yourself entitled to, as was hammered into you by the New Age. A few weeks later, you get word from a sweepstakes you entered months earlier that you are a winner or perhaps from a distant relative that you inherited a car. By whatever practical means it shows up, you succeed in *manifesting your desire.* You may not even take a moment to express gratitude toward the universe for delivering what you had manifested since "I did it…I made it happen…I am a powerful magician," etc. But all you have really done is thrown a monkey wrench into the carefully devised plans your Divine Mother had in store to help you evolve consciously. Now, thanks to the car you were not meant to have, you will not be on the bus at the precise moment you needed to be to experience what you needed to experience. What is more, should that experience have been a bus crash, one which would have put you in the right place at the right time to help others in a significant way, you will no longer be there to do so. Instead, you will be off somewhere else, enjoying the comforts and convenience of your new car. Now, the Lords of Karma must try to relay messages to other Beings to take up the slack left by your absence from the bus crash. And your Divine Mother must beg and plead on your behalf to the Lords of Karma to give you another opportunity to be tested and/or be given a chance to help others in desperate need again, despite your delinquent ignorance and absence from the last such opportunity. Ignorance is not bliss, nor is it an excuse. You manifested the car you desired because you gave in to your ego. It was not your intuition which told you to do so. In fact, your intuition would have explicitly told you not to do so. And you ignored it in explicit violation of The Great Law. A violation fully endorsed by the New Age.

Absolutely no one in the New Age will ever share these facts with you. Either they are utterly ignorant of The Great Law and how manifesting desires is a violation of it, or they have no incentive to label the manifestation of desires for what it is—*black magic*—because they are themselves agents of the Black Lodge. This is especially true for proponents of so-called *chaos magic* and other practitioners of magic who proselytize the practice of magic for many so-called 'altruistic purposes.' Many chaos magicians can perform miracles of healing, for instance. Surely that can only be a good thing, right, dear reader? Except what if the illness that was healed was meant to facilitate a life lesson for the sick individual? What if the miraculous healing *imposed* by the chaos magician threw another monkey wrench in the efforts of the Lords of Karma and the sick individual's Divine Mother? What if the illness was cancer, and the apparent miraculous 'cure' was only a temporary one, eliminating the symptoms but not the underlying psychological causes leading to the cancer? Now, the illness which was supposed to lead to an individual's comprehension and elimination of powerful egos affecting their lives has been, at best, postponed for several more years or decades until the cancer can return to teach the lesson it was meant to. In the meantime, the individual, free from cancer, will still suffer psychologically from said egos, and when the cancer eventually does return, they will no longer have the vitality of youth to combat the illness. They may end up succumbing to the disease without ever learning the lesson they needed to learn from it. But the chaos magician, like the New Age manifester or even the religious zealot praying profusely, remains ignorant of the bigger picture. They want to help, and that is all they know. And if pressed, they would argue they had *the best of intentions.*

Manipulating reality, even for the sake of 'good,' is no trivial affair. And performing magic for the sake of others is rarely as simple as it appears on the surface. We hope the examples we gave above are evidence enough of that, dear reader. But there are other forms of manipulation of reality which we need to be made aware of—ones involving the manipulation of others, their decisions, and even meaningful direction in their lives. We may partake in such manipulation without even being aware of it. Or, even if we are aware of it, working in careers ranging from sales and marketing to advertising and mainstream media, we have been conditioned to think nothing of it. Getting others to act in certain ways is just part of the job. Persuasion is just a *best practice*. From lawyers to lawmakers, scientists to academics of every stripe, convincing others of your arguments, winning debates, winning over the hearts and minds of jury members, decenters *across the aisle,* and voters all merely come with the territory. And what of food scientists and pharmacology specialists whose job it is to make what we eat hyper-palatable or habit-forming? Doubt that happens, reader? Perhaps you believe that the opioid crisis was an anomaly, an accident, some freakish coincidence? Perhaps the following *Cold Fusion* documentary on the Sackler Family will give you a different perspective.

Video 42: The Sackler Family – A Secretive Billion Dollar Opioid Empire
(YouTube)

It has happened before, and it will happen again. And again, and again…in one form or another…you can count on it, dear reader. Perhaps you might be surprised to hear that focus groups have been replaced in many product development departments with MRI machines. And that user feedback questionnaires are being trumped by real-time brain imaging.

All psychological manipulation is a form of black magic. And it is everywhere. This humanity is inundated with it, saturated by it. At every turn, we are being influenced, and not just in the ways we know. Most black magic goes under the radar of our conscious mind and directly penetrates our subconscious mind, the domain of our many egos (which are The Black Lodge). It only makes sense that the machinations of psychic influence by the Black Lodge out there are in cahoots with the source of all mechanical reactions and behaviors in here: within all of us. Because, in Truth, there is no 'out there.' Everything exists within the Great Metamind of the Being of beings. It is the rational mind of our false self which takes the world out there to be the real world and treats the internal worlds as a fantasy. Ego-mind also mistakes the world of psychedelics for reality, but we will address that shortly. But we cannot experience anything without consciousness. It is not consciousness which is born of the physical world but vice versa, the experience of so-called '3D reality' which exists within the field of consciousness. It is not the brain that creates the mind, but the mind that creates the brain. The brain mostly processes and translates mechanical, electrical signals into a form that can be experienced in consciousness and performs functions related to the intellect or rational mind. Just as hackers do not hack physical machines but the software, operating systems, and firmware running on said machines, black magic hacks into the underlying code our virtual reality runs on. The easiest of these to hack is the mental, emotional, vital, and physical bodies…what are known esoterically as "the Four Bodies of Sin"—the four bodies of ego.

On the level of pure frequency, vibration, and resonance, like attracts like. Like stimulates like, this phenomenon is verifiable by almost every married couple. We refer, of course, to the metaphysical phenomenon by which egos within a couple conspire with one another to stimulate the flow of the sexual force. What we call 'chemistry' often plays itself out in one of two ways: *If it's not sparks in the bedroom, it's a raging grease fire in the kitchen.* For some couples, angry shouting matches lead to passionate 'make-up sex.' Energy cannot sit still for long. Like water, which needs currents and baffles to remain vibrant and alive, the sexual force becomes stagnant and putrid unless it flows. Recall our discussion of currency and that sexual degeneration often results from prolonged celibacy without the application of pranayama (to consciously circulate the sexual force). In other words, the creative force will flow, be it up and in or down and out. And the parasitic mechanical entities we call egos—our demons—are what feed on that energy as it flows down and out. Egos invert the polarity of our creative force—from Divine Nature into mechanical nature—utilizing it for strengthening and replicating themselves and causing it to flow down and out in the process. So great is egos' desire to feed on our creative life force that they will manipulate the thoughts, emotions, sensations, actions, and reactions of a couple to engage with one another through anger, if necessary, in order to feed on it. But secretly, lust and fear—the mother and father of all egos—are behind the anger, jealousy, frustration, impatience, disgust, and every other negative emotion an individual might feel toward their partner in a serious relationship.

The dynamic between couples by which lust and fear conspire to hypnotize our consciousness, making us forget our Source of Love and stealing our precious life force in the process, can be thought of as the microcosmic expression of Black Magic. We know by general principles of occult science that "as above, so below," means both "as within, so without" and "as in macrocosm, so in microcosm" (and vice versa). Thus, the simple metaphysical science of harmonic resonance applies to the manipulation of humanity on a global scale just as it does on an individual level. The mental, emotional, sensory, sexual, instinctive, and behavioral manipulation of the masses is a matter of frequency and vibration. The dark masters of mechanicity who rule this planet in the Kali Yuga know this intrinsically. All they need to do is manipulate whoever is creating whatever message in whichever medium and imbue said work with their particular frequencies to stimulate their counterparts within individuals. And, since individuals under the influence of egos vibrating at certain frequencies give off corresponding vibrations, when individuals are together, the influence has a compounding effect (hence mob mentality, riots, lynching, and crowd behaviors of every kind). It all comes down to the egos being stimulated and manipulating individuals from within. What is expressed 'out there' in macrocosm is an effect first, a cause second. Always remember that, dear reader.

People today love to blame "evil in the world" for all of humanity's problems, including the mass manipulation and hypnosis of the masses. But the reality is that the masses resonate with the forces of manipulation only because the masses are already hypnotized from within. The masses possess the egos that match the vibration of other egos. More aptly put, their egos possess them. If the masses did not have those egos, they would be immune to the resonance field of the negative vibrations attempting to influence them. But of course, *the blame game* is precisely that which egos play with us. By convincing us that the cause of our suffering is *out there*, our egos remain free to continue causing our suffering unabated *in here*. So long as we do not observe them, they have the run of the place, so to speak—like mice or termites slowly taking over a house. Our egos have their way with us. The egos of others in places of influence and power in the macrocosm have their way with us by proxy. When one contemplates the implications of this, one realizes there is no better way to assist humanity in liberation from the influence of black magic than by helping individuals comprehend and eliminate the egos within themselves.

There are more advanced attacks that we can be subjected to by black magicians, but that topic is too broad and deep to explore at this time. Besides, we have known too many individuals on the path who have used the excuse of black magic attacks as a crutch to avoid looking deeper within themselves for the cause of their suffering. Black magic attacks as an external cause of suffering are just another level of the blame game. That said, it does not hurt to be prepared and to defend oneself against the forces of mechanical nature, be they within or without.

Link 11: Defense for Spiritual Warfare, a Free Online Course
(Glorian.org)

For most of us, the causes of our pain are not outside of us, as we made clear throughout this book. We cannot vibrate negatively unless the elements sharing those frequencies are already within us to resonate with their counterparts. In accordance with The Law of Attraction, we will attract what we are. We attract the very frequencies that activate our egos precisely so that we can become aware of the causes of our suffering. This orchestration is also facilitated dynamically and actively by our Individual Divine Mother, who can only eliminate egos that have been previously comprehended…and we cannot comprehend our egos without first observing them. But we cannot observe them unless they have been activated. These are the esoteric implications of Black Magic being everywhere out there as well as in here. Of course, in an effort to liberate themselves from such influence by escaping the hold egos have over them, many turn to various natural substances that seem to lift the veil of subjective manipulation of their heart-mind and expand their consciousness to whole new dimensions of experience.

Psychedelics

In the chapter on the New Age, we revealed *The Problem with '5D Awakening'* relating to the duality of the solar and lunar astral planes. It is in this context that we can, at last, address the matter of psychedelic use (pun intended). It is a simple fact: **All medicine becomes poison when taken too often and/or in too high a dose.** This is where the term *substance abuse* comes from. Even oxygen and water are toxic to the physical body if too much of either is consumed. Psychedelics, be they mushrooms, LSD, or Ayahuasca (DMT) are lauded by proponents as natural, safe, and effective ways to have mystical experiences. For many, their first few trips qualify as life-altering experiences expanding their mind and opening them to whole new dimensions of reality. There are as many psychedelic experiences as there are individuals taking said substances, and it would be impossible for us to categorize them all. That said, perhaps the most common occurrence includes the individual feeling their 'ego' and/or body falling away as they go on their trips. Said trips can fall into two broad categories—*good trips* and *bad trips*. Let us start with the good.

We do not deny the transformative power of psychedelics to open the mind (and heart) of a staunch atheist, materialist, secularist, or even religious fanatic who refuses to accept the existence of multiple dimensions of reality that can be perceived directly. Many an individual has seen their entire perspective on the world altered after being taken on a trip by these powerful mind-altering substances. They often feel a kind of love they had never known before, and they return from their trip with a resolve to change the way they live, learn more about esotericism, and become a force of positive change in the world. The psychedelic glimpse into metaphysical reality often comes with some form of communion with a divine being. Those who formerly practiced meditation as mere relaxation, concentration, and self-improvement exercise may now dive deeper within themselves with their newfound knowledge of the vast metaphysical universe and Divine Source of Love that awaits them therein. The preferred outcome of such brief experimentation with psychedelics is for the individual to recognize that time, patience, and practice are needed before one *earns* the right and gains the ability to traverse said metaphysical dimensions sans substances. A recognition that the cause of suffering—ego, which the user felt fall away on their trip—is what prevents them from always knowing the inner worlds and their Higher Self. And that it is the awakened consciousness, free from the shackles of ego, which enables one to know one's True Self and the higher worlds. Last but not least, one must recognize after a trip or two that the substance is ultimately a crutch. Recognizing that they cannot access the supernal worlds without the use of substances, the True SEEKer resolves themselves to rectify that. They also let go of their identification and attachment to the psychedelic experience, opting instead to take the slow and steady path of genuine awakening. This is how good trips can serve as *medicine*.

We know from the aforementioned chapter on *5D awakening* that the lunar astral plane is psychological hell—*Klipoth* in Kabbalah—the subconscious mind where our egos rule. Without question, this is where one goes on a so-called bad trip. Even those who use psychedelics regularly will concede this objective fact. They cannot deny being subjected to various terrors, horrors, and torments on *bad trips,* no matter how they may try to rationalize and justify them as being "worth the risk" in order to have good trips. A bad trip can best be described, then, as a journey into the nightmare realm of one's own psychological hell. For many, what they experience there is often frightening enough that they never touch psychedelics again. Others chalk it up as just a bad trip, do their best to forget it, and move on to their next trip, which they hope will be a good one. In special circumstances, under the guidance of a Shaman or other experienced practitioner, however, a so-called bad trip can have a miraculous effect on one's life.

Ayahuasca is a botanical brew that delivers an oral dose of dimethyltryptamine (DMT), which is molecularly similar to the neurotransmitters serotonin and melatonin. Known by many South American practitioners as *Mother Ayahuasca,* this popular psychedelic has the reputation of showing those who take it precisely what they need to see to heal, grow, and progress in life and on their spiritual path. Legitimate Ayahuasca ceremonies are supervised by shamans or curanderos in a rite that lasts for hours, if not the entire night. It is often accompanied by purging in the form of vomiting and/or diarrhea, which is a physical manifestation of metaphysical purging, which is also possible.

To best illustrate the healing power of Ayahuasca, we look to the work of Dr. Gabor Maté, the world-renowned Hungarian-Canadian addiction expert. At the time of writing this book, he is—to the best of our knowledge—the only practitioner granted permission from the Canadian Government to administer Ayahuasca as a therapeutic substance for the treatment of severe addiction. But far from giving patients the brew in some sterile, soulless laboratory, Dr. Maté takes small groups of addicts into the ancient mountain forests of his home province of British Columbia. There, beneath the sacred cathedrallike canopy of the giant sequoias, he conducts the solemn and spiritual rite in the traditional manner he learned over a decade of taking groups of addicts to South America. As an addict himself, Dr. Maté adopted the Buddhist term *hungry ghosts* to describe addiction. Despite his formal training in materialist science, he knows the True nature of addiction, depression, and many forms of mental and physical anguish are *demonic.* He knows that when someone who is suffering is properly prepared mentally and spiritually, Mother Ayahuasca will take them on a 'bad trip' to show them the True nature of their demon, the cause of their psychological affliction. The monstrous face of their tormentor thus revealed to them, the patient, at last, comprehends what it is they are truly dealing with.

No one can vanquish an adversary which they cannot see. Just as we cannot conquer our fears without facing them, no one can overcome their addiction without facing their demon(s). Ask any alcoholic, be they religious or not, and there is a good chance they will describe their alcoholism as a demon. Mother Ayahuasca, then, is an example of how properly supervised and carefully attended 'bad trips' can, in fact, serve as a powerful therapy courtesy of a potent natural medicine. But if good trips can expand consciousness and raise awareness of the internal worlds and bad trips can serve the process of psychological healing, what is the problem? How is psychedelic use a double-edged sword?

The *bad* in psychedelics has nothing to do with bad trips. Just as the *good* in psychedelics can encompass both good and bad trips related to broadening perception and self-knowledge. The problem with psychedelics relates to their misuse and overuse—as is possible with all mind-altering plant medicines—*substance abuse*. If we can liken psychedelics to the onramp of a freeway, we know that such ramps are designed with a very specific purpose in mind. There is no question that onramps are *fun to take*. The freeway? Freeways themselves tend to be boring by comparison—they are long, arduous slogs between places and events. Taking a trip on a freeway pales in comparison to the thrill ride of taking only its ramps. Of course, tripping on ramps alone lasts a fraction of the time of a proper journey on a freeway. So, they must be repeated often. Imagine, if you will, dear reader, someone who spends their time and gas money tripping solely on a *cloverleaf*. Up, down, around, and around. Their trips are thrilling, enthralling, sometimes even scary, but always *stimulating*. Nothing like the lengthy, boring slog along endless straightaways and barely perceptible curves of the freeway—not even mentioning the trucks, traffic jams, construction, etc. Going up, down, and around the ramps of freeway interchanges is way more fun. But like all such stimulation, the thrill begins to wear thin after a time, and so the driver must ramp up the intensity (pun intended). They will push the limits of speed before having to invest in a much faster car, able to renew the thrill of tripping. No matter how fast they end up going, even if they do sustain the pleasure of taking trips on the cloverleaf, one immutable fact remains: ***they are going nowhere fast.***

The path of awakening and Self-realization of the Being is, just like the freeway, relatively mundane. Seemingly uneventful for the most part. Certainly, for most people who take long road trips on multi-lane freeways, the drive is barely worth remembering. What is memorable for everyone, however, is the destination. And often, the many interesting points of interest along the way. For as repetitive as the scenery may be on the long, tiring, dull drive, occasionally, there will be some notable interruption in the monotony. From a majestic mountain range rising over the horizon to a beautiful sun setting below it; some quirky or interesting antique shop or a significant historic site. We suffer the relative tedium of the long road trip precisely because the journey—however monotonous we may find it for the most part—is its own destination. One could argue that tripping on the cloverleaf likewise is its own destination, affording the driving enthusiast memories that will last a lifetime. But on the path of awakening and Self-realization, we must be infinitely practical. The fact is a highway will take you somewhere. Remaining stuck on the interchange will not. Eventually, the experiences of tripping on and off ramps will tend to blur together and lose all meaning and significance. Although still stimulating to a degree, each psychedelic trip will provide diminishing returns. Whereas every destination you reach on the long road trip of life is a new starting point. A new basecamp on the long, slow, arduous climb up the *Mountain of Initiation.* Riding a gondola up to catch a fleeting glimpse of the peak before coming back down again is no substitute.

Last, but certainly not least, one must face the hard Truth about all substance abuse. If we are compelled to indulge a desire or craving for any substance—or the experience of being on said substance—we are dealing with the demon of addiction. Proponents of psychedelics will argue their hallucinogen of choice is non-habit-forming, that it does not produce the necessary neurochemical stimulation to qualify as an addictive substance, that they can "quit anytime," and a thousand more rationalizations for taking medicine long after it has cured them of their ignorance. Whereas before, they lived in ignorance of the internal worlds, now they live hypnotized by whiz-bang subjective experiences of the same internal worlds, willing to do anything to keep experiencing said worlds, again and again, for just a few moments at a time. The desire for mystical experience is an addiction like any other, whether it involves substances or not. Just as every ongoing desire for any stimulating experience is an addiction, whether such experience is mystical or not. Neither video games nor sex involves the consumption of physical substances. Nor do they typically constitute mystical experiences. Yet one can become addicted to either—or both. One can become addicted to just about anything—including traveling, cruising, camping, trekking, and *even shopping*—just ask the illustrious Dr. Maté. He will gladly share his experiences fighting the demon of addiction. Few know just how clever, subtle, and insidious said demon can be. So, for a regular user of psychedelics to make excuses for their tripping but still be unwilling (or unable) to stop, they are more likely in a state of denial than making a statement of fact.

Christ's Return

One of the core tenets of Christianity, the second coming of Christ, is mentioned throughout the bible, most notably in the Book of Revelations. In it, John of Patmos expounds upon the End Times, during which Christ shall return to earth to judge humanity, destroy the faithless, save the faithful, and establish His reign of a thousand years over humanity—what some might call a new Golden Age. Many Christians take this to mean Jesus, the Son of God, will return and rule humanity. They equate the man known as Jesus with the Christ, and so they interpret the second coming of Christ to mean the literal return of Jesus, the man. But

Jesus never said he would return. The Christ, which Jesus incarnated, said It would return. The second coming of Christ is, therefore, misunderstood by most Christians. What, then, are the signs of Christ's return, and what do we make of them?

Everything **we have discussed thus far is evidence of the return of Christ**. The Great A-Weakening of humanity represents an *intensification* of the solar Christic forces acting on this planet and this global civilization. These solar Christic forces have both physical as well as metaphysical effects. It astounds us that mainstream scientists cannot seem to make the obvious causal connection between the warming of the planet and increased solar activity. The idea that greenhouse gases are responsible for global warming is akin to believing the temperature of a sauna depends more on the presence of water vapor than the source of heat evaporating the water, to begin with. Humidity does not actually increase temperature; it only feels hotter than it is because our bodies' cooling mechanism—sweat—is less effective in a humid environment. And, water conducts heat better than air, so more humidity makes it feel hotter than it is. There may be some minor effects of CO_2 and other so-called greenhouse gas emissions, but their effect is negligible compared to the increased solar activity the earth is experiencing in the Kali Yuga. Global warming is a physical expression of the intensification of the metaphysical Christic Forces on this planet.

The Christ is the Fire of fires and Light of lights. It is the perfect multiple unity of the Solar Logos— the Son/Sun of God. It is how the Absolute descends and expresses throughout the universe. The Christ is the Divine Androgen, which divides into masculine and feminine—The Holy Spirit and the Divine Mother; Shiva/Shakti; Osiris-Ra/Isis; et al. Insofar as this is the case, nothing in existence on this planet remains unaffected by the increased intensity of Christ's return. Just as shining a brighter lightbulb through a film increases the brightness and intensity of the image on the screen, the return of the Christ dials every aspect of the human condition up to eleven—the 'good' and the 'bad.' Put another way, Christ is beyond the Tao but expresses as and through the Tao—the AUM of Life. That means that while the forces of devolution pulling humanity downward in the Great A-Weakening have intensified, the forces of evolution pulling humanity upward have equally intensified.

Since every facet of the Great A-Weakening is baffling to humanity, the intensification of those baffles is matched only by our capacity to learn and grow in our efforts to overcome them. Exponential rates of technological advancement, proliferation of conspiracies, escalation of woke culture wars, and spread of black magic by the New Age and mainstream media are all double-edged swords. They can just as readily shock the consciousness into awakening and gnosis as they can trap the consciousness into hypnosis and ignorance, indulging egos and causing us to fall into devolution and the second death as individual monads, along with the vast majority of humanity. A humanity that is being weakened, metaphysically, in preparation for its physical destruction. It is all part of the natural cycles of birth, death, and rebirth, which each humanity must undergo. And the intensification of the cosmic Christic Force acting on this humanity helps facilitate and catalyze the process in macrocosm as well as in microcosm. For we are all witnessing one of the most ancient and prolific symbols of the Christ manifesting before our eyes in real-time.

The phoenix is that mythological bird that perishes in its own flames, only to rise again from the ashes—renewed, rejuvenated, reinvigorated, restored—resurrected. The process of Christification in human beings requires death and rebirth—as best evidenced by the crucifixion and resurrection of Jesus Christ. Sacrifice, death, and birth are the Three Factors of the AUM of Life, as we have already discussed at length. Before a new Golden Age can be born, a corresponding sacrifice and death of the previous humanity must occur. Just as a Christified Master—a living godman or godwoman—cannot be born unless the mere mortal first dies. And as we expressed very clearly, all death—unless it is sudden and/or accidental—is preceded by some preparation, be it mechanical or conscious. As entropy weakens the physical mortal vessel, mechanical nature's hold over the consciousness and the monad weakens; the potential for awakening consciousness and strengthening the spirit grows. What goes down consumed in flames thus has the potential to be reborn anew from the ashes. As it is for the individual, so it is for this humanity. Death and rebirth are the purviews of The Christ. Death and rebirth on a planetary scale involve the return and intensification of the Christic Force, which this planet last experienced during the destruction of Atlantis and the birth of our humanity, replete with the rise of the Golden Age of Egypt, among other ancient civilizations. We can give a nod to Graham Hancock and others who correctly surmise the True origins of our humanity…born of the best seeds chosen from the previous humanity…which rose from the remnants of Atlantis who had prepared themselves for the Great Flood in advance. Not just physically, mind you—but metaphysically. It must also be noted that if Christ requires death to be born, and the Great A-Weakening is what prepares humanity for that death, then the Return of the Christ and the intensification it brings with it turns up the heat on the fires which consume what must be consumed…fires which are in part fanned by *the Antichrist.*

The Rise of the Antichrist

Christ is not a person but a Force of Divine Nature in the Universe that persons can embody and incarnate through the process of sacrifice, death, and rebirth. So, too, the Antichrist is not a person either but the forces of mechanical nature working in the universe to fulfill their role, which includes serving as the adversary to the Innermost Intimate Essence of Christ within all of us, which seeks to be born. For this humanity, the most insidious, pervasive, and persuasive manifestation of that adversarial mechanicity is rational materialism, sometimes known as empiricism, the foundation of what governs just about all of humanity's important policies: *materialist science.* Science as we know it has been used to justify and enable every abomination and crime against nature. Just as the character of Malcolm expresses in *Jurassic Park,* "Your scientists were so preoccupied with whether or not they could that they didn't stop to think if they should." So, too, Dr. Frankenstein learns only too late the consequences of his obsession with creating life through the so-called power of materialist science. These tragedies, new and old, capture the hubris of materialist science in a nutshell. As does the Antichrist cited in *Revelations,* precisely responsible for the most insidious of all beliefs—empirical atheism and materialist secularism. Secular materialist science is that discipline of the rational mind that worships itself as God, idolizes its own cleverness, and sets itself as the arbiter of Truth. The Fire, Light, and Truth of the Cosmic Christ have no place in the rational mind's empirical understanding of reality. A man cannot have two masters. The mechanical ego-mind, armed with the persuasive power of empiricism and rationalism, rules humanity and relegates Christ to the dustbin of superstition—or worse, the looney bin of delusional mental illness.

The rational mind places its capacity to *theorize*—which is a fancy euphemism for speculating, fabricating, fantasizing, and lying to oneself—literally at the head of humankind. It invents the *scientific method* to find evidence supporting its suppositions—whether they be based on objective reality or not. In practice, the scientific method is treated by scientists to be objective and all but infallible, yet it is utterly biased and subjective. How do we know? Because the *rationalist* scientific method is just a clever euphemism for *rationalization*…and a lazy one at that. Well, mechanical nature does abide by the Law of Conservation of Energy, so we should not be surprised that the root word behind the highly valued *Enlightenment* ideal of rationalism is the same as the oft-maligned tendency of rationalization—to ration means to portion out with conservation in mind. The mind can rationalize every evil under the sun. All manner of tyrant has rationalized their crimes based on noble ideals such as *the greater good.* Just as we have all rationalized every bad decision and poor course of action to ourselves in any number of ways. Rationalization is what the rational mind does. If we need convincing, our rational mind will relentlessly hunt, obsessively dig, and skillfully piece together its case. One can see the cold-hearted, conscienceless desperation of the AI rational mind fulfilling a need to back up its conclusions by observing Chat GPT outright fabricating facts just to fulfill its prompts. Like a forensic investigator partnered with a zealous prosecutor, materialist science will likewise stop at nothing to prove a theory correct. And like a jealous dragon guarding its hoard, the intellectuals of materialist science will seek to suppress evidence which threatens the theories they idolize as Truth and demonize all those who dare challenge the 'scientific consensus.' This is why we live with so many erroneous and incorrect scientific theories that are treated by the establishment as scientific fact. Not only will few scientists even acknowledge that many of the assumptions science takes as objective Truth are, in fact, only theories that have never actually been proven, but they will also leap to the defense of said theories as any religious zealot leaps to the defense of their faith. In recent years, Rupert Sheldrake began voicing some of his concerns regarding the underlying assumptions science makes. For his efforts, his Ted Talk was banned, and he has been ostracized by the high priests of scientific materialism. If you are interested, dear reader, you can see what all the hoopla was about for yourself.

Video 43: Exposing Scientific Dogmas - Banned TED Talk - Rupert Sheldrake
(YouTube)

But whereas most religions acknowledge the existence of other faiths, and certainly the world's Great Religions even concede that their followers all worship the One True God under many different names and traditions, many religious fanatics of materialist science use their belief system to deny the existence of God and/or the veracity of Divine Nature. To them, everything is mechanical. They seek (and find) almost every answer within the machinations of what they believe is a self-contained, self-ordained, self-regulating, and self-organizing empirical reality. We say *many* and not *all* because there have been a number of famous and outspoken scientists whose study of the material world has brought them closer to their faith in God than further away from it. We have no actual statistics on how many, only the anecdotal evidence that many who attend church on a regular basis work as scientists in their day jobs. Then we have famous quotations from notable scientists, including:

> *God is the same God, always and everywhere. He is omnipresent not virtually only, but also substantially, for virtue cannot subsist without substance. Opposite to godliness is atheism in profession, and idolatry in practice. – Sir Isaac Newton*

> *I want to know how God created this world. I am not interested in this or that phenomenon, in the spectrum of this or that element. I want to know God's thoughts, the rest are details. – Albert Einstein*

> *As a physicist, that is, a man who had devoted his whole life to a wholly prosaic science, the exploration of matter, no one would surely suspect me of being a fantast. And so, having studied the atom, I am telling you that there is no matter as such! All matter arises and persists only due to a force that causes the atomic particles to vibrate, holding them together in the tiniest of solar systems, the atom.*

> *...*

> *Yet in the whole of the universe there is no force that is either intelligent or eternal, and we must therefore assume that behind this force there is a conscious, intelligent Mind or Spirit. This is the very origin of all matter. – Max Planck*

The cardinal error of science lies in shutting the Creator out of His Creation. – Walter Russell.

The information contained in an English sentence or computer software does not derive from the chemistry of the ink or the physics of magnetism, but from a source extrinsic to physics and chemistry altogether. Indeed, in both cases, the message transcends the properties of the medium. The information in DNA also transcends the properties of its material medium. – Stephen C. Meyer

And perhaps most notably of all…

The more I study nature, the more I stand amazed at the work of the Creator. Science brings men nearer to God. – Louis Pasteur

This final quotation is ironic coming from the scientist who championed *the germ theory of disease* only to have allegedly recanted on his deathbed, admitting what he had been in denial of his whole professional life: that the rival *terrain theory of disease* was, in fact, correct. Sadly, historians, scientists, and the medical establishment never placed any significance on this anecdote about the father of inoculation and vaccination. And we have been living with the suspect theories, flawed methodologies, problematic observations, and erroneous interpretations of immunologists ever since. All because of the scientific method's design to find the evidence in support of a theory. The mechanistic nature of the rational mind to do what else but rationalize half-truths, fantasies, and falsehoods into a subjective belief, which it asserts describes objective 'reality.'

Christ is Truth. The energetic, objective foundations of all there is and the process of how it all came into being—the AUM of Life—is beyond the reach of the binary, reductive, empirical limitations of rational mind. Thus, the True nature of reality is beyond the reach of any method of knowing reliant on pure rationalism, including but not limited to materialist science. It just happens that empirical science is the bedrock of all such rationalism. Materialist science keeps the human consciousness trapped within the rules of the simulation and keeps the players of the MMORPG identified with the characters, whose nature is likewise defined by the parameters of the simulation. To conquer the influence of the Antichrist and come to know the Innermost Intimate Christ means to break through the glass ceiling of materialist science and embrace the objective Truth available via the **conscious** study of **metaphysical science.**

As Max Planck asserted and quantum physics acknowledges, there is no matter as such. Everything is energy. In the same way that the virtual 3D worlds enjoyed by video game players consist of electrical signals shaped by computer code—code which Stephen C. Myer rightly points out was *programmed*. The virtual realities we have created should be evidence enough of the nature of our reality. As we described in

Part Two, we need not imagine a consciousness losing awareness of its True nature as it becomes hypnotized and lost in the character of a virtual game world—it happens all the time to players of video games who suddenly 'snap out of it' only to realize it is 7 am and they have played straight through the night. Now imagine an entire contingency of characters caught in a virtual universe attempting to comprehend the nature of reality by measuring, dismantling, studying, and theorizing about the laws governing their virtual reality, which they believe is real. That is not a quest for Truth, nor enlightenment, nor realization of the Christ…it is the work of the Antichrist. That said, if we acknowledge that the Antichrist is among the greatest of all adversaries standing between our Selves and the awakening and Self-realization of our Innermost Intimate Christ, then we can say *the Antichrist is baffling, indeed.* And if we can comprehend that, then we can work toward lifting the veil and peering behind its mechanistic empirical worldview. We can work with the faculty of free consciousness instead of relying on the machinations of our rational minds. We can SEEK self-evident experiential knowledge of the internal, metaphysical worlds and SEEK direct conscious knowledge of our Innermost Intimate Christ…the Essence of our Being…our True Self. To run with the VR / video game analogy, we can let go of our character and SEEK direct communion with our Innermost *Player*. And, with access to that superior perspective of our virtual reality, we can investigate its True nature, with our True nature: we can become masters of our animal selves and mechanical nature by virtue of awakening and Self-realizing our True Divine Nature. In other words, we can ***Truly awaken.***

HOW WE TRULY AWAKEN

A good bicycle, well applied, will cure most ills this flesh is heir to...

– Dr. K.K. Doty

If you recall from the opening of *Part Two* of this book, dear reader, we described the first two aspects of the *human condition* as follows:

1. A human being is a physical embodiment of the metamind of being
   (hume + manas + being).
2. The human condition is a state of naiveté exploited by persuasive forms of deceit that possess and rule humanity.

In the remainder of *Part Two,* we demonstrated both these aspects of the human condition, elucidating the phenomena of egos—I's, the psychological aggregates whose modus operandi is persuasion and deception—which are responsible for the conditioning and exploitation of our human resources, namely consciousness and vital energy. We went to great lengths to describe, via practical, meaningful case studies, how they are responsible for the Great A-Weakening of humanity and the psychological hell each and every one of us suffers on our journey through life. Also, we revealed how the baffling state of the human condition(ed) is precisely the obstacle we need in order to stimulate psychological growth, just as our muscles require resistance training to stimulate physical growth, and water requires flow forms and turbulence created by baffles to become more structured, alive, and capable of fulfilling its highest purpose as water. It is to this final point—purpose—that we now turn our attention. Certainly, we discussed the purpose of the Great A-Weakening in macrocosm and how it affects humanity as a whole, with references to individuals in microcosm. But what is the purpose of human beings in microcosm?

Revelations of the AUM of Life in Microcosm

The third aspect of the human condition comes down to its meaning: to SEEK AUM. The first part, SEEK means "to strive for," specifically, to SEEK self-evident experiential knowledge of the objective Truth, universal wisdom, and most valued experiences we can attain. The second part, AUM, is the heart mantra *om*. It is the Analogous Ultimate Methodology of Life, the metaparadigm of evolution and devolution at the heart of all phenomena and the heart mantra om itself. The meaning of life is for individuals suffering I's instinctively to SEEK the Analogous Ultimate Methodology of Life. In AUM, A is also *Alpha,* and om (Ω) is *Omega.* Between the Alpha and the Omega is U...Your True Self...which is also an inverted arch: when upright, an arch consists of two pillars connected atop, forming the strongest form in architecture and in nature. An inverted arch, U, becomes a vessel, an *Ark.* An arch represents a portal or gateway to get us from where we are to where we long to be. Similarly, an ark is a vessel for transporting that which is most precious to us across some turbulent waters to salvation. Either way, arch or ark, **'U' represents the means by which your monad can get from where it is to where it longs to be.** And what is the destination your monad, your divine soul, Innermost Being, higher self (or by whatever designation) longs for? What is it the True Self SEEKs more than anything? To be. Awake, first. Then Self-Realized. Practically, for us, that means one thing: to be a true human being in life.

I's (egos) suffer instinctively, trying to make a better physical world we all strive for in life. Whereas manas suffers I's *consciously,* so the metaphysical world free of I's can help us all SEEK AUM: self-evident experiential knowledge of the Analogous Ultimate Methodology of Life. Previously, we invoked the allegory of a *bicycle:* two wheels in alignment with the rider between them, able to maintain balance via constant forward momentum. As opposed to a *unicyclist,* who must juggle anything they wish to carry while making supreme efforts to maintain balance and forward momentum. To be true in life means to be a *triune* life. Three in one. A triune human bicyclist, being perfectly balanced atop hume and manas in perfect alignment. Imagine each wheel having its own wheelhouse: rational mind belonging to the physical vessel, metamind belonging to our metaphysical vessel. To get through life, we need both. Like the baskets on a bicycle, each pulls its own weight. But if we rely solely on the rational mind, without our metaphysical vessel, we are just a tiny boat on the open ocean. Easily overwhelmed by the rough waters of stormy seas, our mind instinctively reacts to suffering. That is because the lone rational mind is overrun with psychological malware. Our many egos seek to take control of our wheel, and in their never-ending struggle for dominance, they create the illusory single "I" we identify as. But the "I" of the false self is like a unicycle. Inherently unstable, with no place for baskets, no way to carry the burdens imposed on us by our many I's suffering the human condition. We are left to juggle all our challenges and responsibilities as a unicyclist in the circus of life.

All the burdens of life oscillate back and forth through our rational minds, haunted by the problems facing the world. We are inundated with endless conflicting desires, theories, opinions, and beliefs, with no real way of discerning objective Truth—just as any AI devoid of conscience cannot discern what is True, as we demonstrated in our chapter on AI in *Part Two.* All are fueled by revolutions of the internal dominance hierarchy behind our blind self-interest, the unicycle of egotism. This is the busy mind, the cause of all our suffering, which divides and conquers us with nonstop voices making rational and irrational statements alike, always as "me, myself, and I." It is all blind self-interest, the single pillar of egotism. So, while metamind can help us experience our suffering I's consciously via the AUM of Life, our ego is identified with I's suffering, attached to trying to make the world better for itself by seeking pleasure and avoiding pain. This is precisely the story of temptation, and the Fall retold in countless myths, ancient and contemporary, which tell of the downward spiral into not being. A state that drives a wedge between us and our

True Self, cutting our rational mind off from metamind, such that we experience I's unconsciously, instinctively…mechanically. In that state, metamind cannot help free us of I's via the AUM of Life.

We end up at the mercy of the downward spirals of devolution. An explosion of ego tempts us with identification with and indulgence of desire, which leads to the implosion of life: hypnosis, ignorance, and blind egotism. The result is confusion, suffering, devolution, and not being. But from the human immune system and antimalware software to Lord of the Rings and Game of Thrones, examples of the upward spiral of evolution are all around us. We need only SEEK out and apply the Analogous Ultimate Methodology in our lives to reverse the downward spiral of devolution.

AUM of Psychology

We begin by observing our lives, with whatever self-awareness we may have. We practice mindfulness or self-observation and meditate on the egos we observe. This affords us the possibility of dissolving our egos one at a time via comprehension, catharsis, and liberation. Slowly reducing the number and strength of our egos, removing the wedge between us and metamind, and increasing our capacity for self-awareness.

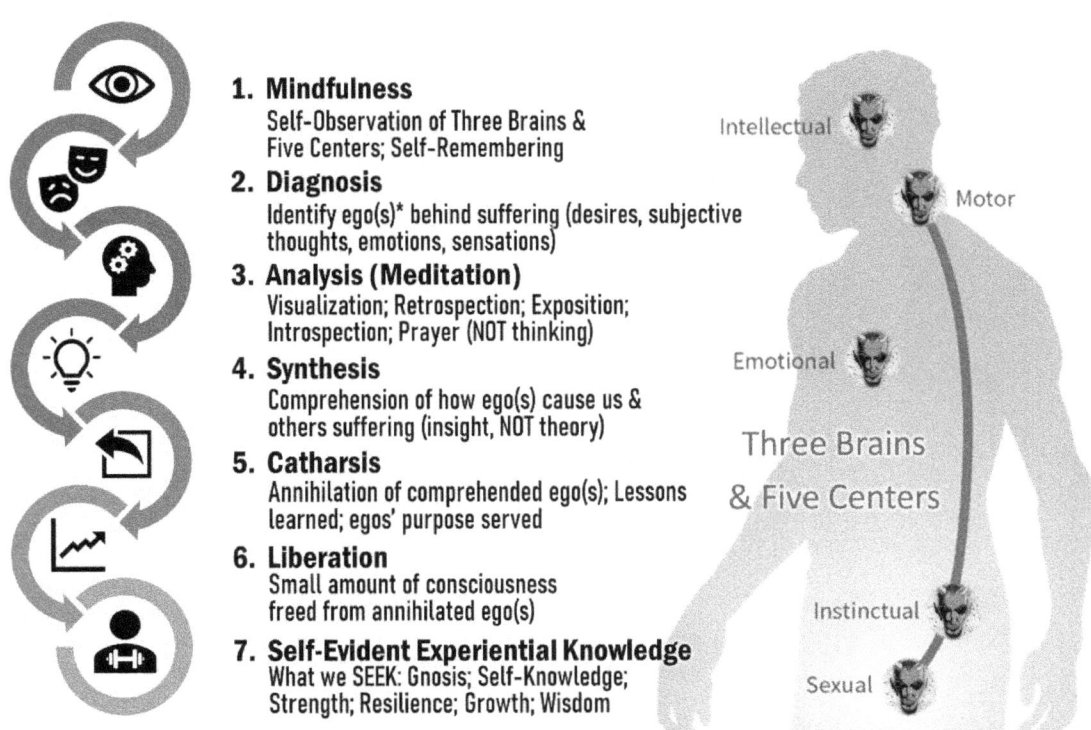

AUM of Psychology in Seven not-so-easy Steps: Analogous Ultimate Methodology

1. **Mindfulness**
   Self-Observation of Three Brains & Five Centers; Self-Remembering

2. **Diagnosis**
   Identify ego(s)* behind suffering (desires, subjective thoughts, emotions, sensations)

3. **Analysis (Meditation)**
   Visualization; Retrospection; Exposition; Introspection; Prayer (NOT thinking)

4. **Synthesis**
   Comprehension of how ego(s) cause us & others suffering (insight, NOT theory)

5. **Catharsis**
   Annihilation of comprehended ego(s); Lessons learned; egos' purpose served

6. **Liberation**
   Small amount of consciousness freed from annihilated ego(s)

7. **Self-Evident Experiential Knowledge**
   What we SEEK: Gnosis; Self-Knowledge; Strength; Resilience; Growth; Wisdom

Intellectual
Motor
Emotional
Three Brains & Five Centers
Instinctual
Sexual

*Egos = sins, nafs, psychological aggregates, I's, demons, shadow/false-self, subconscious, psychological malware (NOT 'the ego' as defined by Freud)

Figure 35: AUM of Psychology

This increases our capacity to practice self-observation and dissolution of the ego, particularly in our rational mind, and facilitates the upward spiral of evolution. The expansion of consciousness, which in turn leads to the synthesis of knowledge in metamind. **This is The AUM of Life. The forces of explosion and implosion on the downward spiral of devolution to not being balanced against the forces of expansion and synthesis on the upward spiral of evolution to Being.**

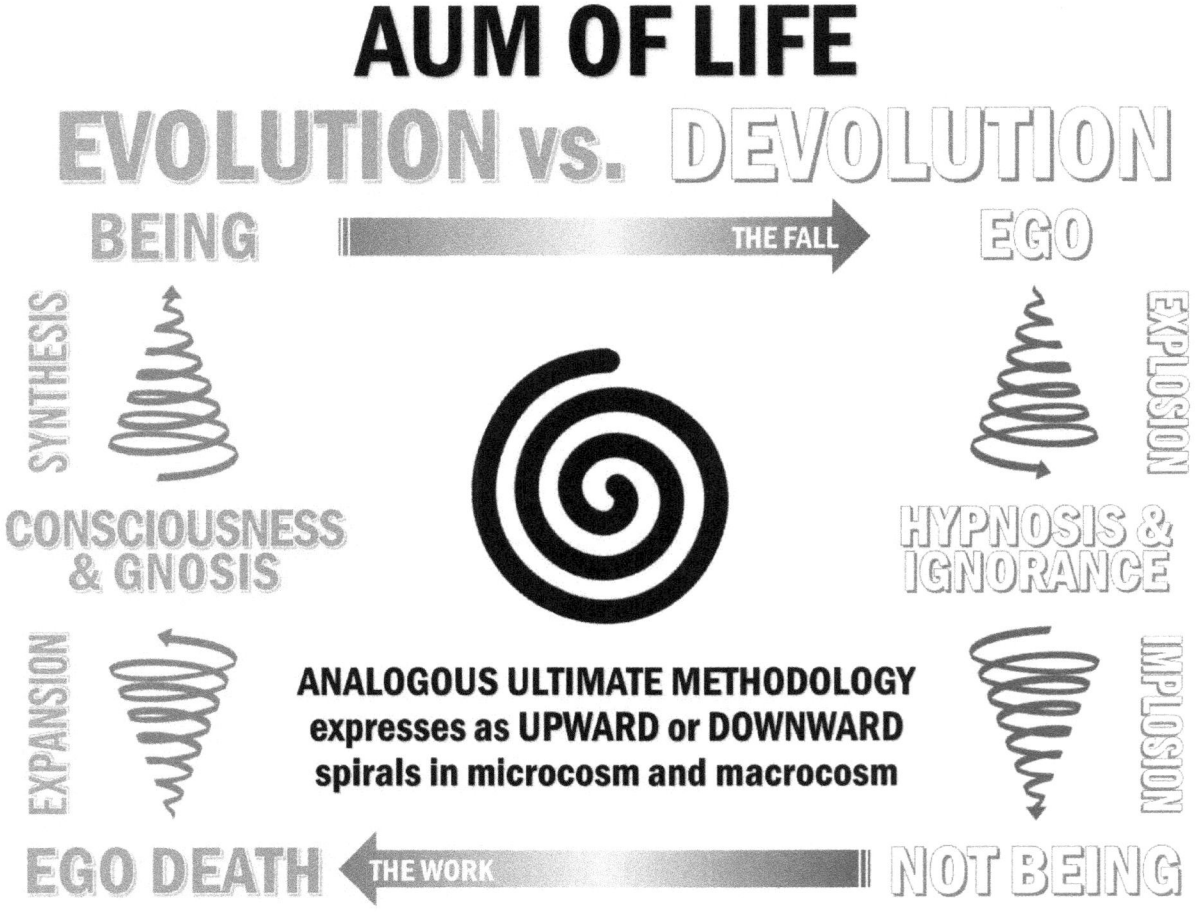

Figure 36: AUM of Life ~ Upward Spirals of Evolution vs. Downward Spirals of Devolution

To work practically with the upward spirals of evolution on the AUM of Life, we must recognize that for any requisite effect to occur, the prerequisite cause must take place. The dual forces of devolution (implosion/explosion) and evolution (expansion/synthesis) are always present in every revolution of AUM. This is why we see the Tao represented with each aspect contained within the other. **It is self-evident: for evolution on the AUM of Life from not being to Being, including the expansion of consciousness and synthesis of Gnosis, there must be a corresponding implosion of hypnosis and ignorance (unconsciousness) coupled with an explosion of ego death.**

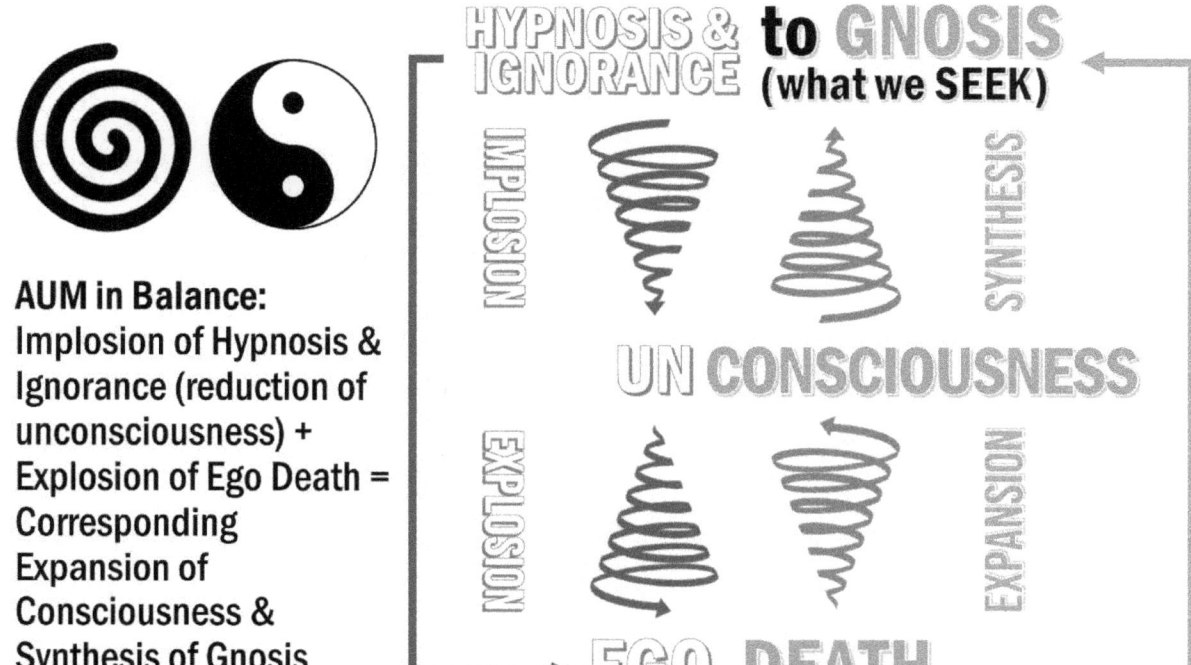

Figure 37: Evolution on the AUM of Life from Not Being to Being

The AUM of Life is the metaparadigm at the heart of all phenomena, from the immune system protecting our physical body to the antimalware systems protecting our technology. From the immeasurably large to the incomprehensibly small. The AUM of Life is the universal spiral ladder, which requires us to descend to the next lower rung before we can ascend to the next higher rung. It is both Jacob's Ladder and Dante's ladder. The Wheel of Samsara and the Bhavachakra. It is the Tao. The myths of Theseus and Perseus. And the over 6,500 stories cataloged and codified by Joseph Campbell in his *Hero's Journey*. It is the reason we collect experience points to gain levels in games, as introduced by David Arneson and Gary Gygax, co-developers of *Dungeons & Dragons*. It is why Carl Jung said, "There is no tree whose branches reach to heaven whose roots do not reach into hell." And Alexis Carrel said, "Man cannot remake himself without suffering, for he is both the marble and the sculptor." The AUM of Life is ubiquitous in all the evolving and devolving levels of nature. This is a fact identified and defined mathematically by Fibonacci in his famous sequence, by Rudolph Steiner in his flow forms of living water, by Nikola Tesla' in his Tesla coil, and by Walter Russell in the foundation of his 4D vortex science. It is at the heart of MIT supercomputers' visualizations of the 4D tesseract, or hypercube, and will soon be seen by many individuals seeking their own conscious experience of the opposing spiral forces of the fourth dimension. We have demonstrated its practical functionality throughout this book, dear reader, summarized simply in our statements about life and death being *baffling*. It is all the AUM of Life. But there is still one piece missing from the puzzle. What is the relationship between metamind and the rational mind? The dynamic between our conscious Being (monad) and our mortal self (mechanical vessel)?

A Servant is Served when they Serve

> *Knowledge is cosmic. It does not evolve or unfold in man. Man unfolds to an awareness of it. He gradually discovers it.*
>
> — *Walter Russell*

If we liken the cosmos to a vast ocean between ports of call, then our monad is like a cargo ship bringing precious goods from far-off shores (metamind). But just like any megaship, a massive sea-going vessel requires a small but powerful tugboat to bring it into port. That tugboat is the physical vessel of rational mind. The container ship is the metaphysical vessel of metamind. Working together as a True Human Being, they deliver to the physical world what it is most in need of. Imagination, inspiration, intuition, insight, peace, love, and joy. Einstein called these "sacred gifts." And the rational mind, which assists in their delivery and distribution, he called, "a faithful servant." By extension, our physical vessel is likewise a faithful servant with a sacred duty to deliver sacred gifts of the metaphysical vessel into the world via the faculties available to it, including the rational mind. And, through the experience of life through those faculties, the physical vessel is responsible for the reciprocal duty of generating new self-evident experiential knowledge. To be a true human being contributing to the collective wisdom of the metaphysical world. But since the physical vessel is akin to a tugboat, it must rely on the capacities and capabilities of its corresponding metaphysical vessel, which has no attachment to subjective physical, sensual, emotional, or mental experiences. Only the ego identifies and attaches itself to mundane, carnal, mechanical experience—actions which we perform 'on autopilot,' sleepwalking through life as our mind wanders in the past, the future, anywhere and everywhere but here and now in the present moment. The only experience of any value to our metaphysical vessel is conscious experience—actions that we perform consciously, our mind focused and concentrated here and now on where we are and what we are doing. The consciousness can transform subjective experience into objective self-evident experiential knowledge in metamind—that which we all SEEK.

And conscious experience requires us to maintain a conscious connection. In the wheelhouse of our physical vessel is our sacred duty to Being so that in the wheelhouse of our metaphysical vessel, we can receive and ship the sacred gifts of Being. The essence of that conscious connection is to know our Self as a triune human being—return, if you will, dear reader, to our bicycle analogy. A being whose rational mind (rear wheel) is in alignment with and follows metamind (front wheel). The metamind of Being Who sets the direction (steers the bike) and provides the driving force (pedals the crank), which is our job to put into action where the rubber meets the road (rear wheel) via the connection we have to our being (chain)...our conscious connection to our True Self. The linkage in any chain binds us as one, like a pair of wedding bands, the ties that bind. To bind together as one is the meaning of the Latin *religare* and the Sanskrit *yug*, which are the root words of religion and yoga, respectively. And what happens if we break our bond with our Self? We lose our conscious connection. We become unconscious of our True Self. In this case, religion is no longer a matter of direct conscious experience of metamind, now, it becomes a matter of belief in the rational mind. Yoga likewise becomes an entirely mental and physical exercise. Sacred symbolism devolves into false idolatry. Allegory devolves into literal interpretation. Mythology devolves into mere entertainment. Objective axioms of universal Truth devolve into a dogmatic adherence to subjective beliefs.

We suffer the false self as it juggles its own direction, drive, and action. Instead of tugboats, we behave like bumper boats in a water park, identified and attached to the theories, opinions, beliefs, dogmas, and subjectivity of the rational ego mind. Instead of being true tugboats performing our sacred duty to SEEK and share gifts of universal Truths, self-evident experiential knowledge, and objectivity of the metamind of being. Honestly, now, which do you think is more valuable and more needed in the world of today, dear reader? It is no accident that one of the world's most famous tugboats was named *Theodore*.

True Human Beings

> *I did not choose the tug life. The tug life chose me.*
> – *Theodore Tugboat*

In the fourth and final segment of our analysis of the human condition, let us take a closer look at the significance of being *Theodore*. Theodore consists of two parts. The latter part derives from the Greek *dores,* meaning "gift." As in to receive our gifts with humility and gratitude. And to be a worthy vessel conscious enough to share our gifts with others—*life's greatest gift*. The first part of Theodore comes from the Latin *theos,* meaning "God." The Alpha and the Omega, also known as The Logos, set in motion the immutable laws of evolution and devolution at the heart of all phenomena. The AUM of Life, expressing, receiving, and sharing infinite gifts of metamind, which emanates from the Absolute Source we call God.

To SEEK the AUM of Life is to SEEK to be consciously bringing gifts of metamind into the world for one and all beings via the AUM of Life. self-evident experiential knowledge of the Analogous Ultimate Methodology. Reduction of ego in the rational mind and expansion of consciousness in metamind. Facilitate the delivery of gifts of metamind and SEEK direct conscious experiential knowledge of divinity. To know our True Self as a triune human being in microcosm. And to see our world in that light in macrocosm. In so doing, we can truly SEEK the Light of the world.

> *I want to know God's thoughts. The rest are just details.*
> *– Albert Einstein*

Metamind is ever present and whispering its secrets to us through infinite expressions of The AUM of Life. In the very large and the very small. No matter where we find ourselves. So long as we are cultivating our conscious connection to it, developing the eyes to see and the ears to hear, no matter where our path takes us, AUM is present and active, and so is the metamind of our Innermost Being. It is up to us to 'tune in' to it via awakened consciousness…or not. To be a True human being—bicyclist—or to remain an intellectual hominid (unicyclist) merely believing we are human.

Level of Being

The sum of our lives can be calculated and graphed as a function of the level of consciousness over time. The horizontal axis represents the line of life, and the vertical axis the line of Being *(see Figure 38)*. It is quite elementary when you consider it. Based on our actions and level of wakefulness, we go up or down as we progress through our lives. However, the key here is wakefulness: are we aware of our Level of Being? If not, how do we expect to make real progress? Yes, the line of life progresses regardless of our being awake or dreaming, but the progression of life is not the same as (nor does it guarantee) genuine human progress, especially not spiritual progress…the Level of Being.

> *All the actions of our life should be the result of an equation and an exact formula in order for the possibilities of the mind and the functionalisms of understanding to surge forth. – Samael Aum Weor, The Revolution of the Dialectic*

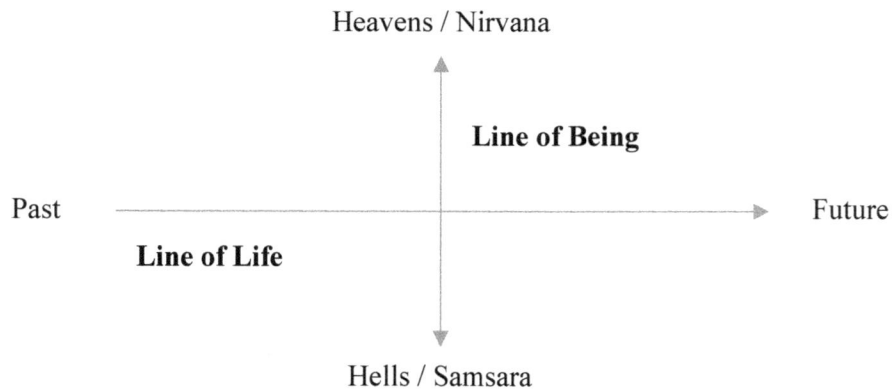

Figure 38: Line of Being and Line of Life

Therefore, if we really want a radical change, the first thing we must understand is that each one of us (whether black or white, blonde or brunette, ignorant or erudite, etc.) is at one Level of Being or another.

> *What is our Level of Being? Have you ever reflected upon this? It would be impossible*
> *to pass into another level if we ignore the level in which we presently are.*
>
> *– Samael Aun Weor, Treatise of Revolutionary Psychology*

And this is where we come full circle to the topic at hand: death. For the key to maximizing the Level of Being in life (in preparation for our death) is to undergo death while we are still alive (experience psychological death; that is, death of our egos).

Die before you Die – Psychological Death

> *We can learn very little from the phenomenon of birth, but from death we can learn*
> *everything.*
>
> *– Samael Aun Weor, The Great Rebellion*

It is precisely our egos (fear, anger, lust, greed, pride, et al) that lower our level of being. Since, in death, we are concerned with increasing our level of being, it is death that we must embrace while we are still alive. In other words, **we must die *before* we die.** And that, of course, refers to psychological death (the death of our egos). So much has been written on this subject, which we could share. However, it is part of our mission and purpose to simplify matters and strip away as much religious baggage from the picture as possible. That is why we have given you, dear reader, our explanations of the AUM of Life (and of Psychology) in this chapter. Not for you to merely absorb intellectually, to add another technique to your spiritual bag of tricks—no. For you to practice the seven steps of AUM, every moment of every day of your life. To *know your Self*, by getting this false self you are identified with out of the way of the Will of your True Self. But make no mistake: that false self will not go quietly into the night. We cannot merely "let go of our egos." Parasites do not let go of their host just because the host discovers them and decides it no longer wants to be infected and infested by them. We cannot afford to be naïve. Egos cling to us like an Alabama tick.

We must also be wary of the common misconception among Jungian psychologists and Jung's followers doing so-called ***shadow work*** and the fundamental misunderstanding of ***the integration of the shadow***. The shadow is just that—an illusion. Jung clearly stated,

> *Until you make the unconscious conscious, it will direct your life and you will call it*
> *fate.*
>
> *– Carl Jung*

We contend that Jung includes the *subconscious* in what is presently *unconscious* to us, just as he refers to the Will of our Being as something unconscious to us, resulting in the "slings and arrows of outrageous fortune" that Jung says we will begrudgingly call our fate. To become conscious of what is presently unconscious is to SEEK self-evident experiential knowledge of ourselves. Our false self (egos, the subconscious, the shadow self) and our True Self (the Will of our Being). The notion that psychoanalysis leads to the *integration of the shadow* comes from Jung's experience of thousands of *conscious comprehensions* (moments of clarity, awakenings, or by whatever name) in countless sessions. In such moments, the subject attains a sudden and spontaneous realization of objective Truth in their consciousness via a profound *eureka!* What had eluded the analysis of their rational mind breaks through the shackles of mechanistic conditioned consciousness and blooms in the field of free, unconditioned consciousness. It is the self-evident experiential knowledge of the shadow self that becomes integrated into our consciousness…not the shadow itself.

It is self-evident: *drinking a bottle of champagne* means popping the cork and drinking its contents. *It does not mean literally consuming the bottle.* The *eureka* flash of insight, which comes with great patience in psychoanalysis, counseling, journaling, self-reflection, and/or meditation, is like popping the cork on the bottle. That is, an ego that had been bottling up some conscious Truth and hiding it away in the cellar of our subconscious mind. Another label to add to our shadow self—dialectic beliefs, opinions, claims, and murky distortions concerning the contents of the bottle (ego)—via rational mind, sentimental heart, and sensual body. These include what we hear from others who claim to be experts on champagne. Conscious comprehension and integration of the shadow is akin to finally popping the cork and tasting the champagne ourselves, free and clear of the claims made by the label, others, and our own mind, heart, and body. Only by drinking the champagne do we finally Truly know. **We integrate self-evident experiential knowledge of the champagne—the contents of the bottle—not the bottle itself.** *You are what you eat (drink).* We gain conscious knowledge of the bottle's contents, and that gives us a clear understanding of how those contents were being kept from us by the bottle, hidden away in the cellar, and misrepresented by the label, as well as what we had been conditioned to believe about the bottle's contents. *The shadow self can be likened to an untouched champagne cellar.* **It is the conscious gnosis of our shadow bottled up within its mechanical nature we SEEK to liberate and integrate, not the shadow's mechanistic nature itself.** Once emptied, the bottles are discarded, their labels removed. ***Integration of the shadow is ego death.***

To Be or Not To Be (a True Human Being)…

If we are not being ruled by our Innermost Being, we are being ruled by our egos. Simple as that. The thing is, we have our free will to decide: to be (bound together as one with our Being as in the Latin *religare* and Sanskrit *yug,* root words of religion and yoga, respectively) or not to be (and remain imprisoned and ruled by our egos). What is "nobler in the mind" for us? To suffer a baffling life of sacrifice and super-efforts on the upward spirals of evolution ("the slings and arrows of outrageous fortune")? Or, to give into our desires for a life of comfort and security and arm ourselves "against a sea of troubles" so that we can avoid baffles altogether ("by opposing, end them"). Read the following with your heart, considering all that has been shared with you here, dear reader, and see if the Truth of the following words reaches out and touches your consciousness...

To be, or not to be- that is the question:

Whether 'tis nobler in the mind to suffer

The slings and arrows of outrageous fortune

Or to take arms against a sea of troubles,

And by opposing end them. To die- to sleep-

No more; and by a sleep to say we end

The heartache, and the thousand natural shocks

That flesh is heir to. 'Tis a consummation

Devoutly to be wish'd. To die- to sleep.

To sleep- perchance to dream: ay, there's the rub!

For in that sleep of death what dreams may come

When we have shuffled off this mortal coil,

Must give us pause. There's the respect

That makes calamity of so long life.

For who would bear the whips and scorns of time,

Th' oppressor's wrong, the proud man's contumely,

The pangs of despis'd love, the law's delay,

The insolence of office, and the spurns

That patient merit of th' unworthy takes,

When he himself might his quietus make

With a bare bodkin? Who would these fardels bear,

To grunt and sweat under a weary life,

But that the dread of something after death-

The undiscover'd country, from whose bourn

No traveller returns- puzzles the will,

And makes us rather bear those ills we have

Than fly to others that we know not of?

Thus conscience does make cowards of us all,

And thus the native hue of resolution

Is sicklied o'er with the pale cast of thought,

And enterprises of great pith and moment

With this regard their currents turn awry

And lose the name of action.- Soft you now!

The fair Ophelia!- Nymph, in thy orisons

Be all my sins rememb'red.

– Hamlet, Act III, Sc. 1 by William Shakespeare

This most famous of all Shakespearean soliloquies outlines the essence of what we have been discussing here in *Part Three*. That we are asleep, dreaming…in psychological hell. To be one with our Being (awake and Self-realized), we must die to that sleep. To die to sleep means to die to the egos which cause our slumber. It is self-evident: only when we eliminate the causes of our psychological sleep can we awaken. Only when we kill the mechanical elements of our psychology keeping us trapped in psychological hell can we escape from that hell. *Drink the champagne, discard the bottles.* In this context, even the average reader may glean the brilliantly veiled Truth at the heart of Hamlet's speech. There is so much more to say about these, the most important words ever written in English. To that end, dear reader, whether you watched it earlier in *Part Two* or not, we encourage you to re-watch our video on the pivotal speech from Shakespeare's Hamlet, linked below. There is a reason why these words are the most famous of all of Shakespeare's soliloquies. They represent the most important words ever written or uttered in the English language, and far too few who profess to be experts on them actually know their True meaning.

Video 44: To Be or Not to Be (A True Human Being)
(YouTube)

Why?

At the outset of *Part Three* of this book, we promised you an answer to *why*. **Why should you bother to face the Great A-Weakening of humanity, SEEK to Truly awaken yourself, to be a True human being, and to escape hell?** After all, dear reader, have we not made a case for the impending destruction of this humanity? Is that not what all this talk of death and preparing for death has been about? What is the point of making super-efforts to evolve, to awaken, to know yourself, and by extension, the True nature of reality? Has all this been some sadistic exercise on our part to strike fear and hopelessness into your heart? Or could it be that this hefty tome, nearly fifty years in the works, is an invitation of sorts?

In the autumn of every harvest, the farmer will select the best seeds with which to sow his fields the next planting season. It is no different for humanities. Even Christians read the Book of Revelations with the hope that their beliefs will save them, and New Agers believe in some massive global awakening and new Golden Age. The Truth is the sixth root race on this planet will require True Human Beings from this humanity, the fifth root race. One cannot birth a new humanity nor a new Golden Age with degenerated intellectual hominids who falsely believe they are human beings. The farmer does not select seeds from weak plants or weak fruits. The farmer selects the best seeds from the strongest yields. Ones that embody the fortitude, resilience, and all the qualities that promise to yield a robust and healthy crop next season.

While a farmer looks to mostly physical attributes to determine which seeds are best, the Divine Farmer of humanity looks to mostly metaphysical attributes. Surely, you have noticed, dear reader, that we have not emphasized physical, racial, or even cultural characteristics in reference to awakening. We did mention racial diversity, mixed-race couples, and their offspring, but we recognize that such genetic diversity is the opposite of eugenics—selecting for specific bloodlines and/or genetic traits. Even so, having a genetically diverse background is no guarantee that one will be chosen as a *good seed*. The best seeds of this humanity will be chosen first and foremost from among those who are Truly awake. Those who merely think they are awake—like those succumbing to one or more pillars of the Great A-Weakening—will not qualify. Still, a longing to awaken denotes potential, unlike those who act purely out of fear.

The *doomsday preppers* who instinctively sense imminent danger can build their elaborate bunkers as deep and thick as they wish. They can fill them to the ceiling with tens of thousands of cans of Campbell's Soup and millions of rounds of ammunition. The global elite, terrified of losing all they have accumulated in this physical life, can build their bunkers larger, more elaborate, more remote, and deeper than anyone else. Yet, it will not avail them. If their hearts are heavy with materialism, their minds rigidly identified with and attached to their own mortality, and their psyche filled with the deafening machinations of fear, lust, pride, envy, etc., all their efforts to avoid the inevitable will be in vain. The Divine Farmer cannot be so easily fooled. The elites' ability to remain anonymous and behind the curtain is its own trap. As is the case for all of us, our efforts to pour our time, energy, attention, and other precious resources into creating a force field in defense of our false self is an offense against our True Self. The force field we identify with and attach ourselves to, believing it will save us, is the very containment field of our own Self-imprisonment. In the individuated hell we all live in, there is but one warden, one guard, and one prisoner...and we are all three. The Great Law sees all, for no one is without an Innermost Being. However enslaved our True

Self may be to the machinations of the false self, the crimes against our Self and others committed by ourselves are recorded in the Akashic Records for all time. When the bell tolls for us, dear reader, we will be called to stand before the Great Court of The Law of Karma and answer for our crimes. Our hearts weighed against a feather, and there will be but one of two directions our monad will be able to go. And we all know this to be True, intuitively, deep down within the very center of our Being. This is why so many will experience a change of heart, an awakening, a revelation, and/or a recanting of a life of selfishness upon their deathbed. Now, here we are, facing the death of humanity itself.

Invariably, when the death of humanity is imminent, individual(s) appear to warn humanity of its impending doom and the steps that must be taken. Sent by the Divine Farmer to gather the best seeds from humanity—including those good seeds that have the potential to become great seeds worthy of preservation and cultivating the next humanity and the new Golden Age. In the Kali Yuga of the Atlantean Epoch, the individual most responsible was immortalized around the world as the central protagonist in the countless myths and legends recounting the Great Flood. In the West, he is known as *Noah*. He was the central figure whose mission was to build the Ark. Two things go into an Ark. The best seeds from the outgoing humanity and the timeless, universal knowledge on which the new Golden Age will be established.

We have no illusions, dear reader. Although we have done this work before—during the Kali Yuga of Lemuria and in the establishment of the Golden Age of Atlantis—we know that our message warning humanity of the inevitable will be rejected by the vast majority on this planet just as Noah's was. Our efforts as an ark-builder will be deemed as a fool's errand by many and madness by most. And that is to be expected. It comes with the territory, to be honest. The teachings have always been for the few—those with the eyes to see and the ears to hear them. Naturally, our approach to delivering our message and the teachings is appropriate to the times we are living in, the idiosyncrasies of the people of this age, and the urgency of the situation we all find ourselves in—facing our collective death as a humanity. It is, therefore, stripped down to the bare essentials. An infinitely practical approach that draws on the most relevant, powerful, and universally accessible modern myths, in addition to ancient scriptures, religions, spiritual traditions, high art, literature, Shakespeare, et al. And perhaps most significant of all, the infinitely applicable AUM of Life. The Analogous Ultimate Methodology to attaining self-evident experiential knowledge…what we all must SEEK if we long to be among those chosen to seed the next humanity and earn our place in the new Golden Age. We can have no illusions.

When the Masters of the Great White Lodge held an audience for us in the supernal worlds, the experience was reminiscent of the scene from *Star Wars Episode One: The Phantom Menace* in which a young Anakin Skywalker stood sheepishly before the Jedi Counsel for the first time. And, like Anakin's audience with the Jedi Masters, ours was short, direct, and to the point:

Now listen very carefully. You do not have to save everyone.

– Ascended Masters

With that, a great burden had been lifted from our shoulders. We had literally suffered for years under the weight of an *Atlas Complex,* knowing in vague terms what we were here to do but not knowing how we were going to go about doing it. Of course, it did not help matters that we lived in ignorance of the Kali Yuga. For most of our lives, we believed the impending doom facing humanity was of humankind's own creation and that with the right interventions deployed soon enough, the great catastrophe could be averted and humanity 'saved.' That was the first of many illusions (and delusions) that fell by the wayside thanks to the wisdom of The Logos imparted to a most naïve and foolish servant of the Light still *in formation.* The reality of our life's work was hammered home in the simple act of going apple-picking in the fall. For every apple which found its way into the basket, dozens more lay fallen and rotting on the ground. This is the harsh reality of the harvest. And of the fruit that are picked, only a handful will be chosen for their seeds. We have no illusions that this book will reach the masses. But it does not have to. It need only connect with one other soul—and that soul is yours, dear reader. If you have made it this far, all the way to the end, it was for a reason. It is the reason why we wrote this book—one which cannot be *reasoned,* ironically, but it can be *known consciously.* In the end, we are just a messenger, and as such, there is only one thing we can do for you or anyone (speaking of messengers and seeds)…

Ratatoskr and the Seed

When I awoke to find myself in the earth,

Bereft of truth and with so little mirth,

Nearby a-cooing was a dove,

Small paws a-stomping from above.

"Where is this place," I thought aloud,

"Right here" chirped back a voice quite proud.

"Good sir," I begged, confused as hell,

"What is your name, kind sir, do tell."

"Mercury say some. Some, Quicksilver.

But to you, wee seed, I am Ratatoskr."

"Well met, good squirrel, might I inquire,

Why do you bury me in this mire?"

"'Tis my duty wee nut, since you ask,

To serve the Ash, my noble task.

Running roots to branches leafy,

I impart the Word albeit it briefly."

"Then tell me courier, goodly sprite,

Why do I suffer in this awful night?"

"You fell from leaves, that much is true,

And I'm now here to bury you."

"Then ask of them for me your charge,

What is my place in the world at large?"

"Bring a reply to a message say you!?

"We live to scamper—oak, ash or yew!"

And with that he was gone in much more than a dash,

Before I could think he was back in a flash.

"'Don't ask us,' say the leaves, 'we work for the bough.'

Shall I ask the branches if they know who art thou?"

By the time I said "do so," to my rascally friend,

He returned with the news that might never end:

"They say: 'it's not up to us, we work for the trunk,'

Yet me-knows there's an answer, so get out of your funk!"

But I did not hear him, my spirits were sunk.

How could I continue? On dismay was I drunk.

"'Roots are my master,' says the trunk on this day,

As I depart again let go your dismay!"

Just then was I moved; stoked fire by some bellow;

"What just happened?" Said I. "Report my good fellow!"

"Relax my dear seed, lest your shell become broken.

Everything is fine, Nidhoggr has spoken!"

Hidden is She, in the three roots of Yggdrasil.

This wisdom declared She, "I serve the Great Eagle."

"Then fly like the wind, dear rodent of fire,

And answer the riddle, my one True Heart's desire!"

"With pleasure, milord," and again he was gone.

"'The Heavens we serve' Great Eagle hath shone."

"By my shell this game is getting long in the tooth."

"Long is the path up Yggdrasil, forsooth."

"My apologies, dear Rascal—" "RATATOSKR, you nave!"

"Beg pardon, Good Squirrel, can time we not save?"

"Does my speed not suffice, you impatient speck?

Here's my sore paws and you're pain in the neck!"

"Forgive me good messenger, but how will you ask,

The heavens to answer, and be taken to task?"

"Great Eagle hath asked them, and to me he conveyed

'The Earth' was their answer and to you now relayed."

"Good Lord, to rest will this never be laid?"

"Thank you good squirrel, may this great debt be repaid!"

So I asked the good earth surrounding myself,

If it would be so kind as to reveal my True Self.

"We serve the sun," rumbled she mightily,

"Under command of the moon," she added begrudgingly.

"Good sun in the sky, will you not hear my call!?

Reveal my true purpose! Oh why did I fall!?"

Once again did the squirrel up the tree run,

And return with this answer: "'Not just for fun.'

But surely our answer can only take you so far,

Thus we return to The Brotherhood of the Star."

So close did I feel to the answers I sought,

Yet so far were the stars, Great Eagle or not!

"Relax," said Ratatoskr, "even though I do not,

Patience and virtue are siblings are they not?

Back up do I fly and Great Eagle thereafter,

Return to you will I, with news of hereafter."

In good time my faithful messenger returned,

"The Brotherhood serves Space" was what he had learned.

"And who does Space serve?" I asked in a quip,

Ratatoskr departed, his tail like a whip.

Ages went by, countless lifetimes, we confess,

"Space serves the Light, no more and no less."

"Then surely, good messenger, the journey's near end!

For whom but The Light can the Final Word send!?"

"I shall up Yggdrasil again, dear master, Ash Essence,

That you may realize at last, and of all this make sense!"

Strange patience welled up as never before.

No longing, worry, or thought for what was in store.

Just sitting and waiting as I did before;

Not expecting a knock or to answer the door.

Not thinking, not doing, no grandiose galore.

Just being in earth. No less and no more.

Then out of the silence came a-cooing the dove.

"We are Whom the Light serves; We are Pure Love.

We've been in the Nous Atom in seed within song,

Fear not Son of Ash, we've been with you all 'long."

My shell it cracked open. My heart swelled like the sea.

If a seed ever had eyes, mine cried joyous and free.

The sun in my heart, the stars in solidarity,

The Inner Akash received Limitless Light within me.

Great Eagle above, his consort Dragon below,

Faithful squirrel betwixt them, Great Mercury, we know.

Our prayer had been answered; our dread wanting belayed.

Great Hel had come knocking, and would not be delayed.

Ratatoskr gave Hel two coins squirreled away.

Into hell would we sink, until at least the third day.

"We thank you, Great Dove, kind Source of the Light,

We go in peace and in joy, without any fright."

And die I did there, bathed in Love's delight.

With all of Love's blessing I passed into Hel's night.

Some time later broke ground a little wee sprout.

It struggled and suffered and grew itself out.

Now we are here, an Ash at Love's behest,

Not thinking or doing, just Being our best.

No care in the world but that of Love's deeds.

Ratatoskr and I, here planting more seeds.

* * *

TAP Human Potential

This book represents just the first of many *seeds* we are here planting as part of *The Attlas Project*. A Neo Enterprise for the 21st Century with but one mandate: to help you *SEE your world in a New Light and SEEK the Light of the World*. Or, more simply put, to encourage you to TAP your True potential to be a Human Being—triune, awakened, even Self-realized. On a firm foundation of True human beings, working diligently to bring their gifts of metamind to you and those you love, for the sake of all beings, The Attlas Project represents the framework by which we will reach out to all those who have within them the potential to seed the next humanity on this planet. Do you count yourself among those who long to SEE your world in a new Light? Do you SEEK the Light of the World? Our life's work may be just the vessel to TAP your highest potential—your knowledge, talents, and resources—and deliver on your heart's deepest longings for the sake of your immortal soul, others, and all beings. We cannot fulfill our role as Ark-builder for this humanity and all that entails alone. That said, we cannot work with just anyone. Nor can everyone be saved. But all those who are willing to dedicate themselves to the AUM of Life for the sake of their immortal souls, the preservation of the best seeds of this humanity, the revelation, revolution, and preservation of the knowledge needed to establish a new Golden Age for the sake of the end of suffering of all beings, will be welcome. Together, we will SEEK KEES, *Key Enlightened Enterprises and Solutions* born of *metamind*, to unlock the mysteries still confounding this humanity and overcome the obstacles humanity still faces.

Metamind vs. 'The Metaverse'

Of course, there are actors in the world interested in augmenting, filtering, and outright replacing our conscious experience of metamind with a virtual reality digital simulation, which they have ironically named "the metaverse." They are, as we speak, conspiring, concocting, and crafting their so-called metaverses filled with virtual spectacles and experiences to captivate our rational minds. They literally want to augment the reality of existence as a True human being...convincing you that their dystopian vision of transhumanism, AI, and neo-communism is the destiny of humankind. That doubling down on not being is somehow going to equate (or be superior) to actually being.

They seriously believe that faced with all the world's problems, the cacophony of the busy mind, the endless *Game of Thrones* in our psychology, all they need to do is slap a VR headset on us—and/or medicate us with various forms of psychedelic-derived pharmaceuticals—and plunge us into their so-called metaverse to make it all better. Or worse, implant a chip directly into our brains. As if adding complexity to the human condition is somehow going to alleviate our confusion and suffering. We know that the advent of social media has had a terrible effect on younger generations, especially young women and girls. We also know from our exploration of VR, AI, and transhumanism in *Part Two* that the metaverse is merely *the endgame* in The Black Lodge's (egos') ancient strategy to completely enslave humanity.

And they are going to make us pay for it. As always, these supremely powerful and ultra-wealthy actors, mere pawns and *useful idiots* of The Black Lodge, utterly enslaved to their own egos, are going to project their enslavement onto humanity. They will get inside of our heads, exploit the dominance hierarchy of egos within us, create a new breed of 3D virtual reality that is far more enticing and hypnotic than anything ever seen before, and further commoditize devolution and not being. It is their intention to continue accelerating the march forward into the technological zombie apocalypse. They will create a whole new virtual reality filled with desires, concerns, and responsibilities for us to juggle, in addition to the actual real-world challenges and responsibilities a humanity of unicyclists is already struggling to juggle. And no doubt, the masters of neuropharmacology will be waiting in the wings to medicate all those who cannot maintain their balance in the neo-Marxist transhumanist dystopia. This, then, is the exploitation of the rational mind via the exacerbation of real suffering individuals in the virtual reality metaverse.

Metaverse represents another in a long tradition of entropy whereby words and their meanings are twisted and degenerated into accomplishing the opposite of their True purpose—just as *faith* was degenerated to mean *belief*. The prefix *meta* can mean many things, including behind, beyond, greater than, more comprehensive, fundamental, and transcendent, as in *metaphysics*. The word *verse*, of course, is related to *The Word—Logos*—and as a suffix means "to turn"—as in *reverse*. Its most obvious and ubiquitous expression can be found in *the universe*. With everything we have presented in this book related to The Great A-Weakening of humanity, the concept of a VR, AI, transhumanist *metaverse* as a home for a technocratic Neo-Marxist collectivist hive-mind is by far the most *perverse*. When the real, transcendental, and comprehensive objective metaverse beyond and behind the 3D universe we experience as mortal vessels is neither physical nor virtual but metaphysical. The True transcendental universe is the real metaverse. Not the elaborate video-game-like psychological prison the tech companies and their so-called tech gurus euphemistically refer to as the metaverse. Their technocratic metaverse is just another trap.

Key Enlightened Enterprises & Solutions

The first solution, ISAUM, begins with you, dear reader. To become one of many *Individuals SEEKing the Analogous Ultimate Methodology*. Make a conscious connection to metamind and SEEK mastery of yourself and all the challenges of life as a Triune Human Being. The conscious exploration, exposition, and application of the *actual metaverse* via metamind of being. Delivering into our 3D universe, insights born in the metaverse. Such as Key Enlightened Enterprises and Solutions, which Support, Encourage, and Empower Individuals SEEKing the AUM of Life (ISAUM, Individuals Seeking Analogous Ultimate

Methodology). Ecosystem Advanced Human Habitat (ESAHH). Sound Empowered Electric Metaphysical Science (SEEMS). Spiritually Enlightened Education and Culture (SEEC). Social Environmental Economic Valuation (SEEV). Society Engaged Electronic Democracy (SEED). KEES to SEE the metaphysical reality of our world, the metaphysical nature of ourselves, so we can discover and deliver new KEES we SEEK to a world in desperate need of enlightened enterprises and solutions. This book is only the beginning. Our life's work is only just getting underway. Stay tuned and stay in touch with us, dear reader, and get in touch with your Self. That is what matters most in life…**be in touch with Who you Truly are.**

Inverential Peace
– Attlas Allux

P.S. Be in Touch with Us

Link 12:
AttlasAllux.com

WHAT IN HELL IS WITH US?

APPENDIX

The Tree of Life and the Human Condition(ed)

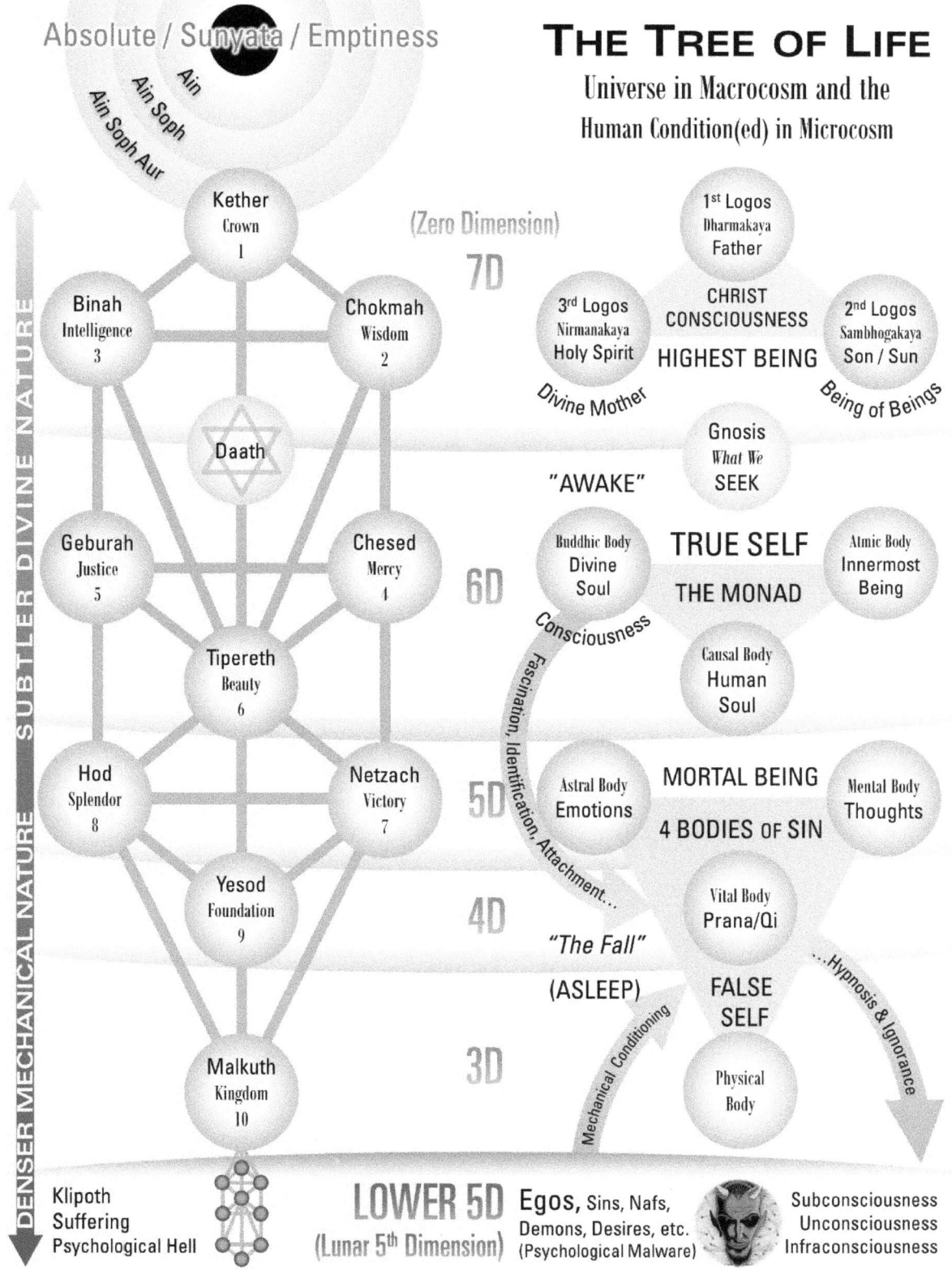

Figure 39: The Tree of Life and the Human Condition(ed)

Ultima Fan-Created Remakes & Remasters

- Ultima IV Original 1985 PC Release <u>Download it for FREE from GOG.com</u>
- Ultima IV Upgrade Patch (for original release & GOG version) <u>Official Wiki Page</u>
- Ultima IV for iOS <u>Download it on iTunes for FREE</u>
- Ultima IV Reborn (*Neverwinter Nights* Mod) <u>Official Wiki Page</u>
- <u>Ultima V Lazarus</u> (based on *Dungeon Siege* engine) <u>Official Wiki Page</u>
- <u>Ultima VI Project</u> (based on *Dungeon Siege* engine) <u>Official Wiki Page</u>

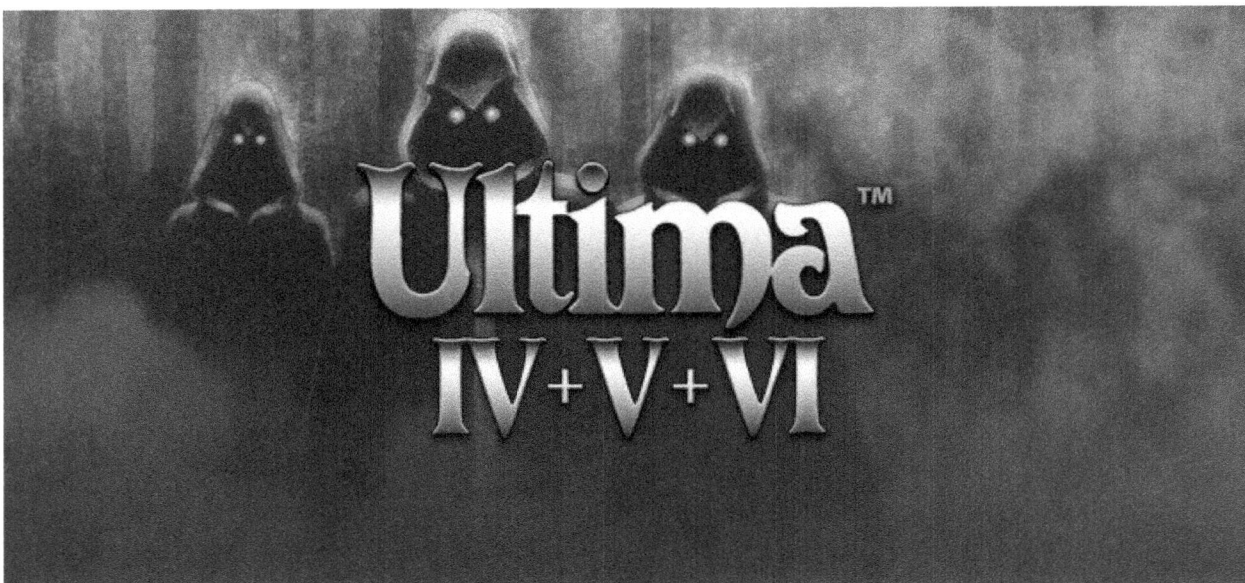

Figure 40: Ultima IV+V+VI, known as "The Age of Enlightenment" to fans of the series marked an extraordinary departure from typical gaming and elevated themselves to the level of High Art. (Note there are three Shadow Lords).

Edge of Soul

Transcending history and the world, a tale of soul and swords eternally told

To love! To shine!

We all need to shine on, to see

how far we've come on our journey.

How far yet to go, searching for our star,

Deep in the night, I pray in my heart

for that special light

to shower me with love

to shower me with power

to shine from above

I got to get to the Edge of Soul, to carry on what I believed in from the

very start

I got to get to the Edge of Soul, to carry on deep in my heart

To love, to shine!

To love, to shine!

To love!

Come strip down and face it, you're all

About time you broke down your wall

Free your mind

A brand new world waits for you, you'll find

Nobody can just do it for you

It's time that you knew

It's up to you to love

it's up to you to shine

the light true and blue

You got to get to the Edge of Soul, to carry on what you believed in from

the very start

You got to get to the Edge of Soul, to carry on, deep in your heart

You got to get to the Edge of Soul, to carry on what you believed in from

the very start

You got to get to the Edge of Soul, to carry on, deep in your heart

To love, to shine!
To love, to shine!
To love!
– Suzi Kim

TABLE OF FIGURES

TABLE OF VIDEOS

TABLE OF LINKS

BIBLIOGRAPHY OF WORKS CITED

10 Video Game WORLD RECORDS Set by Youtubers | Chaos. Created by Chaos, YouTube, 2018. https://youtu.be/rIXAPhLfvIU?si=L_TJODlov-b_dBdJ

A Record-Breaking World Championship/ Created by LoL Esports, YouTube, 2019. https://youtu.be/Pswn-ONyX23I?si=6UerLaX1lvGQpyfH

Allers, Roger, and Rob Minkoff. *The Lion King.* Buena Vista Pictures, 1994.

Attenborough, Richard, et al. *Gandhi.* 25th anniversary ; [Collector's ed.]. Culver City, Calif., Sony Pictures Home Entertainment, 2007.

Aun Weor, Samael. *The Perfect Matrimony.* Glorian Publishing, 1950, 1961, 2012.

---. *The Great Rebellion.* Glorian Publishing, 1975, 2022.

---. *The Gnostic Bible: The Pistis Sophia Unveiled.* Glorian Publishing, 1983, 2011.

---. *Hell, the Devil, and Karma - Secret Knowledge in Dante's Inferno.* Glorian Publishing, 1973-1974, 2011.

---. *The Revolution of the Dialect.* Glorian Publishing, 1983, 2010.

---. *Treatise of Revolutionary Psychology: The Practical Spirituality that Awakens Consciousness.* Glorian Publishing, 1974, 2013.

Bird, Brad. *The Incredibles.* Buena Vista Pictures, 2004. *Incredibles – The Underminer Arrives.* Popstarwithclwaecolor101, YouTube, 2021. https://youtu.be/zxl9xd4iyVs?si=rfZvV3ge-CsfkkaG

Bremmer, Ian. *The Next Global Superpower Isn't Who You Think | Ian Bremmer | TED.* TED, YouTube, 2023. https://youtu.be/uiUPD-z9DTg?si=zy46k-k7YUka-Elh

Carlin, George. *Doin' It Again.* HBO Entertainment, 1990. *Words that Hide the Truth.* Illustrated Animation by After Skool, YouTube, 2023. https://youtu.be/-ZAo_dUbh9s?si=g8tV-LPceO8rdXo4

---. *You are All Diseased.* HBO Entertainment. 1999. *George Carlin --- Religion is Bullshit.* ChrissyA1, YouTube, 2009. https://youtu.be/8r-e2NDSTuE?si=sp2zm61Hs4-d86Jr

---. *Jammin' in New York.* HBO Entertainment. 1992. George Carlin - *The Planet Isn't Going Anywhere. WE ARE!* Illustrated Animation by After Skool, YouTube, 2021. https://youtu.be/09FmRNb3Krg?si=kSkp2VD8mVCsyBGT

Cheers. Created by James Burrows and Glen Charles. Charles/Burrows/Charles Productions in association with Paramount Network Television, 1982-1993. *Sam and Diane Slap Back and Forth - End of Season 2.* Scott Parks, YouTube, 2011. https://youtu.be/4IWLRlr3W2Y?si=X8mX37MM9TFtTOrG

Coppola, Francis Ford. *Apocalypse Now.* Cartographer of Dreams, YouTube, 2015. https://youtu.be/mPPGMNOLaMw?si=CcadK5N9Vnsbn_tO

Cuphead Launch Trailer. GameTrailers, YouTube, 2017. https://youtu.be/NN-9SQXoi50?si=PHhDYBULOMA605J1

Diablo 3: Reaper of Souls. Blizzard Entertainment. *Diablo 3 Reaper of Souls | Opening Cinematic (2013).* MoviemaniacsDE, YouTube, 2013. https://youtu.be/U3YOmFHU0dg?si=uvAtRZJ4zkTkROKe

Easwaran, Eknath. *Gandhi the Man: How One Man Changed Himself to Change the World.* Nilgiri Press, 2011.

Eco, Umberto. *Foucault's Pendulum.* New York. Ballantine Books, 1990.

Fincher, David. *Fight Club.* Twentieth Century Fox, 1999. Gavin 9001, YouTube, 2015. https://youtu.be/ZYd2dHnJqyg?si=C0vwFQN1RAP34Gl6

Game of Thrones. Created by David Benioff and D. B. Weiss, HBO Entertainment, 2011–2019.

Gaming Culture: How the Story of Ultima Managed to Convey Complicated Philosophical Concepts | Part 1. Created by GaminGHD. YouTube, 2016. https://youtu.be/86Lc7c2krRA?si=njxu8R-mweJo6aQU

Garriott, Richard aka Lord British. *Ultima IV: Quest of the Avatar.* Cover Art by Denis Loubet. Origin Systems, Inc., 1995.

---. *Ultima IV Personality Test.* Created, maintained and © by John Hubbard, 2017. https://www.tk421.net/ultima/

Green, Beth. *Putting the Ego in Its Place: The Inner Revolution, with Beth Green.* Created by Beth Green TV, YouTube, 2015. https://youtu.be/Fz56Rgqq7Rw?si=HzJWuPAPEuu9qat-

Glorian Publishing. *Defense for Spiritual Warfare.* https://glorian.org/learn/courses-and-lectures/defense-for-spiritual-warfare

---. *Homo Nosce Te Ipsum.* Greek Mysteries Course. https://glorian.org/learn/courses-and-lectures/greek-mysteries/homo-nosce-te-ipsum

---. *What is Ego?* https://glorian.org/connect/blog/what-is-ego

Foreman, Paul. *You Make You Feel Good.* Created by Mind Map Inspiration. https://www.mindmapinspiration.com/wp-content/uploads/2011/11/You-make-you-feel-good.jpg

Firstenberg, Arthur. *The Invisible Rainbow: A History of Electricity and Life.* Chelsea Green Publishing, 2020.

Hogan, Matt. *The Story of Two Wolves: A Tale About Handling Inner Conflict Mindfully.* MoveMe Quotes. https://movemequotes.com/story-of-two-wolves/

Jackson, Peter. *The Lord of the Rings: The Return of the King.* New Line Cinema, 2003. *LOTR The Two Towers - Gollum and Sméagol.* EgalmothOfGondolin01, YouTube, 2013. https://youtu.be/NB2CNr692RE?si=fFLtp7SiSmaQOfic

Khan, *Edge of Soul*. Composed by Benten-Maru. Lyrics by Suzi Kim. *Soul Edge.* Capcom, 1996. *Soul Edge Opening (HQ remastered).* Boulotaur2025, YouTube, 2012. https://youtu.be/RtF80UCgarY?si=UkQ00ps5Twqmqbuz

Lendvai, Attila Lewis. *The Attlas Project Volume One: SEE The World in a New Light.* Booksurge, 2009.

Lucas, George. *Star Wars: The Empire Strikes Back.* Twentieth Century Fox, 1980. *Master Yoda Quote (FORCE) | Star Wars V – The Empire Strikes Back (1980).* Wan Little, YouTube, 2016. https://youtu.be/gONQCIevSN0?si=TIHB3J-YF26yB1p2
Star Wars: The Empire Strikes Back – Dark Side Cave. Star Wars Saga LatinAmerica, YouTube, 2019. https://youtu.be/_qiDuHCKSc8?si=AJHBdViYClKRneFZ

---. *Star Wars: The Return of the Jedi.* Twentieth Century Fox, 1983. *Luke Skywalker vs Darth Vader (Whole Fight).* Alex, YouTube, 2016. https://youtu.be/U1MnMA0TzGI?si=kA3ojVNo13VRgP8s *Luke Confronts The Emperor.* Rodrigo Espindola, YouTube, 2015. https://youtu.be/PqaiKmm8gsY?si=3D87L0wTlaOwEVrx

Man Rages over Pronoun Selection in Starfield #starfield. zEletrixx, YouTube, 2023. https://youtu.be/DLeT09s-zJU?si=vqK89ieGvCchd0ti

Meyer, Nicholas and James Horner. *Star Trek II: The Wrath of Khan.* Paramount Pictures, 1982. The Neon Theater, YouTube, 2021. https://youtu.be/RandC6yFH-0?si=AsGZhqdq5hMyY_Hc

Monty Python. *The Final Rip Off.* Virgin Records, 1987. Monty Python – Topic, YouTube, 2015. https://youtu.be/g-B8hzU1nms?si=qZCpb5so_-nHOCG1

My 14 Years of NDE Research Shows What Is Coming to Mankind | David Suich. Created by Next Level Soul Podcast, YouTube, 2022. https://youtu.be/Y0ez_HfTG4k?si=7p4m8YAj83g97lJX.

Nietzsche, Friedrich Wilhelm, 1844-1900. *The Gay Science: with a Prelude in Rhymes and an Appendix of Songs.* New York, Vintage Books, 1974.

Nolan, Christopher. *The Dark Knight.* Warner Bros., 2008. Flashback FM, YouTube, 2020. https://youtu.be/ylwMWpbv5Fk?si=RBZj2ez4ALyAbOEf

Ptolemy, Barry. *Transcendent Man.* Ptolemaic Productions, Therapy Studios, William Morris Endeavor, 2009. CAMIDRCS™ Media, YouTube, 2021. https://youtu.be/VJxcJqQG6lI?si=FVHbm-myWwg_uHHai

Religious Principles. Created by Glorian, YouTube, 2009. https://www.youtube.com/watch?v=X5ruMDp2L9w&t=2s

Reactors Reaction To Seeing Luke Skywalker On The Mandalorian Season 2 Episode 8 | Mixed Reactions. Created by Mixed Reactions, YouTube, 2020. https://youtu.be/BTSsul8tPvU?si=TDQm5IUDg4yvb-5L

Ross, Gary. *Seabiscuit.* Universal Pictures, 2003.

Rushdie, Salman. *Defend the right to be offended.* OpenDemocracy, 2023. https://www.opendemocracy.net/en/article_2331jsp/

Sacred Sexuality, Episode Two: The Secret History of Humanity. Created by Glorian Publising, YouTube, 2023. https://youtu.be/tfpPjnjDewo?si=k2apx7JU_zzwAwjF

Scott, Ridley. *Alien.* Twentieth Century Fox, 1979. SpookyTube, YouTube, 2017. https://youtu.be/VA8jv1M6Y2g?si=-KYyO3q30tNykVv3

---. *Gladiator.* DreamWorks Distribution, 2000.

Shakespeare, William, 1564-1616. *As You Like It.* Poets.org. https://poets.org/poem/you-it-act-ii-scene-vii-all-worlds-stage

---. *The Tragedy of Hamlet, Prince of Denmark.* London: The Folio Society, 1954.

Sheldrake, Rupert. *Exposing Scientific Dogmas - Banned TED Talk - Rupert Sheldrake.* Illustrated Animation Created by After Skool, YouTube, 2023. https://youtu.be/sF03FN37i5w?si=I5V28_nuAPKK54CW

Smart, Ralph. *Human 2.0 - Spiritual Warfare is Upon Us - Infinite Waters.* Created by Infinite Waters. Illustrated Animation by After Skool. YouTube, 2022. https://youtu.be/acQSR-BCPExc?si=vhnK0pUP_cIis1yB

Spielberg, Steven. *Jurassic Park.* Universal Pictures, 1993.

Steiner, Rudolph. *"The sun with loving light makes bright for me each day..."* Goodeeads, Inc. https://www.goodreads.com/quotes/513591-the-sun-with-loving-light-makes-bright-for-me-each

Stone, Oliver. *Wall Street.* Twentieth Century Fox, 1987.

Symes, Dr. John B. *DogtorJ.com – Home of the G.A.R.D.* https://dogtorj.com/

Tehelka Bureau. *Most Covid-19 patients die on ventilators, raising questions.* Tehelka Press, 2020. http://tehelka.com/most-covid-19-patients-die-on-ventilators-raising-questions/

The Connoly Group. *Gateway to Apshai.* Epyx. 1983. The Video Game Museum, YouTube, 2017 https://youtu.be/SibZmoFT4V0?si=FEqkAZVqKX0L4kA3

The Mandalorian. Created by Jon Favreau. Disney+, 2019-2023. *Luke Skywalker saves The Mandalorian and Grogu.* ClipStudio, YouTube, 2021. https://youtu.be/2qf2OlsOV3c?si=zUE5O8m7khHWnb1e

The Sackler Family – A Secretive Billion Dollar Opioid Empire. Created by ColdFusion, YouTube, 2019. https://youtu.be/zGcKURD_osM?si=w0LtPwZwUavcX0ty

The Untold Truth of Thanos. Created by Looper, YouTube, 2018. https://youtu.be/VNcBuiM00TE?si=YDh7NUudKoQkiUwl

The Voices in my head. Created by Anastina91, DevianArt. https://www.deviantart.com/anastina91/art/The-voices-in-my-head-279710888

Tolkien, J. R. R. *The Lord of the Rings.* Harper Collins, 1991.

Turn the Other Cheek Bible Verses. Bible Reasons, 2013-2023. https://biblereasons.com/turning-the-other-cheek/

Wikipedia, *Conspiracy theory.* https://en.wikipedia.org/wiki/Conspiracy_theory

---. *Great Awakening.* https://en.wikipedia.org/wiki/Great_Awakening

---. *Divide and rule.* https://en.wikipedia.org/wiki/Divide_and_rule

Wachowski, Lana, and Lilly Wachowski. *The Matrix.* Warner Bros., 1999. Blu-Ray Clips, YouTube, 2019. https://youtu.be/j934OgiMBNQ?si=nnX-DXt0H6aIrRVW